Hana & Hina

AFTER ♡ SCHOOL

story & art
MILK MORINAGA

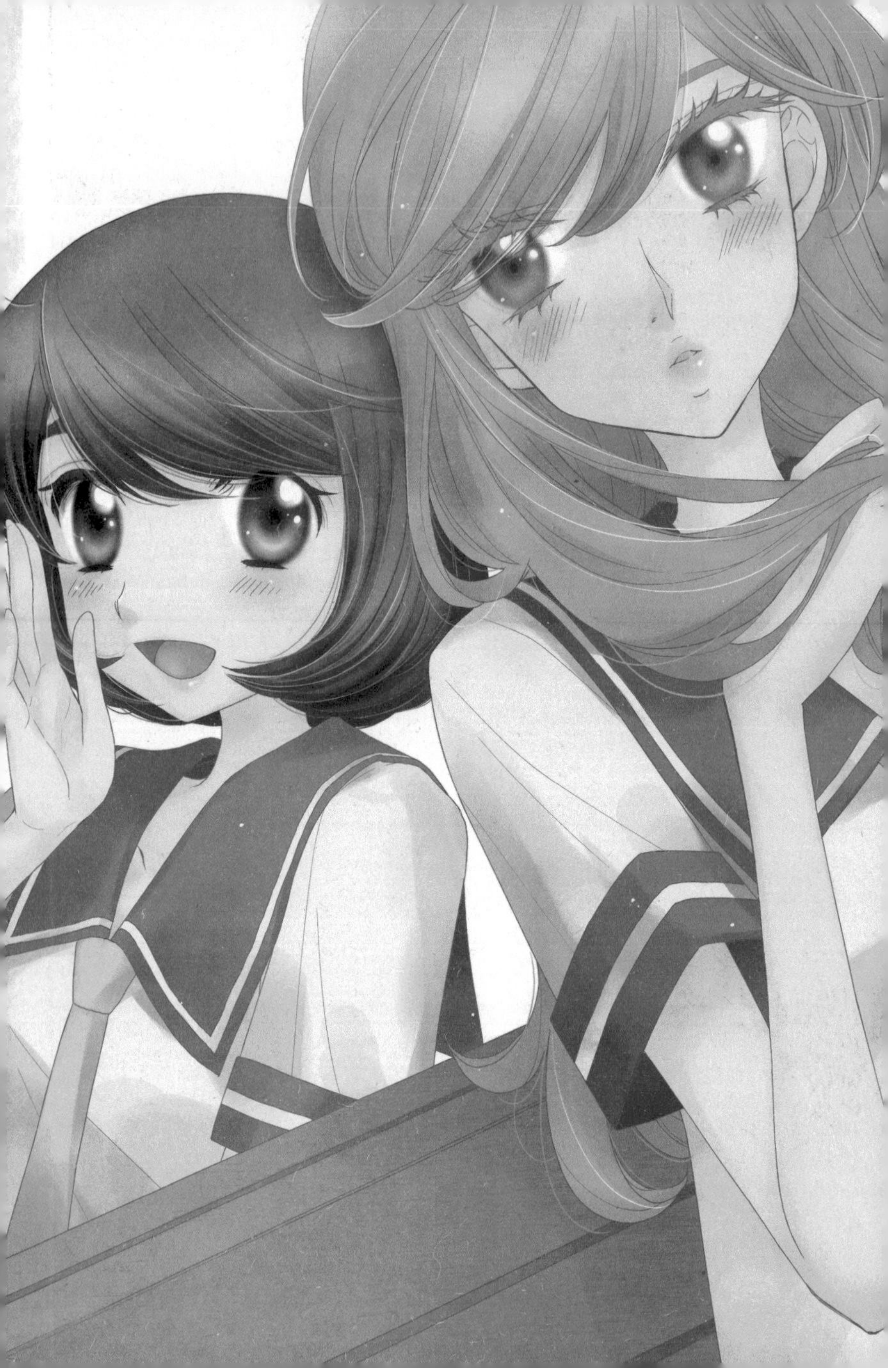

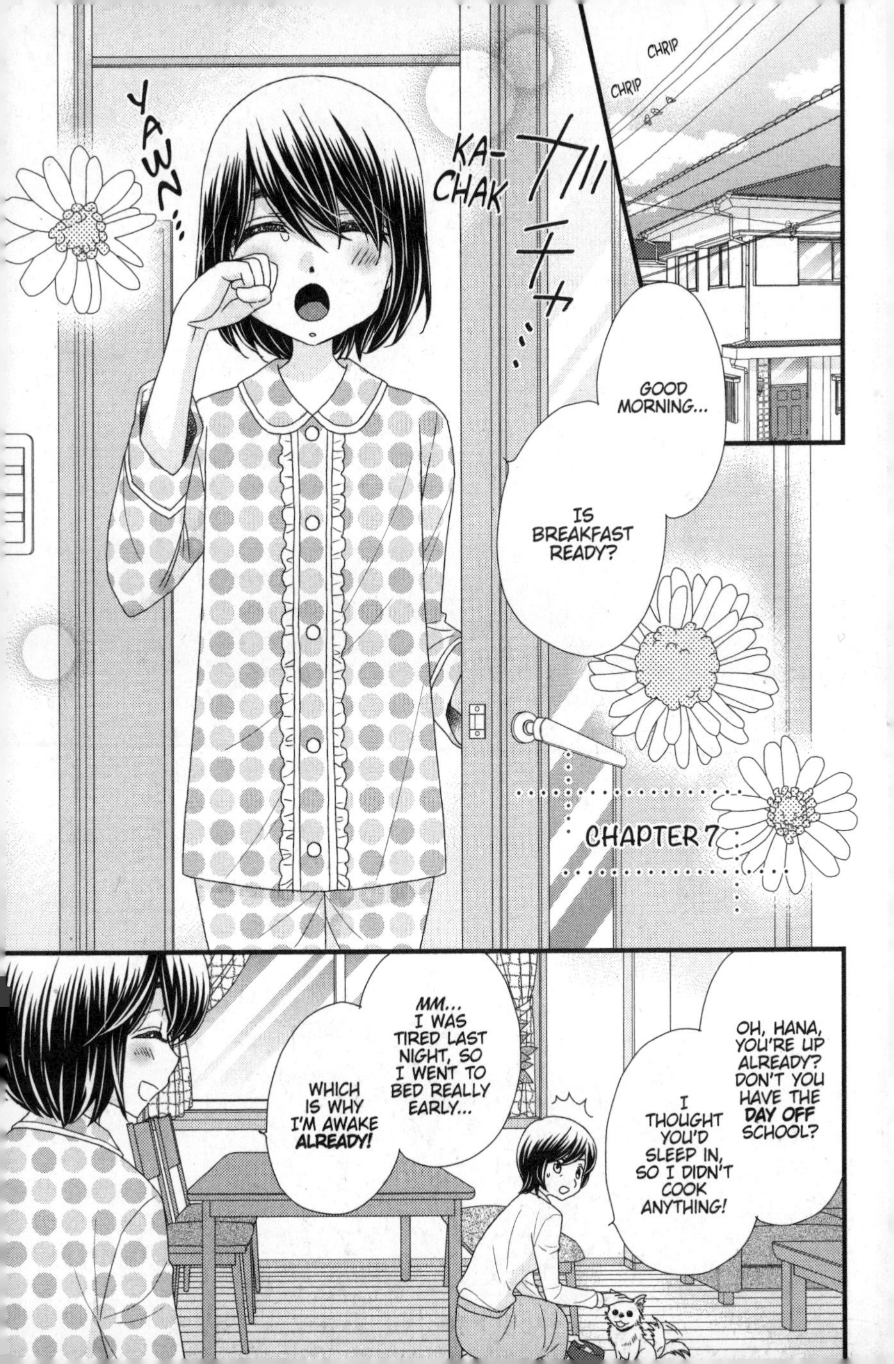
CHRIP
CHRIP
KA-CHAK
YAWN...
GOOD MORNING...
IS BREAKFAST READY?
CHAPTER 7
OH, HANA, YOU'RE UP ALREADY? DON'T YOU HAVE THE DAY OFF SCHOOL?
I THOUGHT YOU'D SLEEP IN, SO I DIDN'T COOK ANYTHING!
MM... I WAS TIRED LAST NIGHT, SO I WENT TO BED REALLY EARLY...
WHICH IS WHY I'M AWAKE ALREADY!

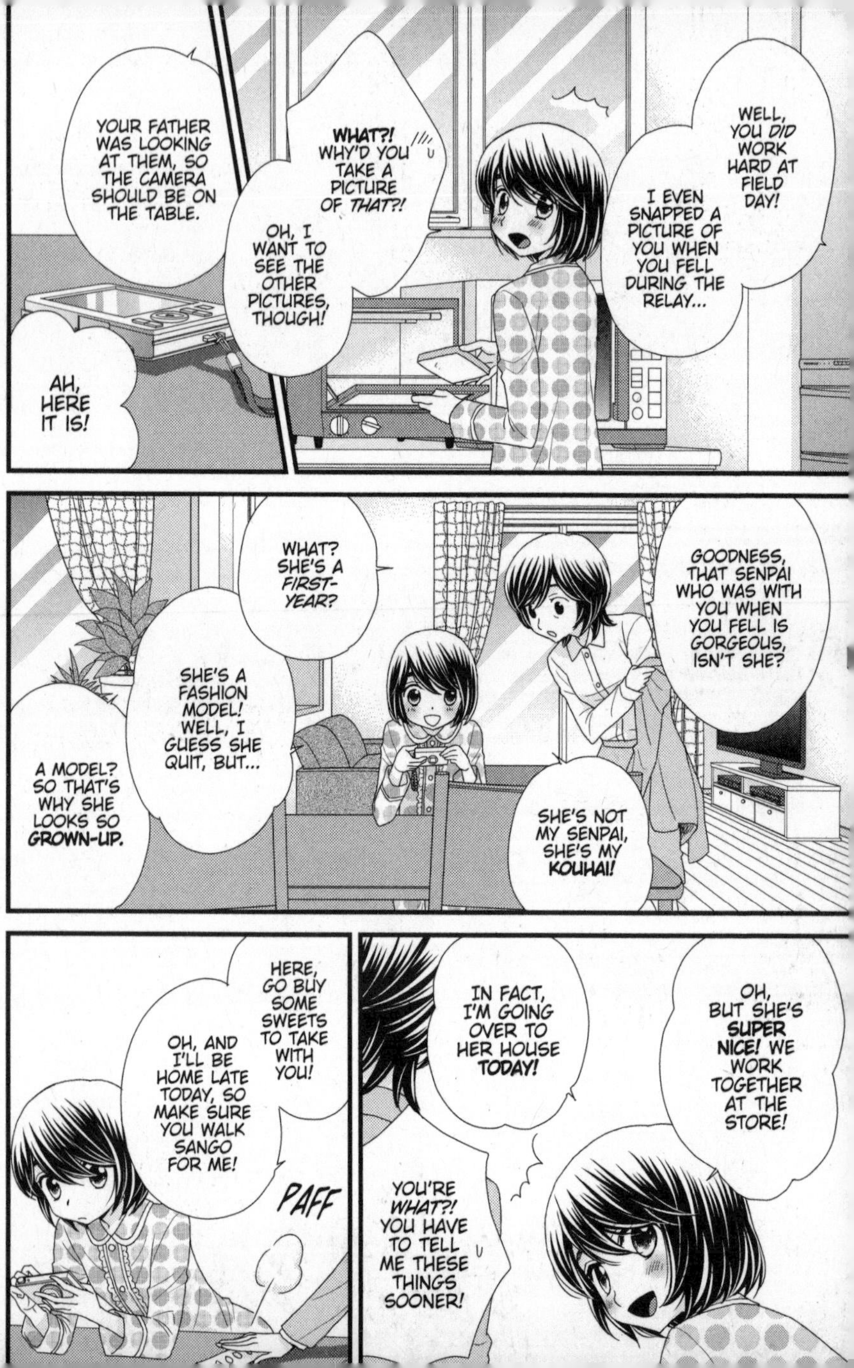

WELL, YOU DID WORK HARD AT FIELD DAY!
I EVEN SNAPPED A PICTURE OF YOU WHEN YOU FELL DURING THE RELAY...
WHAT?! WHY'D YOU TAKE A PICTURE OF THAT?!
OH, I WANT TO SEE THE OTHER PICTURES, THOUGH!
YOUR FATHER WAS LOOKING AT THEM, SO THE CAMERA SHOULD BE ON THE TABLE.
AH, HERE IT IS!
GOODNESS, THAT SENPAI WHO WAS WITH YOU WHEN YOU FELL IS GORGEOUS, ISN'T SHE?
SHE'S NOT MY SENPAI, SHE'S MY KOUHAI!
WHAT? SHE'S A FIRST-YEAR?
SHE'S A FASHION MODEL! WELL, I GUESS SHE QUIT, BUT...
A MODEL? SO THAT'S WHY SHE LOOKS SO GROWN-UP.
OH, BUT SHE'S SUPER NICE! WE WORK TOGETHER AT THE STORE!
IN FACT, I'M GOING OVER TO HER HOUSE TODAY!
YOU'RE WHAT?! YOU HAVE TO TELL ME THESE THINGS SOONER!
HERE, GO BUY SOME SWEETS TO TAKE WITH YOU!
OH, AND I'LL BE HOME LATE TODAY, SO MAKE SURE YOU WALK SANGO FOR ME!
PAFF

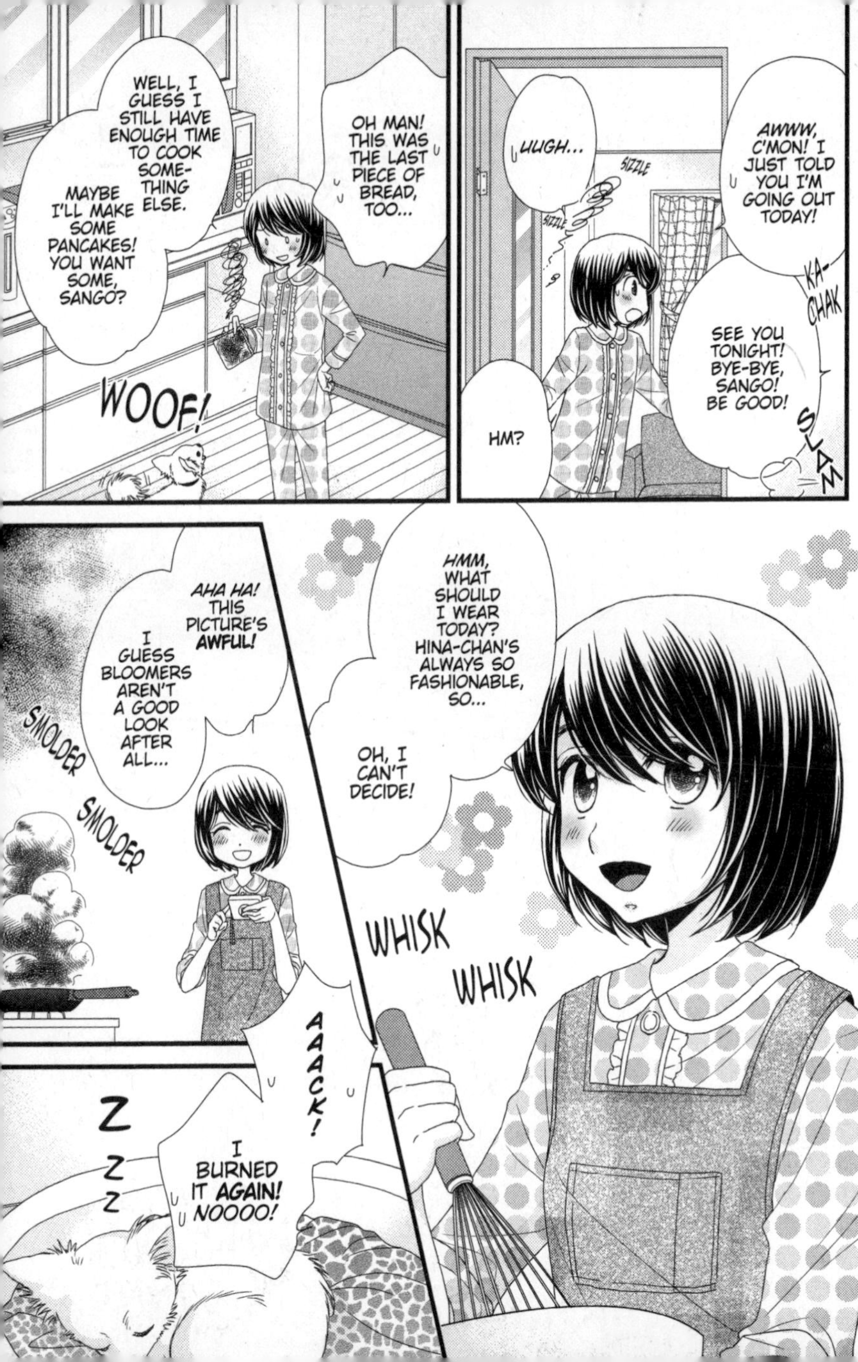
AWWW, C'MON! I JUST TOLD YOU I'M GOING OUT TODAY!
UGH...
SIZZLE
SIZZLE
KA-CHAK
SEE YOU TONIGHT! BYE-BYE, SANGO! BE GOOD!
SLAM
HM?
OH MAN! THIS WAS THE LAST PIECE OF BREAD, TOO...
WELL, I GUESS I STILL HAVE ENOUGH TIME TO COOK SOME-THING ELSE.
MAYBE I'LL MAKE SOME PANCAKES! YOU WANT SOME, SANGO?
WOOF!
HMM, WHAT SHOULD I WEAR TODAY? HINA-CHAN'S ALWAYS SO FASHIONABLE, SO...
OH, I CAN'T DECIDE!
WHISK
WHISK
AHA HA! THIS PICTURE'S AWFUL!
I GUESS BLOOMERS AREN'T A GOOD LOOK AFTER ALL...
SMOLDER
SMOLDER
AAAACK!
I BURNED IT AGAIN! NOOOO!
Z
Z
Z

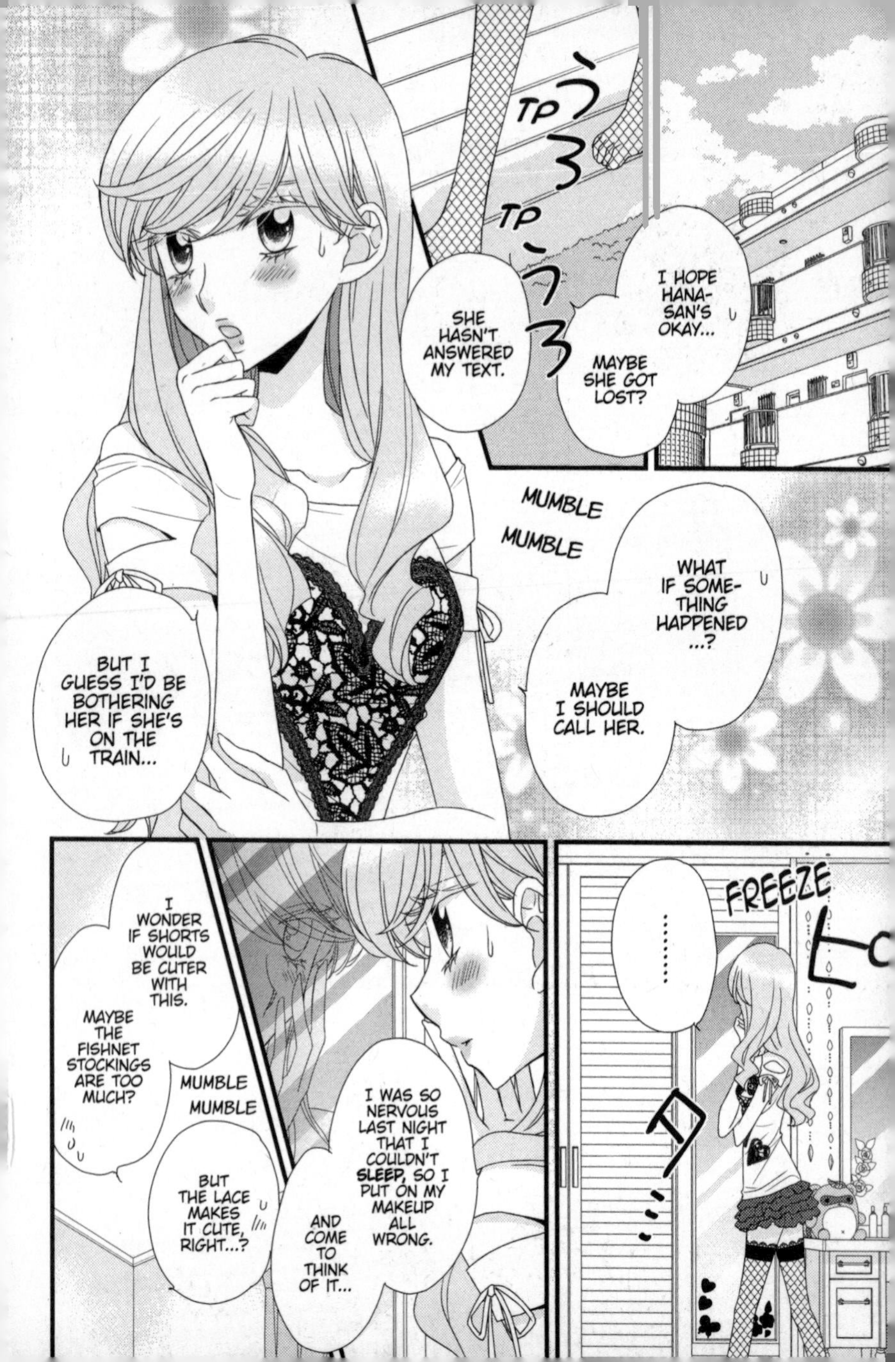
I HOPE HANA-SAN'S OKAY...
MAYBE SHE GOT LOST?
TP
TP
SHE HASN'T ANSWERED MY TEXT.
MUMBLE
MUMBLE
WHAT IF SOMETHING HAPPENED...?
MAYBE I SHOULD CALL HER.
BUT I GUESS I'D BE BOTHERING HER IF SHE'S ON THE TRAIN...
FREEZE
......
I WAS SO NERVOUS LAST NIGHT THAT I COULDN'T SLEEP, SO I PUT ON MY MAKEUP ALL WRONG.
AND COME TO THINK OF IT...
I WONDER IF SHORTS WOULD BE CUTER WITH THIS.
MAYBE THE FISHNET STOCKINGS ARE TOO MUCH?
MUMBLE
MUMBLE
BUT THE LACE MAKES IT CUTE, RIGHT...?

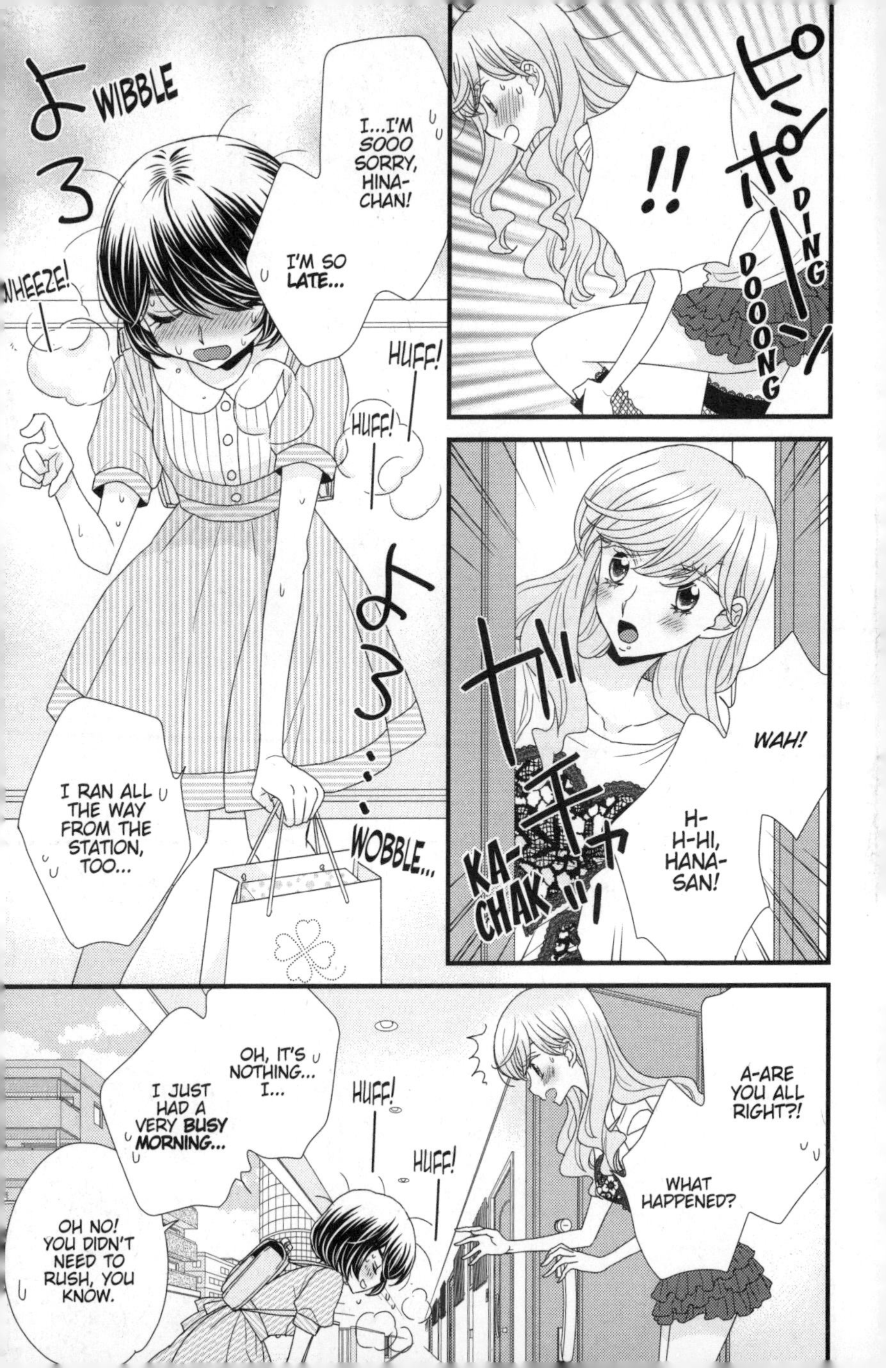
ピンポーン
DING DOOOONG
!!
ガチャ
KA-CHAK
WAH!
H-H-HI, HANA-SAN!
よろ
WIBBLE
I...I'M SOOO SORRY, HINA-CHAN!
I'M SO LATE...
WHEEZE!
HUFF!
HUFF!
よろ...
WOBBLE...
I RAN ALL THE WAY FROM THE STATION, TOO...
A-ARE YOU ALL RIGHT?!
WHAT HAPPENED?
OH, IT'S NOTHING... I...
I JUST HAD A VERY BUSY MORNING...
HUFF!
HUFF!
OH NO! YOU DIDN'T NEED TO RUSH, YOU KNOW.

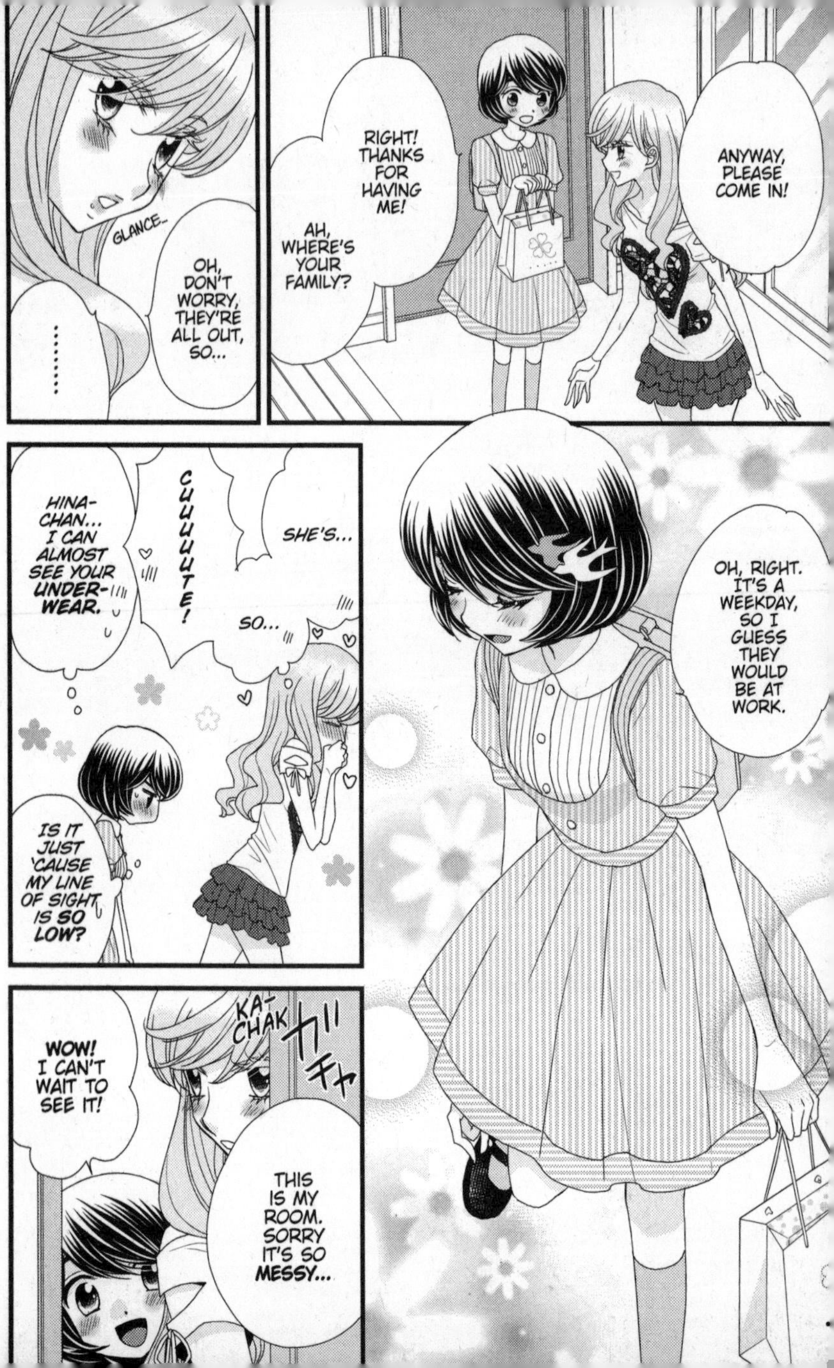
ANYWAY, PLEASE COME IN!
RIGHT! THANKS FOR HAVING ME!
AH, WHERE'S YOUR FAMILY?
GLANCE...
OH, DON'T WORRY, THEY'RE ALL OUT, SO...
......
OH, RIGHT. IT'S A WEEKDAY, SO I GUESS THEY WOULD BE AT WORK.
SHE'S...
SO...
CUUUUUTE!
HINA-CHAN... I CAN ALMOST SEE YOUR UNDERWEAR.
IS IT JUST 'CAUSE MY LINE OF SIGHT IS SO LOW?
KA-CHAK
ガチャ
THIS IS MY ROOM. SORRY IT'S SO MESSY...
WOW! I CAN'T WAIT TO SEE IT!

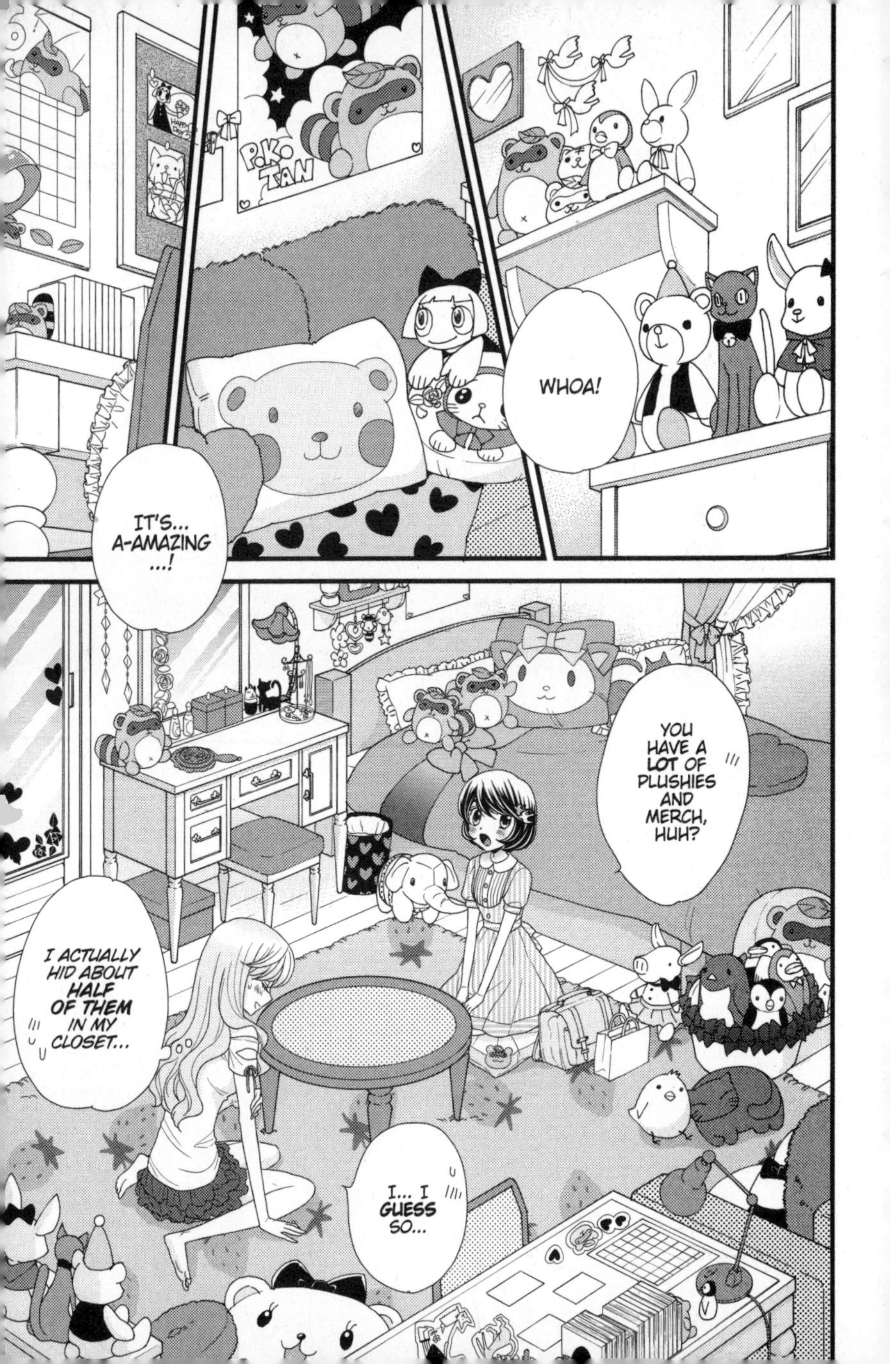
WHOA!
IT'S... A-AMAZING ...!
YOU HAVE A **LOT** OF PLUSHIES AND MERCH, HUH?
I ACTUALLY HID ABOUT **HALF OF THEM** IN MY CLOSET...
I... I **GUESS** SO...

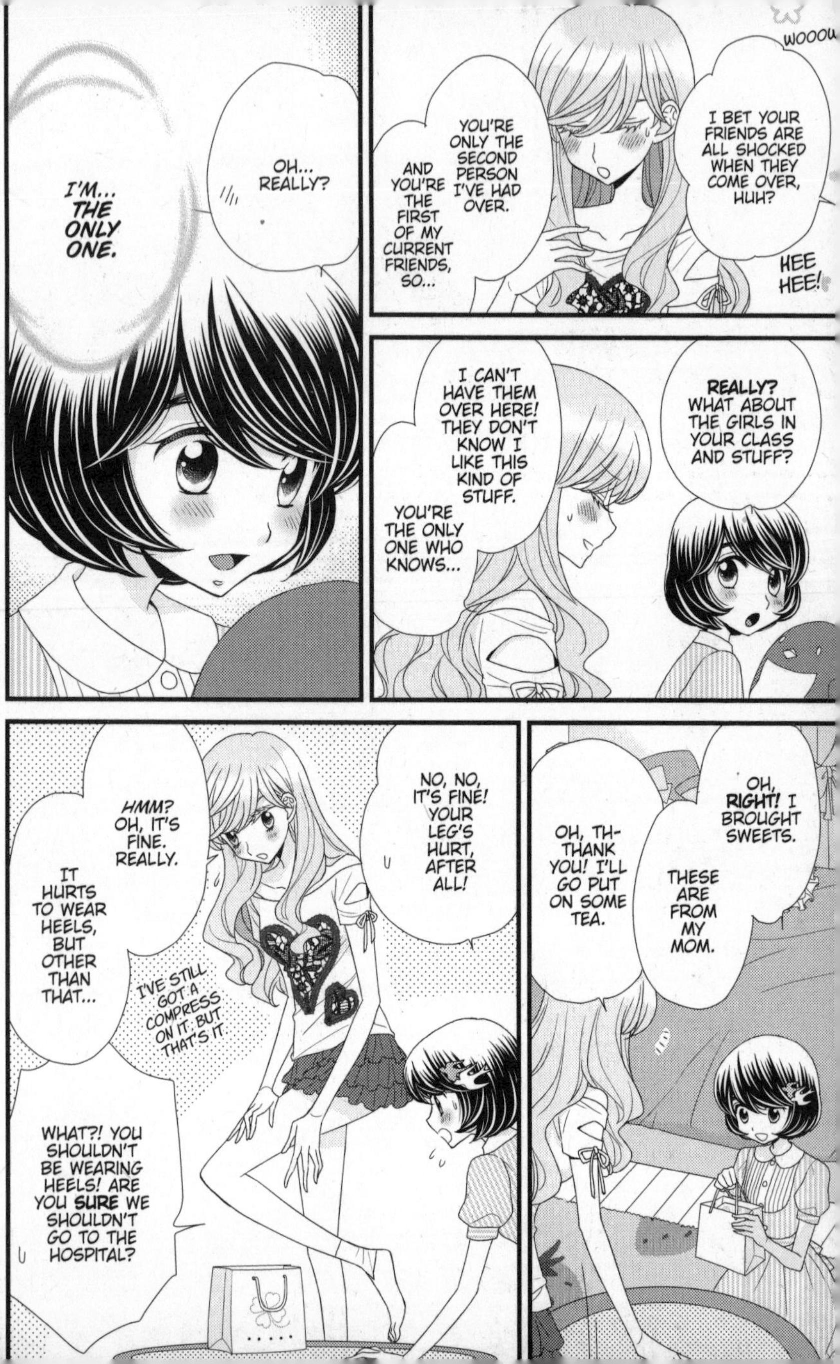
WOOOU
I BET YOUR FRIENDS ARE ALL SHOCKED WHEN THEY COME OVER, HUH?
HEE HEE!
YOU'RE ONLY THE SECOND PERSON I'VE HAD OVER.
AND YOU'RE THE FIRST OF MY CURRENT FRIENDS, SO...
REALLY? WHAT ABOUT THE GIRLS IN YOUR CLASS AND STUFF?
I CAN'T HAVE THEM OVER HERE! THEY DON'T KNOW I LIKE THIS KIND OF STUFF.
YOU'RE THE ONLY ONE WHO KNOWS...
OH... REALLY?
I'M... THE ONLY ONE.
OH, RIGHT! I BROUGHT SWEETS.
THESE ARE FROM MY MOM.
OH, TH-THANK YOU! I'LL GO PUT ON SOME TEA.
NO, NO, IT'S FINE! YOUR LEG'S HURT, AFTER ALL!
HMM? OH, IT'S FINE. REALLY.
IT HURTS TO WEAR HEELS, BUT OTHER THAN THAT...
I'VE STILL GOT A COMPRESS ON IT. BUT THAT'S IT.
WHAT?! YOU SHOULDN'T BE WEARING HEELS! ARE YOU SURE WE SHOULDN'T GO TO THE HOSPITAL?

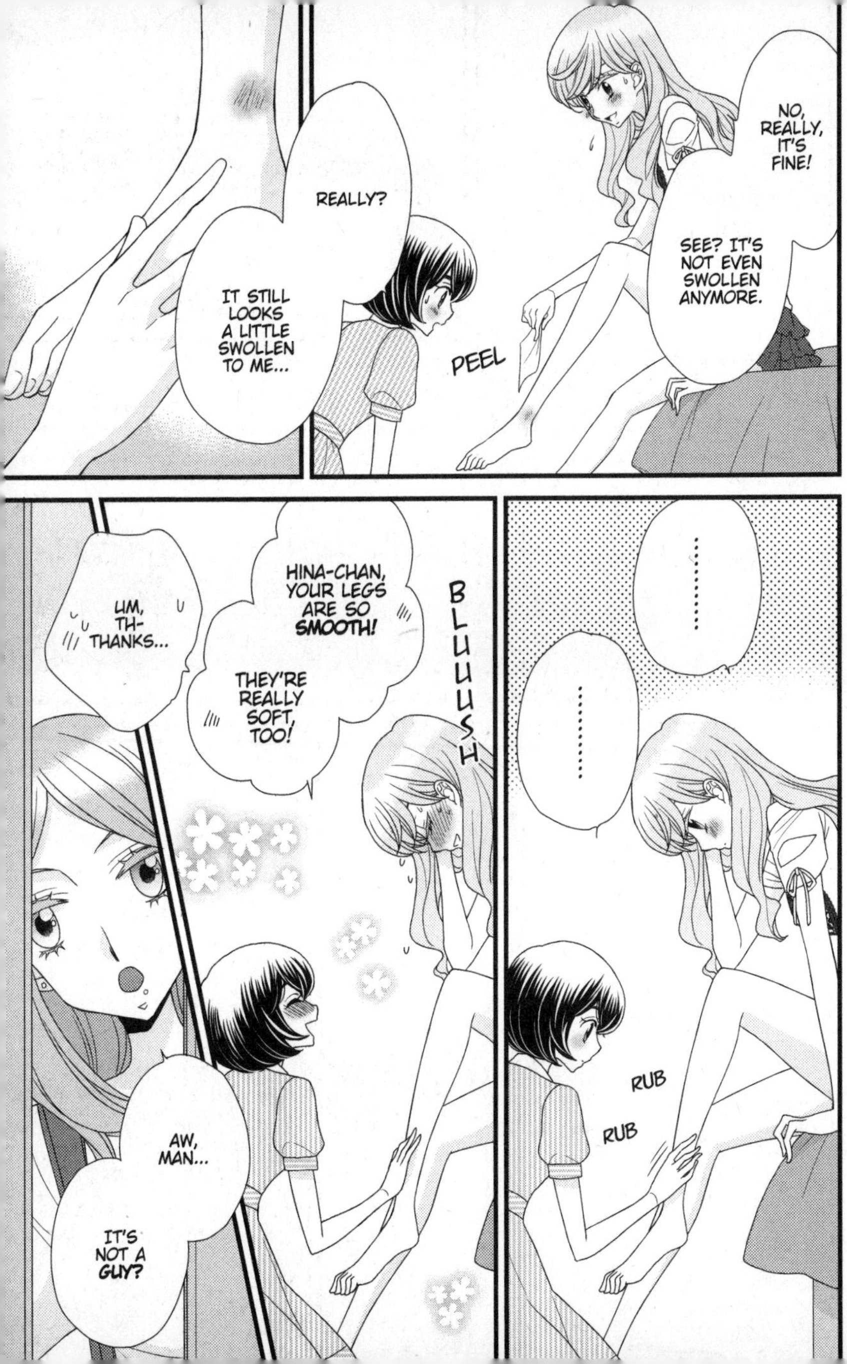
NO, REALLY, IT'S FINE!
SEE? IT'S NOT EVEN SWOLLEN ANYMORE.
PEEL
REALLY?
IT STILL LOOKS A LITTLE SWOLLEN TO ME...
......
......
RUB
RUB
HINA-CHAN, YOUR LEGS ARE SO **SMOOTH!**
THEY'RE REALLY SOFT, TOO!
BLUUUSH
UM, TH-THANKS...
AW, MAN...
IT'S NOT A **GUY?**

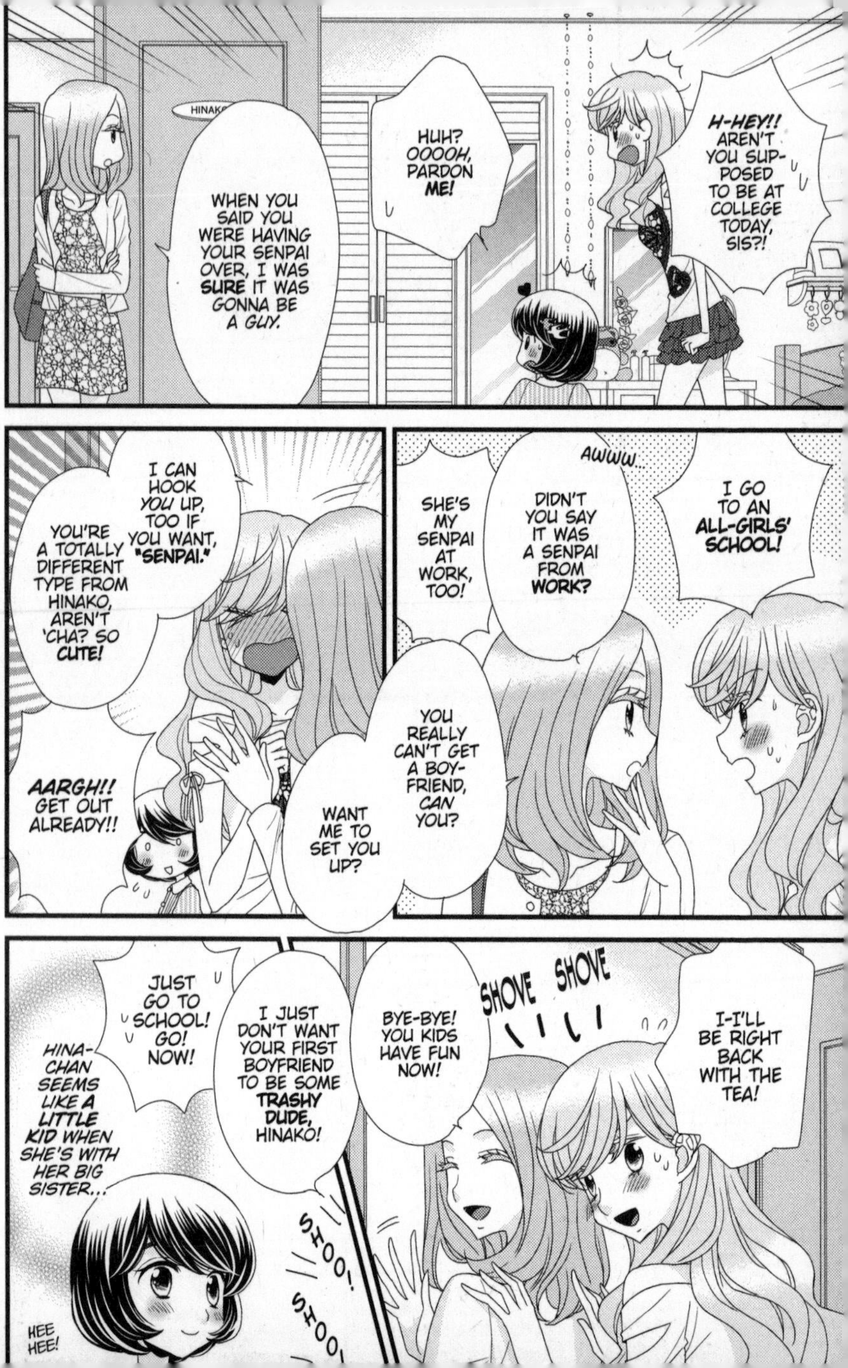
H-HEY!! AREN'T YOU SUP-POSED TO BE AT COLLEGE TODAY, SIS?!
HUH? OOOOH, PARDON ME!
WHEN YOU SAID YOU WERE HAVING YOUR SENPAI OVER, I WAS SURE IT WAS GONNA BE A GUY.
I GO TO AN ALL-GIRLS' SCHOOL!
AWWW...
DIDN'T YOU SAY IT WAS A SENPAI FROM WORK?
SHE'S MY SENPAI AT WORK, TOO!
YOU REALLY CAN'T GET A BOY-FRIEND, CAN YOU?
WANT ME TO SET YOU UP?
I CAN HOOK YOU UP, TOO IF YOU WANT, "SENPAI."
YOU'RE A TOTALLY DIFFERENT TYPE FROM HINAKO, AREN'T 'CHA? SO CUTE!
AARGH!! GET OUT ALREADY!!
I-I'LL BE RIGHT BACK WITH THE TEA!
SHOVE SHOVE
BYE-BYE! YOU KIDS HAVE FUN NOW!
I JUST DON'T WANT YOUR FIRST BOYFRIEND TO BE SOME TRASHY DUDE, HINAKO!
JUST GO TO SCHOOL! GO! NOW!
SHOO! SHOO!
HINA-CHAN SEEMS LIKE A LITTLE KID WHEN SHE'S WITH HER BIG SISTER...
HEE HEE!

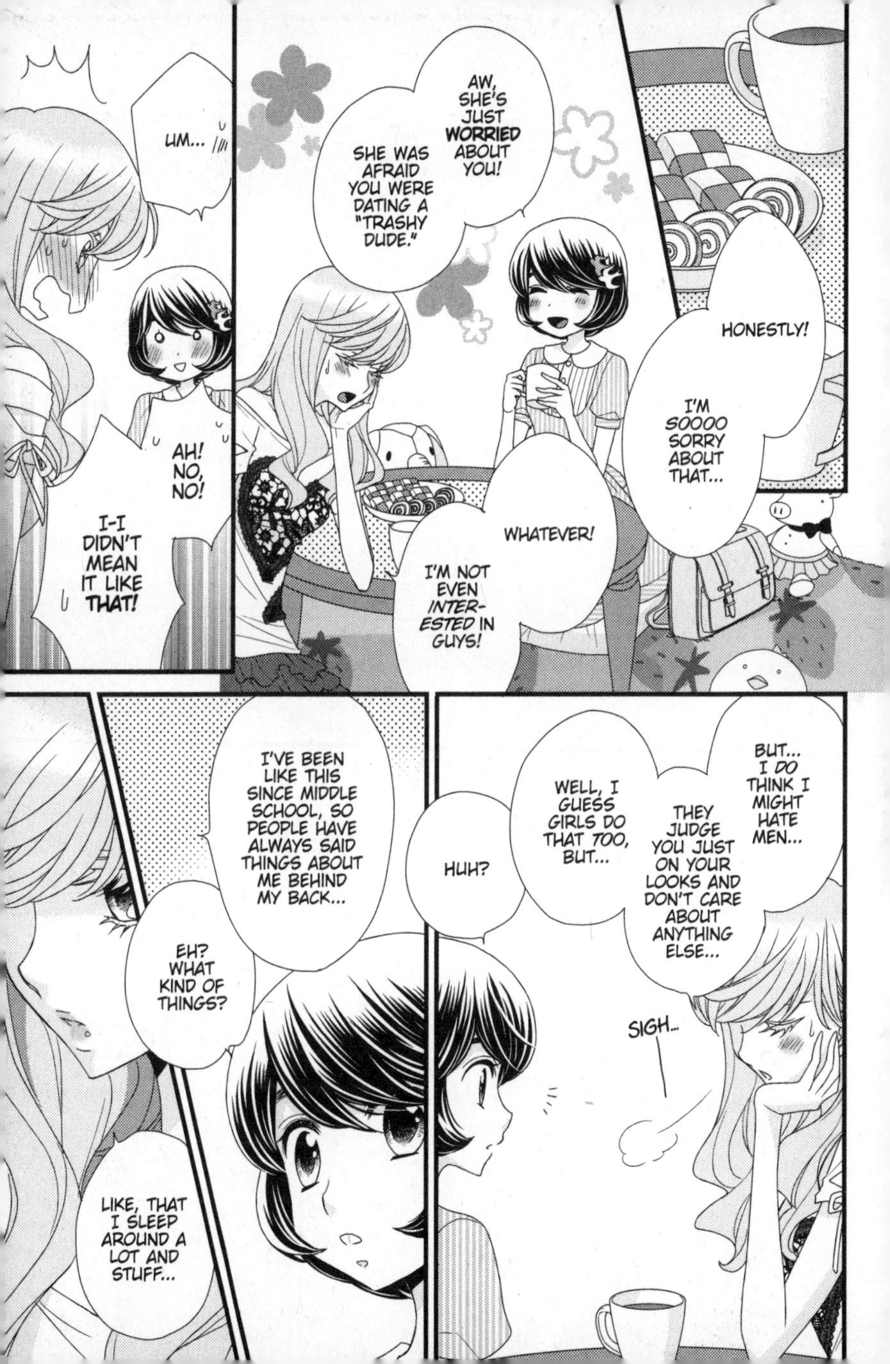
HONESTLY!
I'M SOOOO SORRY ABOUT THAT...
AW, SHE'S JUST WORRIED ABOUT YOU!
SHE WAS AFRAID YOU WERE DATING A "TRASHY DUDE."
WHATEVER!
I'M NOT EVEN INTERESTED IN GUYS!
UM...
AH! NO, NO!
I-I DIDN'T MEAN IT LIKE THAT!
BUT... I DO THINK I MIGHT HATE MEN...
THEY JUDGE YOU JUST ON YOUR LOOKS AND DON'T CARE ABOUT ANYTHING ELSE...
WELL, I GUESS GIRLS DO THAT TOO, BUT...
HUH?
SIGH...
I'VE BEEN LIKE THIS SINCE MIDDLE SCHOOL, SO PEOPLE HAVE ALWAYS SAID THINGS ABOUT ME BEHIND MY BACK...
EH? WHAT KIND OF THINGS?
LIKE, THAT I SLEEP AROUND A LOT AND STUFF...

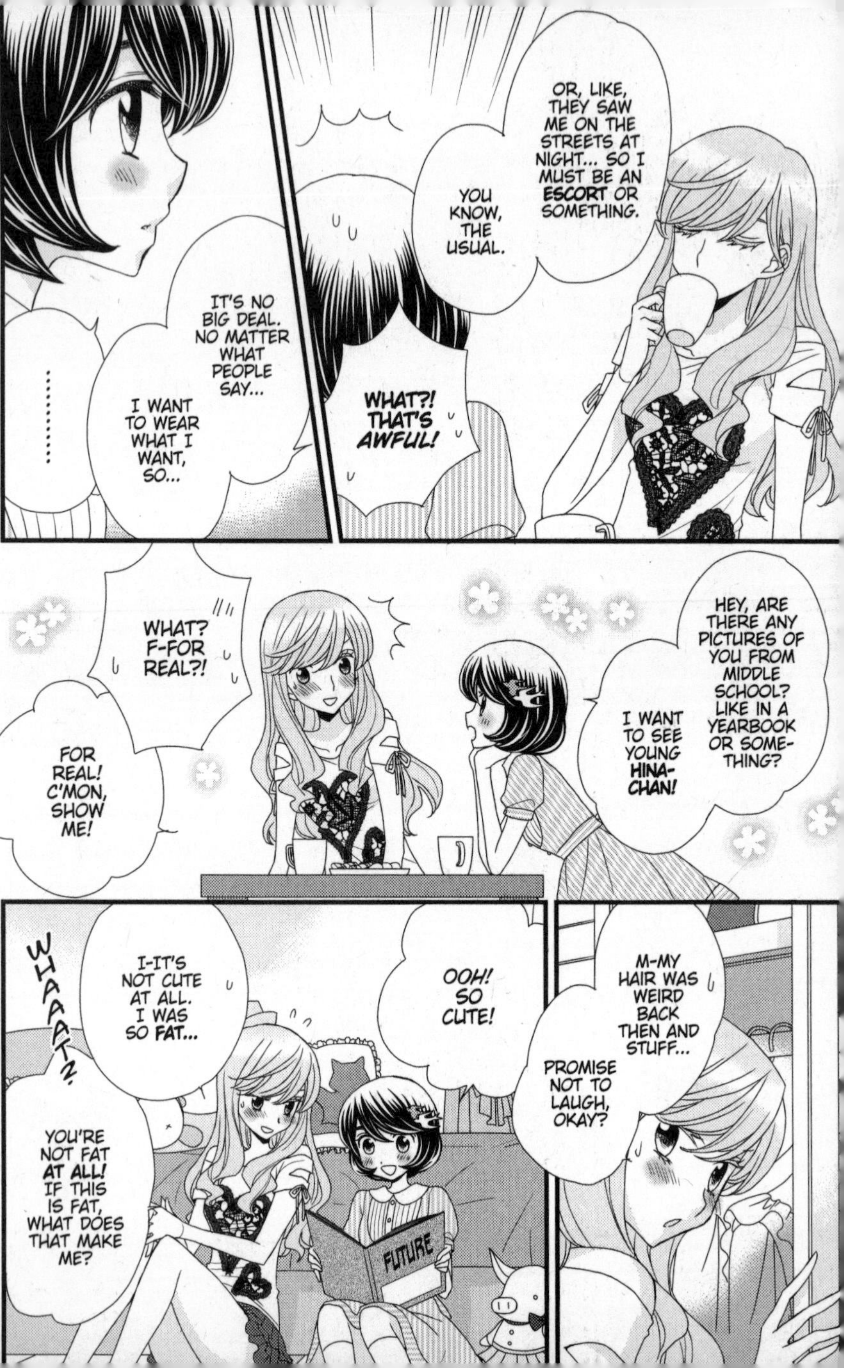
OR, LIKE, THEY SAW ME ON THE STREETS AT NIGHT... SO I MUST BE AN ESCORT OR SOMETHING.
YOU KNOW, THE USUAL.
WHAT?! THAT'S AWFUL!
IT'S NO BIG DEAL. NO MATTER WHAT PEOPLE SAY...
I WANT TO WEAR WHAT I WANT, SO...
......
HEY, ARE THERE ANY PICTURES OF YOU FROM MIDDLE SCHOOL? LIKE IN A YEARBOOK OR SOMETHING?
I WANT TO SEE YOUNG HINA-CHAN!
WHAT? F-FOR REAL?!
FOR REAL! C'MON, SHOW ME!
M-MY HAIR WAS WEIRD BACK THEN AND STUFF...
PROMISE NOT TO LAUGH, OKAY?
OOH! SO CUTE!
I-IT'S NOT CUTE AT ALL. I WAS SO FAT...
WHAAAT?!
YOU'RE NOT FAT AT ALL! IF THIS IS FAT, WHAT DOES THAT MAKE ME?
FUTURE

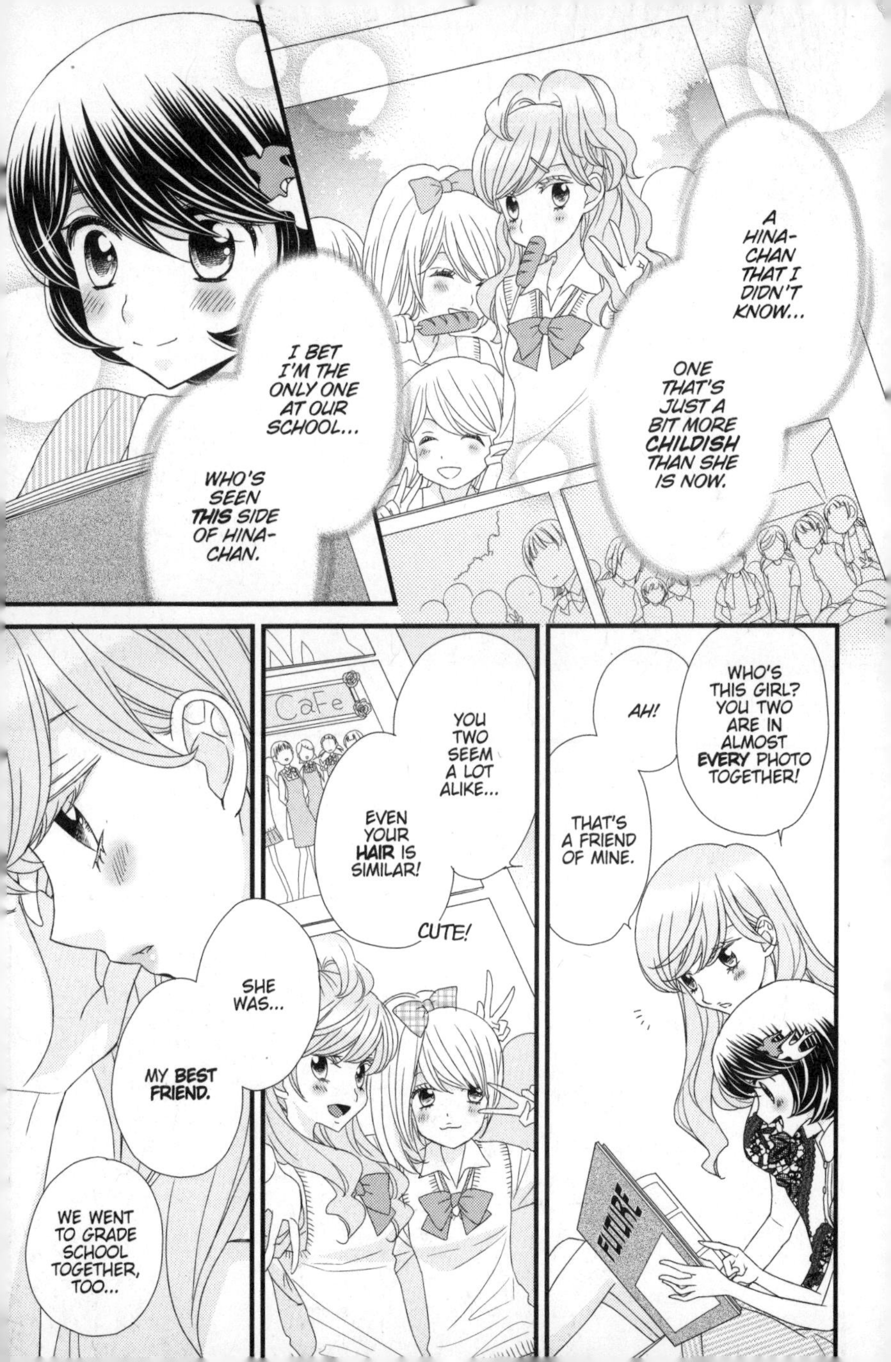
A HINA-CHAN THAT I DIDN'T KNOW...
ONE THAT'S JUST A BIT MORE **CHILDISH** THAN SHE IS NOW.
I BET I'M THE ONLY ONE AT OUR SCHOOL...
WHO'S SEEN **THIS** SIDE OF HINA-CHAN.
WHO'S THIS GIRL? YOU TWO ARE IN ALMOST **EVERY** PHOTO TOGETHER!
AH!
THAT'S A FRIEND OF MINE.
FUTURE
CaFe
YOU TWO SEEM A LOT ALIKE...
EVEN YOUR **HAIR** IS SIMILAR!
CUTE!
SHE WAS...
MY **BEST FRIEND.**
WE WENT TO GRADE SCHOOL TOGETHER, TOO...

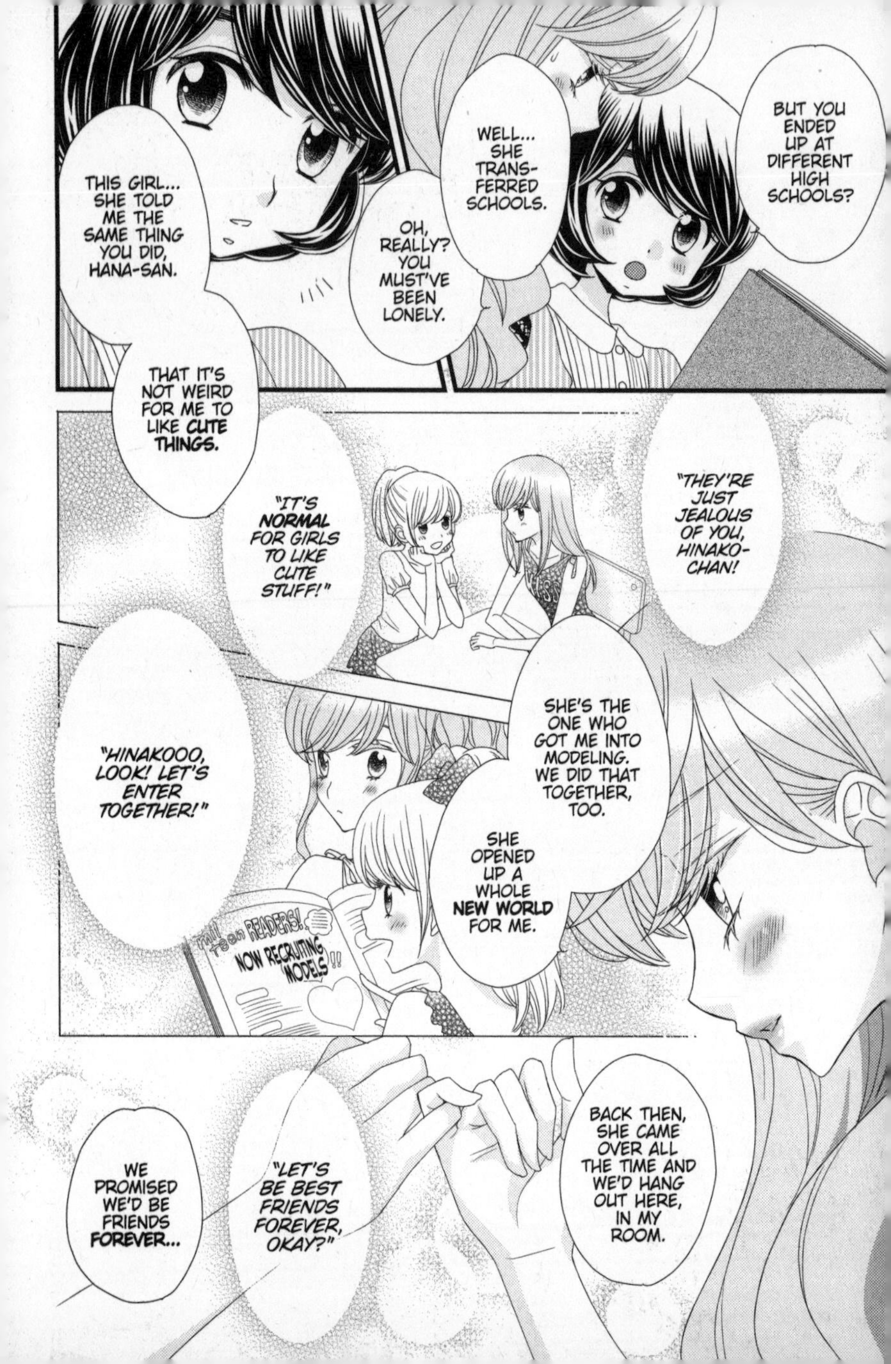
BUT YOU ENDED UP AT DIFFERENT HIGH SCHOOLS?
WELL... SHE TRANS-FERRED SCHOOLS.
OH, REALLY? YOU MUST'VE BEEN LONELY.
THIS GIRL... SHE TOLD ME THE SAME THING YOU DID, HANA-SAN.
THAT IT'S NOT WEIRD FOR ME TO LIKE **CUTE THINGS.**
"THEY'RE JUST JEALOUS OF YOU, HINAKO-CHAN!
"IT'S **NORMAL** FOR GIRLS TO LIKE CUTE STUFF!"
SHE'S THE ONE WHO GOT ME INTO MODELING. WE DID THAT TOGETHER, TOO.
SHE OPENED UP A WHOLE **NEW WORLD** FOR ME.
"HINAKOOO, LOOK! LET'S ENTER TOGETHER!"
mil teen READERS!
NOW RECRUITING MODELS!!
BACK THEN, SHE CAME OVER ALL THE TIME AND WE'D HANG OUT HERE, IN MY ROOM.
"LET'S BE BEST FRIENDS FOREVER, OKAY?"
WE PROMISED WE'D BE FRIENDS **FOREVER...**

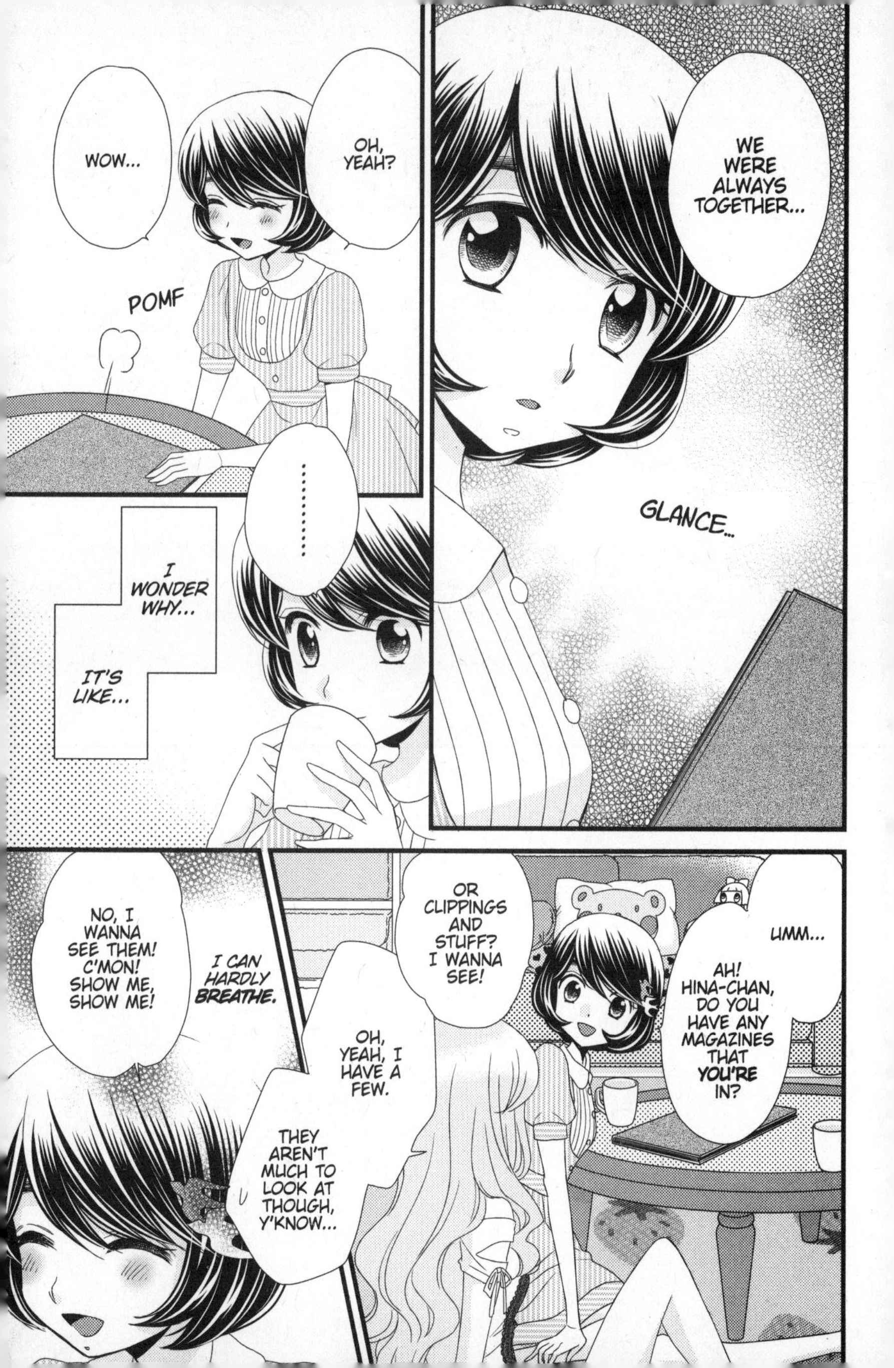
WE WERE ALWAYS TOGETHER...
GLANCE...
OH, YEAH?
WOW...
POMF
....
I WONDER WHY...
IT'S LIKE...
UMM...
AH! HINA-CHAN, DO YOU HAVE ANY MAGAZINES THAT YOU'RE IN?
OR CLIPPINGS AND STUFF? I WANNA SEE!
OH, YEAH, I HAVE A FEW.
THEY AREN'T MUCH TO LOOK AT THOUGH, Y'KNOW...
I CAN HARDLY BREATHE.
NO, I WANNA SEE THEM! C'MON! SHOW ME, SHOW ME!

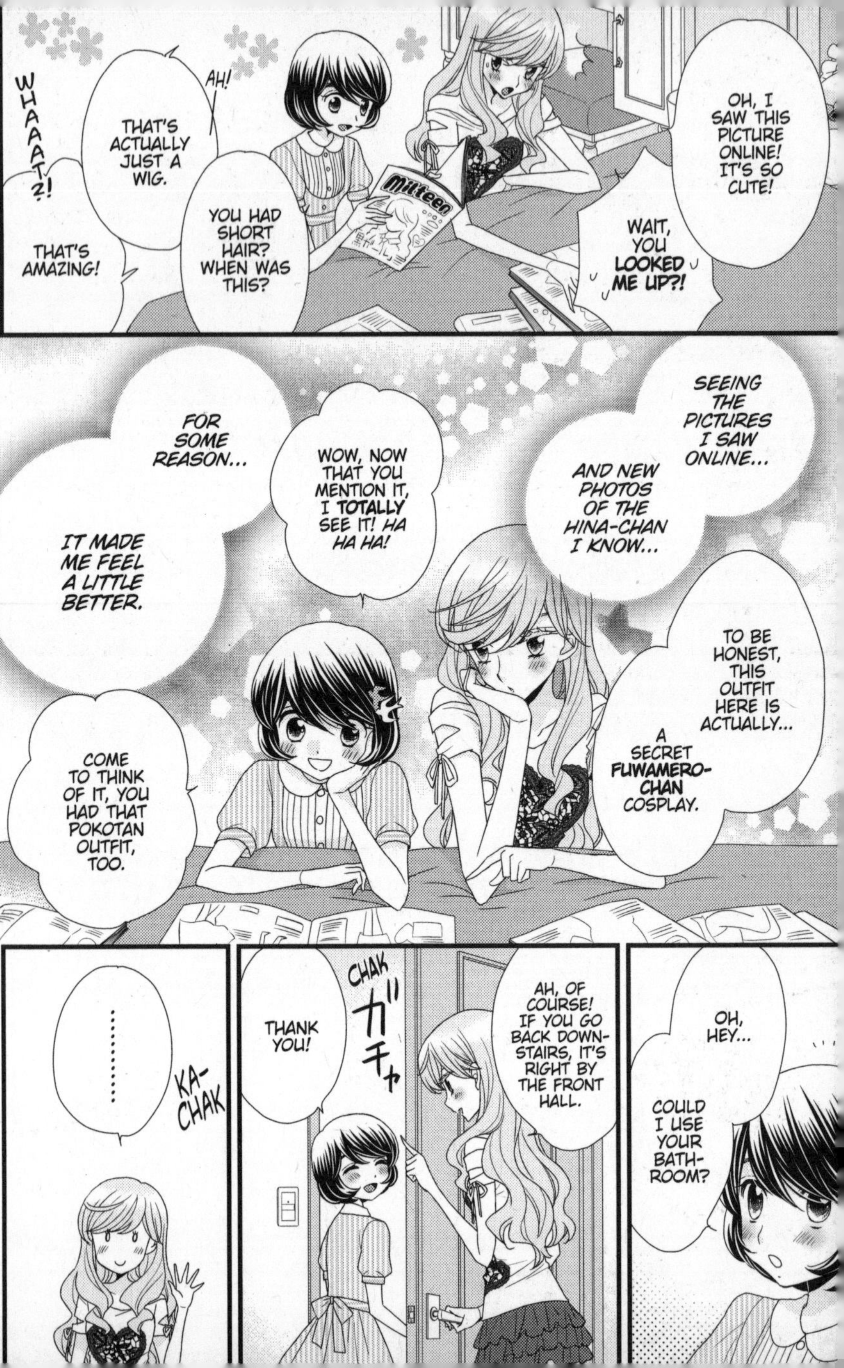

OH, I SAW THIS PICTURE ONLINE! IT'S SO CUTE!
WAIT, YOU LOOKED ME UP?!
AH!
THAT'S ACTUALLY JUST A WIG.
YOU HAD SHORT HAIR? WHEN WAS THIS?
WHAAAT?!
THAT'S AMAZING!
SEEING THE PICTURES I SAW ONLINE...
AND NEW PHOTOS OF THE HINA-CHAN I KNOW...
WOW, NOW THAT YOU MENTION IT, I TOTALLY SEE IT! HA HA HA!
FOR SOME REASON...
IT MADE ME FEEL A LITTLE BETTER.
TO BE HONEST, THIS OUTFIT HERE IS ACTUALLY...
A SECRET FUWAMERO-CHAN COSPLAY.
COME TO THINK OF IT, YOU HAD THAT POKOTAN OUTFIT, TOO.
OH, HEY...
COULD I USE YOUR BATHROOM?
AH, OF COURSE! IF YOU GO BACK DOWN-STAIRS, IT'S RIGHT BY THE FRONT HALL.
CHAK
ガチャ
THANK YOU!
....
KA-CHAK

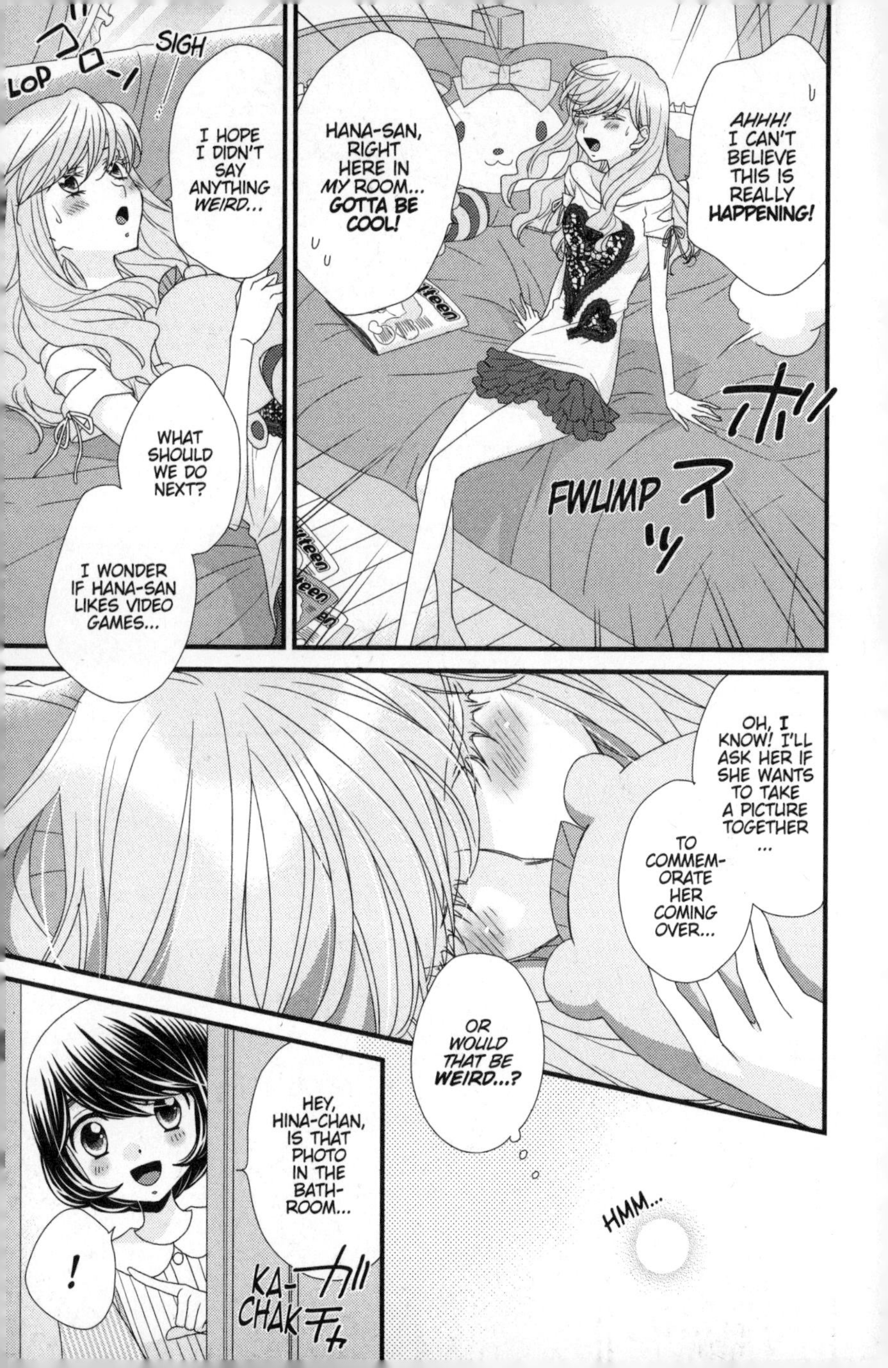
AHHH! I CAN'T BELIEVE THIS IS REALLY HAPPENING!
HANA-SAN, RIGHT HERE IN MY ROOM... GOTTA BE COOL!
FWLUMP
SIGH
LOP
I HOPE I DIDN'T SAY ANYTHING WEIRD...
WHAT SHOULD WE DO NEXT?
I WONDER IF HANA-SAN LIKES VIDEO GAMES...
OH, I KNOW! I'LL ASK HER IF SHE WANTS TO TAKE A PICTURE TOGETHER...
TO COMMEM-ORATE HER COMING OVER...
OR WOULD THAT BE WEIRD...?
HMM...
HEY, HINA-CHAN, IS THAT PHOTO IN THE BATH-ROOM...
KA-CHAK
!

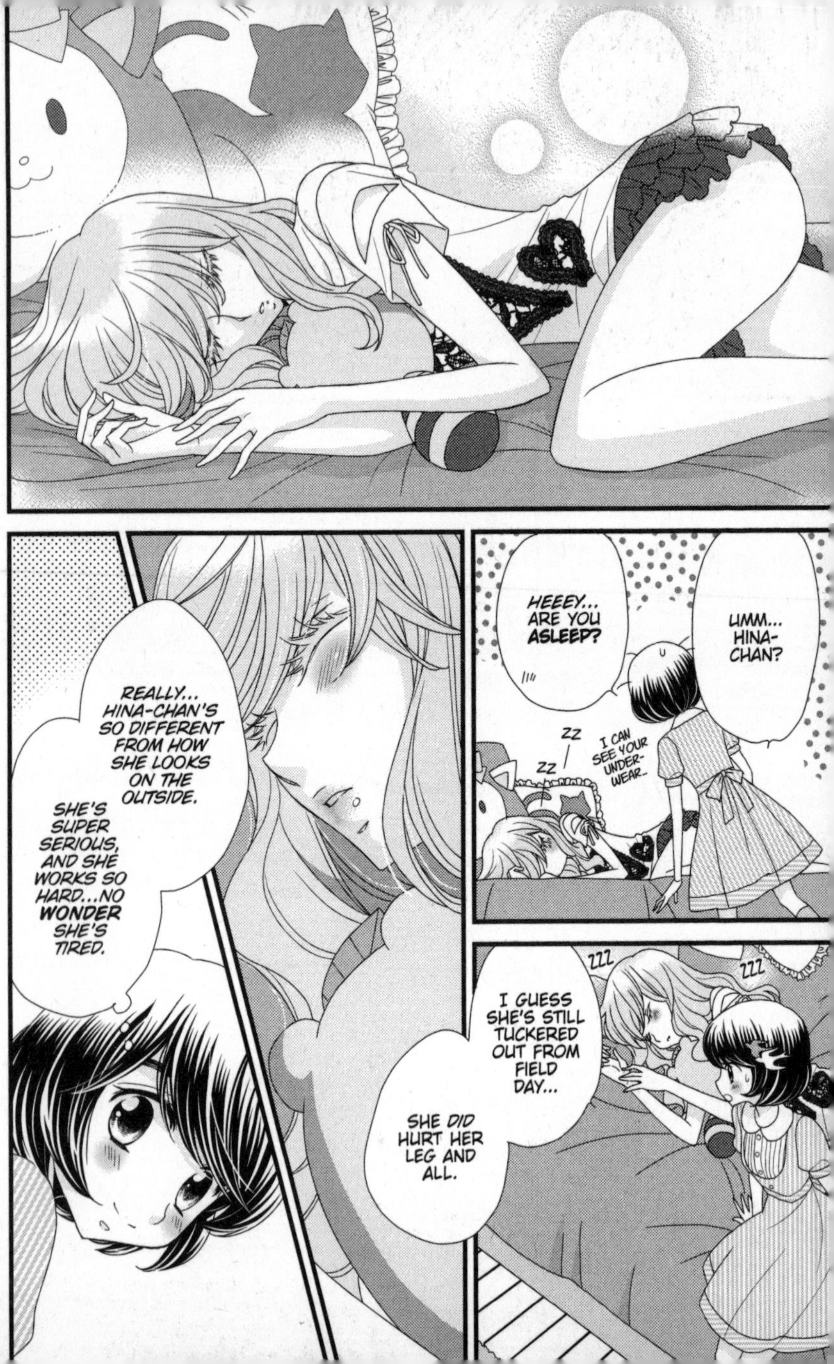
UMM... HINA-CHAN?
HEEEY... ARE YOU ASLEEP?
I CAN SEE YOUR UNDER-WEAR..
ZZ
ZZ
ZZZ
ZZZ
I GUESS SHE'S STILL TUCKERED OUT FROM FIELD DAY...
SHE DID HURT HER LEG AND ALL.
REALLY... HINA-CHAN'S SO DIFFERENT FROM HOW SHE LOOKS ON THE OUTSIDE.
SHE'S SUPER SERIOUS, AND SHE WORKS SO HARD...NO WONDER SHE'S TIRED.

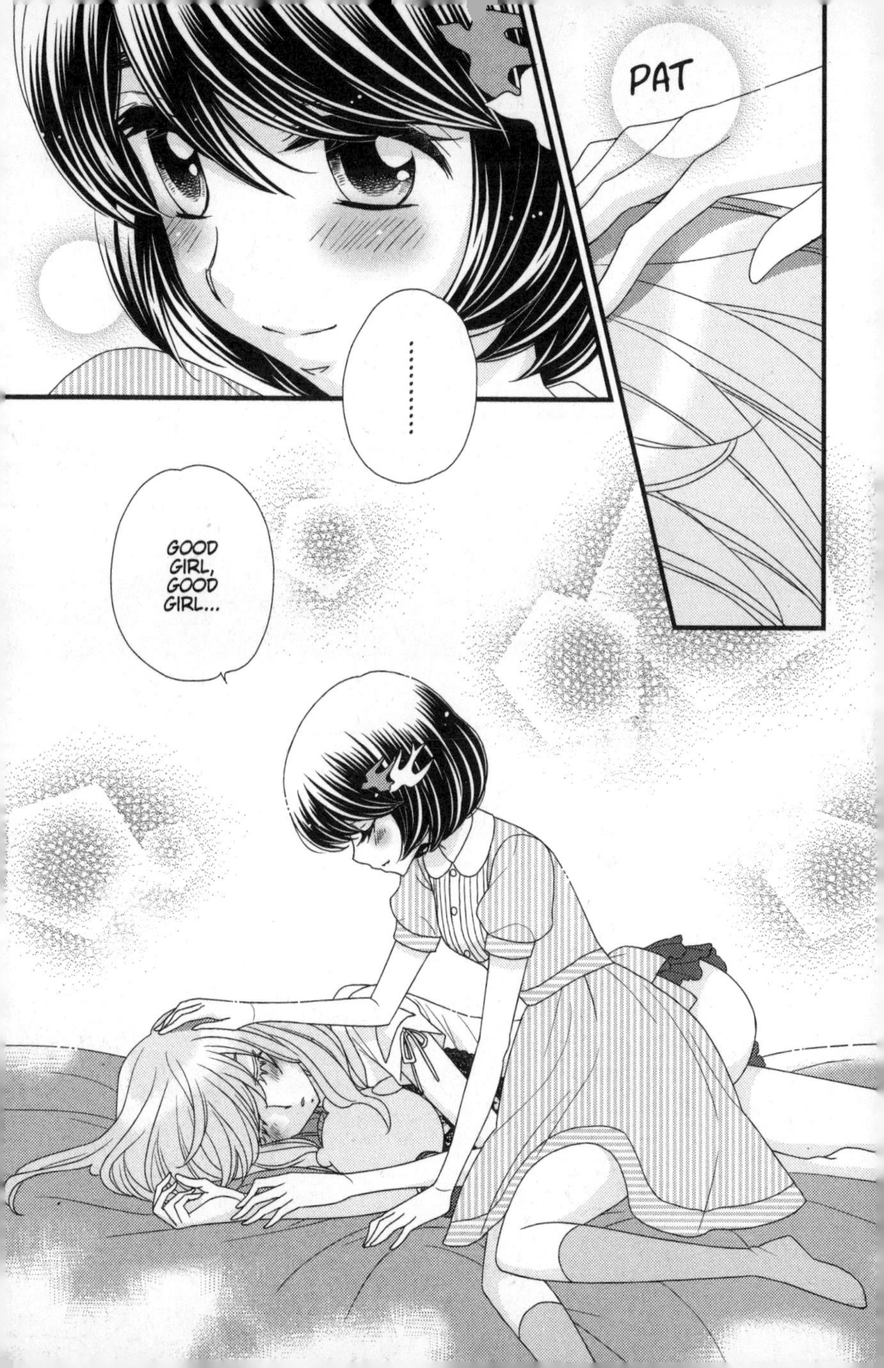
PAT
....
GOOD GIRL, GOOD GIRL...

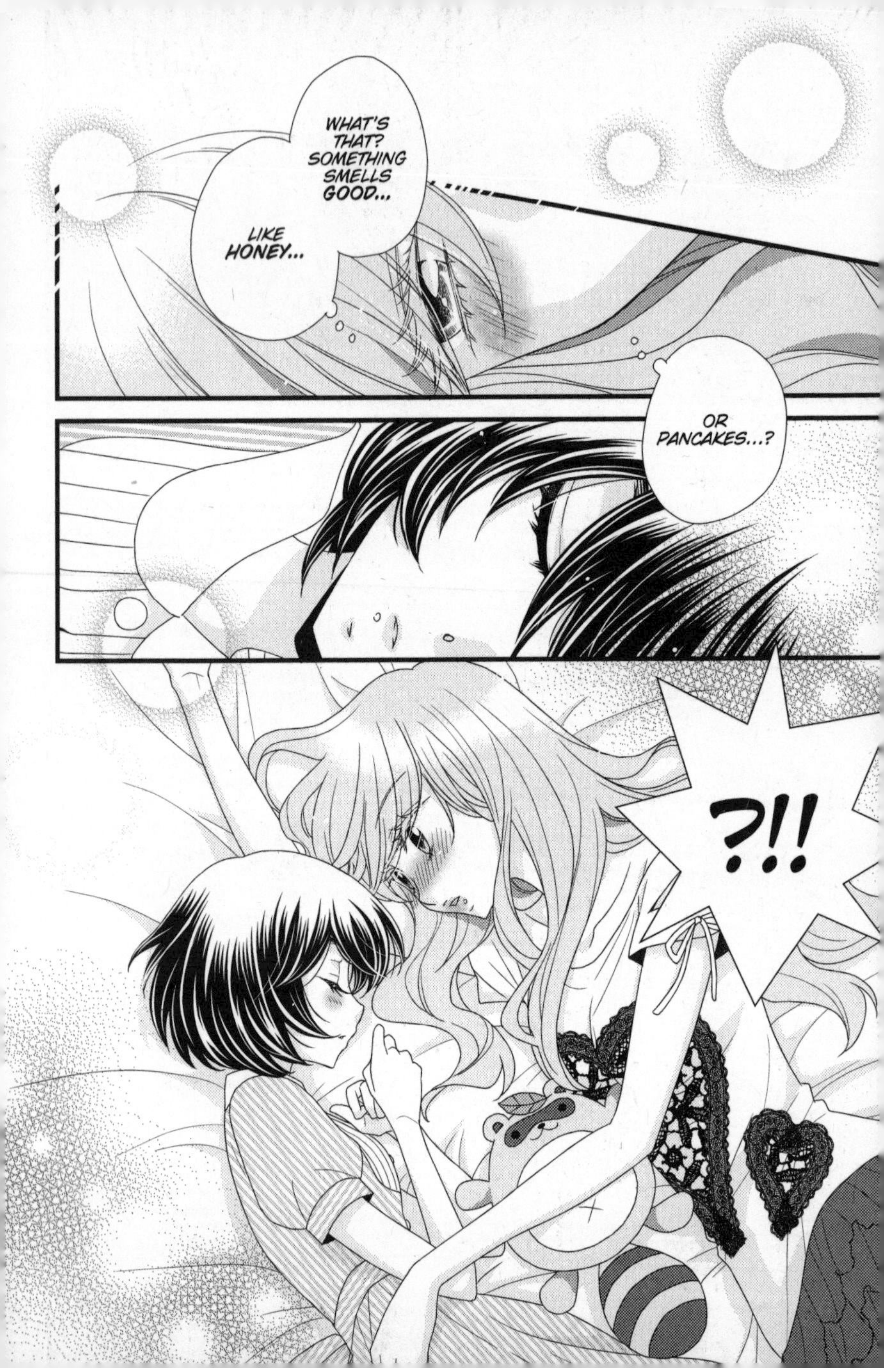
WHAT'S THAT? SOMETHING SMELLS GOOD...
LIKE HONEY...
OR PANCAKES...?
?!!

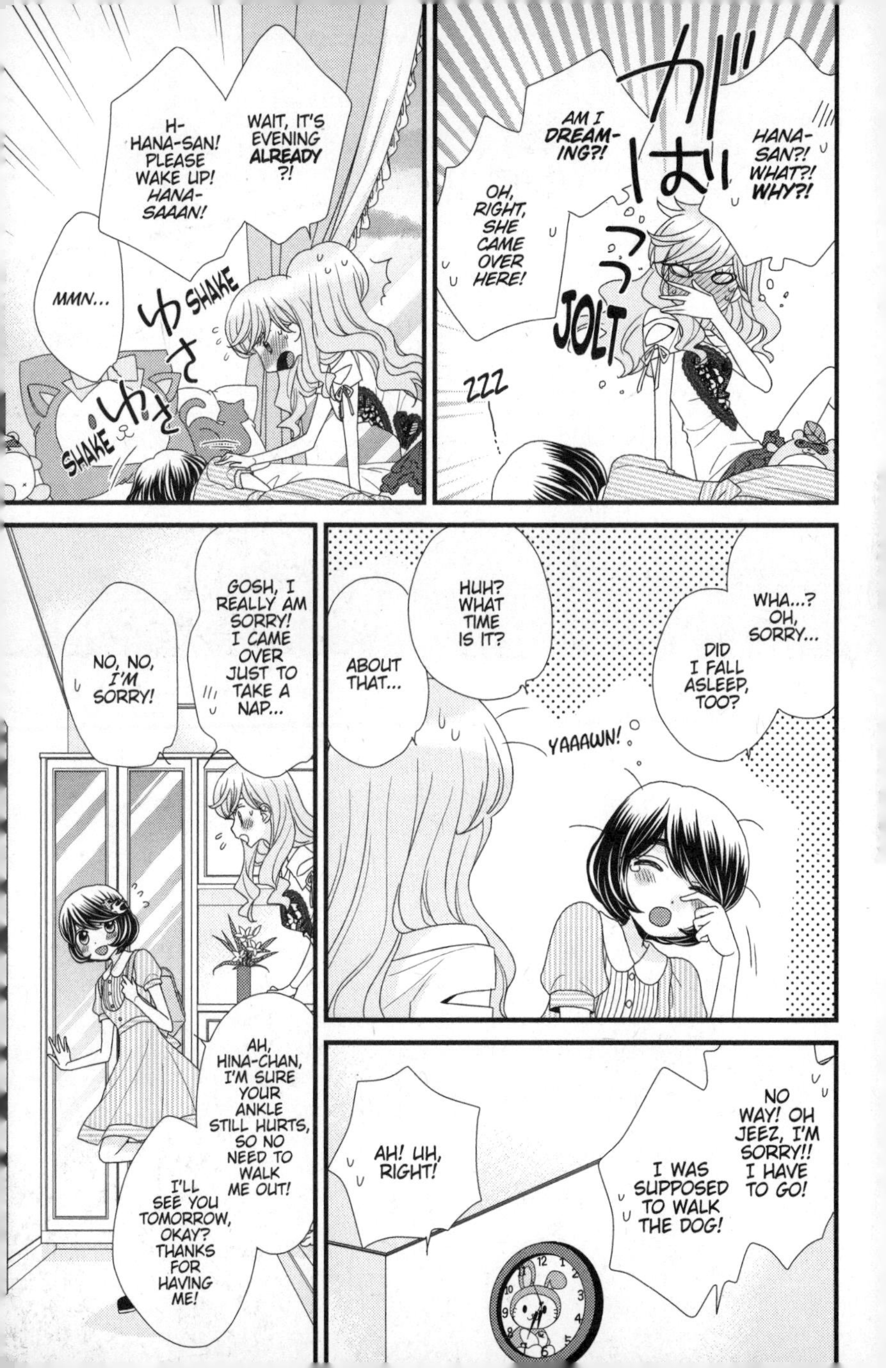
がばっ
JOLT
HANA-SAN?! WHAT?! WHY?!
AM I DREAMING?!
OH, RIGHT, SHE CAME OVER HERE!
ZZZ
WAIT, IT'S EVENING ALREADY?!
H-HANA-SAN! PLEASE WAKE UP! HANA-SAAAN!
MMN...
ゆさ SHAKE
ゆさ SHAKE
WHA...? OH, SORRY...
DID I FALL ASLEEP, TOO?
YAAAWN!
HUH? WHAT TIME IS IT?
ABOUT THAT...
NO WAY! OH JEEZ, I'M SORRY!! I HAVE TO GO!
I WAS SUPPOSED TO WALK THE DOG!
AH! UH, RIGHT!
GOSH, I REALLY AM SORRY! I CAME OVER JUST TO TAKE A NAP...
NO, NO, I'M SORRY!
AH, HINA-CHAN, I'M SURE YOUR ANKLE STILL HURTS, SO NO NEED TO WALK ME OUT!
I'LL SEE YOU TOMORROW, OKAY? THANKS FOR HAVING ME!

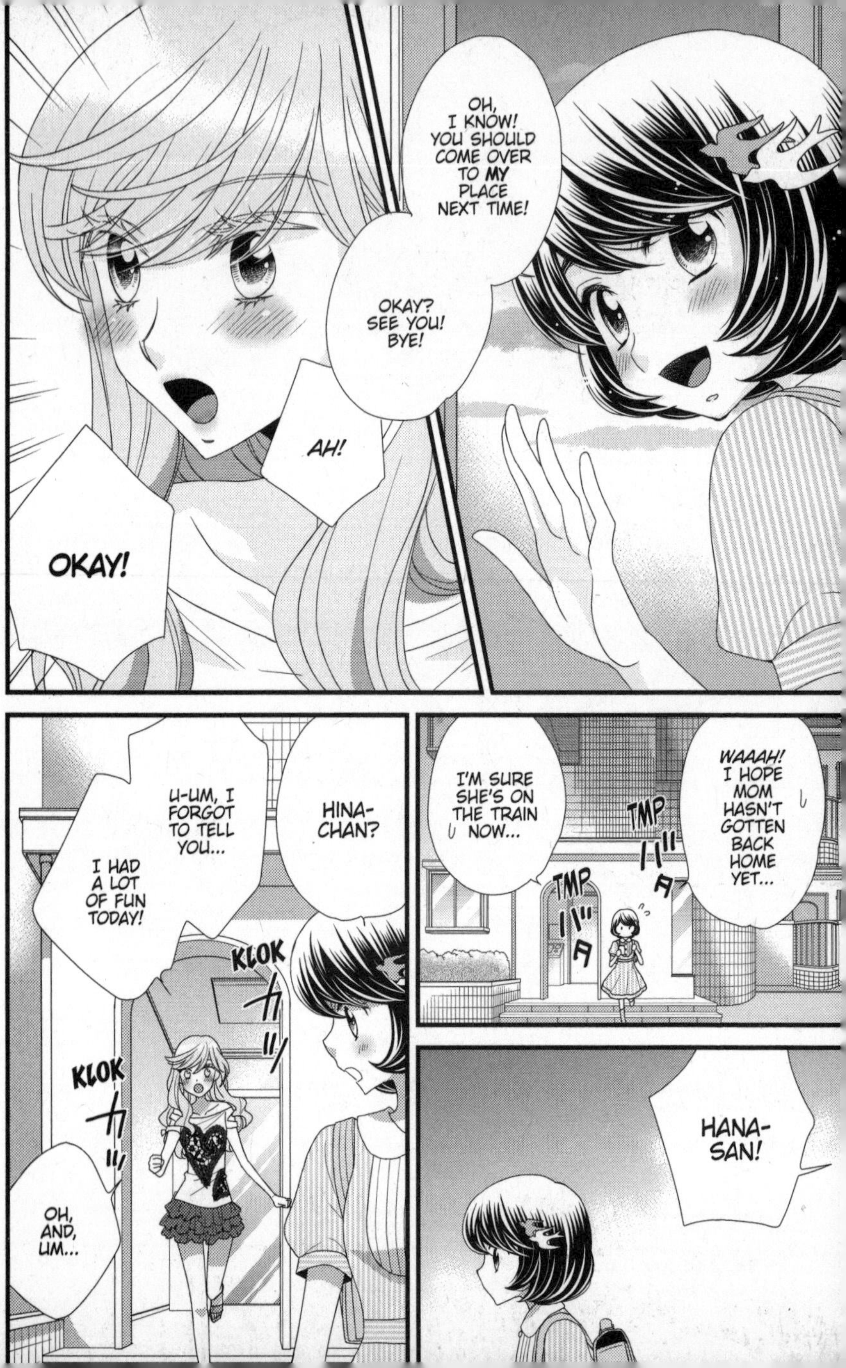
OH, I KNOW! YOU SHOULD COME OVER TO MY PLACE NEXT TIME!
OKAY? SEE YOU! BYE!
AH!
OKAY!
WAAAH! I HOPE MOM HASN'T GOTTEN BACK HOME YET...
TMP
TMP
I'M SURE SHE'S ON THE TRAIN NOW...
HANA-SAN!
HINA-CHAN?
U-UM, I FORGOT TO TELL YOU...
I HAD A LOT OF FUN TODAY!
KLOK
KLOK
OH, AND, UM...

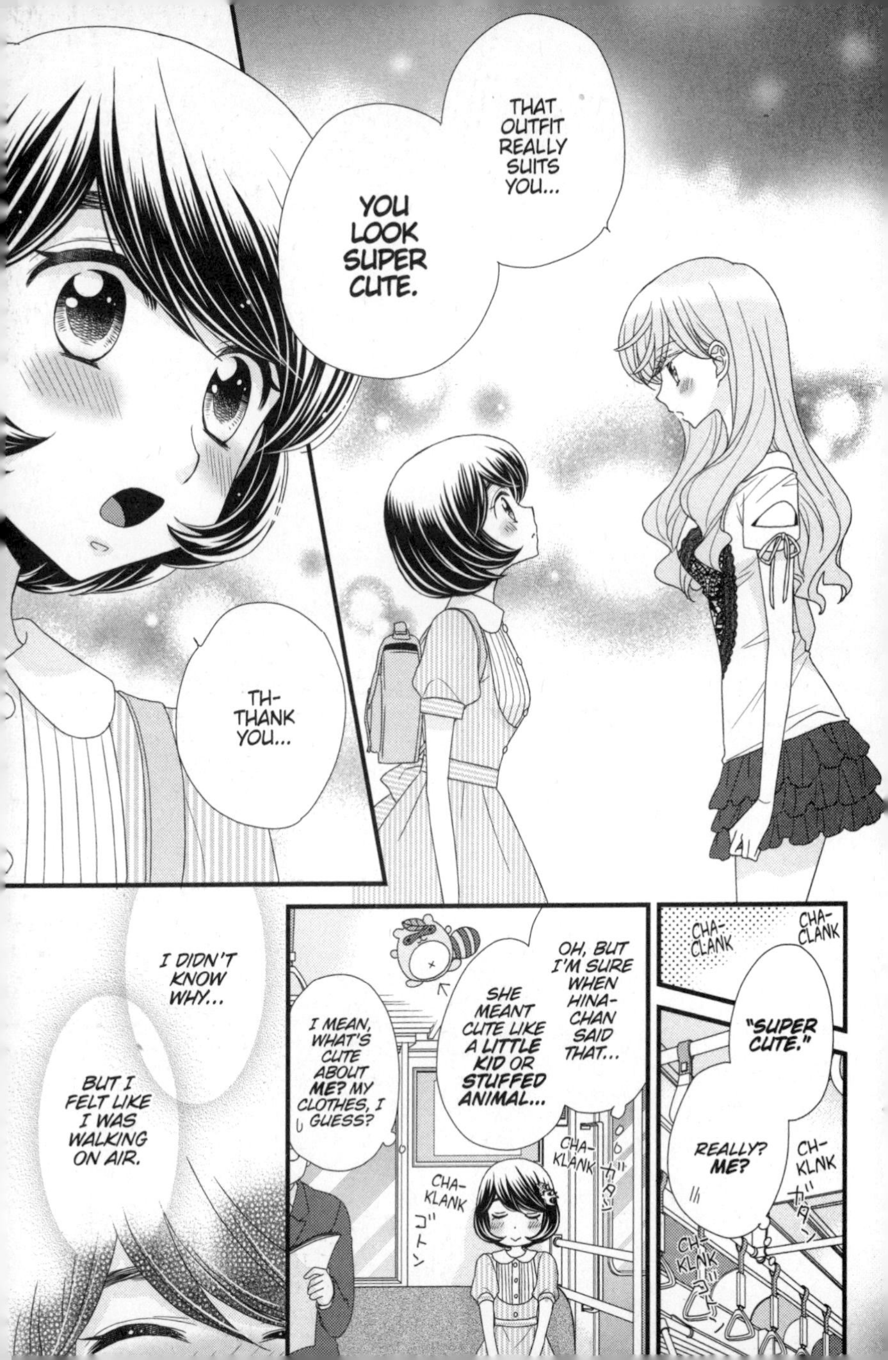
THAT OUTFIT REALLY SUITS YOU...
YOU LOOK SUPER CUTE.
TH-THANK YOU...
CHA-CLANK
CHA-CLANK
"SUPER CUTE."
CH-KLNK
REALLY? ME?
CH-KLNK
OH, BUT I'M SURE WHEN HINA-CHAN SAID THAT...
SHE MEANT CUTE LIKE A LITTLE KID OR STUFFED ANIMAL...
I MEAN, WHAT'S CUTE ABOUT ME? MY CLOTHES, I GUESS?
CHA-KLANK
CHA-KLANK
I DIDN'T KNOW WHY...
BUT I FELT LIKE I WAS WALKING ON AIR.

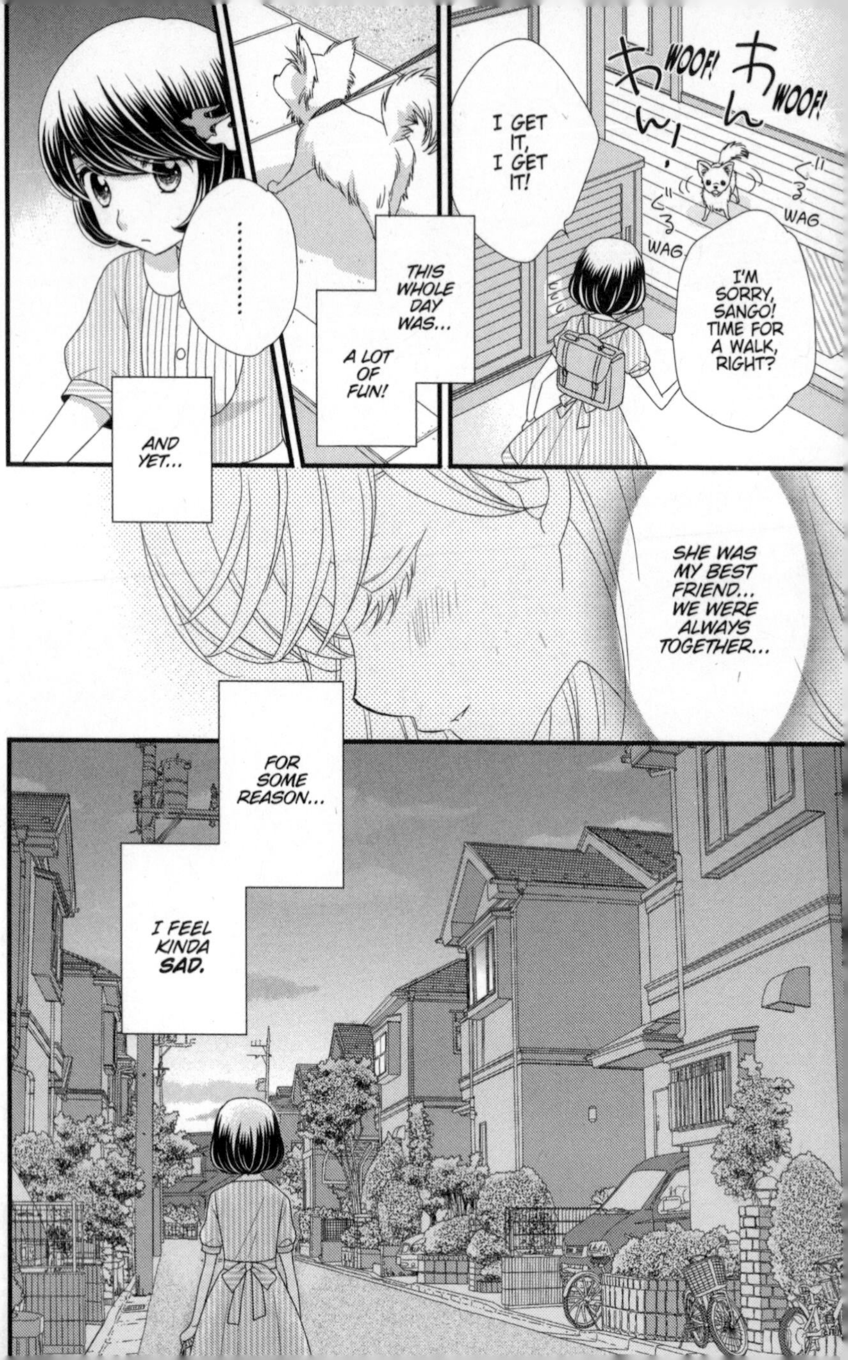

WOOF!
WOOF!
WAG
WAG
I'M SORRY, SANGO! TIME FOR A WALK, RIGHT?
I GET IT, I GET IT!
THIS WHOLE DAY WAS...
A LOT OF FUN!
......
AND YET...
SHE WAS MY BEST FRIEND... WE WERE ALWAYS TOGETHER...
FOR SOME REASON...
I FEEL KINDA SAD.

Hana & Hina
AFTER ♡ SCHOOL

Hana & Hina

AFTER ♡ SCHOOL

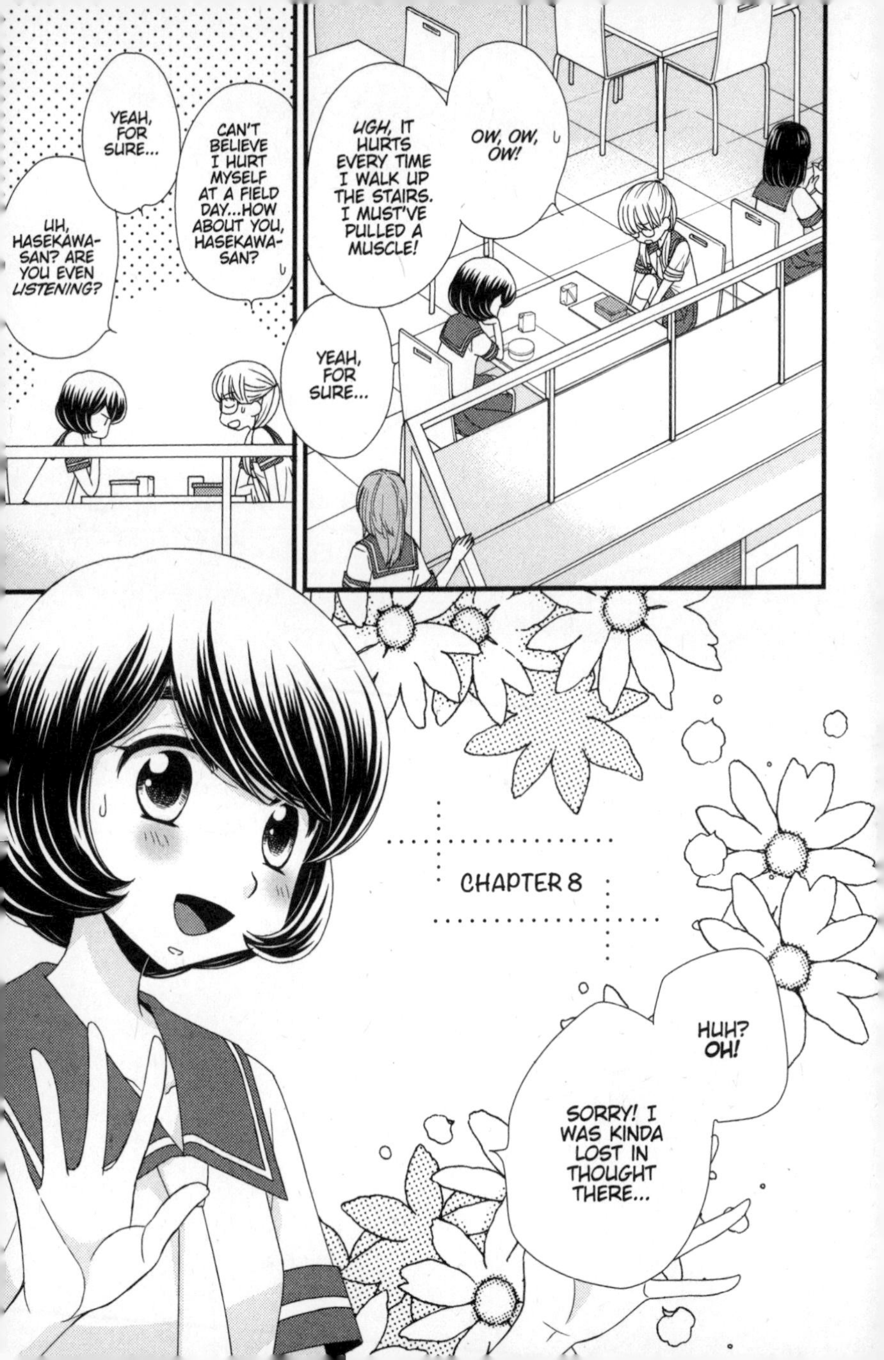
OW, OW, OW!
UGH, IT HURTS EVERY TIME I WALK UP THE STAIRS. I MUST'VE PULLED A MUSCLE!
YEAH, FOR SURE...
CAN'T BELIEVE I HURT MYSELF AT A FIELD DAY...HOW ABOUT YOU, HASEKAWA-SAN?
YEAH, FOR SURE...
UH, HASEKAWA-SAN? ARE YOU EVEN LISTENING?
CHAPTER 8
HUH? OH!
SORRY! I WAS KINDA LOST IN THOUGHT THERE...

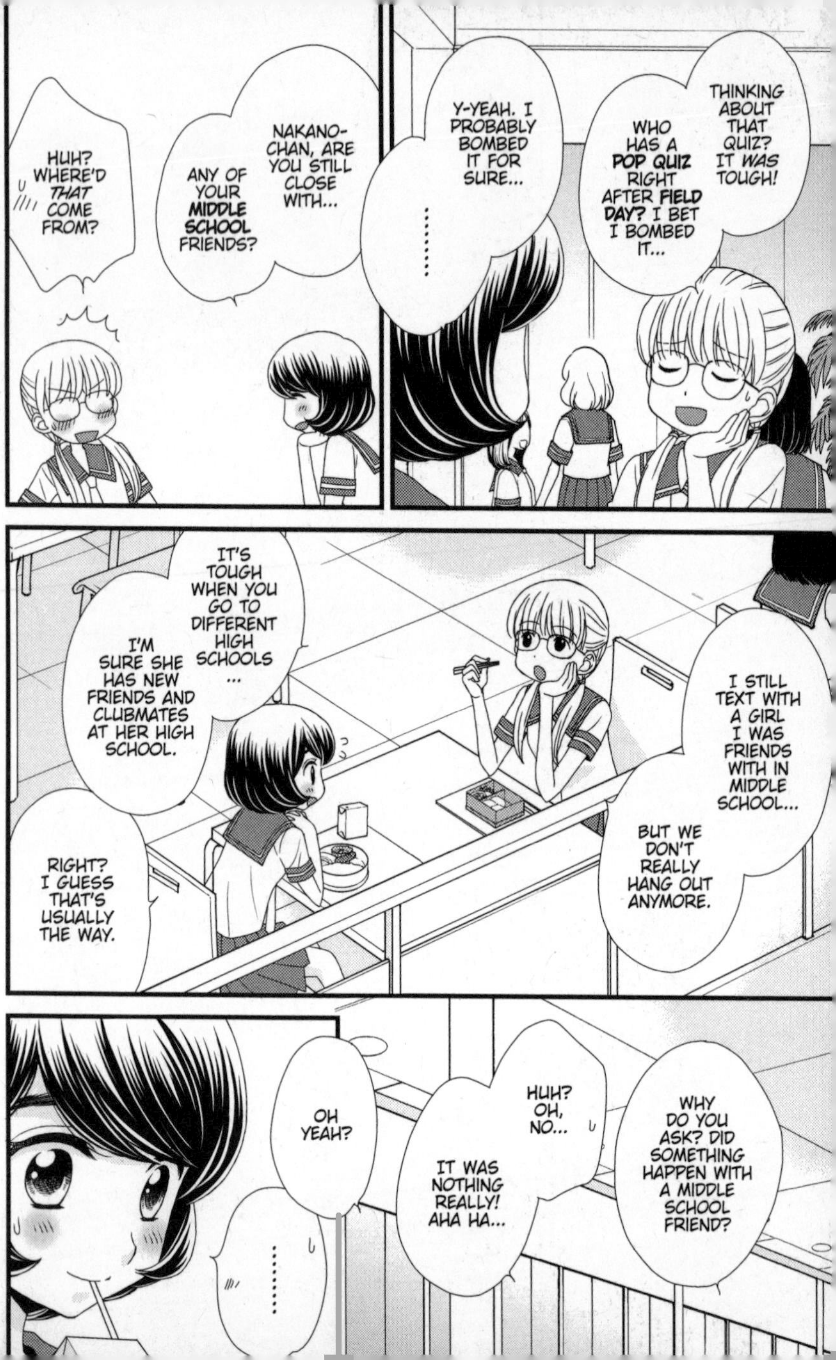
THINKING ABOUT THAT QUIZ? IT WAS TOUGH!
WHO HAS A POP QUIZ RIGHT AFTER FIELD DAY? I BET I BOMBED IT...
Y-YEAH. I PROBABLY BOMBED IT FOR SURE...
......
NAKANO-CHAN, ARE YOU STILL CLOSE WITH...
ANY OF YOUR MIDDLE SCHOOL FRIENDS?
HUH? WHERE'D THAT COME FROM?
I STILL TEXT WITH A GIRL I WAS FRIENDS WITH IN MIDDLE SCHOOL...
BUT WE DON'T REALLY HANG OUT ANYMORE.
IT'S TOUGH WHEN YOU GO TO DIFFERENT HIGH SCHOOLS ...
I'M SURE SHE HAS NEW FRIENDS AND CLUBMATES AT HER HIGH SCHOOL.
RIGHT? I GUESS THAT'S USUALLY THE WAY.
WHY DO YOU ASK? DID SOMETHING HAPPEN WITH A MIDDLE SCHOOL FRIEND?
HUH? OH, NO...
IT WAS NOTHING REALLY! AHA HA...
OH YEAH?
......

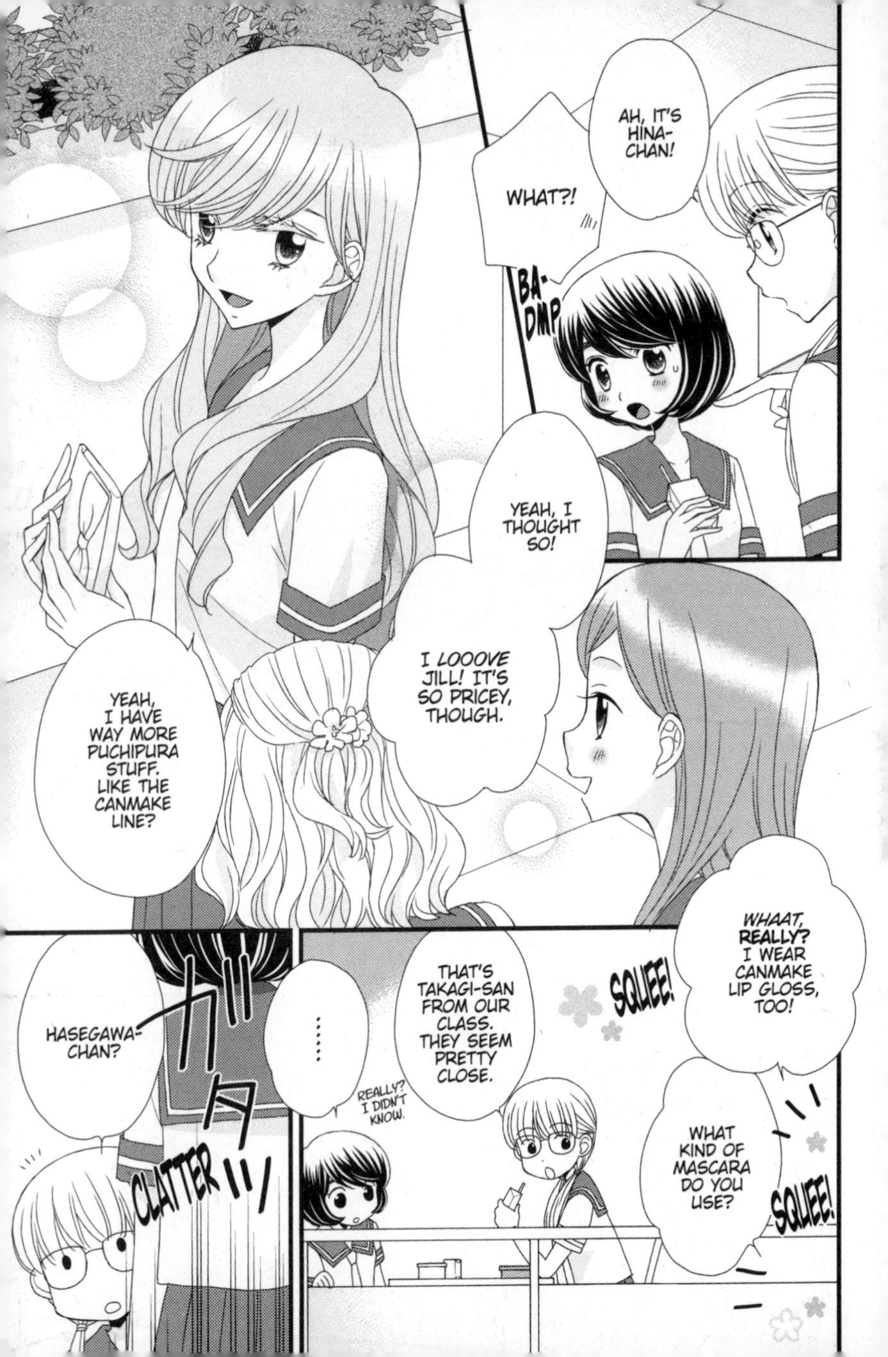
AH, IT'S HINA-CHAN!
WHAT?!
BA-DMP
YEAH, I THOUGHT SO!
I *LOOOVE* JILL! IT'S SO PRICEY, THOUGH.
YEAH, I HAVE WAY MORE PUCHIPURA STUFF. LIKE THE CANMAKE LINE?
WHAAT, **REALLY?** I WEAR CANMAKE LIP GLOSS, TOO!
SQUEE!
WHAT KIND OF MASCARA DO YOU USE?
SQUEE!
THAT'S TAKAGI-SAN FROM OUR CLASS. THEY SEEM PRETTY CLOSE.
REALLY? I DIDN'T KNOW.
......
HASEGAWA-CHAN?
CLATTER

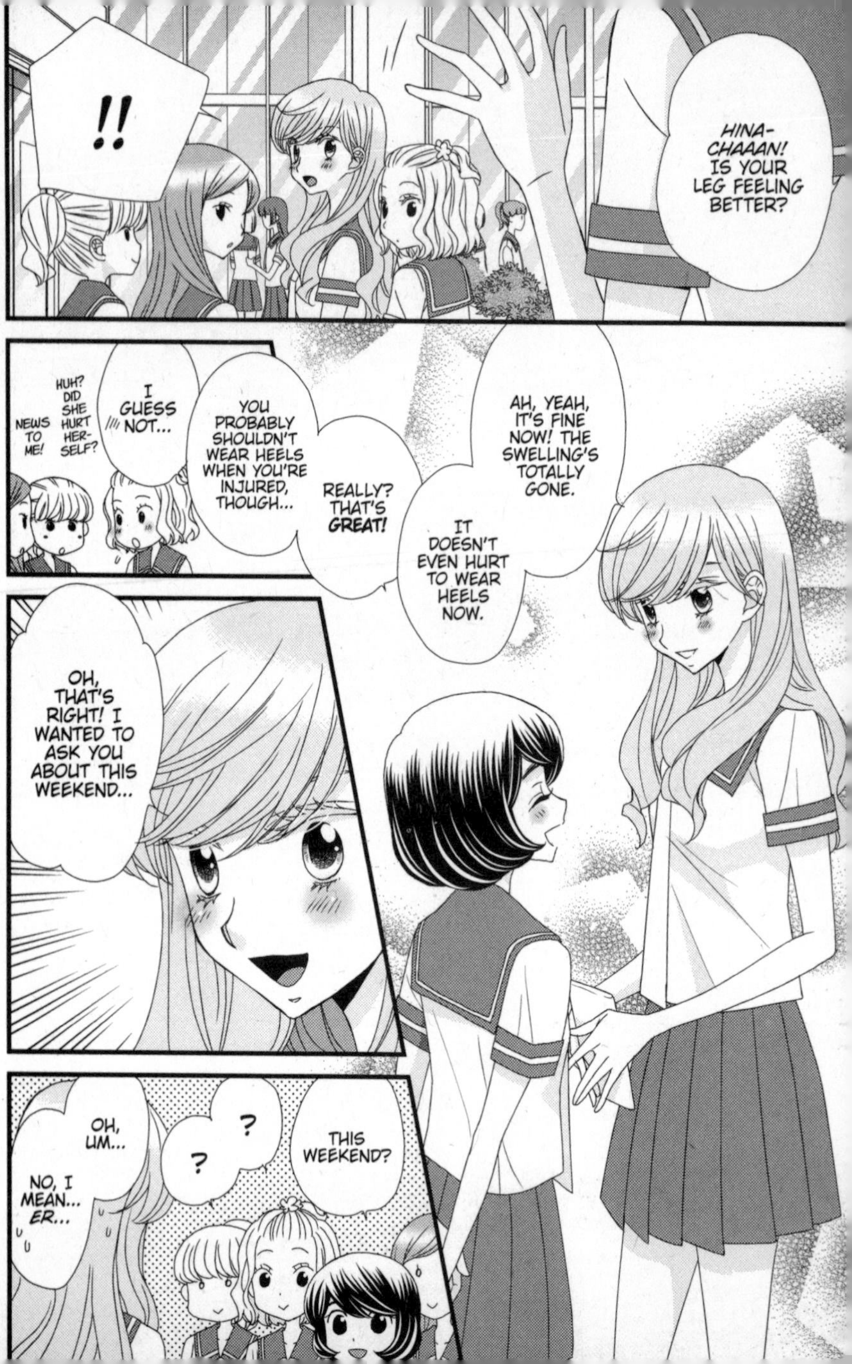
HINA-CHAAAN! IS YOUR LEG FEELING BETTER?
!!
AH, YEAH, IT'S FINE NOW! THE SWELLING'S TOTALLY GONE.
IT DOESN'T EVEN HURT TO WEAR HEELS NOW.
REALLY? THAT'S GREAT!
YOU PROBABLY SHOULDN'T WEAR HEELS WHEN YOU'RE INJURED, THOUGH...
I GUESS NOT...
HUH? DID SHE HURT HER-SELF?
NEWS TO ME!
OH, THAT'S RIGHT! I WANTED TO ASK YOU ABOUT THIS WEEKEND...
THIS WEEKEND?
? ?
OH, UM...
NO, I MEAN... ER...

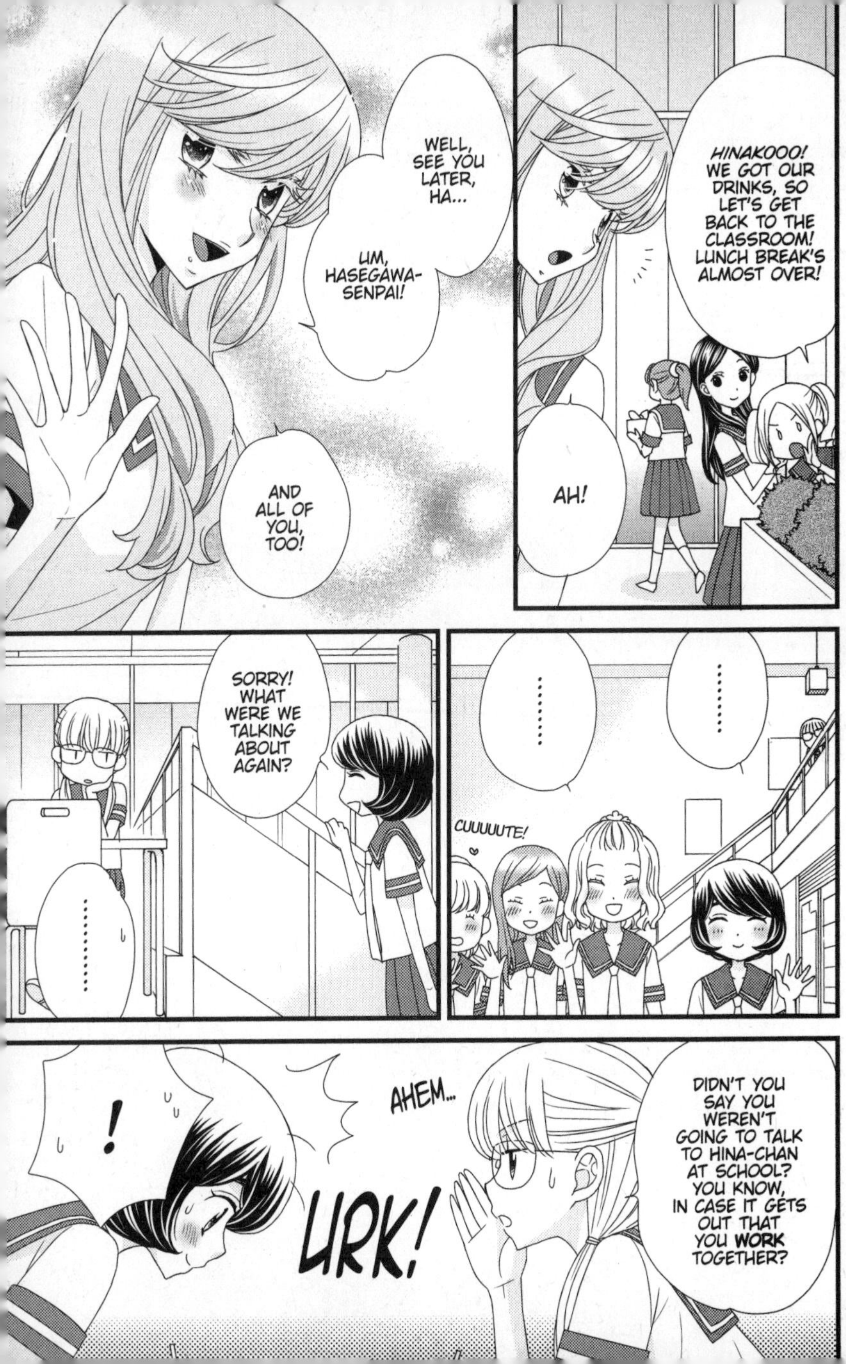
HINAKOOO! WE GOT OUR DRINKS, SO LET'S GET BACK TO THE CLASSROOM! LUNCH BREAK'S ALMOST OVER!
AH!
WELL, SEE YOU LATER, HA...
UM, HASEGAWA-SENPAI!
AND ALL OF YOU, TOO!
......
......
CUUUUUTE!
SORRY! WHAT WERE WE TALKING ABOUT AGAIN?
......
DIDN'T YOU SAY YOU WEREN'T GOING TO TALK TO HINA-CHAN AT SCHOOL? YOU KNOW, IN CASE IT GETS OUT THAT YOU WORK TOGETHER?
AHEM...
URK!
!

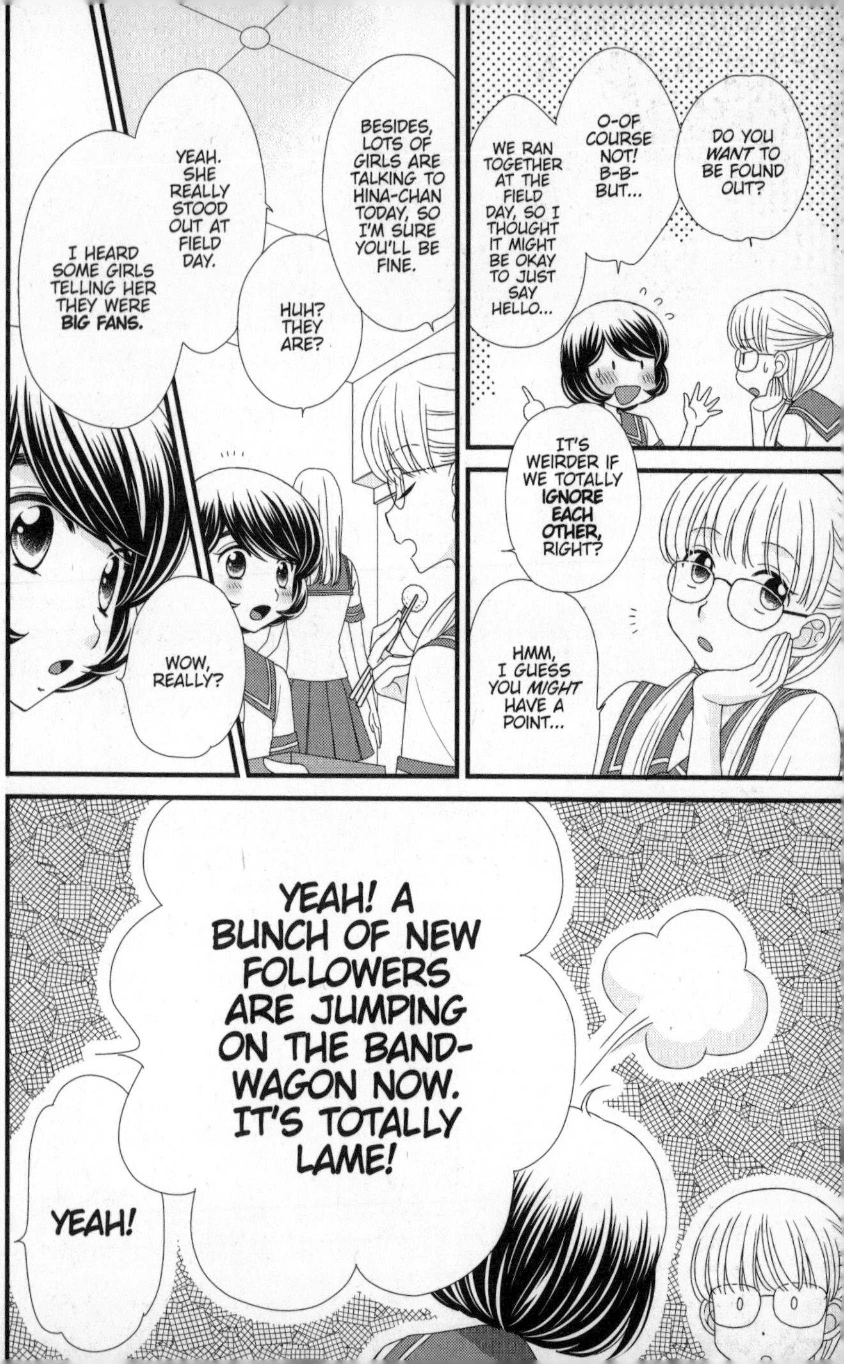
DO YOU WANT TO BE FOUND OUT?
O-OF COURSE NOT! B-B-BUT...
WE RAN TOGETHER AT THE FIELD DAY, SO I THOUGHT IT MIGHT BE OKAY TO JUST SAY HELLO...
IT'S WEIRDER IF WE TOTALLY IGNORE EACH OTHER, RIGHT?
HMM, I GUESS YOU MIGHT HAVE A POINT...
BESIDES, LOTS OF GIRLS ARE TALKING TO HINA-CHAN TODAY, SO I'M SURE YOU'LL BE FINE.
HUH? THEY ARE?
YEAH. SHE REALLY STOOD OUT AT FIELD DAY.
I HEARD SOME GIRLS TELLING HER THEY WERE BIG FANS.
WOW, REALLY?
YEAH! A BUNCH OF NEW FOLLOWERS ARE JUMPING ON THE BAND-WAGON NOW. IT'S TOTALLY LAME!
YEAH!

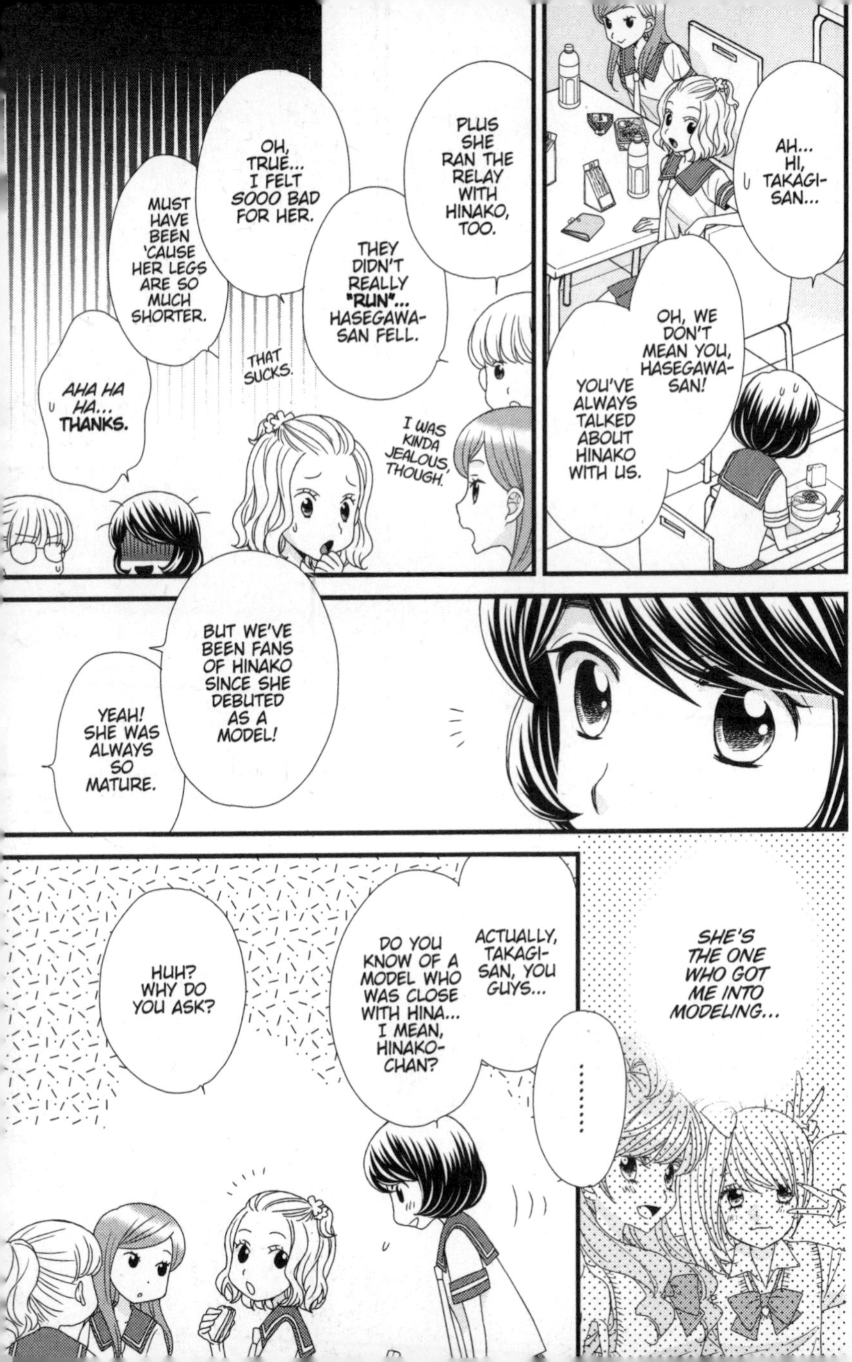
AH... HI, TAKAGI-SAN...
OH, WE DON'T MEAN YOU, HASEGAWA-SAN!
YOU'VE ALWAYS TALKED ABOUT HINAKO WITH US.
PLUS SHE RAN THE RELAY WITH HINAKO, TOO.
OH, TRUE... I FELT SOOO BAD FOR HER.
THEY DIDN'T REALLY "RUN"... HASEGAWA-SAN FELL.
MUST HAVE BEEN 'CAUSE HER LEGS ARE SO MUCH SHORTER.
THAT SUCKS.
I WAS KINDA JEALOUS, THOUGH.
AHA HA HA... THANKS.
BUT WE'VE BEEN FANS OF HINAKO SINCE SHE DEBUTED AS A MODEL!
YEAH! SHE WAS ALWAYS SO MATURE.
SHE'S THE ONE WHO GOT ME INTO MODELING...
......
ACTUALLY, TAKAGI-SAN, YOU GUYS...
DO YOU KNOW OF A MODEL WHO WAS CLOSE WITH HINA... I MEAN, HINAKO-CHAN?
HUH? WHY DO YOU ASK?

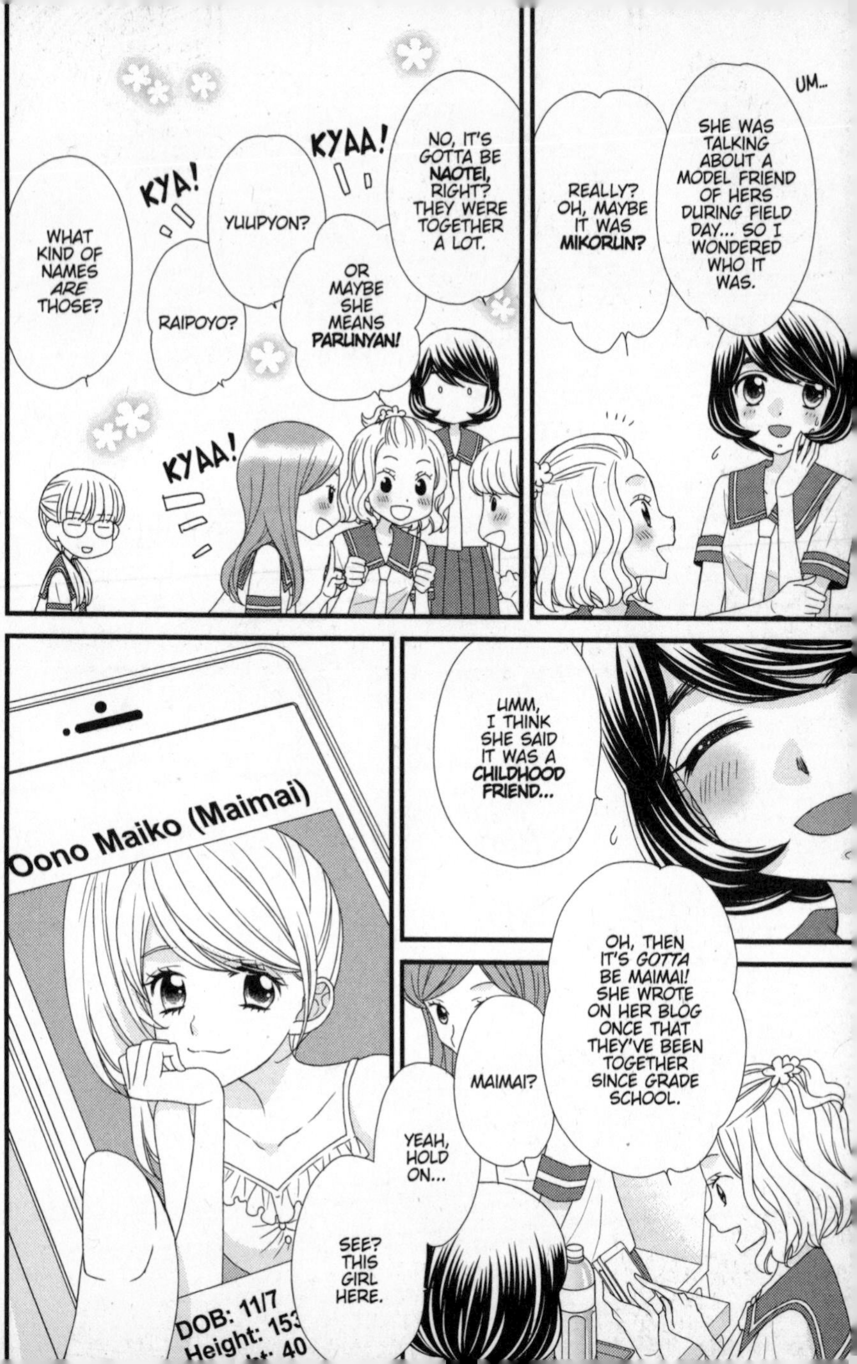
UM...
SHE WAS TALKING ABOUT A MODEL FRIEND OF HERS DURING FIELD DAY... SO I WONDERED WHO IT WAS.
REALLY? OH, MAYBE IT WAS MIKORUN?
NO, IT'S GOTTA BE NAOTEI, RIGHT? THEY WERE TOGETHER A LOT.
KYAA!
YUUPYON?
KYA!
OR MAYBE SHE MEANS PARUNYAN!
RAIPOYO?
WHAT KIND OF NAMES ARE THOSE?
KYAA!
UMM, I THINK SHE SAID IT WAS A CHILDHOOD FRIEND...
OH, THEN IT'S GOTTA BE MAIMAI! SHE WROTE ON HER BLOG ONCE THAT THEY'VE BEEN TOGETHER SINCE GRADE SCHOOL.
MAIMAI?
YEAH, HOLD ON...
SEE? THIS GIRL HERE.
Oono Maiko (Maimai)
DOB: 11/7
Height: 153

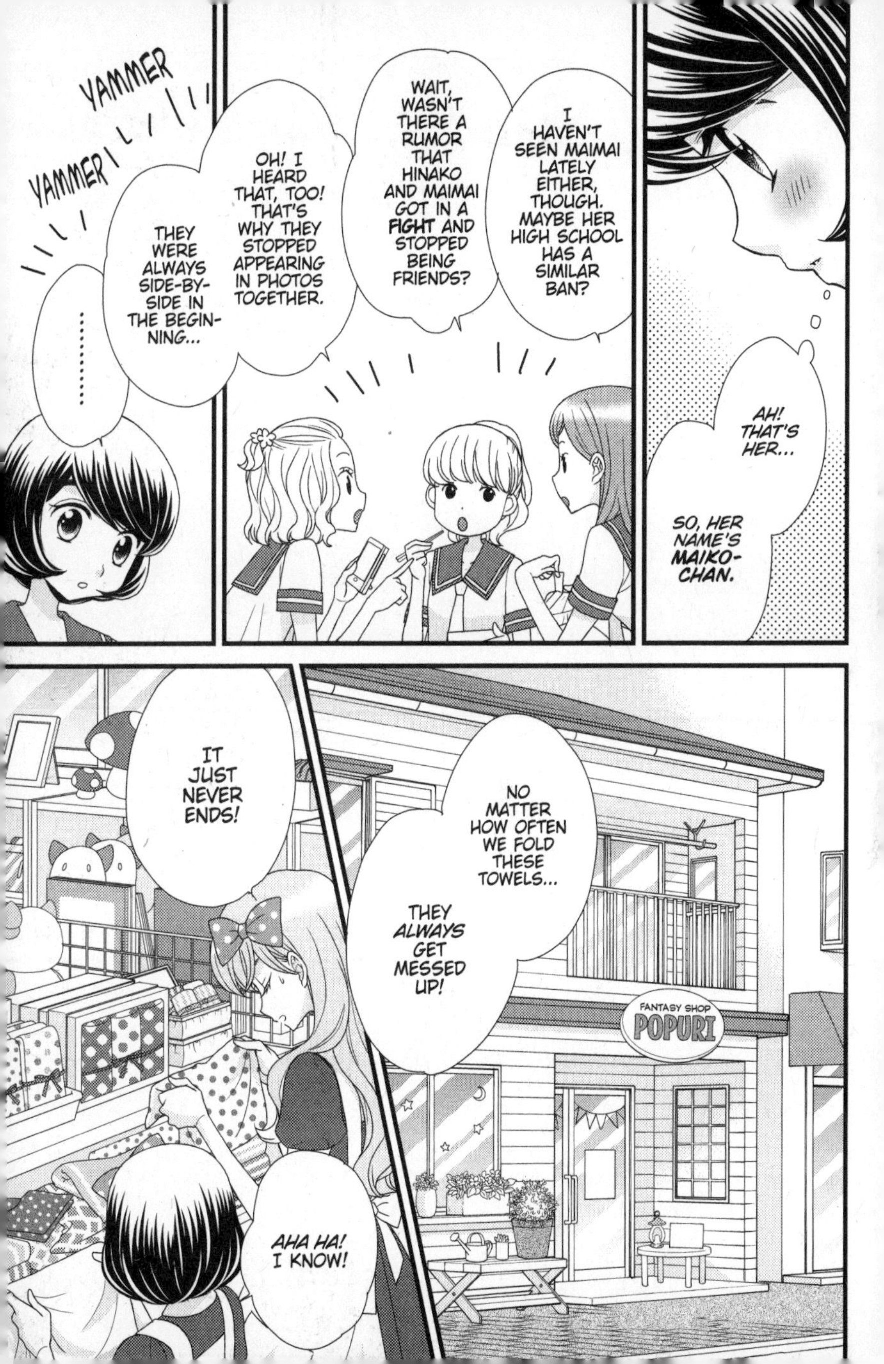
AH! THAT'S HER...
SO, HER NAME'S MAIKO-CHAN.
I HAVEN'T SEEN MAIMAI LATELY EITHER, THOUGH. MAYBE HER HIGH SCHOOL HAS A SIMILAR BAN?
WAIT, WASN'T THERE A RUMOR THAT HINAKO AND MAIMAI GOT IN A FIGHT AND STOPPED BEING FRIENDS?
OH! I HEARD THAT, TOO! THAT'S WHY THEY STOPPED APPEARING IN PHOTOS TOGETHER.
YAMMER
YAMMER
THEY WERE ALWAYS SIDE-BY-SIDE IN THE BEGIN-NING...
......
FANTASY SHOP
POPURI
NO MATTER HOW OFTEN WE FOLD THESE TOWELS...
THEY ALWAYS GET MESSED UP!
IT JUST NEVER ENDS!
AHA HA! I KNOW!

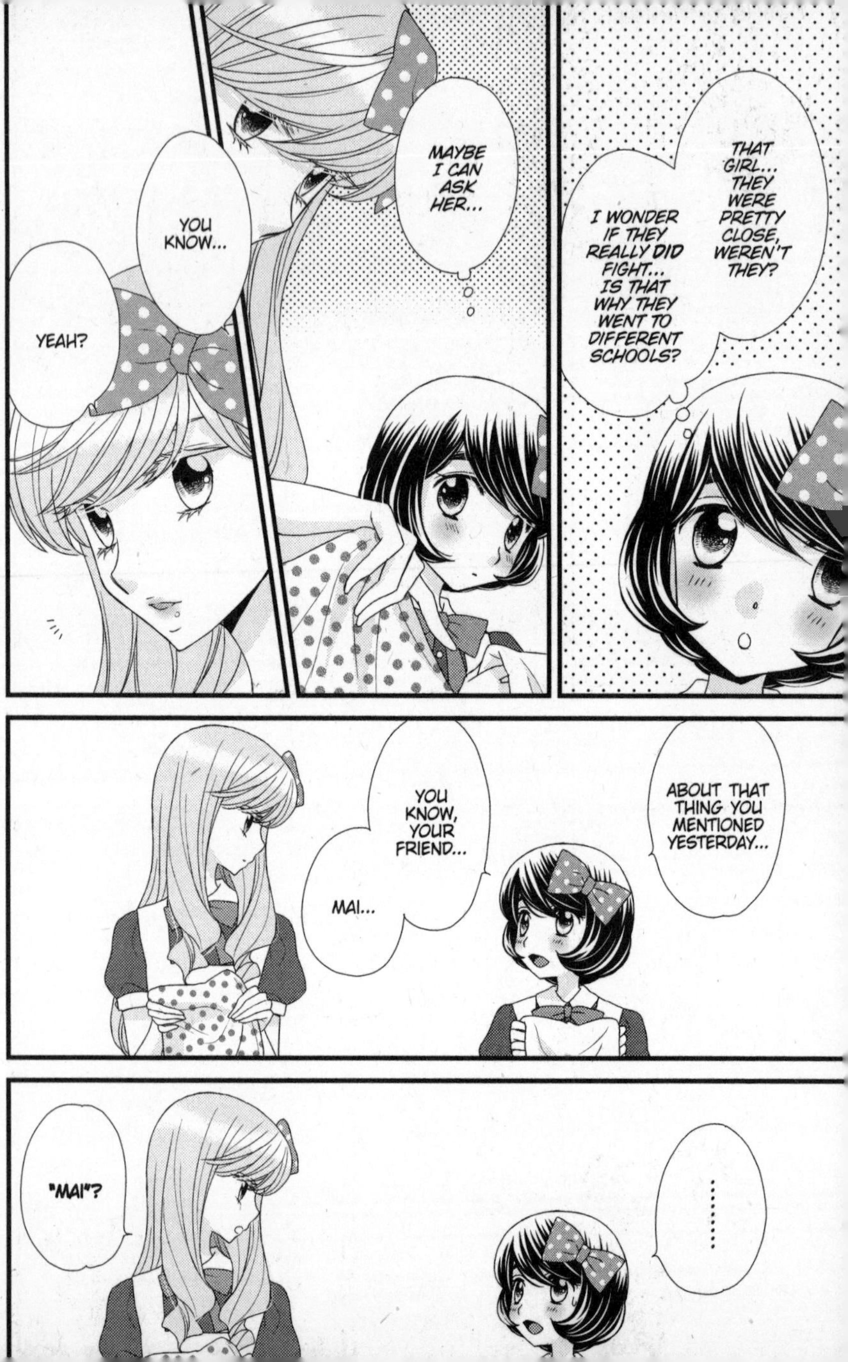
THAT GIRL... THEY WERE PRETTY CLOSE, WEREN'T THEY?
I WONDER IF THEY REALLY DID FIGHT... IS THAT WHY THEY WENT TO DIFFERENT SCHOOLS?
MAYBE I CAN ASK HER...
YOU KNOW...
YEAH?
ABOUT THAT THING YOU MENTIONED YESTERDAY...
YOU KNOW, YOUR FRIEND...
MAI...
......
"MAI"?

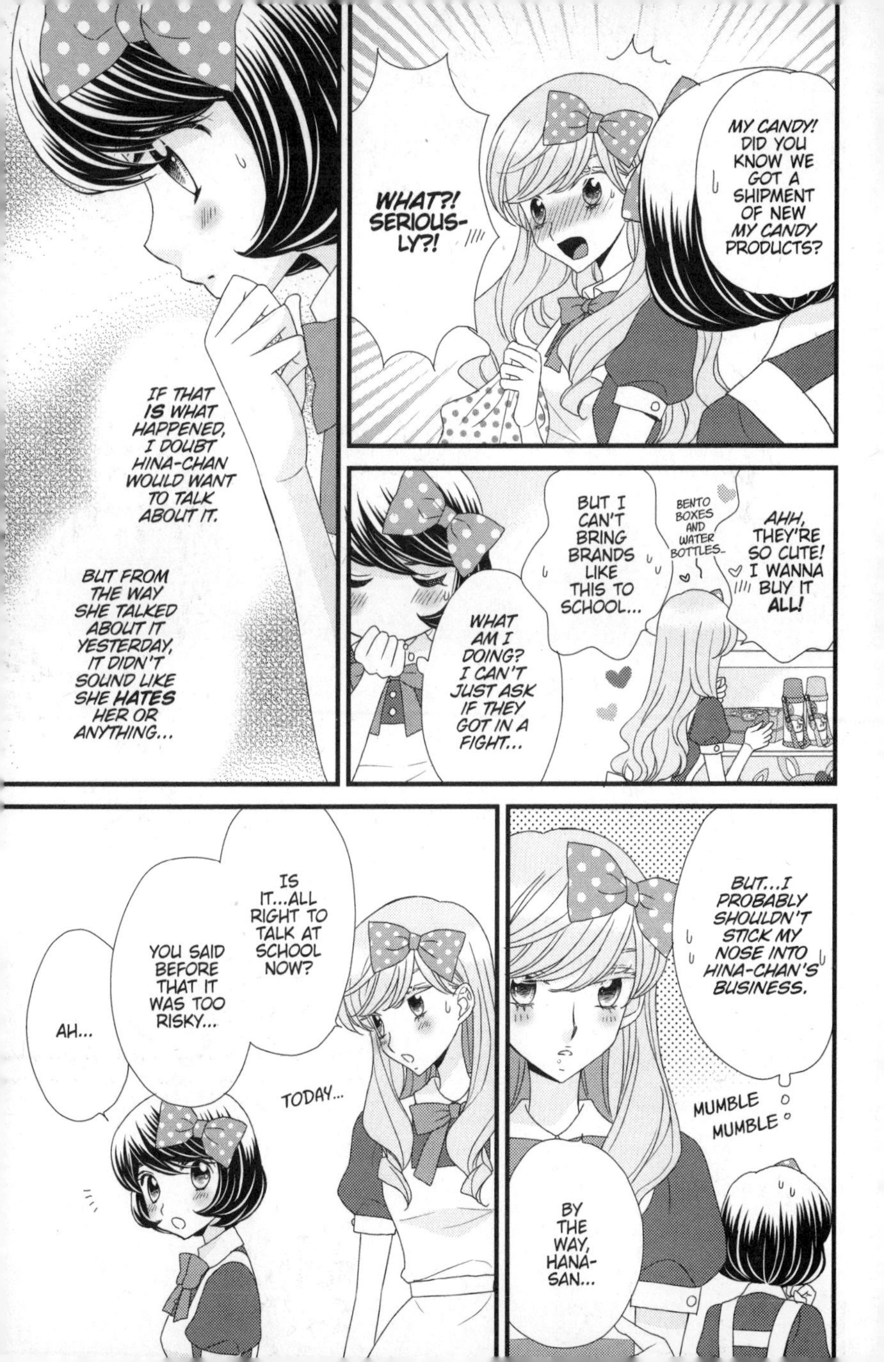
MY CANDY! DID YOU KNOW WE GOT A SHIPMENT OF NEW MY CANDY PRODUCTS?
WHAT?! SERIOUSLY?!
AHH, THEY'RE SO CUTE! I WANNA BUY IT ALL!
BENTO BOXES AND WATER BOTTLES...
BUT I CAN'T BRING BRANDS LIKE THIS TO SCHOOL...
WHAT AM I DOING? I CAN'T JUST ASK IF THEY GOT IN A FIGHT...
IF THAT IS WHAT HAPPENED, I DOUBT HINA-CHAN WOULD WANT TO TALK ABOUT IT.
BUT FROM THE WAY SHE TALKED ABOUT IT YESTERDAY, IT DIDN'T SOUND LIKE SHE HATES HER OR ANYTHING...
BUT...I PROBABLY SHOULDN'T STICK MY NOSE INTO HINA-CHAN'S BUSINESS.
MUMBLE MUMBLE
BY THE WAY, HANA-SAN...
TODAY...
IS IT...ALL RIGHT TO TALK AT SCHOOL NOW?
YOU SAID BEFORE THAT IT WAS TOO RISKY...
AH...

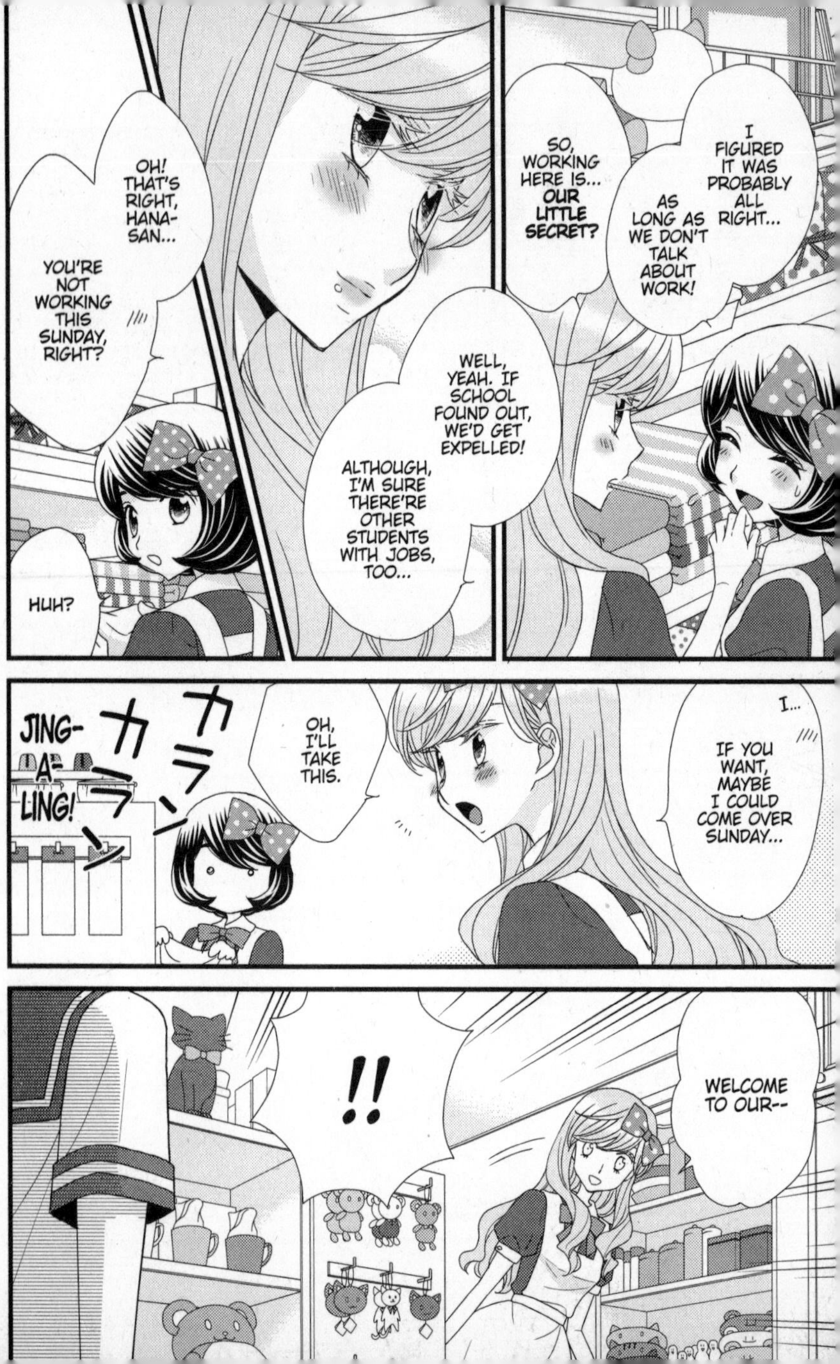
I FIGURED IT WAS PROBABLY ALL RIGHT...
AS LONG AS WE DON'T TALK ABOUT WORK!
SO, WORKING HERE IS... **OUR LITTLE SECRET?**
WELL, YEAH. IF SCHOOL FOUND OUT, WE'D GET EXPELLED!
ALTHOUGH, I'M SURE THERE'RE OTHER STUDENTS WITH JOBS, TOO...
OH! THAT'S RIGHT, HANA-SAN...
YOU'RE NOT WORKING THIS SUNDAY, RIGHT?
HUH?
I...
IF YOU WANT, MAYBE I COULD COME OVER SUNDAY...
OH, I'LL TAKE THIS.
カランカラン
JING-A-LING!
WELCOME TO OUR--
!!

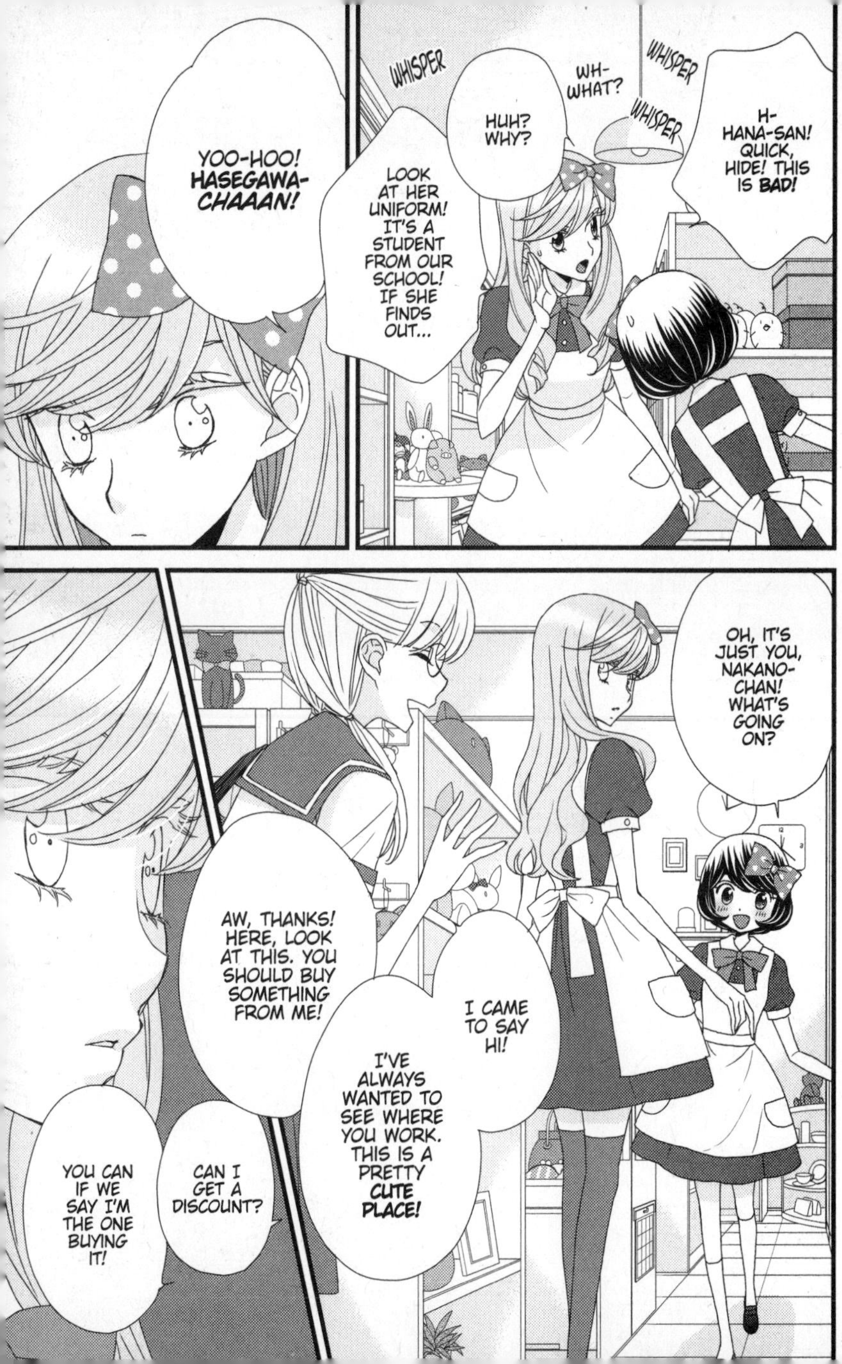
H- HANA-SAN! QUICK, HIDE! THIS IS **BAD!**
WHISPER
WHISPER
WH- WHAT?
HUH? WHY?
WHISPER
LOOK AT HER UNIFORM! IT'S A STUDENT FROM OUR SCHOOL! IF SHE FINDS OUT...
YOO-HOO! **HASEGAWA-CHAAAN!**
OH, IT'S JUST YOU, NAKANO-CHAN! WHAT'S GOING ON?
I CAME TO SAY HI!
I'VE ALWAYS WANTED TO SEE WHERE YOU WORK. THIS IS A PRETTY **CUTE PLACE!**
AW, THANKS! HERE, LOOK AT THIS. YOU SHOULD BUY SOMETHING FROM ME!
CAN I GET A DISCOUNT?
YOU CAN IF WE SAY I'M THE ONE BUYING IT!

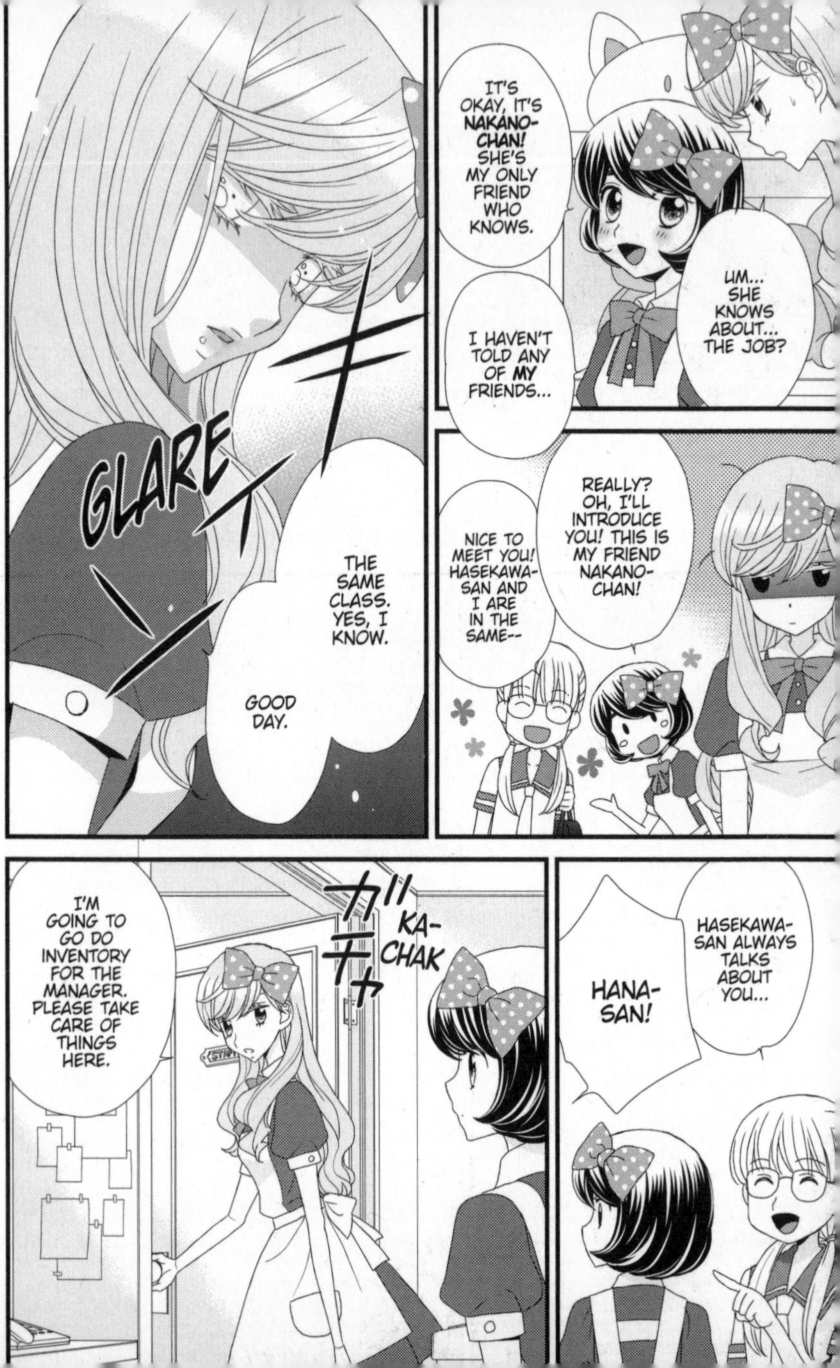
UM... SHE KNOWS ABOUT... THE JOB?
IT'S OKAY, IT'S NAKANO-CHAN! SHE'S MY ONLY FRIEND WHO KNOWS.
I HAVEN'T TOLD ANY OF MY FRIENDS...
REALLY? OH, I'LL INTRODUCE YOU! THIS IS MY FRIEND NAKANO-CHAN!
NICE TO MEET YOU! HASEKAWA-SAN AND I ARE IN THE SAME--
GLARE
THE SAME CLASS. YES, I KNOW.
GOOD DAY.
HASEKAWA-SAN ALWAYS TALKS ABOUT YOU...
HANA-SAN!
カチャ KA-CHAK
I'M GOING TO GO DO INVENTORY FOR THE MANAGER. PLEASE TAKE CARE OF THINGS HERE.

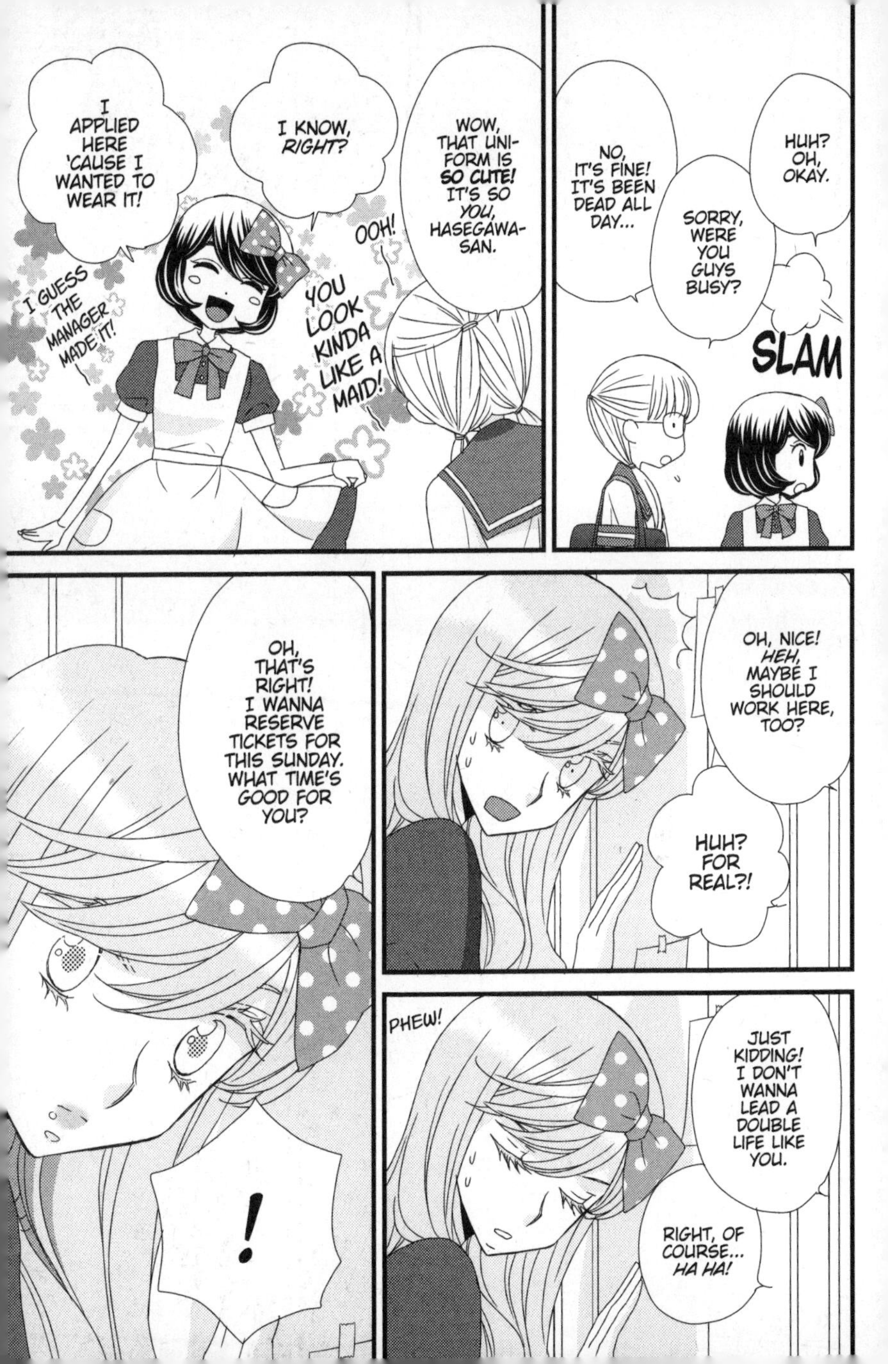
HUH? OH, OKAY.
NO, IT'S FINE! IT'S BEEN DEAD ALL DAY...
SORRY, WERE YOU GUYS BUSY?
SLAM
WOW, THAT UNI-FORM IS **SO CUTE!** IT'S SO *YOU*, HASEGAWA-SAN.
OOH!
I KNOW, *RIGHT?*
YOU LOOK KINDA LIKE A MAID!
I APPLIED HERE 'CAUSE I WANTED TO WEAR IT!
I GUESS THE MANAGER MADE IT!
OH, NICE! *HEH*, MAYBE I SHOULD WORK HERE, TOO?
HUH? FOR REAL?!
JUST KIDDING! I DON'T WANNA LEAD A DOUBLE LIFE LIKE YOU.
PHEW!
RIGHT, OF COURSE... *HA HA!*
OH, THAT'S RIGHT! I WANNA RESERVE TICKETS FOR THIS SUNDAY. WHAT TIME'S GOOD FOR YOU?
!

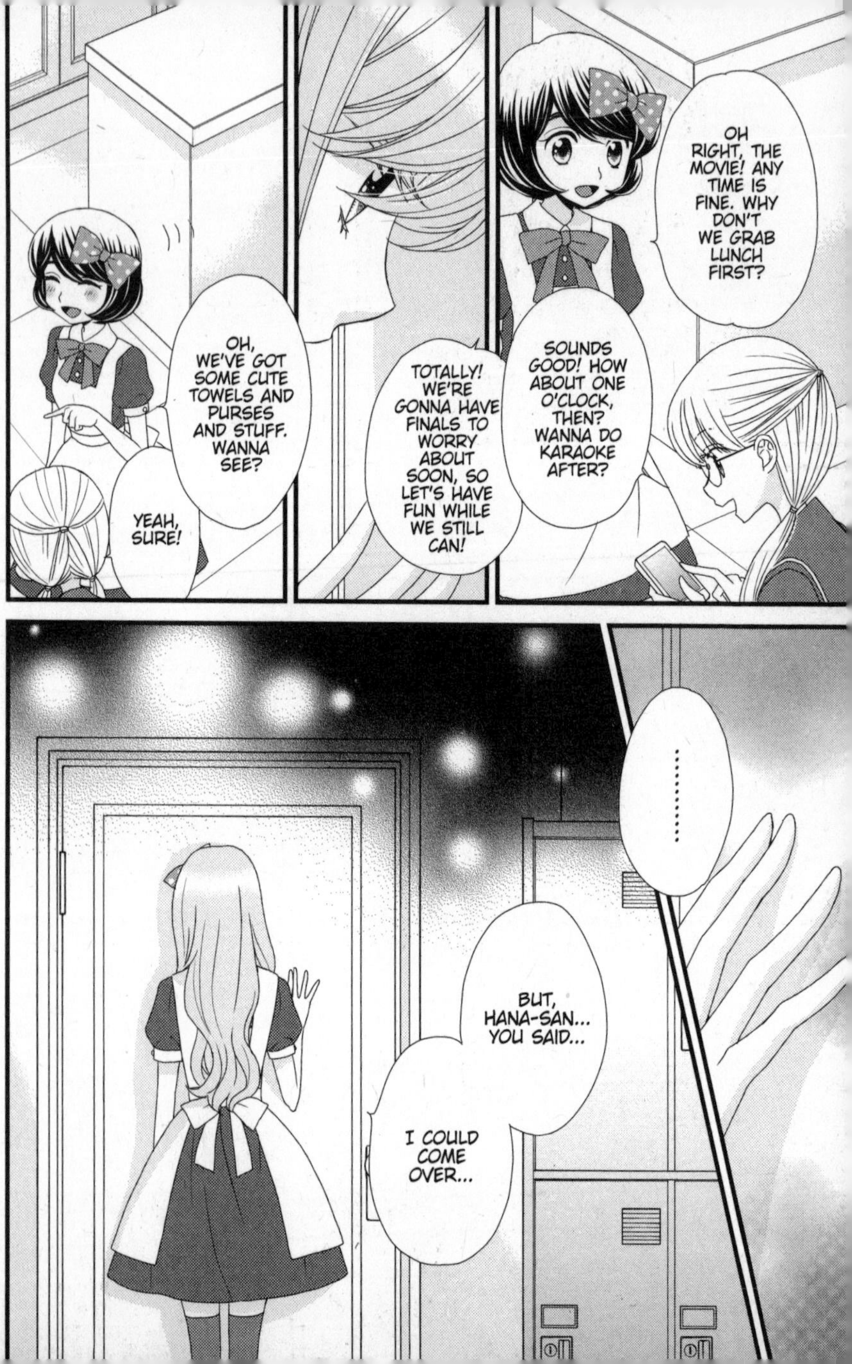
OH RIGHT, THE MOVIE! ANY TIME IS FINE. WHY DON'T WE GRAB LUNCH FIRST?
SOUNDS GOOD! HOW ABOUT ONE O'CLOCK, THEN? WANNA DO KARAOKE AFTER?
TOTALLY! WE'RE GONNA HAVE FINALS TO WORRY ABOUT SOON, SO LET'S HAVE FUN WHILE WE STILL CAN!
OH, WE'VE GOT SOME CUTE TOWELS AND PURSES AND STUFF. WANNA SEE?
YEAH, SURE!
......
BUT, HANA-SAN... YOU SAID...
I COULD COME OVER...

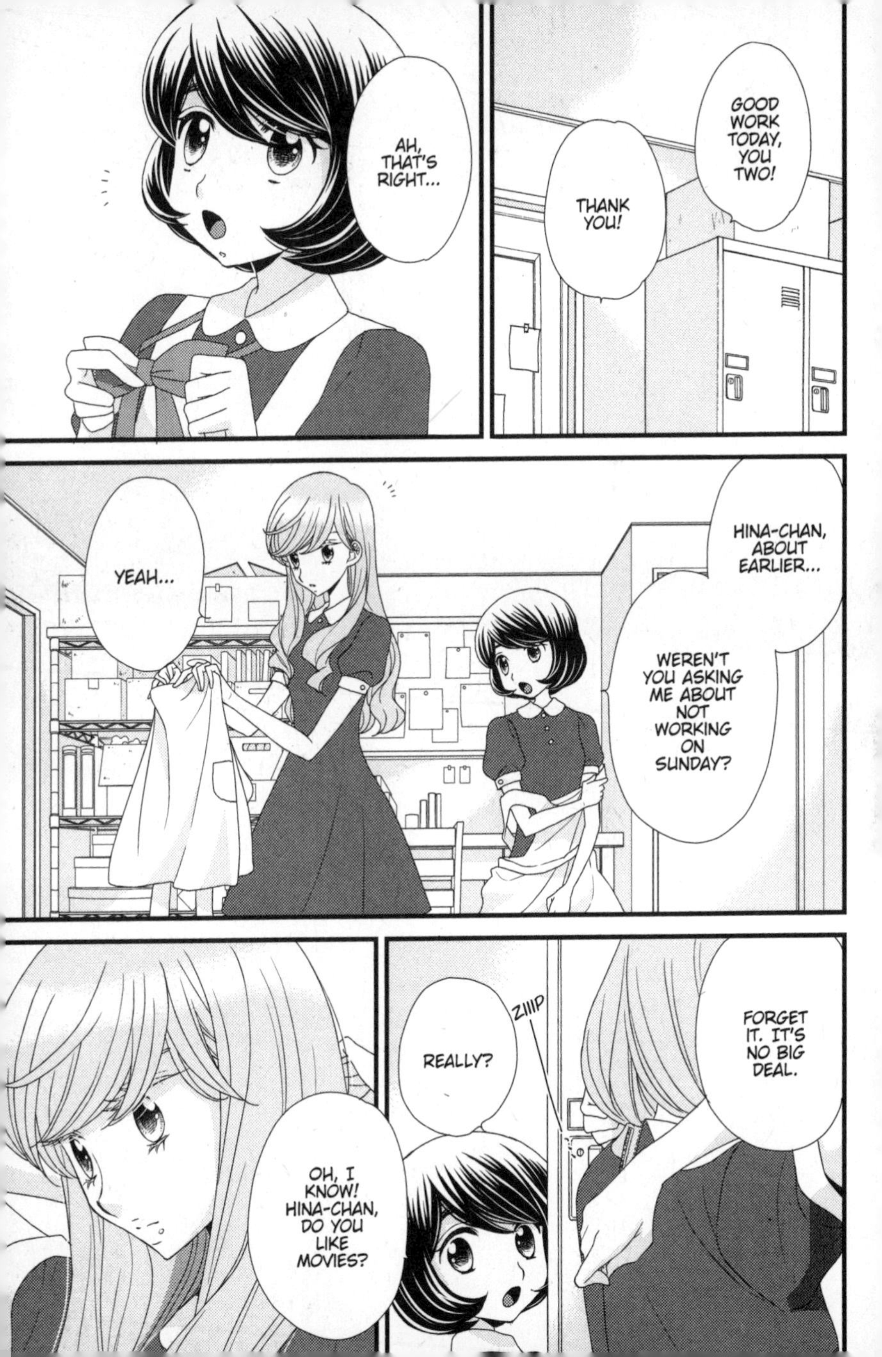
GOOD WORK TODAY, YOU TWO!
THANK YOU!
AH, THAT'S RIGHT...
HINA-CHAN, ABOUT EARLIER...
WEREN'T YOU ASKING ME ABOUT NOT WORKING ON SUNDAY?
YEAH...
FORGET IT. IT'S NO BIG DEAL.
ZIIIP
REALLY?
OH, I KNOW! HINA-CHAN, DO YOU LIKE MOVIES?

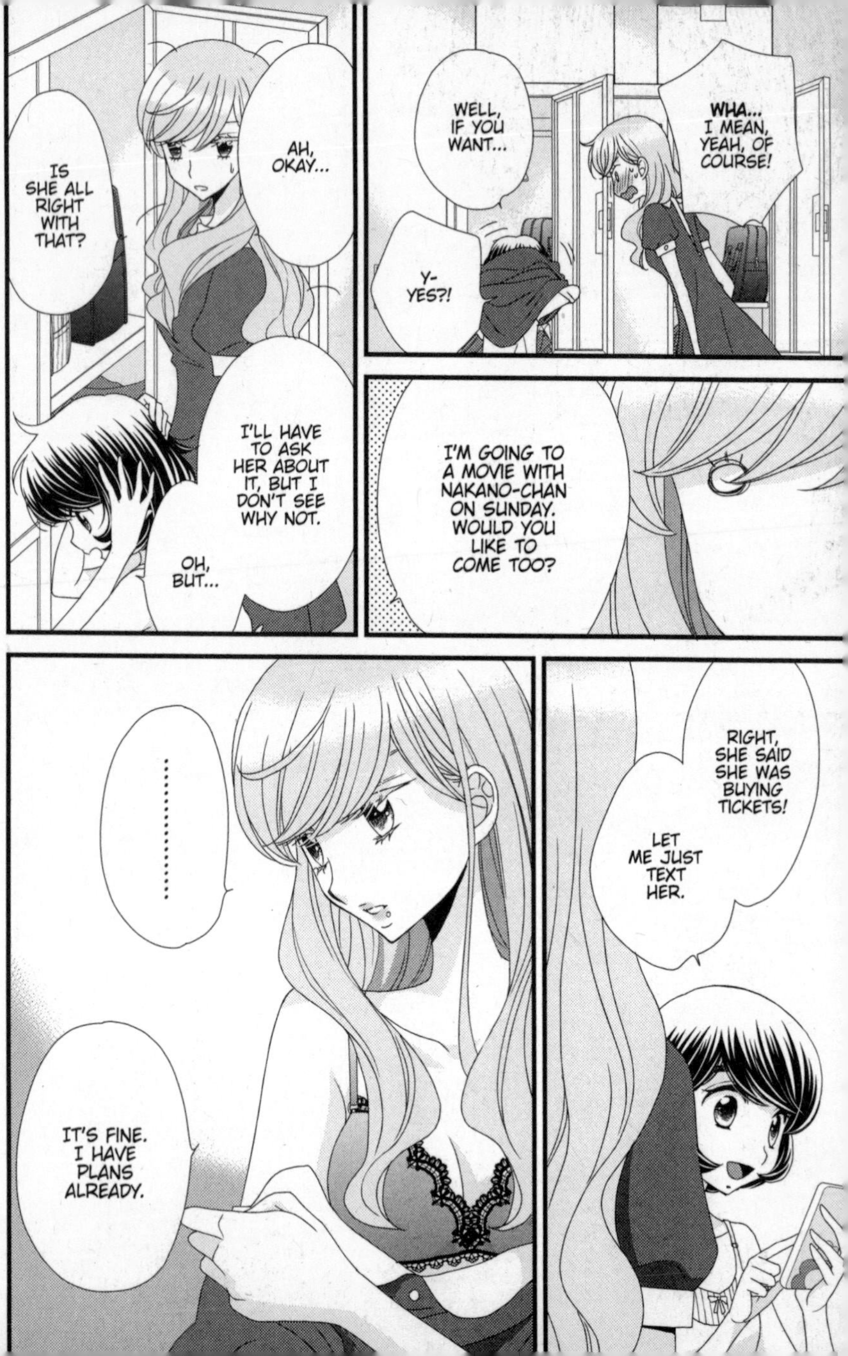
WHA... I MEAN, YEAH, OF COURSE!
WELL, IF YOU WANT...
Y- YES?!
I'M GOING TO A MOVIE WITH NAKANO-CHAN ON SUNDAY. WOULD YOU LIKE TO COME TOO?
AH, OKAY...
IS SHE ALL RIGHT WITH THAT?
I'LL HAVE TO ASK HER ABOUT IT, BUT I DON'T SEE WHY NOT.
OH, BUT...
RIGHT, SHE SAID SHE WAS BUYING TICKETS!
LET ME JUST TEXT HER.
....
IT'S FINE. I HAVE PLANS ALREADY.

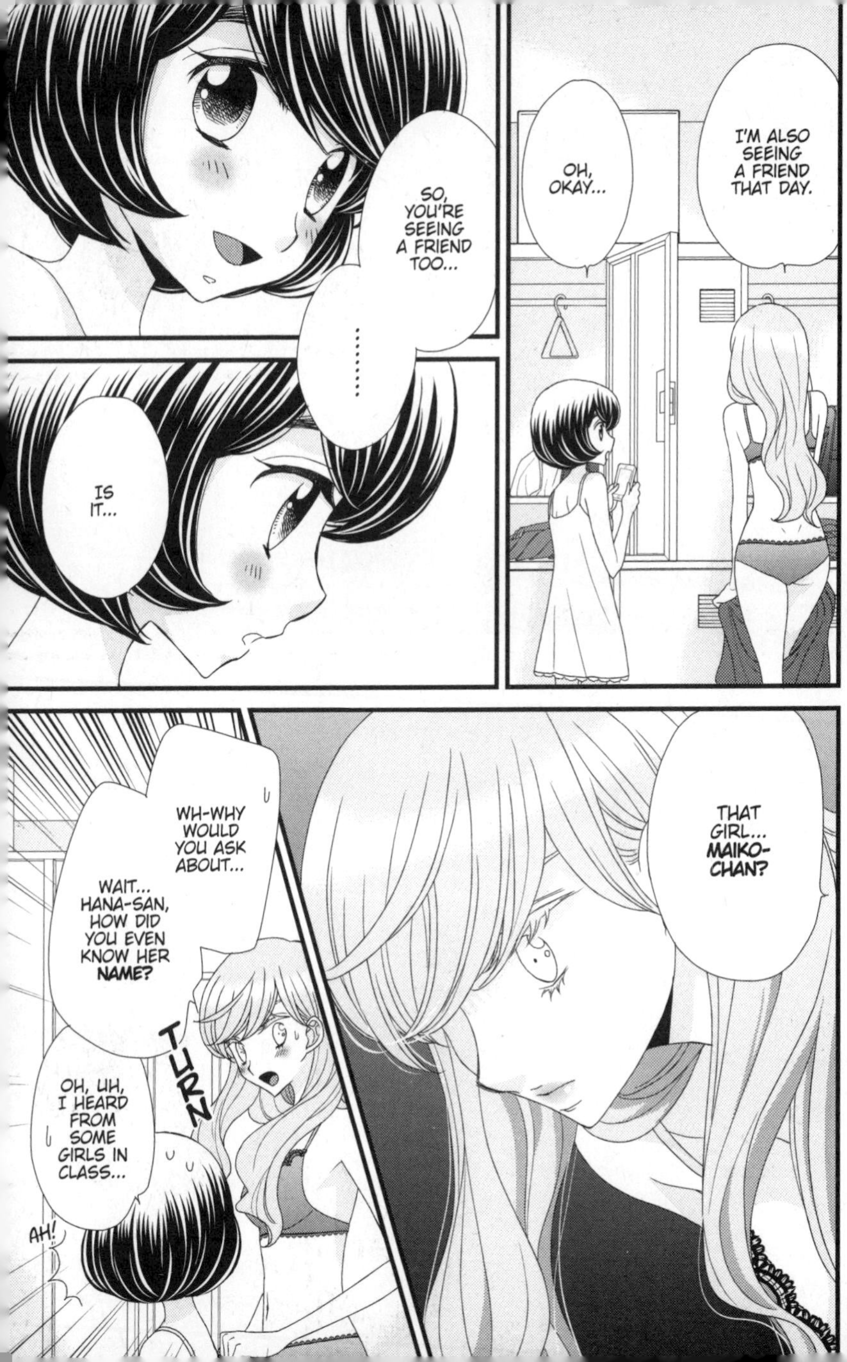
I'M ALSO SEEING A FRIEND THAT DAY.
OH, OKAY...
SO, YOU'RE SEEING A FRIEND TOO...
......
IS IT...
THAT GIRL... **MAIKO-CHAN?**
WH-WHY WOULD YOU ASK ABOUT...
WAIT... HANA-SAN, HOW DID YOU EVEN KNOW HER **NAME?**
TURN
OH, UH, I HEARD FROM SOME GIRLS IN CLASS...
AH!

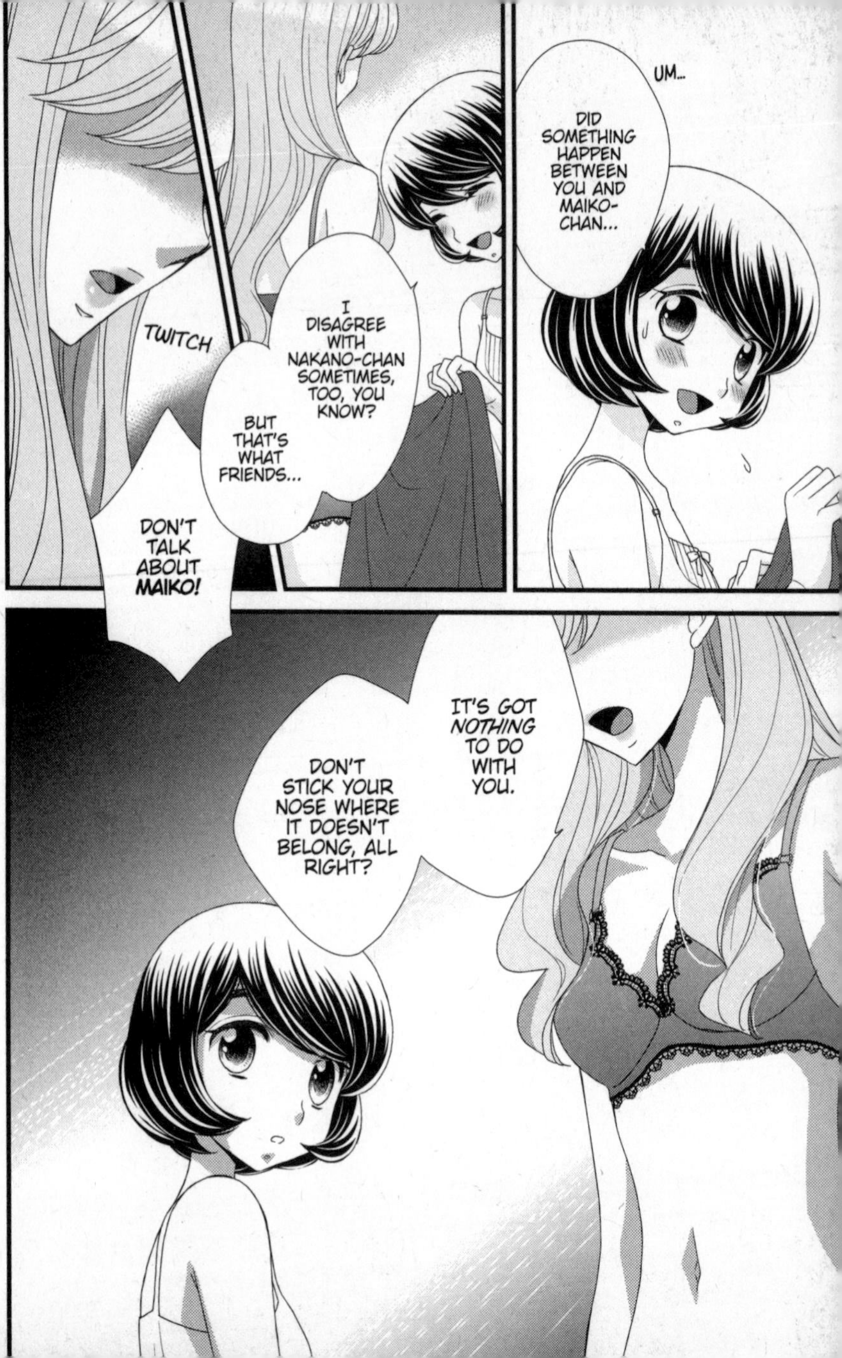
UM...
DID SOMETHING HAPPEN BETWEEN YOU AND MAIKO-CHAN...
I DISAGREE WITH NAKANO-CHAN SOMETIMES, TOO, YOU KNOW?
BUT THAT'S WHAT FRIENDS...
TWITCH
DON'T TALK ABOUT MAIKO!
IT'S GOT NOTHING TO DO WITH YOU.
DON'T STICK YOUR NOSE WHERE IT DOESN'T BELONG, ALL RIGHT?

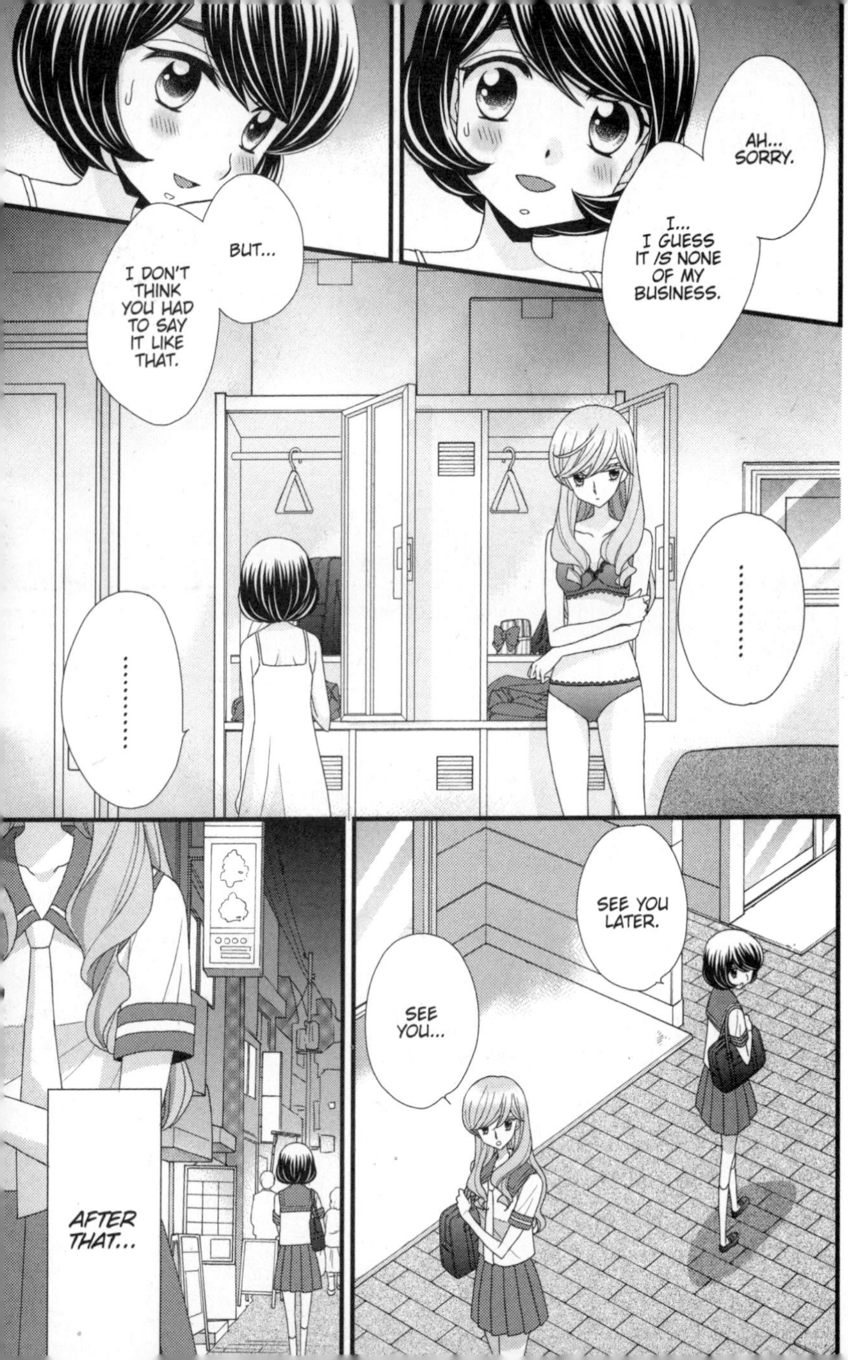
AH... SORRY.
I... I GUESS IT IS NONE OF MY BUSINESS.
BUT...
I DON'T THINK YOU HAD TO SAY IT LIKE THAT.
......
......
SEE YOU LATER.
SEE YOU...
AFTER THAT...

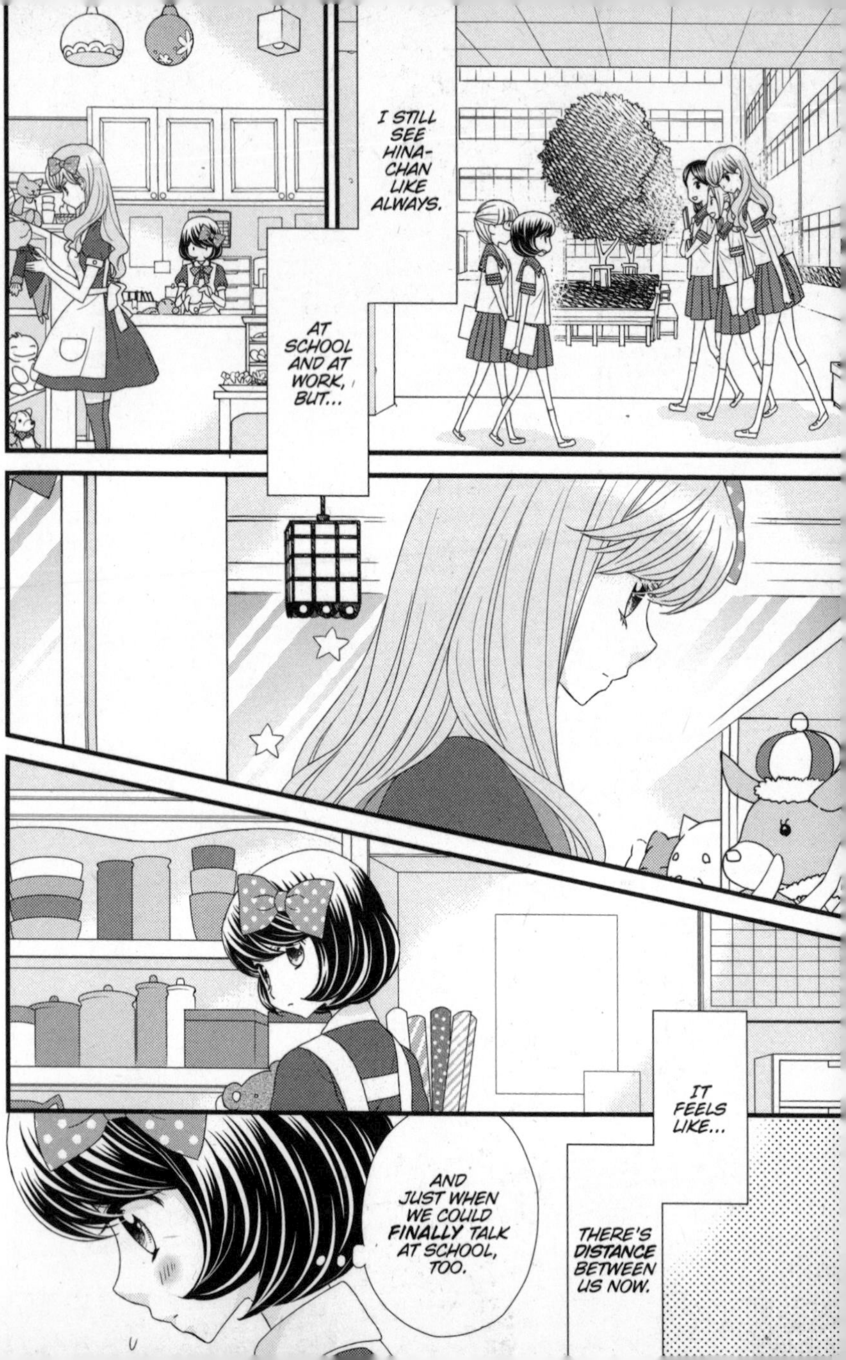
I STILL SEE HINA-CHAN LIKE ALWAYS.
AT SCHOOL AND AT WORK, BUT...
IT FEELS LIKE...
THERE'S DISTANCE BETWEEN US NOW.
AND JUST WHEN WE COULD FINALLY TALK AT SCHOOL, TOO.

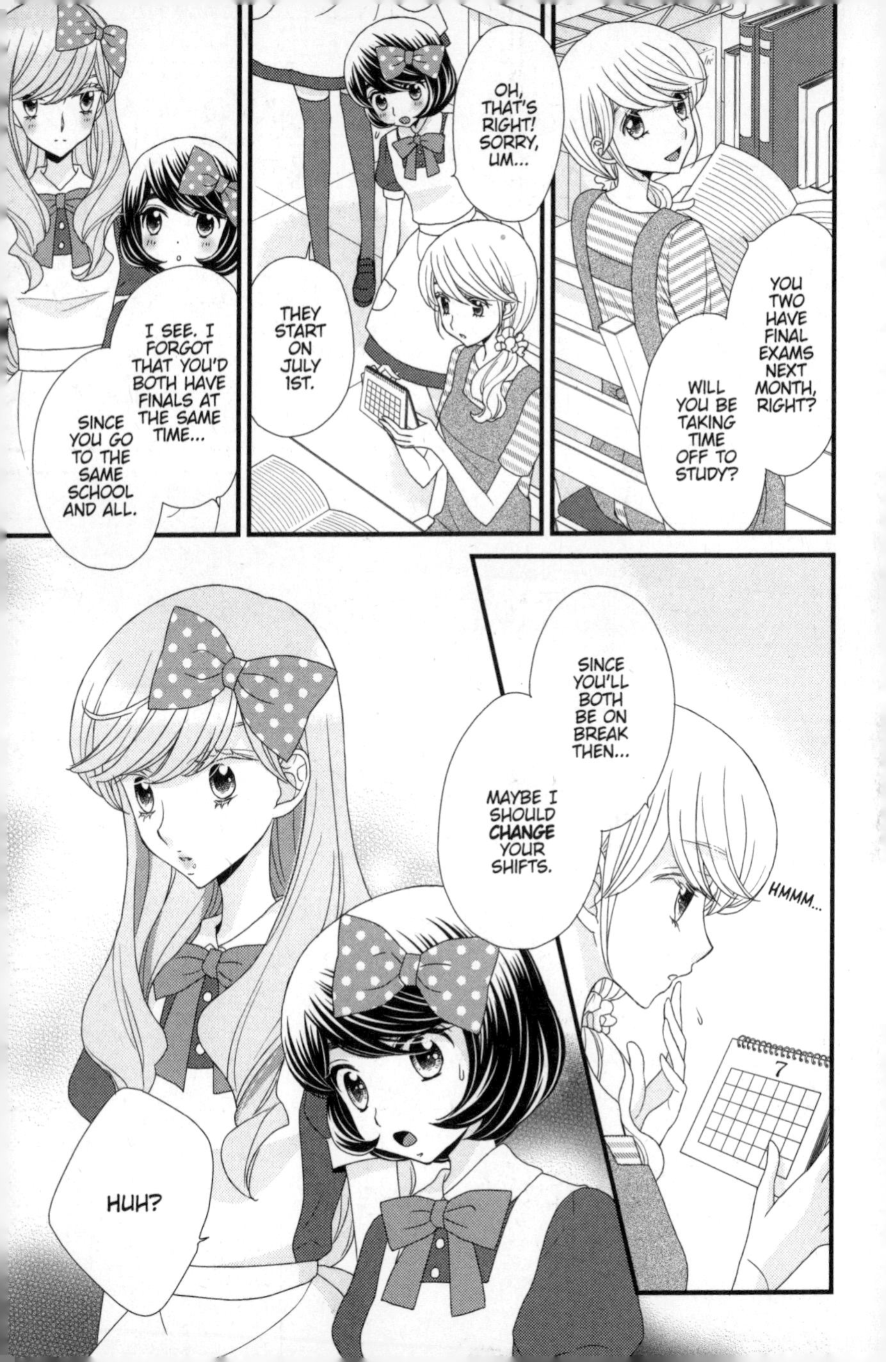
YOU TWO HAVE FINAL EXAMS NEXT MONTH, RIGHT?
WILL YOU BE TAKING TIME OFF TO STUDY?
OH, THAT'S RIGHT! SORRY, UM...
THEY START ON JULY 1ST.
I SEE. I FORGOT THAT YOU'D BOTH HAVE FINALS AT THE SAME TIME...
SINCE YOU GO TO THE SAME SCHOOL AND ALL.
SINCE YOU'LL BOTH BE ON BREAK THEN...
MAYBE I SHOULD **CHANGE** YOUR SHIFTS.
HMMM...
HUH?

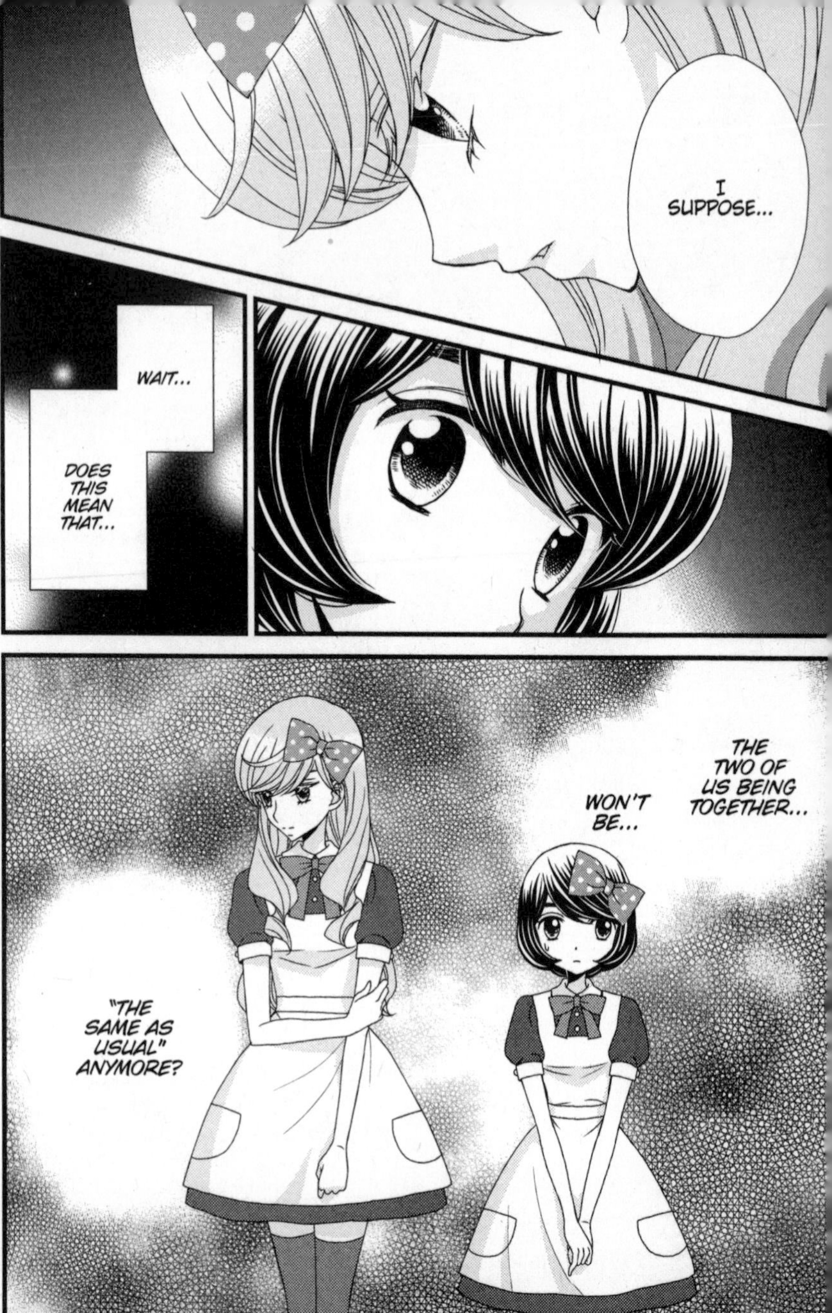
I SUPPOSE...
WAIT...
DOES THIS MEAN THAT...
THE TWO OF US BEING TOGETHER...
WON'T BE...
"THE SAME AS USUAL" ANYMORE?

end

Hana & Hina
AFTER♡SCHOOL

Hana & Hina

AFTER SCHOOL

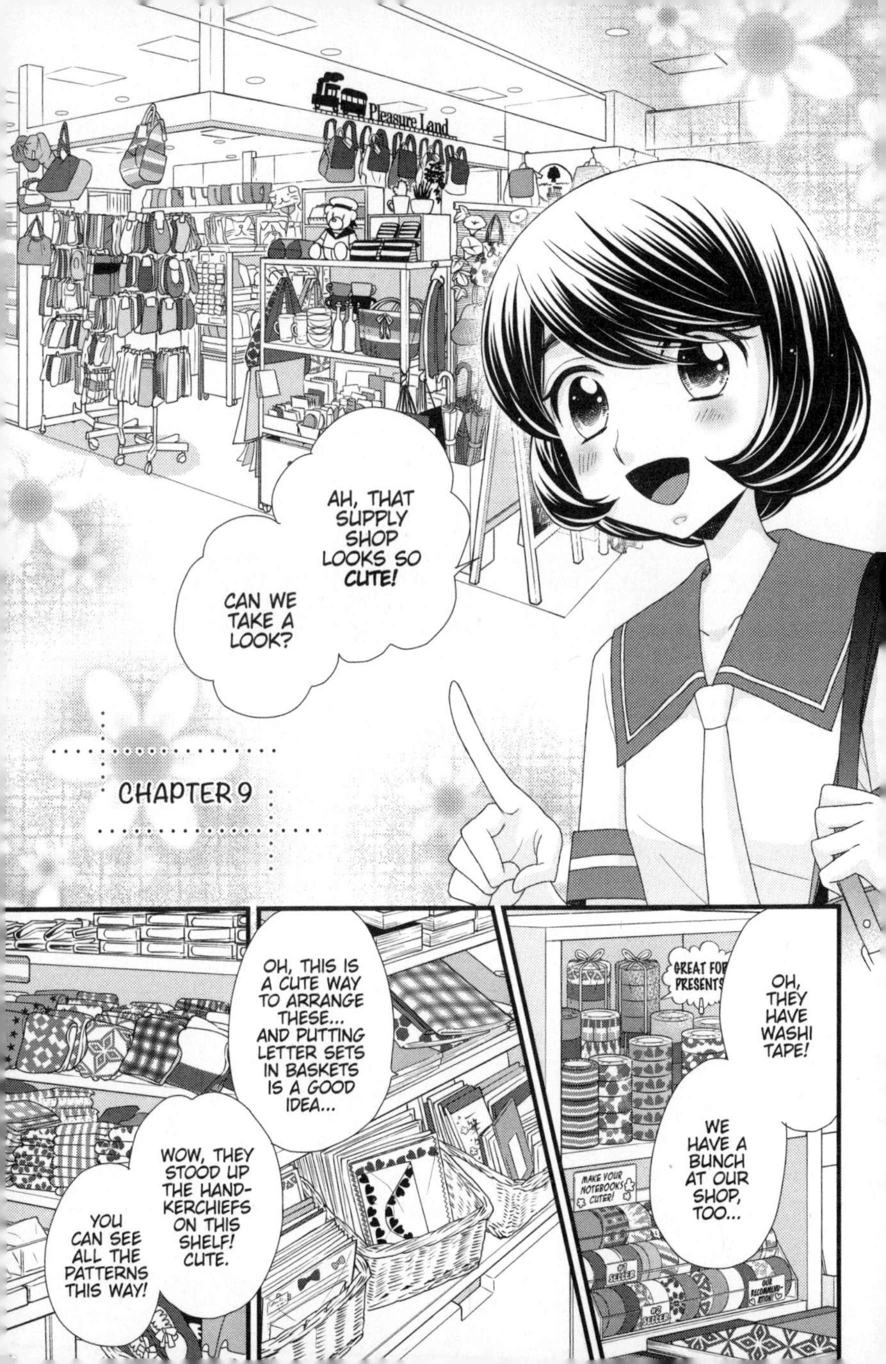
Pleasure Land
AH, THAT SUPPLY SHOP LOOKS SO CUTE!
CAN WE TAKE A LOOK?
CHAPTER 9
OH, THEY HAVE WASHI TAPE!
WE HAVE A BUNCH AT OUR SHOP, TOO...
GREAT FOR PRESENTS
MAKE YOUR NOTEBOOKS CUTER!
#1 SELLER
#2 SELLER
OUR RECOMMENDATION
OH, THIS IS A CUTE WAY TO ARRANGE THESE... AND PUTTING LETTER SETS IN BASKETS IS A GOOD IDEA...
WOW, THEY STOOD UP THE HAND-KERCHIEFS ON THIS SHELF! CUTE.
YOU CAN SEE ALL THE PATTERNS THIS WAY!

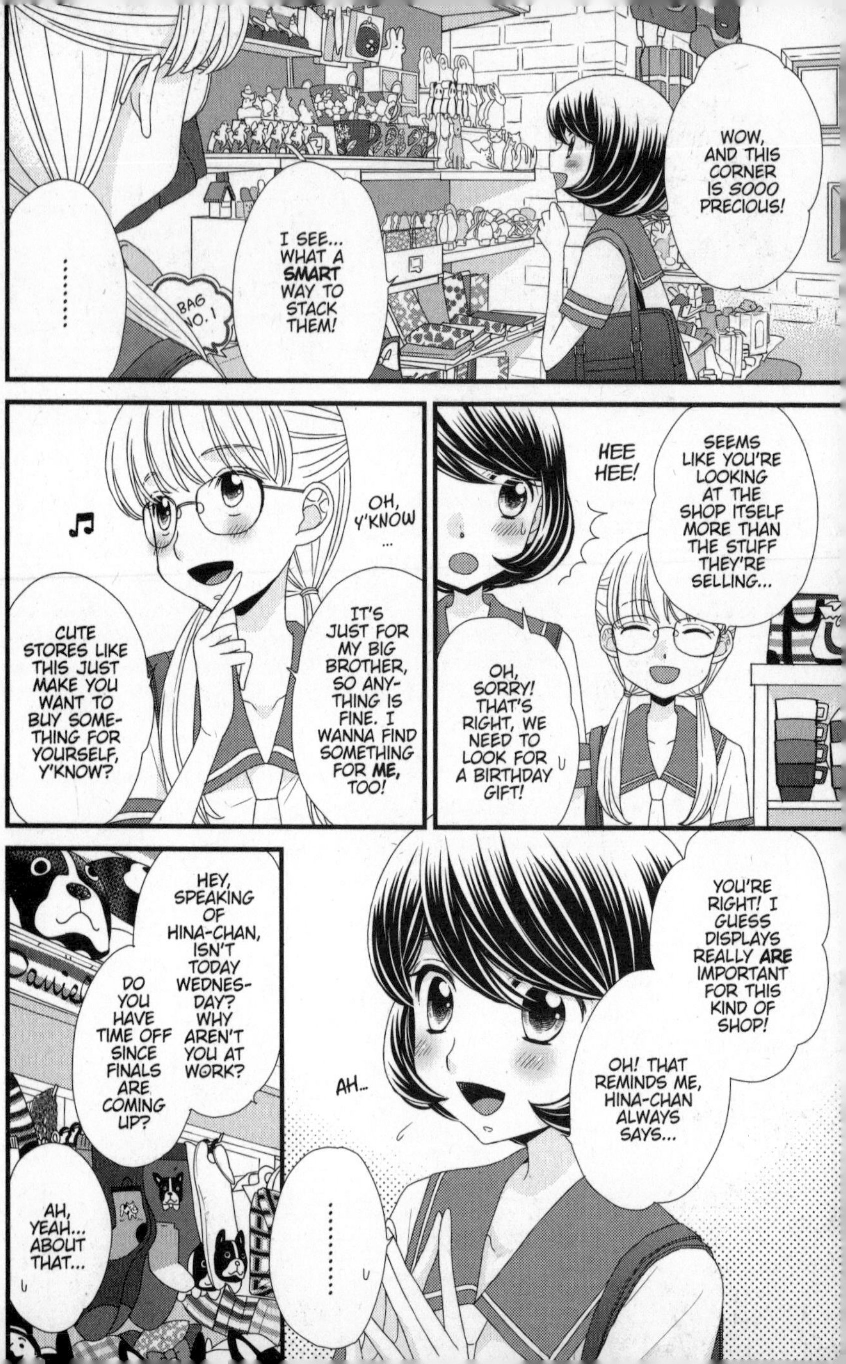
WOW, AND THIS CORNER IS SOOO PRECIOUS!
I SEE... WHAT A SMART WAY TO STACK THEM!
BAG NO. 1
......
SEEMS LIKE YOU'RE LOOKING AT THE SHOP ITSELF MORE THAN THE STUFF THEY'RE SELLING...
HEE HEE!
OH, SORRY! THAT'S RIGHT, WE NEED TO LOOK FOR A BIRTHDAY GIFT!
OH, Y'KNOW ...
IT'S JUST FOR MY BIG BROTHER, SO ANYTHING IS FINE. I WANNA FIND SOMETHING FOR ME, TOO!
CUTE STORES LIKE THIS JUST MAKE YOU WANT TO BUY SOMETHING FOR YOURSELF, Y'KNOW?
YOU'RE RIGHT! I GUESS DISPLAYS REALLY ARE IMPORTANT FOR THIS KIND OF SHOP!
OH! THAT REMINDS ME, HINA-CHAN ALWAYS SAYS...
AH...
......
HEY, SPEAKING OF HINA-CHAN, ISN'T TODAY WEDNESDAY? WHY AREN'T YOU AT WORK?
DO YOU HAVE TIME OFF SINCE FINALS ARE COMING UP?
AH, YEAH... ABOUT THAT...

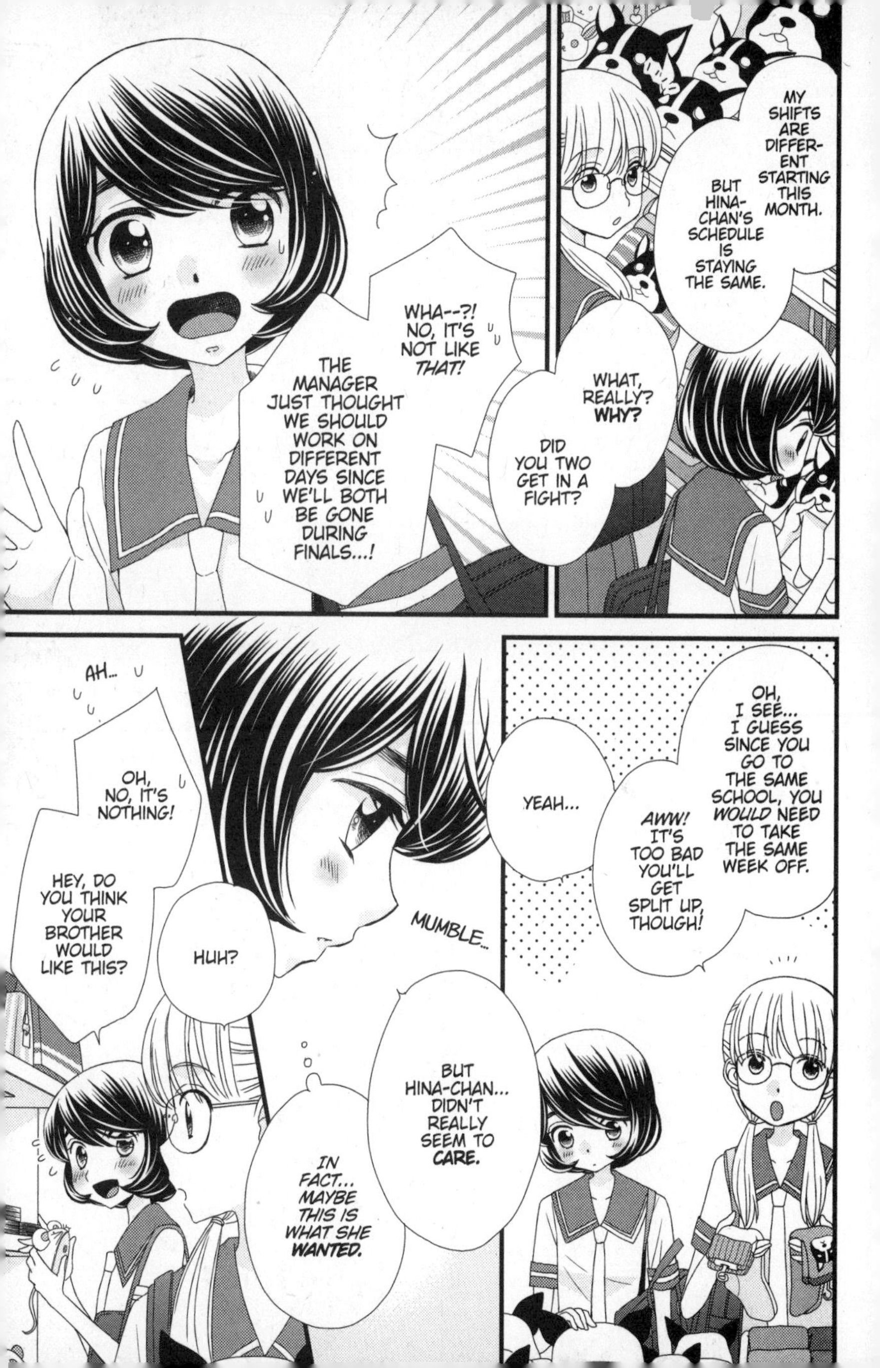
MY SHIFTS ARE DIFFERENT STARTING THIS MONTH.
BUT HINA-CHAN'S SCHEDULE IS STAYING THE SAME.
WHAT, REALLY? WHY?
DID YOU TWO GET IN A FIGHT?
WHA--?! NO, IT'S NOT LIKE THAT!
THE MANAGER JUST THOUGHT WE SHOULD WORK ON DIFFERENT DAYS SINCE WE'LL BOTH BE GONE DURING FINALS...!
OH, I SEE... I GUESS SINCE YOU GO TO THE SAME SCHOOL, YOU WOULD NEED TO TAKE THE SAME WEEK OFF.
AWW! IT'S TOO BAD YOU'LL GET SPLIT UP, THOUGH!
YEAH...
MUMBLE...
BUT HINA-CHAN... DIDN'T REALLY SEEM TO CARE.
IN FACT... MAYBE THIS IS WHAT SHE WANTED.
AH...
OH, NO, IT'S NOTHING!
HEY, DO YOU THINK YOUR BROTHER WOULD LIKE THIS?
HUH?

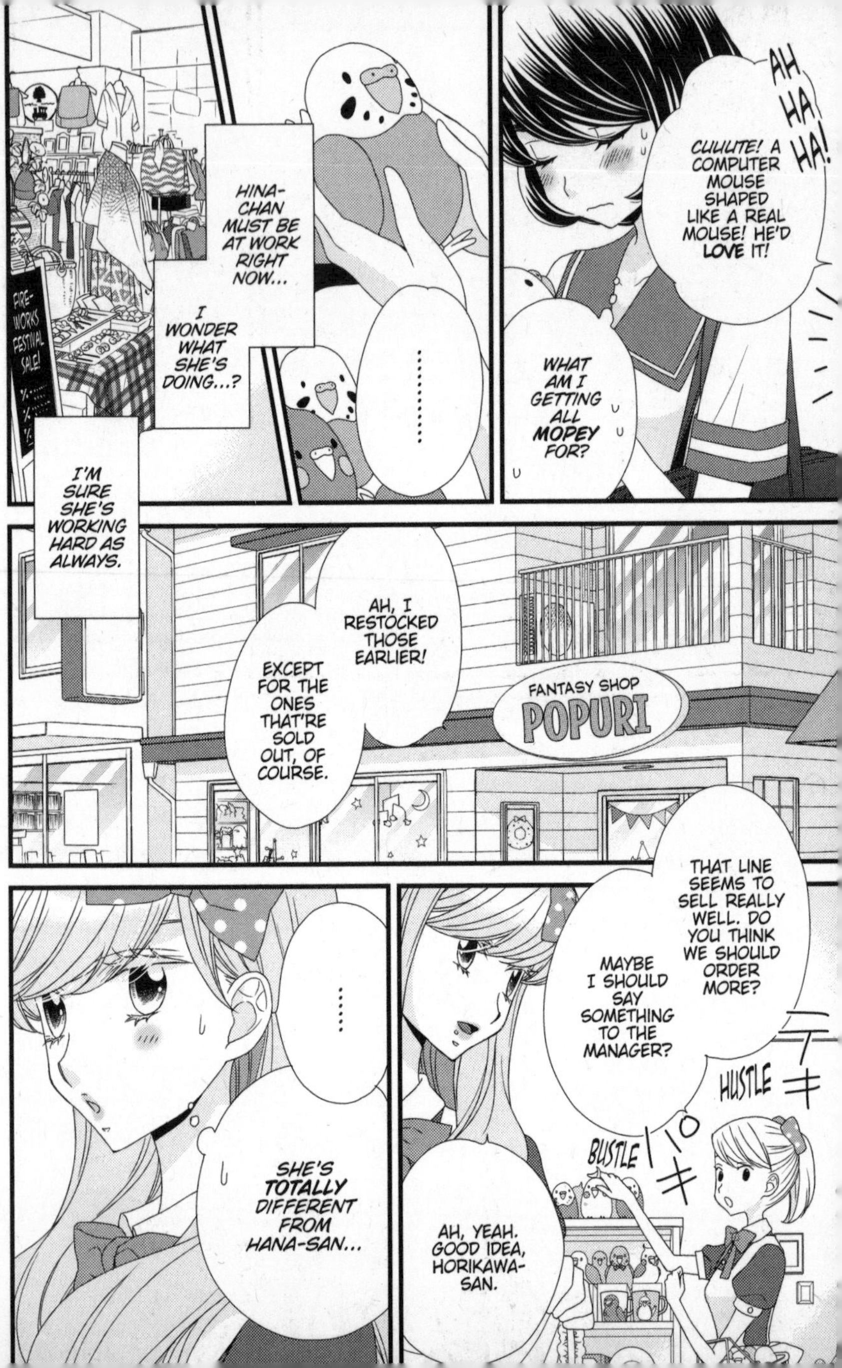
AH HA HA!
CUUUTE! A COMPUTER MOUSE SHAPED LIKE A REAL MOUSE! HE'D **LOVE** IT!
WHAT AM I GETTING ALL **MOPEY** FOR?
HINA-CHAN MUST BE AT WORK RIGHT NOW...
I WONDER WHAT SHE'S DOING...?
FIRE-WORKS FESTIVAL SALE!
......
I'M SURE SHE'S WORKING HARD AS ALWAYS.
AH, I RESTOCKED THOSE EARLIER!
EXCEPT FOR THE ONES THAT'RE SOLD OUT, OF COURSE.
FANTASY SHOP POPURI
THAT LINE SEEMS TO SELL REALLY WELL. DO YOU THINK WE SHOULD ORDER MORE?
MAYBE I SHOULD SAY SOMETHING TO THE MANAGER?
HUSTLE
BUSTLE
AH, YEAH. GOOD IDEA, HORIKAWA-SAN.
......
SHE'S **TOTALLY** DIFFERENT FROM HANA-SAN...

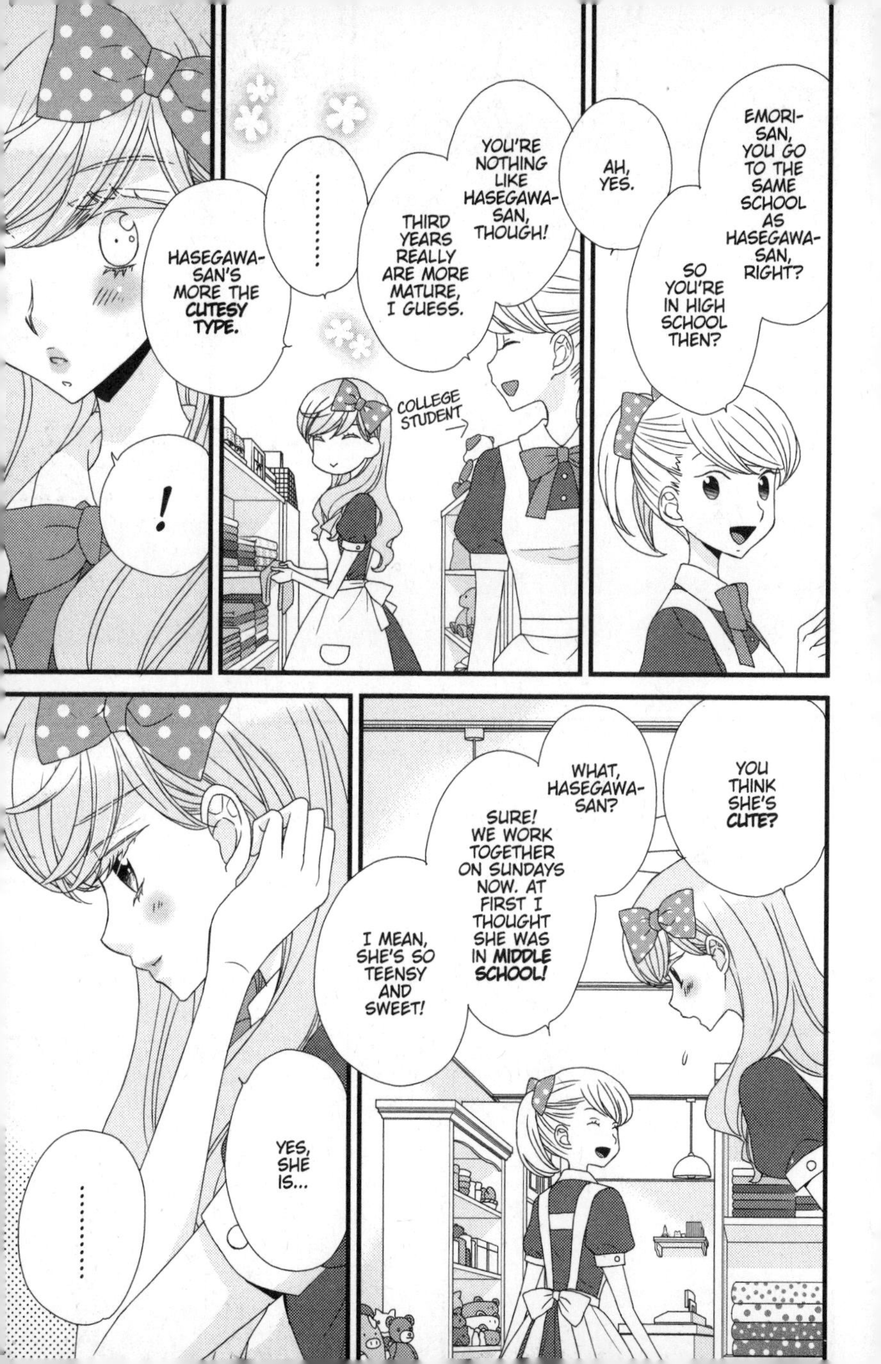
EMORI-SAN, YOU GO TO THE SAME SCHOOL AS HASEGAWA-SAN, RIGHT?
SO YOU'RE IN HIGH SCHOOL THEN?
AH, YES.
YOU'RE NOTHING LIKE HASEGAWA-SAN, THOUGH!
THIRD YEARS REALLY ARE MORE MATURE, I GUESS.
COLLEGE STUDENT
……
HASEGAWA-SAN'S MORE THE **CUTESY TYPE.**
!
YOU THINK SHE'S **CUTE?**
WHAT, HASEGAWA-SAN?
SURE! WE WORK TOGETHER ON SUNDAYS NOW. AT FIRST I THOUGHT SHE WAS IN **MIDDLE SCHOOL!**
I MEAN, SHE'S SO TEENSY AND SWEET!
YES, SHE IS...
……

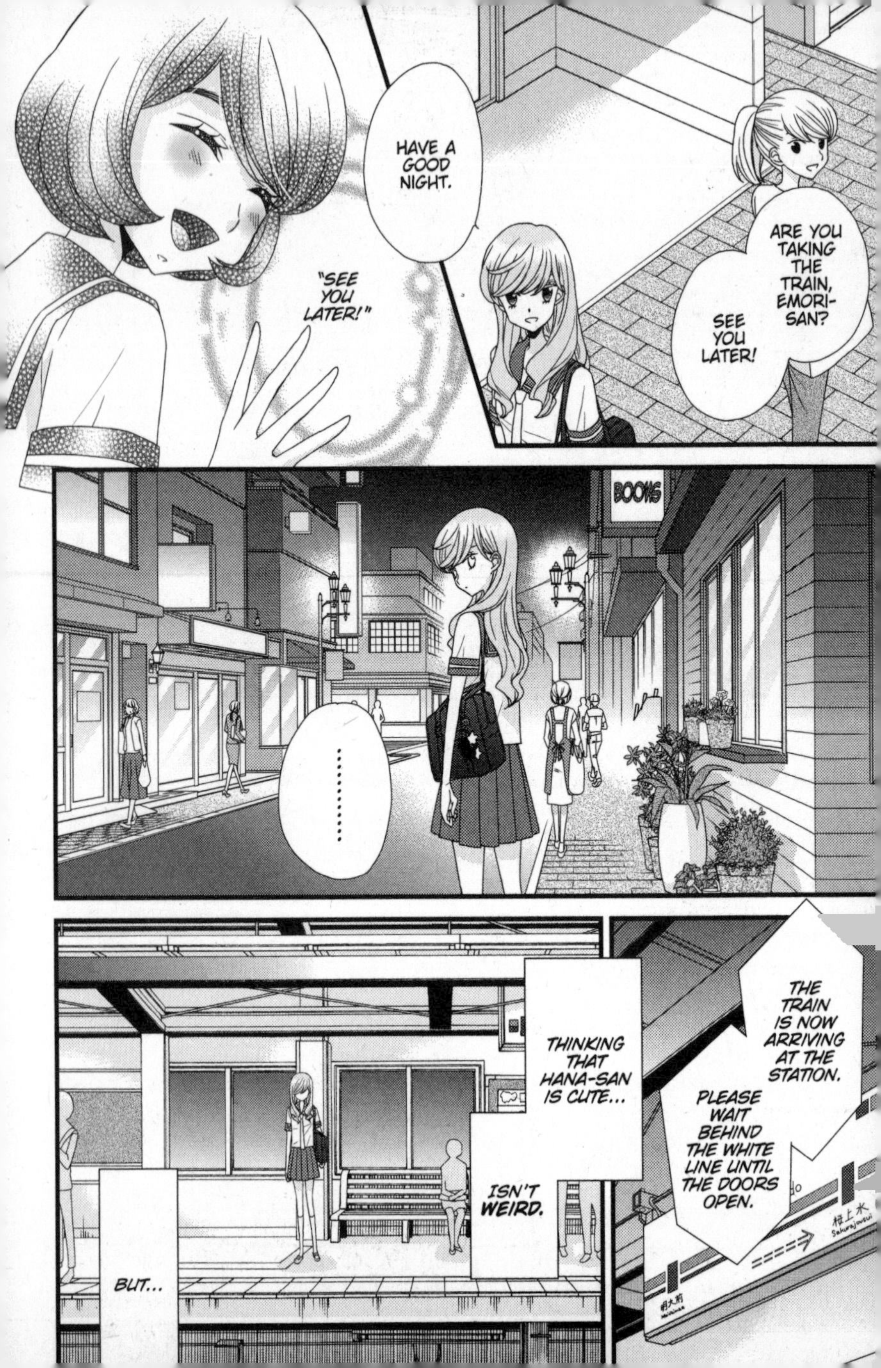
ARE YOU TAKING THE TRAIN, EMORI-SAN?
SEE YOU LATER!
HAVE A GOOD NIGHT.
"SEE YOU LATER!"
BOOKS
......
THE TRAIN IS NOW ARRIVING AT THE STATION.
PLEASE WAIT BEHIND THE WHITE LINE UNTIL THE DOORS OPEN.
THINKING THAT HANA-SAN IS CUTE...
ISN'T WEIRD.
BUT...

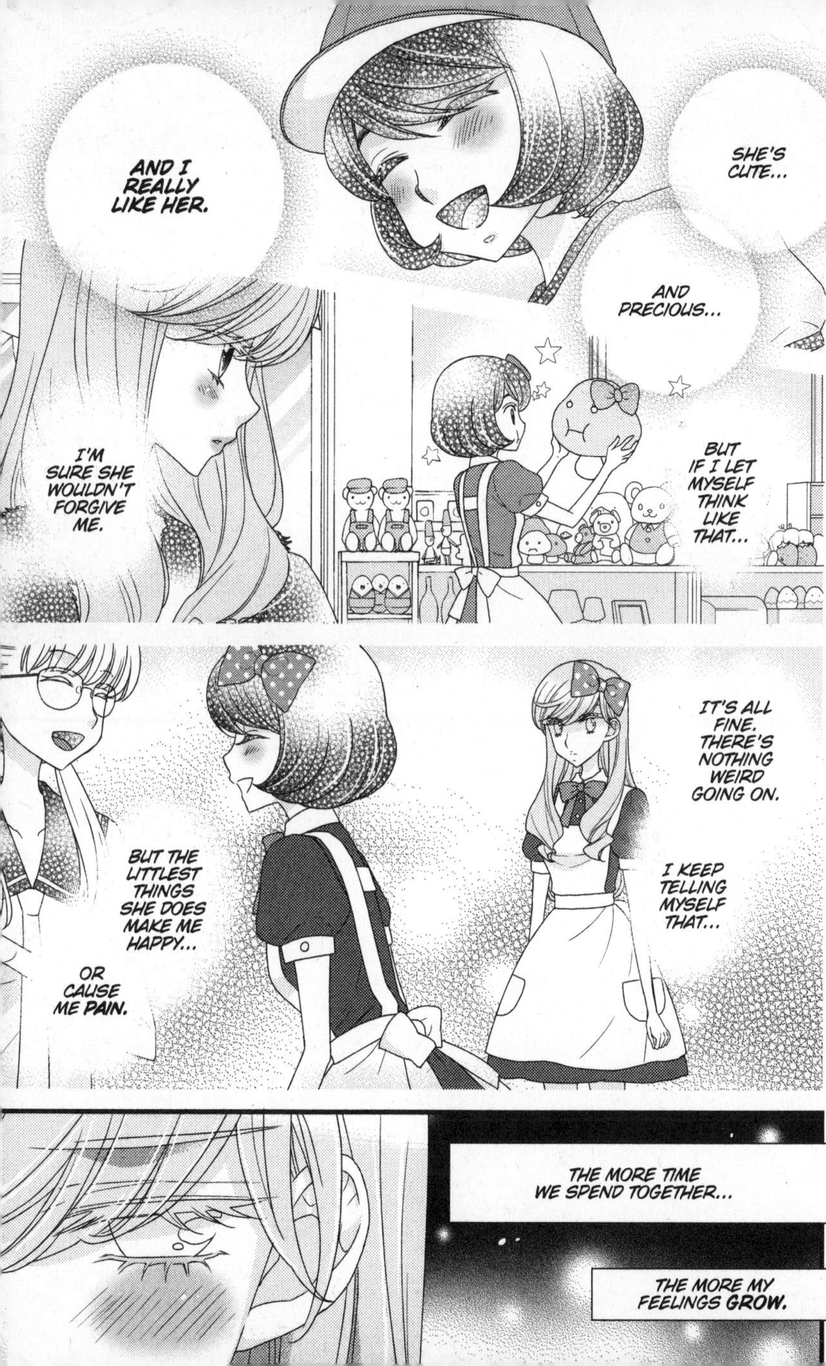
SHE'S CUTE...
AND PRECIOUS...
AND I REALLY LIKE HER.
BUT IF I LET MYSELF THINK LIKE THAT...
I'M SURE SHE WOULDN'T FORGIVE ME.
IT'S ALL FINE. THERE'S NOTHING WEIRD GOING ON.
I KEEP TELLING MYSELF THAT...
BUT THE LITTLEST THINGS SHE DOES MAKE ME HAPPY...
OR CAUSE ME **PAIN.**
THE MORE TIME WE SPEND TOGETHER...
THE MORE MY FEELINGS **GROW.**

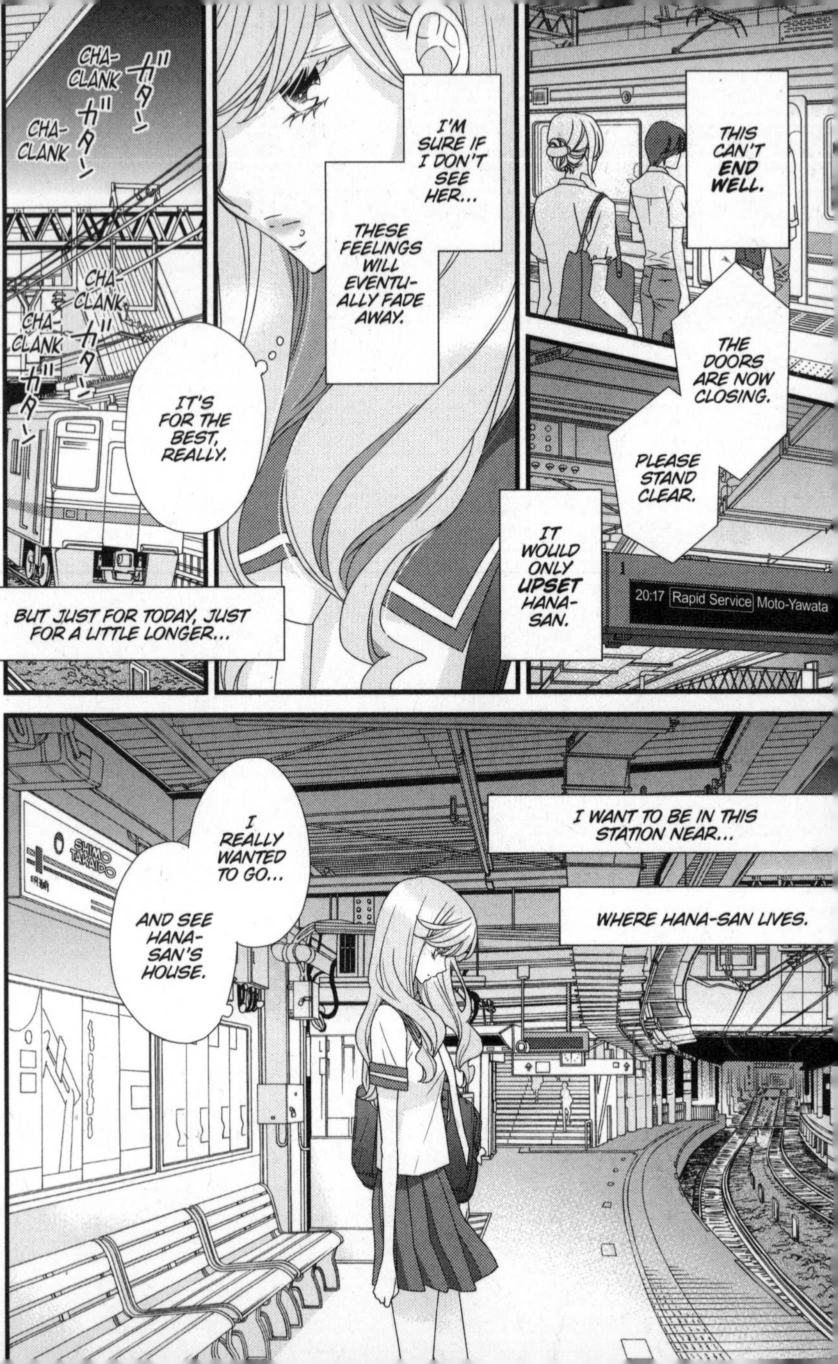
THIS CAN'T END WELL.
THE DOORS ARE NOW CLOSING.
PLEASE STAND CLEAR.
IT WOULD ONLY UPSET HANA-SAN.
20:17 Rapid Service Moto-Yawata
I'M SURE IF I DON'T SEE HER...
THESE FEELINGS WILL EVENTUALLY FADE AWAY.
IT'S FOR THE BEST, REALLY.
CHA-CLANK
CHA-CLANK
CHA-CLANK
CHA-CLANK
BUT JUST FOR TODAY, JUST FOR A LITTLE LONGER...
I WANT TO BE IN THIS STATION NEAR...
WHERE HANA-SAN LIVES.
I REALLY WANTED TO GO...
AND SEE HANA-SAN'S HOUSE.
SHIMO TAKAIDO

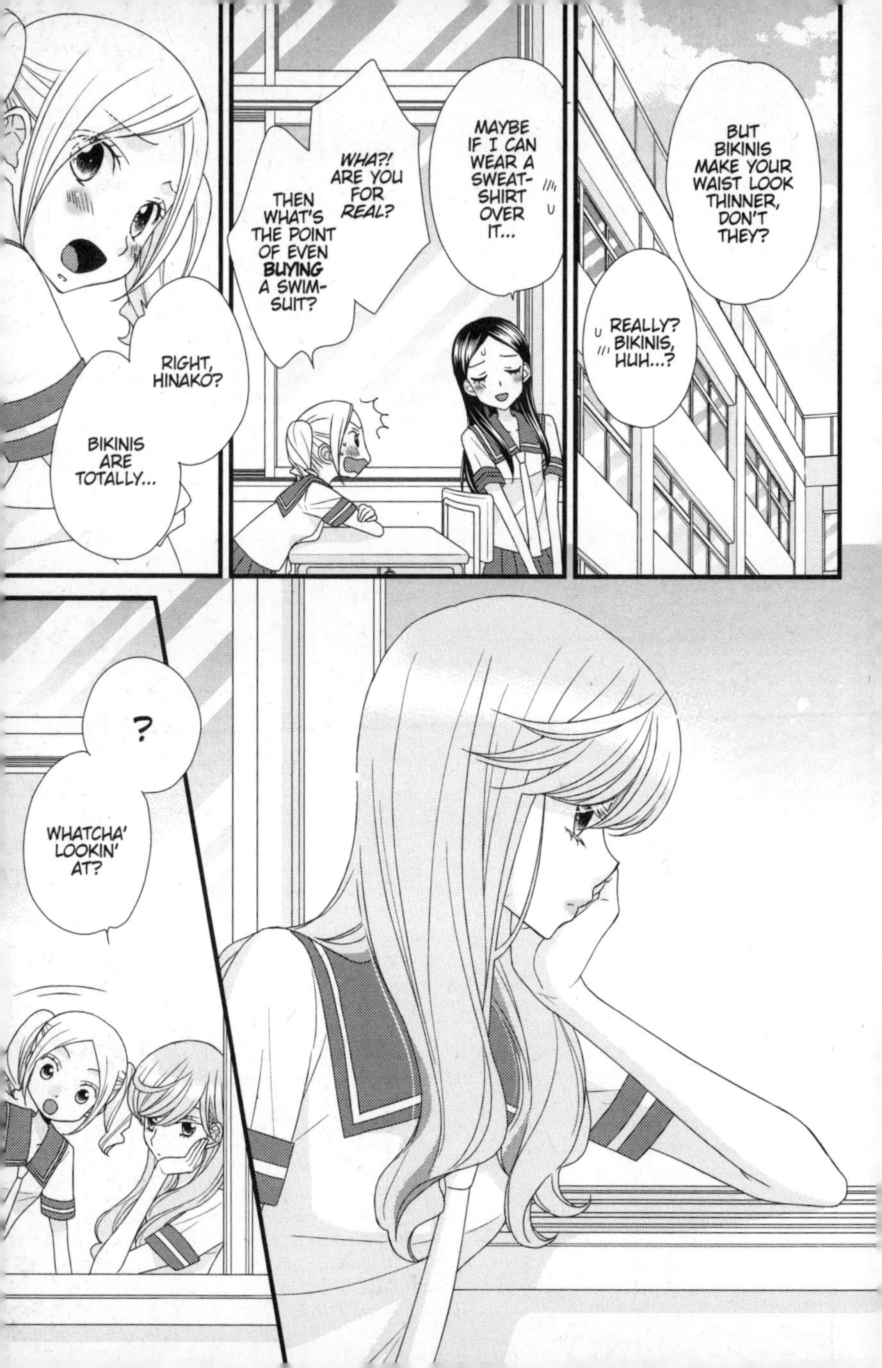
BUT BIKINIS MAKE YOUR WAIST LOOK THINNER, DON'T THEY?
REALLY? BIKINIS, HUH...?
MAYBE IF I CAN WEAR A SWEAT-SHIRT OVER IT...
WHA?! ARE YOU FOR REAL?
THEN WHAT'S THE POINT OF EVEN BUYING A SWIM-SUIT?
RIGHT, HINAKO?
BIKINIS ARE TOTALLY...
?
WHATCHA' LOOKIN' AT?

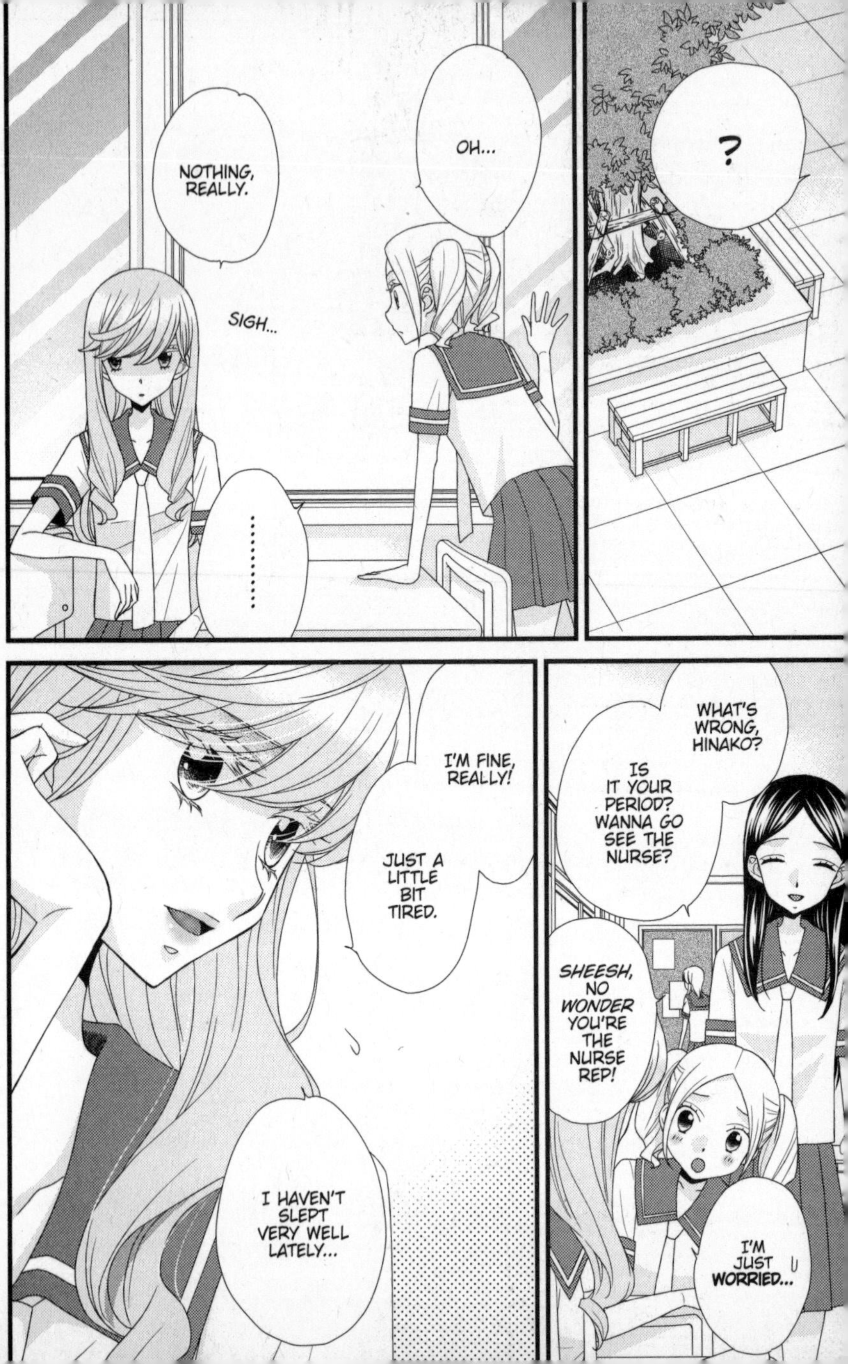
?
OH...
NOTHING, REALLY.
SIGH...
......
WHAT'S WRONG, HINAKO?
IS IT YOUR PERIOD? WANNA GO SEE THE NURSE?
SHEESH, NO WONDER YOU'RE THE NURSE REP!
I'M JUST WORRIED...
I'M FINE, REALLY!
JUST A LITTLE BIT TIRED.
I HAVEN'T SLEPT VERY WELL LATELY...

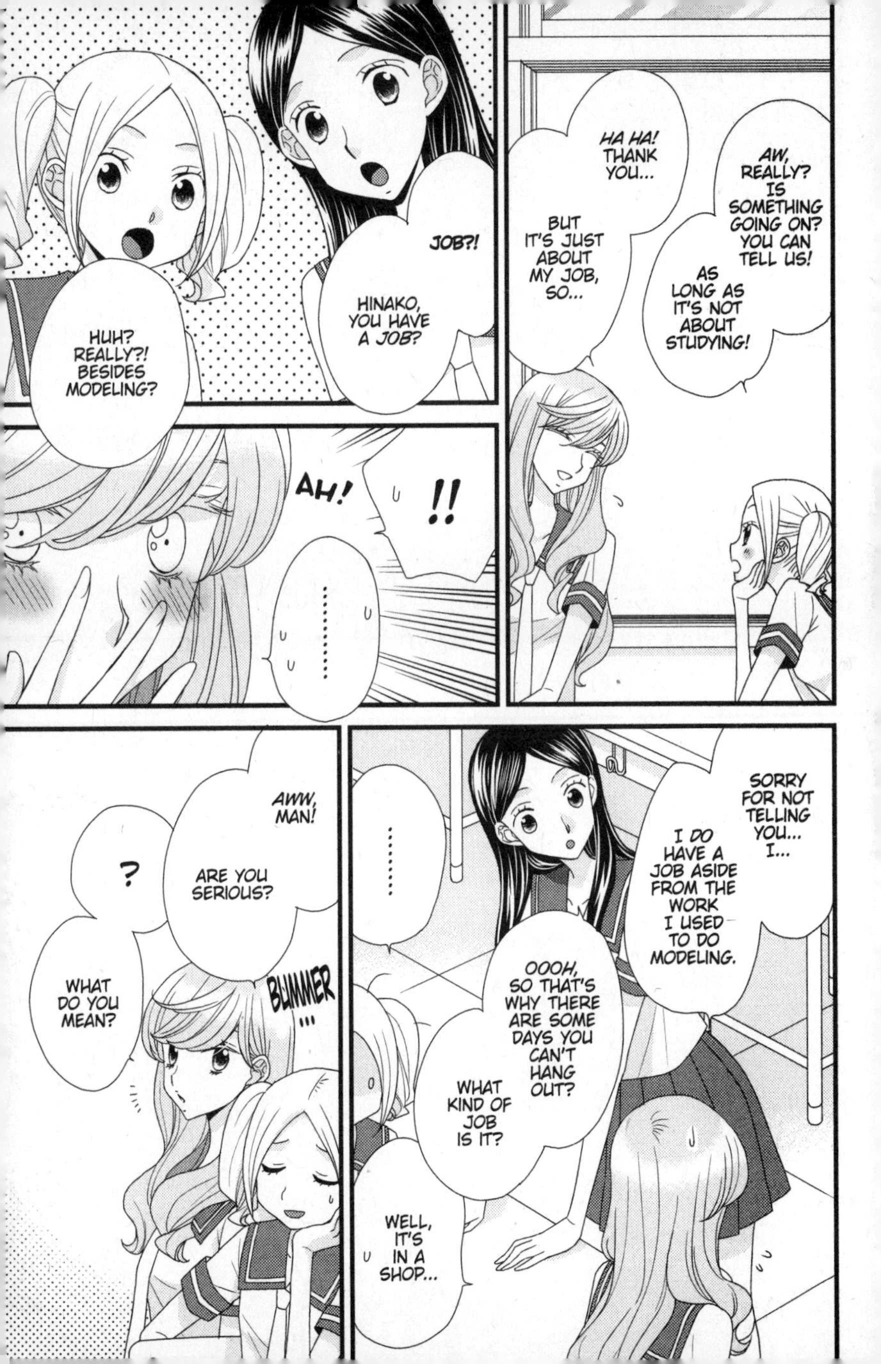
AW, REALLY? IS SOMETHING GOING ON? YOU CAN TELL US!
AS LONG AS IT'S NOT ABOUT STUDYING!
HA HA! THANK YOU...
BUT IT'S JUST ABOUT MY JOB, SO...
JOB?!
HINAKO, YOU HAVE A JOB?
HUH? REALLY?! BESIDES MODELING?
AH!
!!
......
SORRY FOR NOT TELLING YOU... I...
I DO HAVE A JOB ASIDE FROM THE WORK I USED TO DO MODELING.
......
OOOH, SO THAT'S WHY THERE ARE SOME DAYS YOU CAN'T HANG OUT?
WHAT KIND OF JOB IS IT?
WELL, IT'S IN A SHOP...
AWW, MAN!
ARE YOU SERIOUS?
BUMMER...
?
WHAT DO YOU MEAN?

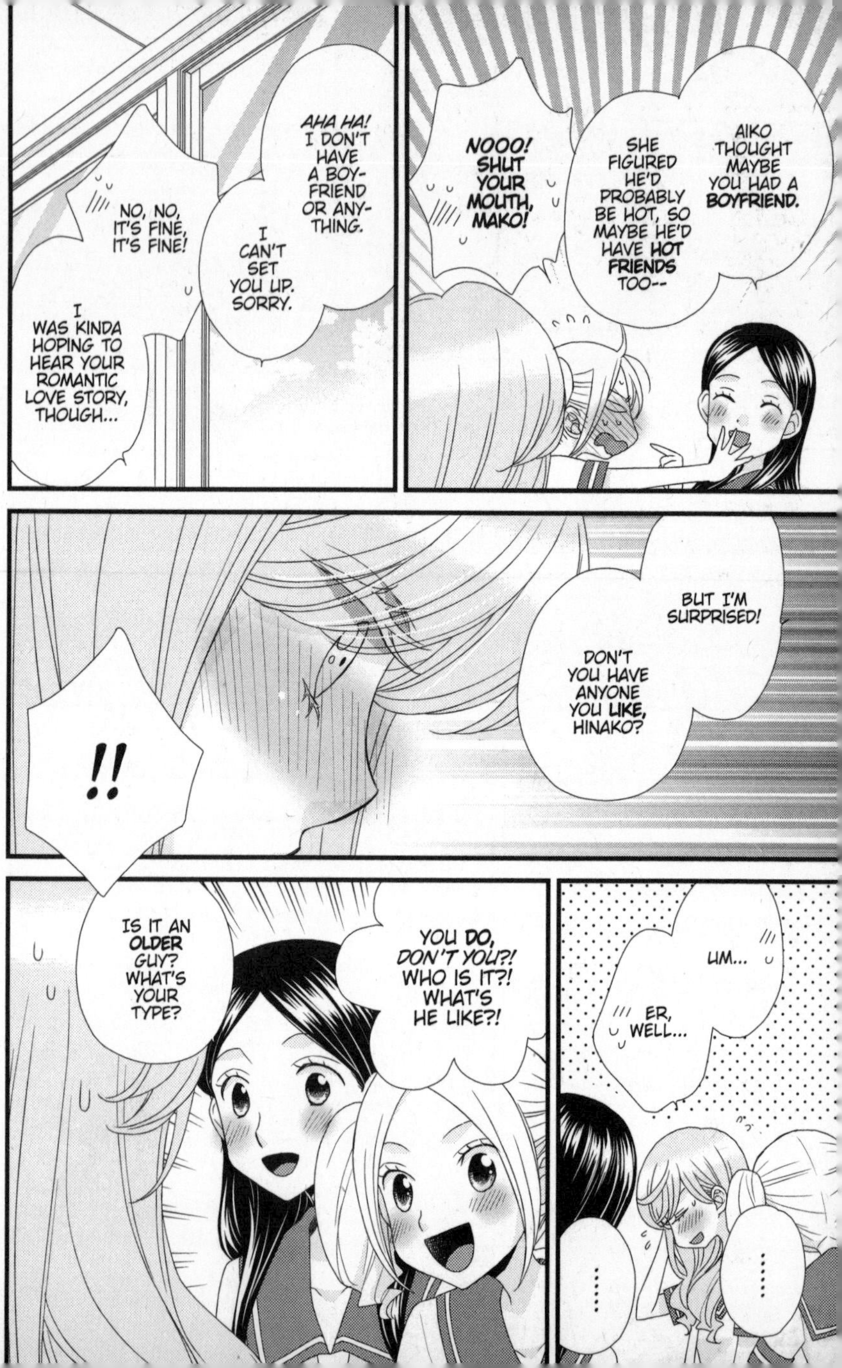
AIKO THOUGHT MAYBE YOU HAD A BOYFRIEND.
SHE FIGURED HE'D PROBABLY BE HOT, SO MAYBE HE'D HAVE HOT FRIENDS TOO--
NOOO! SHUT YOUR MOUTH, MAKO!
AHA HA! I DON'T HAVE A BOY-FRIEND OR ANY-THING.
I CAN'T SET YOU UP. SORRY.
NO, NO, IT'S FINE, IT'S FINE!
I WAS KINDA HOPING TO HEAR YOUR ROMANTIC LOVE STORY, THOUGH...
BUT I'M SURPRISED!
DON'T YOU HAVE ANYONE YOU LIKE, HINAKO?
!!
UM...
ER, WELL...
......
......
YOU DO, DON'T YOU?! WHO IS IT?! WHAT'S HE LIKE?!
IS IT AN OLDER GUY? WHAT'S YOUR TYPE?

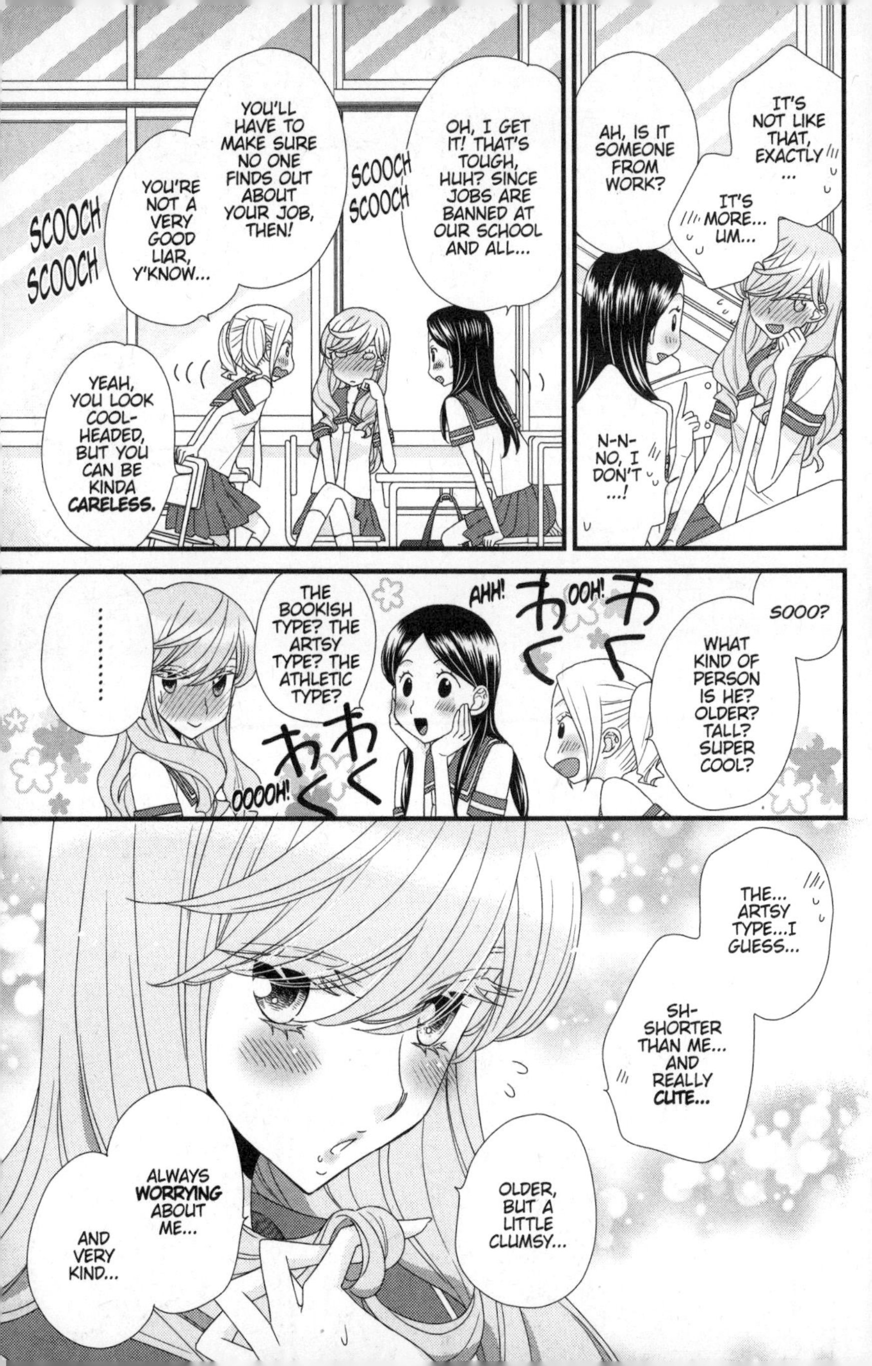
IT'S NOT LIKE THAT, EXACTLY...
IT'S MORE... UM...
AH, IS IT SOMEONE FROM WORK?
N-N-NO, I DON'T ...!
OH, I GET IT! THAT'S TOUGH, HUH? SINCE JOBS ARE BANNED AT OUR SCHOOL AND ALL...
SCOOCH SCOOCH
YOU'LL HAVE TO MAKE SURE NO ONE FINDS OUT ABOUT YOUR JOB, THEN!
YOU'RE NOT A VERY GOOD LIAR, Y'KNOW...
SCOOCH SCOOCH
YEAH, YOU LOOK COOL-HEADED, BUT YOU CAN BE KINDA CARELESS.
SOOO?
WHAT KIND OF PERSON IS HE? OLDER? TALL? SUPER COOL?
おく
OOH!
AHH!
THE BOOKISH TYPE? THE ARTSY TYPE? THE ATHLETIC TYPE?
わくく
OOOOH!
....
THE... ARTSY TYPE...I GUESS...
SH-SHORTER THAN ME... AND REALLY CUTE...
OLDER, BUT A LITTLE CLUMSY...
ALWAYS WORRYING ABOUT ME...
AND VERY KIND...

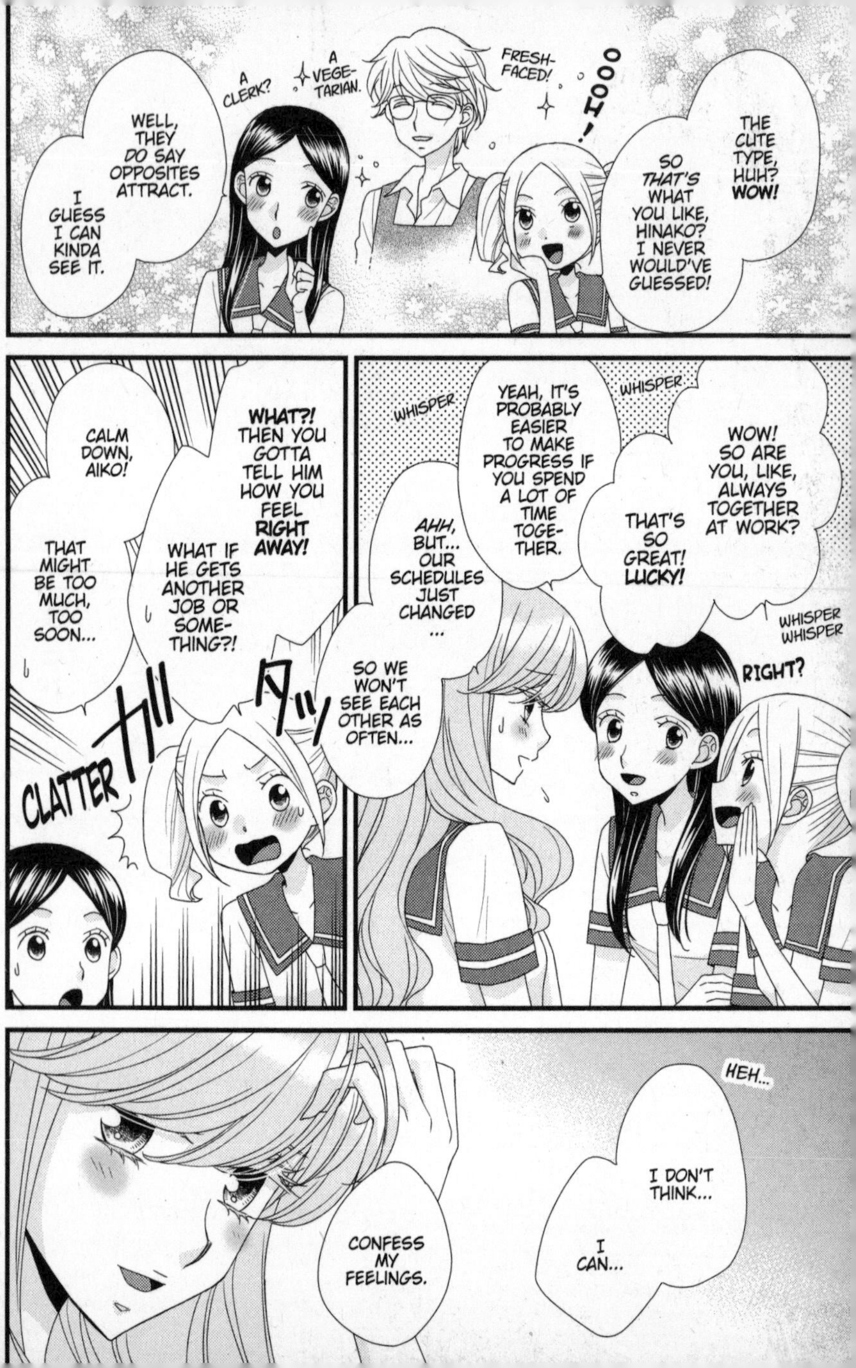
THE CUTE TYPE, HUH? WOW!
SO THAT'S WHAT YOU LIKE, HINAKO? I NEVER WOULD'VE GUESSED!
OOOH!
FRESH-FACED!
A VEGE-TARIAN.
A CLERK?
WELL, THEY DO SAY OPPOSITES ATTRACT.
I GUESS I CAN KINDA SEE IT.
WHISPER
WOW! SO ARE YOU, LIKE, ALWAYS TOGETHER AT WORK?
THAT'S SO GREAT! LUCKY!
WHISPER WHISPER
RIGHT?
YEAH, IT'S PROBABLY EASIER TO MAKE PROGRESS IF YOU SPEND A LOT OF TIME TOGE-THER.
WHISPER
AHH, BUT... OUR SCHEDULES JUST CHANGED...
SO WE WON'T SEE EACH OTHER AS OFTEN...
WHAT?! THEN YOU GOTTA TELL HIM HOW YOU FEEL RIGHT AWAY!
WHAT IF HE GETS ANOTHER JOB OR SOME-THING?!
CLATTER
CALM DOWN, AIKO!
THAT MIGHT BE TOO MUCH, TOO SOON...
HEH...
I DON'T THINK...
I CAN...
CONFESS MY FEELINGS.

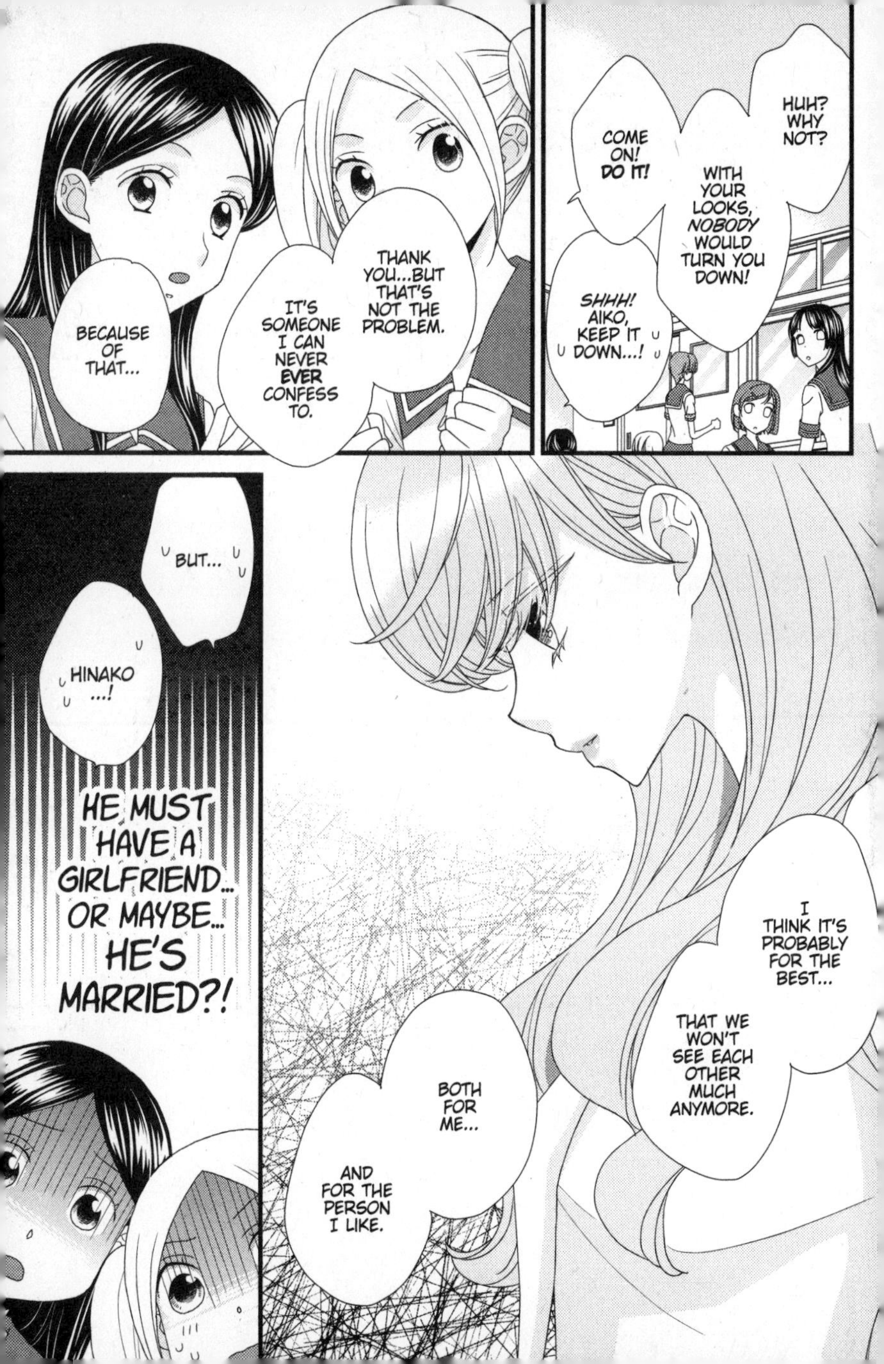
HUH? WHY NOT?
COME ON! DO IT!
WITH YOUR LOOKS, NOBODY WOULD TURN YOU DOWN!
SHHH! AIKO, KEEP IT DOWN...!
THANK YOU...BUT THAT'S NOT THE PROBLEM.
IT'S SOMEONE I CAN NEVER EVER CONFESS TO.
BECAUSE OF THAT...
I THINK IT'S PROBABLY FOR THE BEST...
THAT WE WON'T SEE EACH OTHER MUCH ANYMORE.
BOTH FOR ME...
AND FOR THE PERSON I LIKE.
BUT...
HINAKO...!
HE MUST HAVE A GIRLFRIEND... OR MAYBE... HE'S MARRIED?!

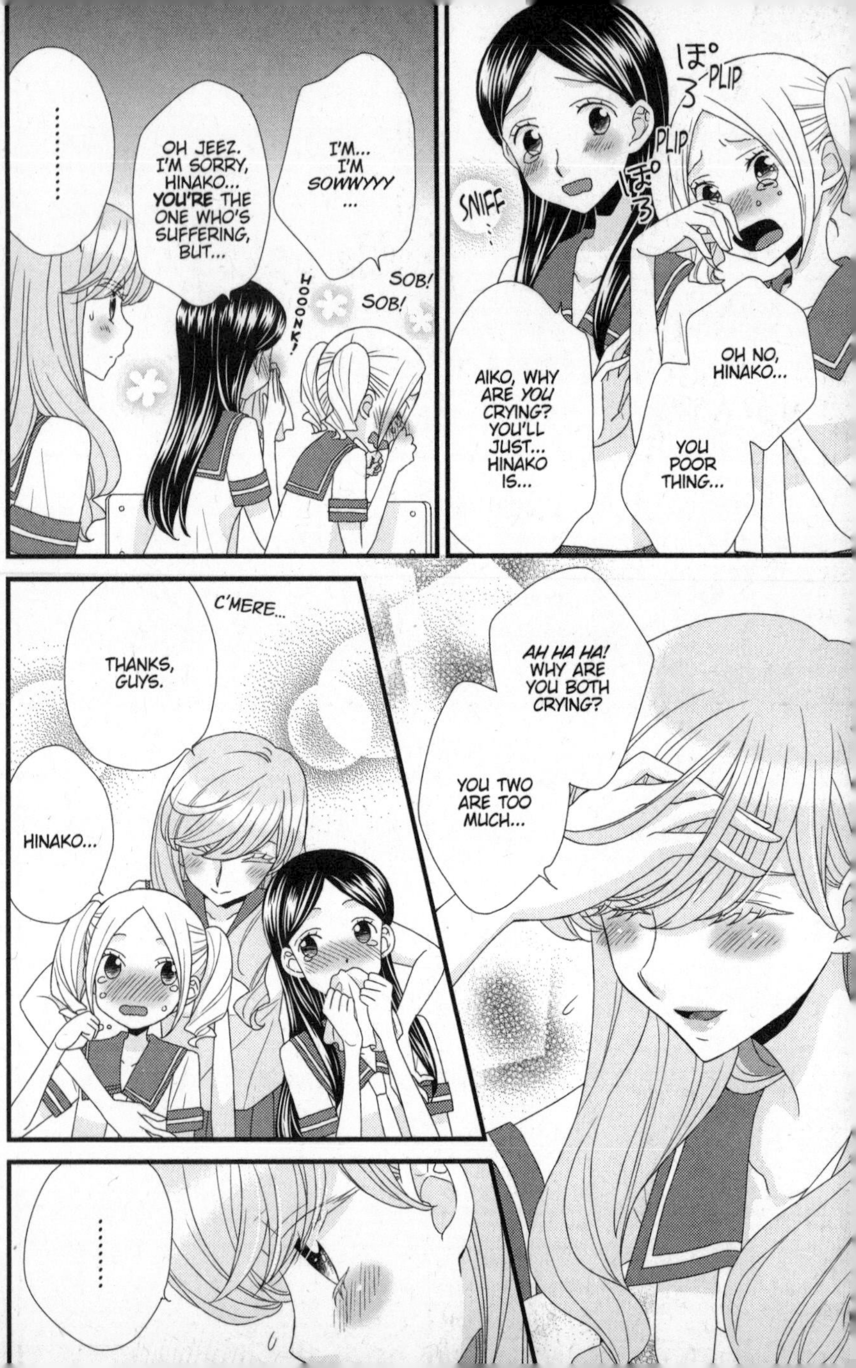
ぽろ PLIP
PLIP ぽろ
SNIFF
OH NO, HINAKO...
YOU POOR THING...
AIKO, WHY ARE *YOU* CRYING? YOU'LL JUST... HINAKO IS...
I'M... I'M *SOWWYYY* ...
SOB! SOB!
HOOOONK!
OH JEEZ. I'M SORRY, HINAKO... **YOU'RE** THE ONE WHO'S SUFFERING, BUT...
......
AH HA HA! WHY ARE YOU BOTH CRYING?
YOU TWO ARE TOO MUCH...
C'MERE...
THANKS, GUYS.
HINAKO...
......

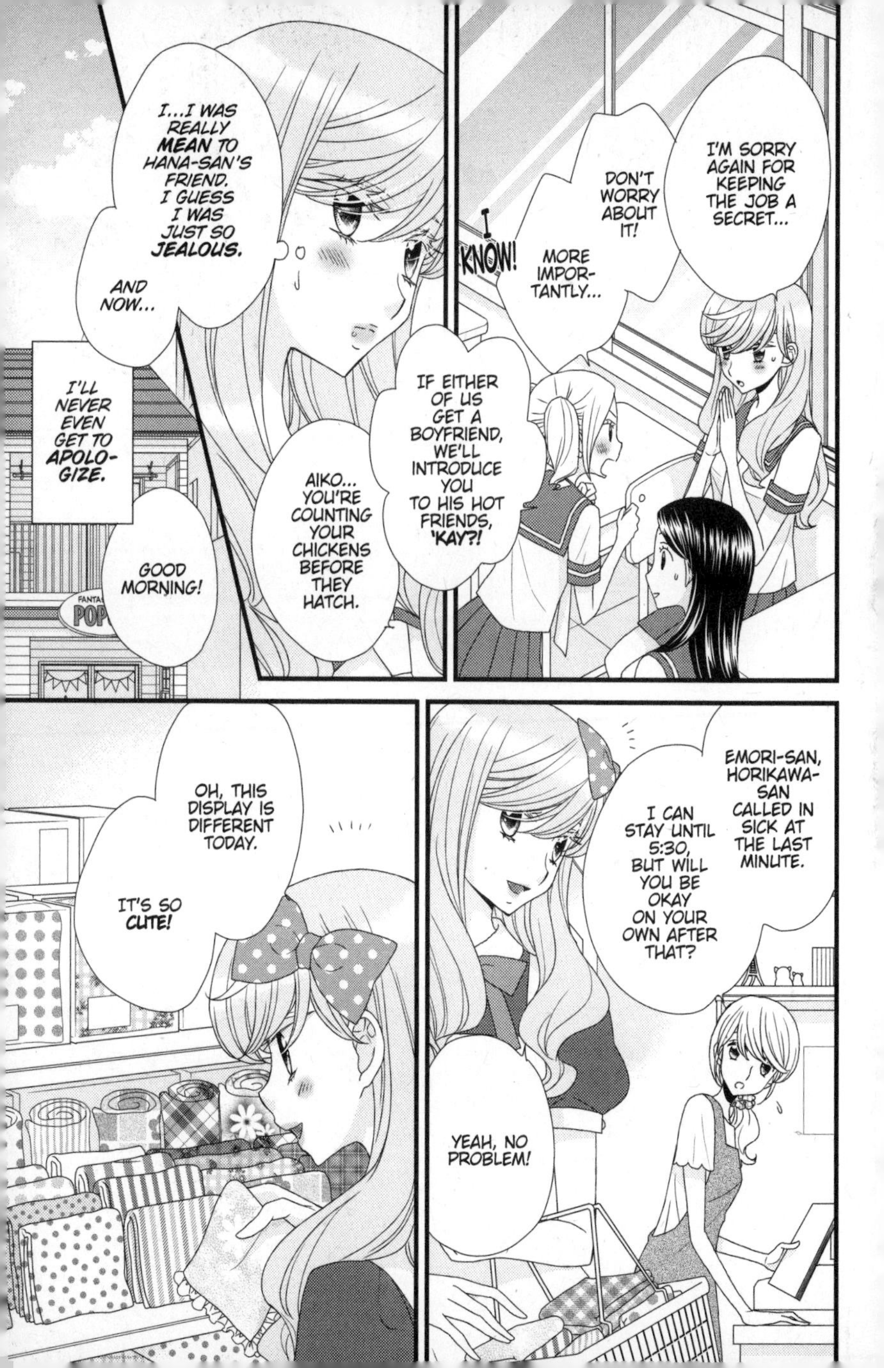
I'M SORRY AGAIN FOR KEEPING THE JOB A SECRET...
DON'T WORRY ABOUT IT!
MORE IMPORTANTLY...
I KNOW!
IF EITHER OF US GET A BOYFRIEND, WE'LL INTRODUCE YOU TO HIS HOT FRIENDS, 'KAY?!
AIKO... YOU'RE COUNTING YOUR CHICKENS BEFORE THEY HATCH.
I...I WAS REALLY MEAN TO HANA-SAN'S FRIEND. I GUESS I WAS JUST SO JEALOUS.
AND NOW...
I'LL NEVER EVEN GET TO APOLOGIZE.
GOOD MORNING!
EMORI-SAN, HORIKAWA-SAN CALLED IN SICK AT THE LAST MINUTE.
I CAN STAY UNTIL 5:30, BUT WILL YOU BE OKAY ON YOUR OWN AFTER THAT?
YEAH, NO PROBLEM!
OH, THIS DISPLAY IS DIFFERENT TODAY.
IT'S SO CUTE!

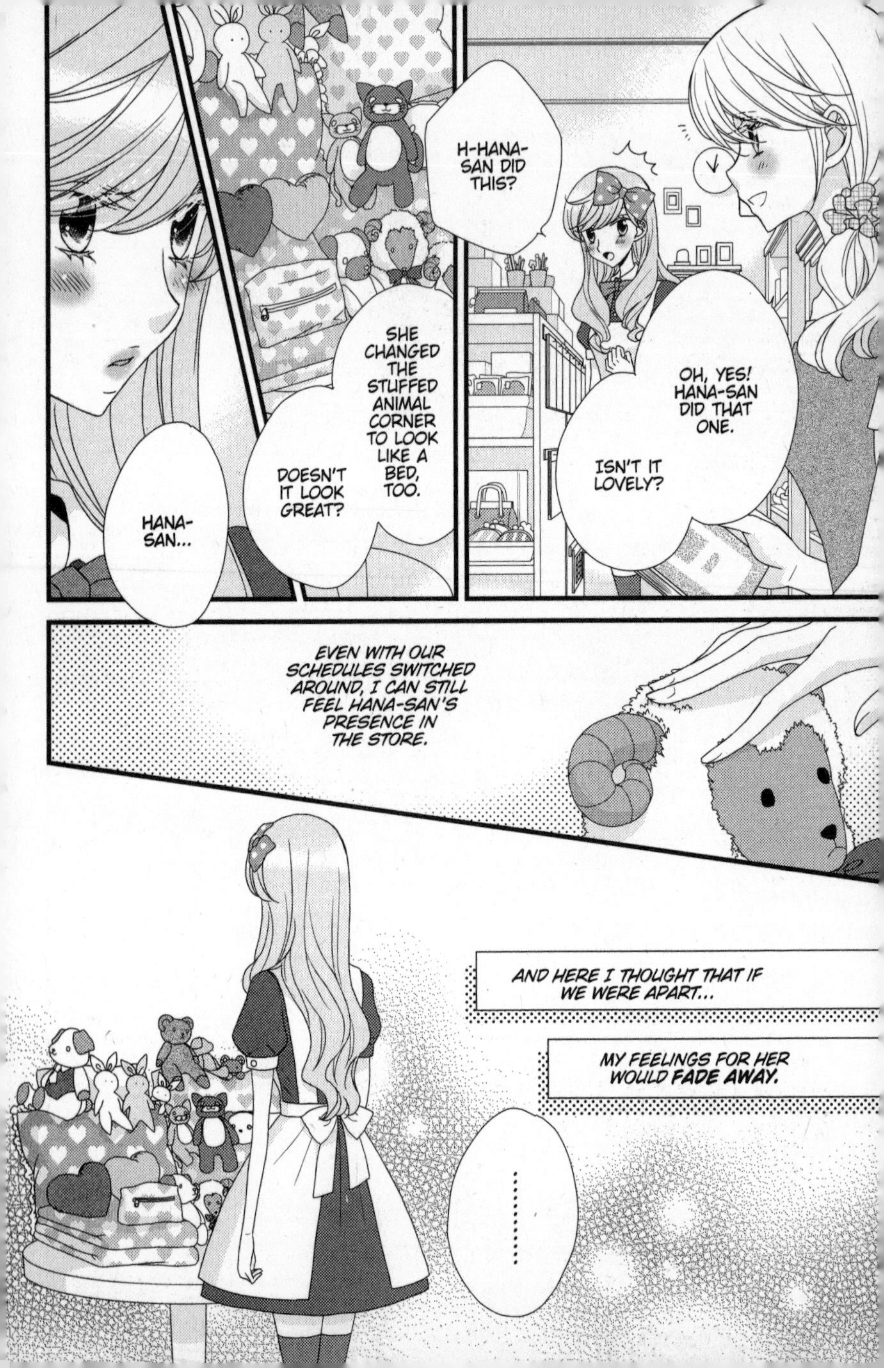
H-HANA-SAN DID THIS?
OH, YES! HANA-SAN DID THAT ONE.
ISN'T IT LOVELY?
SHE CHANGED THE STUFFED ANIMAL CORNER TO LOOK LIKE A BED, TOO.
DOESN'T IT LOOK GREAT?
HANA-SAN...
EVEN WITH OUR SCHEDULES SWITCHED AROUND, I CAN STILL FEEL HANA-SAN'S PRESENCE IN THE STORE.
AND HERE I THOUGHT THAT IF WE WERE APART...
MY FEELINGS FOR HER WOULD **FADE AWAY.**
......

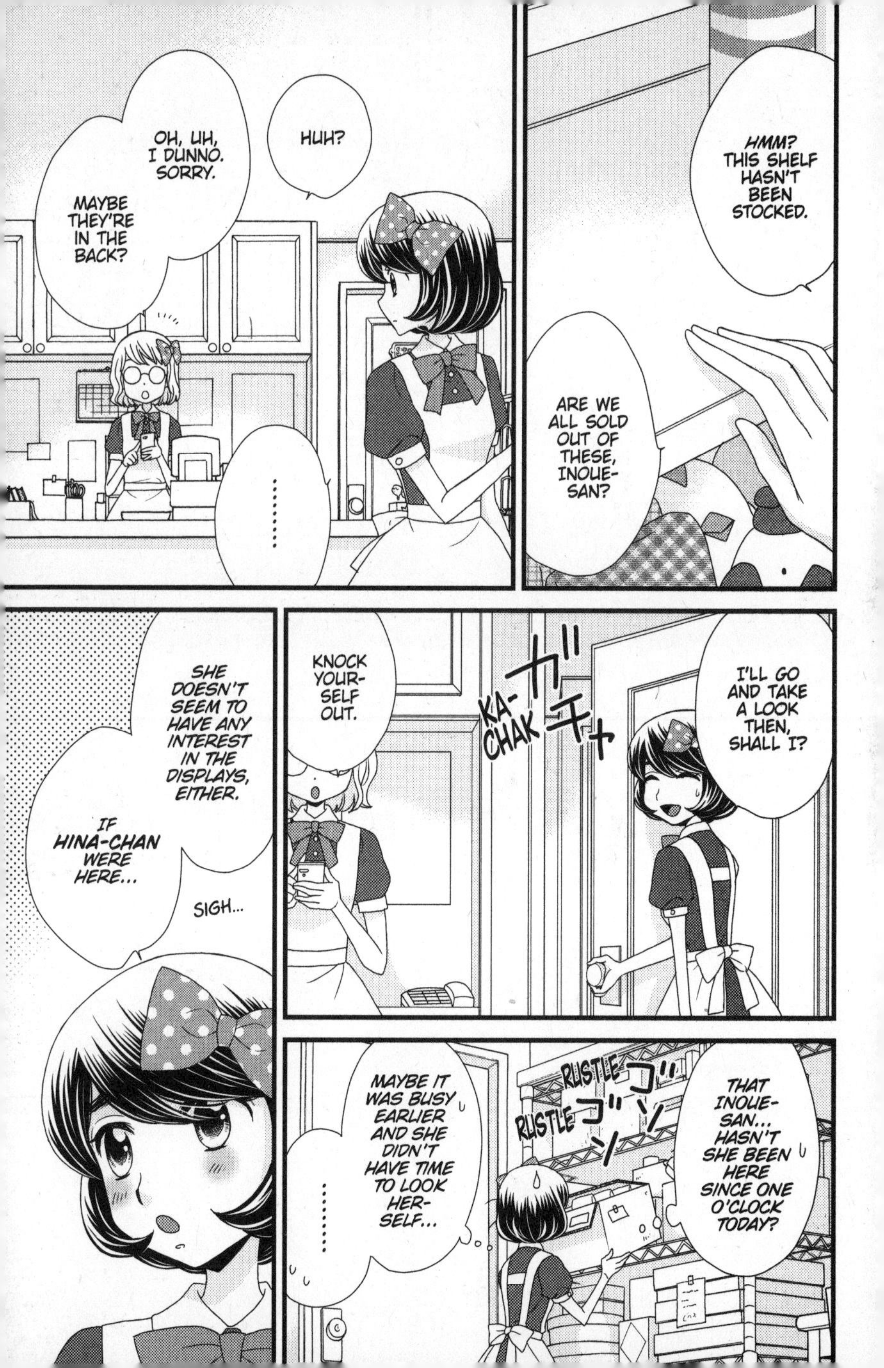
HMM? THIS SHELF HASN'T BEEN STOCKED.
ARE WE ALL SOLD OUT OF THESE, INOUE-SAN?
HUH?
OH, UH, I DUNNO. SORRY.
MAYBE THEY'RE IN THE BACK?
....
I'LL GO AND TAKE A LOOK THEN, SHALL I?
KA-CHAK
ガチャ
KNOCK YOURSELF OUT.
THAT INOUE-SAN... HASN'T SHE BEEN HERE SINCE ONE O'CLOCK TODAY?
RUSTLE RUSTLE
ゴソゴソ
MAYBE IT WAS BUSY EARLIER AND SHE DIDN'T HAVE TIME TO LOOK HERSELF...
....
SHE DOESN'T SEEM TO HAVE ANY INTEREST IN THE DISPLAYS, EITHER.
IF HINA-CHAN WERE HERE...
SIGH...

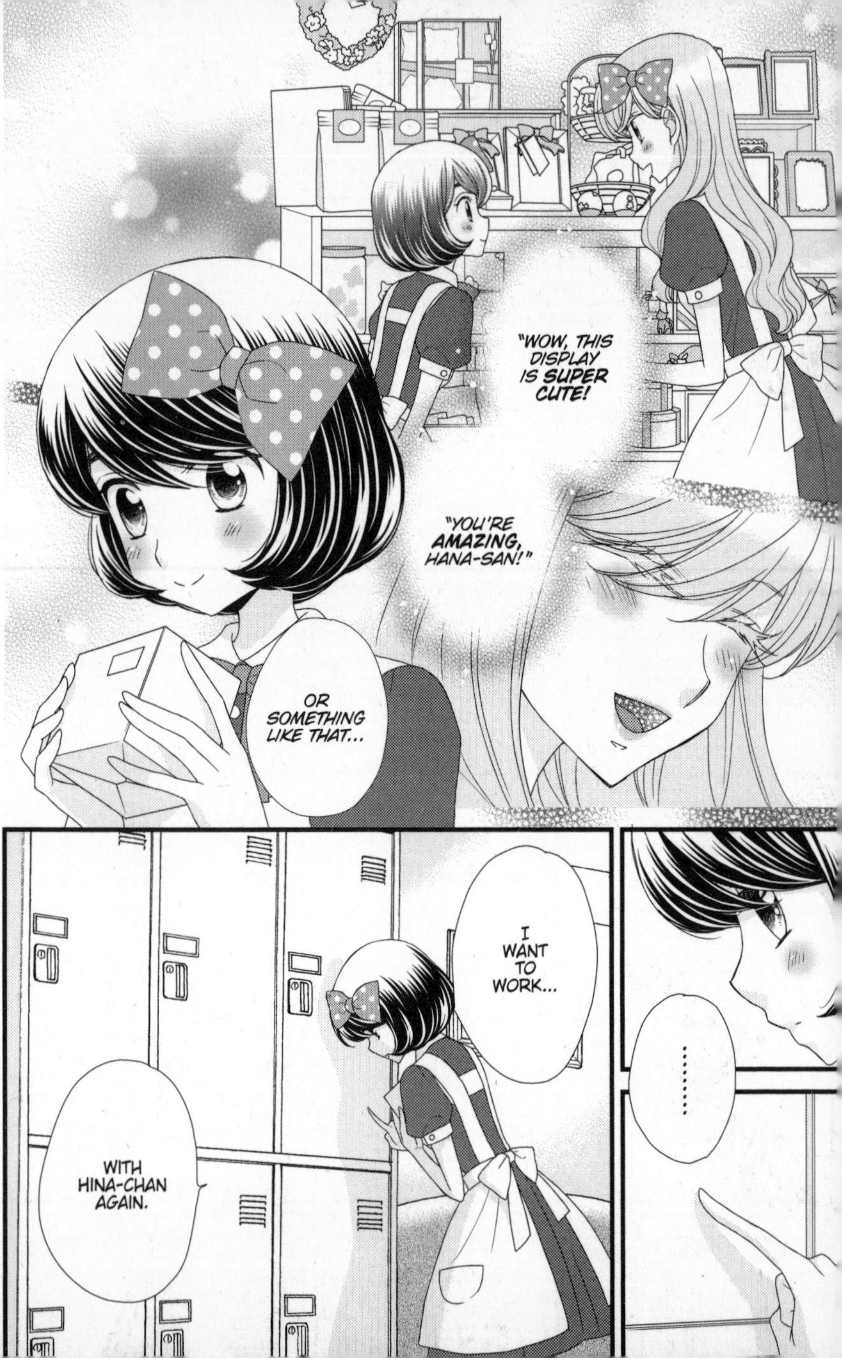
"WOW, THIS DISPLAY IS SUPER CUTE!
"YOU'RE AMAZING, HANA-SAN!"
OR SOMETHING LIKE THAT...
......
I WANT TO WORK...
WITH HINA-CHAN AGAIN.

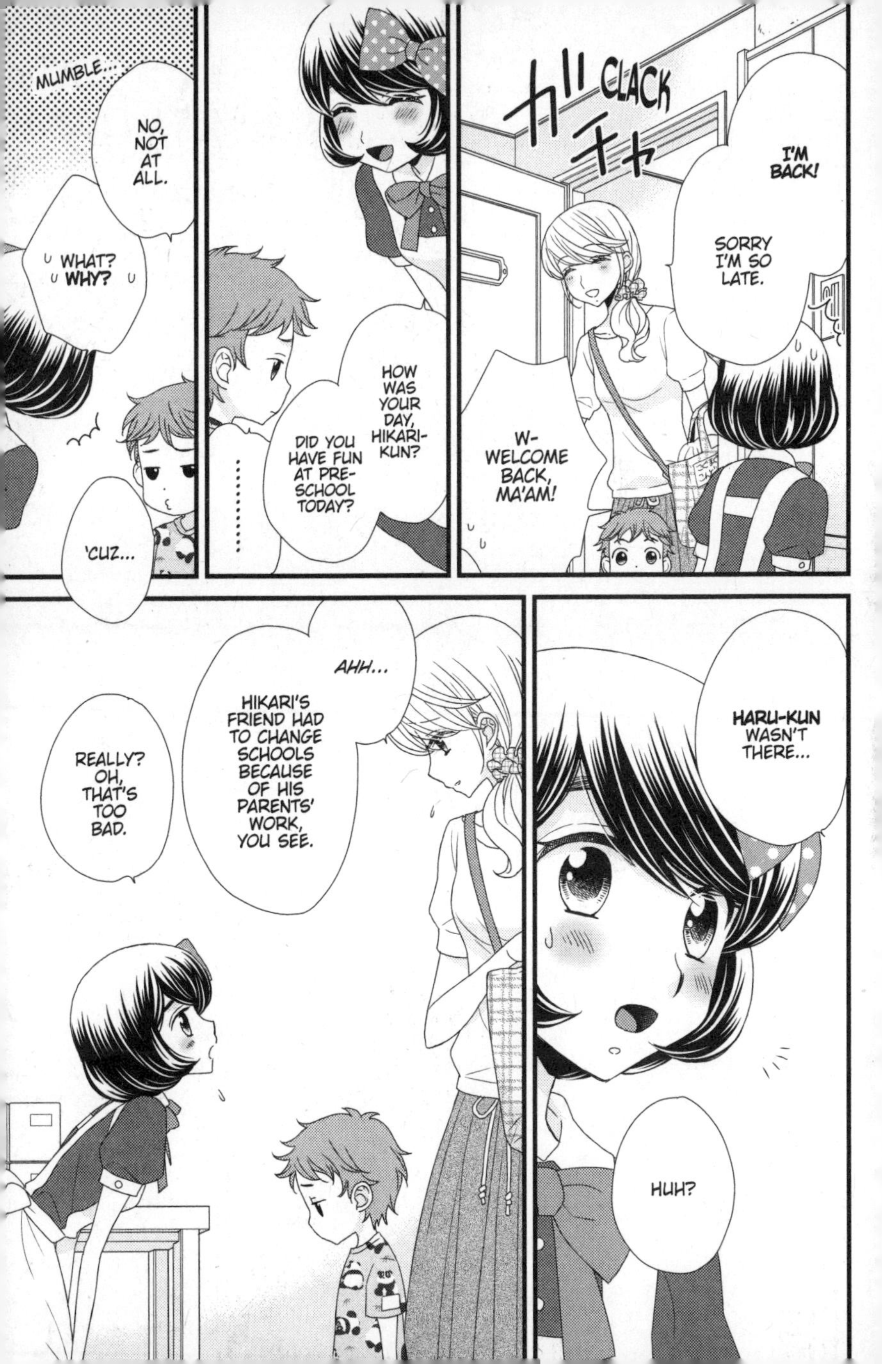

カチャ
CLACK
I'M BACK!
SORRY I'M SO LATE.
W- WELCOME BACK, MA'AM!
HOW WAS YOUR DAY, HIKARI-KUN?
DID YOU HAVE FUN AT PRE-SCHOOL TODAY?
......
MUMBLE...
NO, NOT AT ALL.
WHAT? WHY?
'CUZ...
HARU-KUN WASN'T THERE...
HUH?
AHH...
HIKARI'S FRIEND HAD TO CHANGE SCHOOLS BECAUSE OF HIS PARENTS' WORK, YOU SEE.
REALLY? OH, THAT'S TOO BAD.

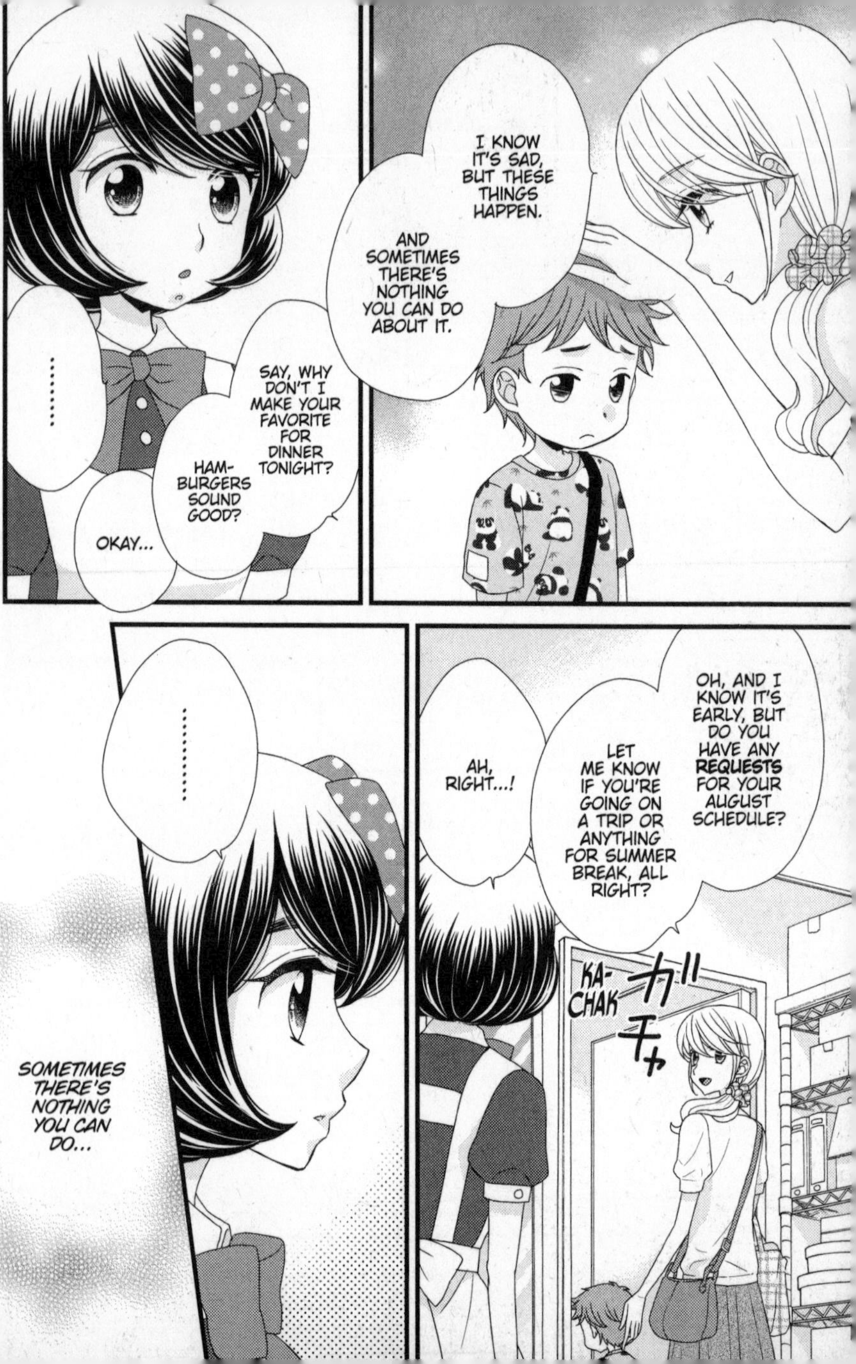
I KNOW IT'S SAD, BUT THESE THINGS HAPPEN.
AND SOMETIMES THERE'S NOTHING YOU CAN DO ABOUT IT.
SAY, WHY DON'T I MAKE YOUR FAVORITE FOR DINNER TONIGHT?
HAM-BURGERS SOUND GOOD?
......
OKAY...
OH, AND I KNOW IT'S EARLY, BUT DO YOU HAVE ANY **REQUESTS** FOR YOUR AUGUST SCHEDULE?
LET ME KNOW IF YOU'RE GOING ON A TRIP OR ANYTHING FOR SUMMER BREAK, ALL RIGHT?
AH, RIGHT...!
KA-CHAK
......
SOMETIMES THERE'S NOTHING YOU CAN DO...

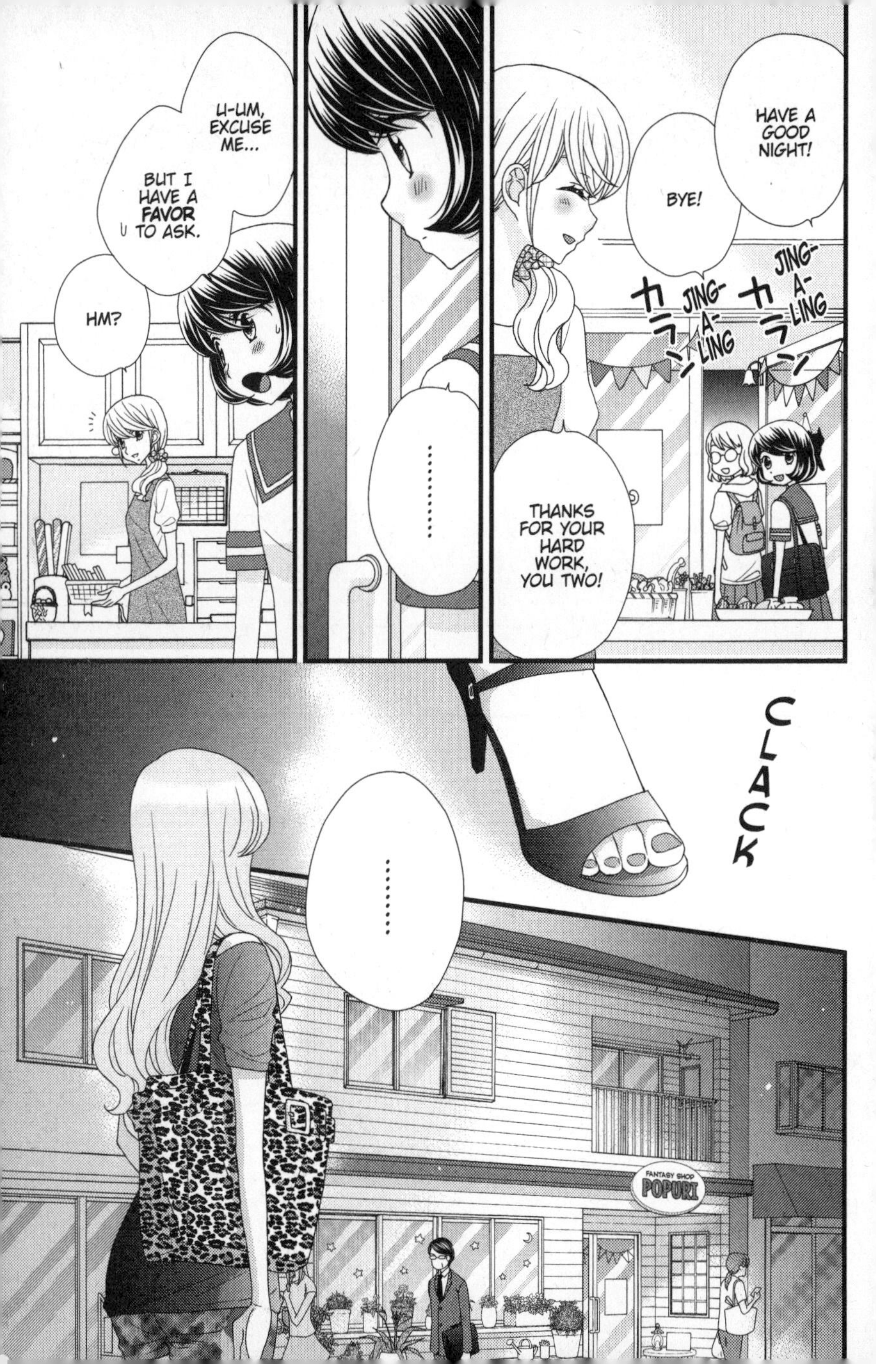
HAVE A GOOD NIGHT!
BYE!
JING-A-LING
カラン
JING-A-LING
カラン
THANKS FOR YOUR HARD WORK, YOU TWO!
......
U-UM, EXCUSE ME...
BUT I HAVE A FAVOR TO ASK.
HM?
CLACK
......
FANTASY SHOP
POPURI

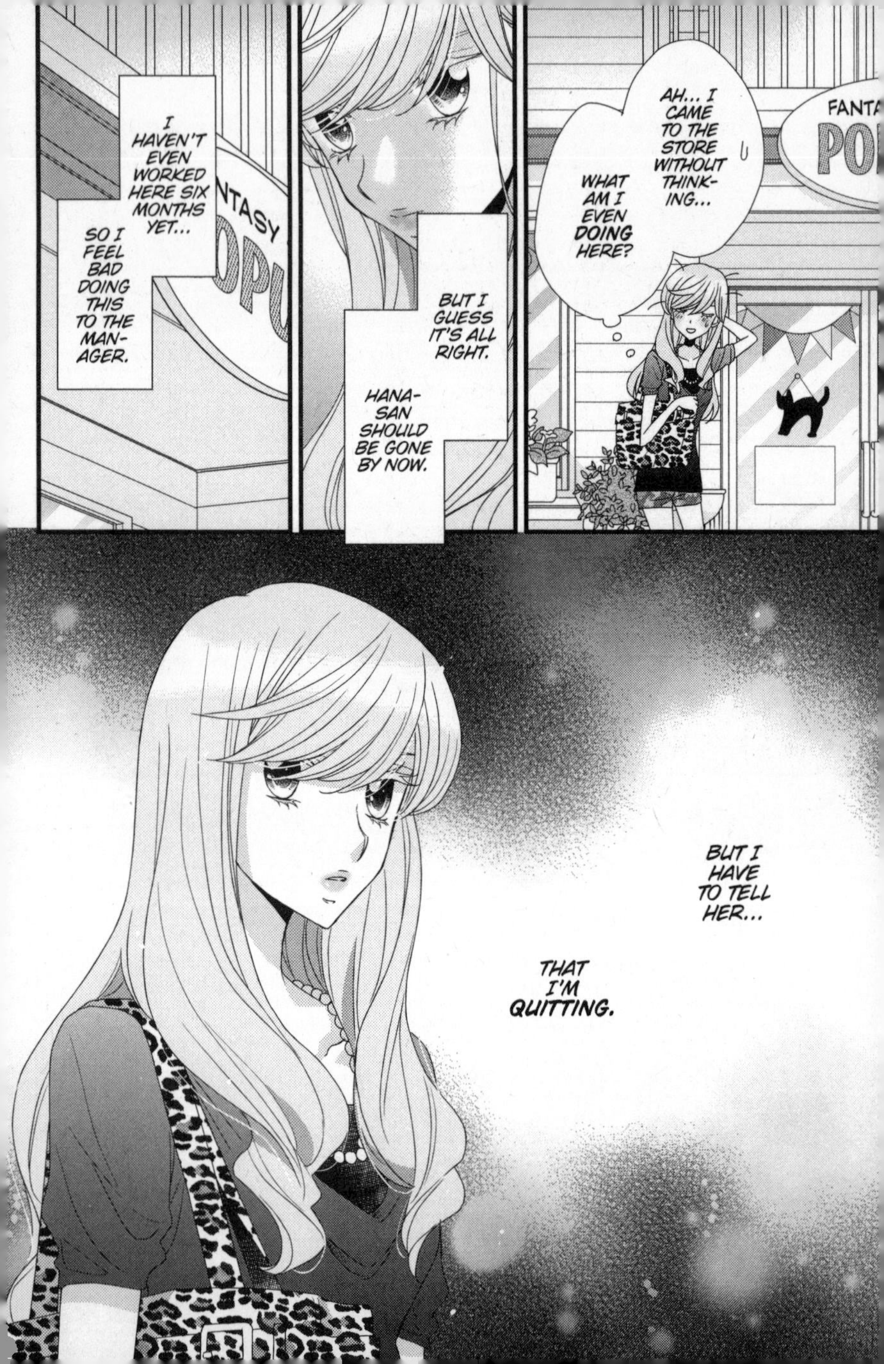

AH... I CAME TO THE STORE WITHOUT THINKING... WHAT AM I EVEN DOING HERE?
BUT I GUESS IT'S ALL RIGHT.
HANA-SAN SHOULD BE GONE BY NOW.
I HAVEN'T EVEN WORKED HERE SIX MONTHS YET...
SO I FEEL BAD DOING THIS TO THE MANAGER.
BUT I HAVE TO TELL HER...
THAT I'M QUITTING.

Hana & Hina
AFTER♡SCHOOL

Hana & Hina

AFTER♥SCHOOL

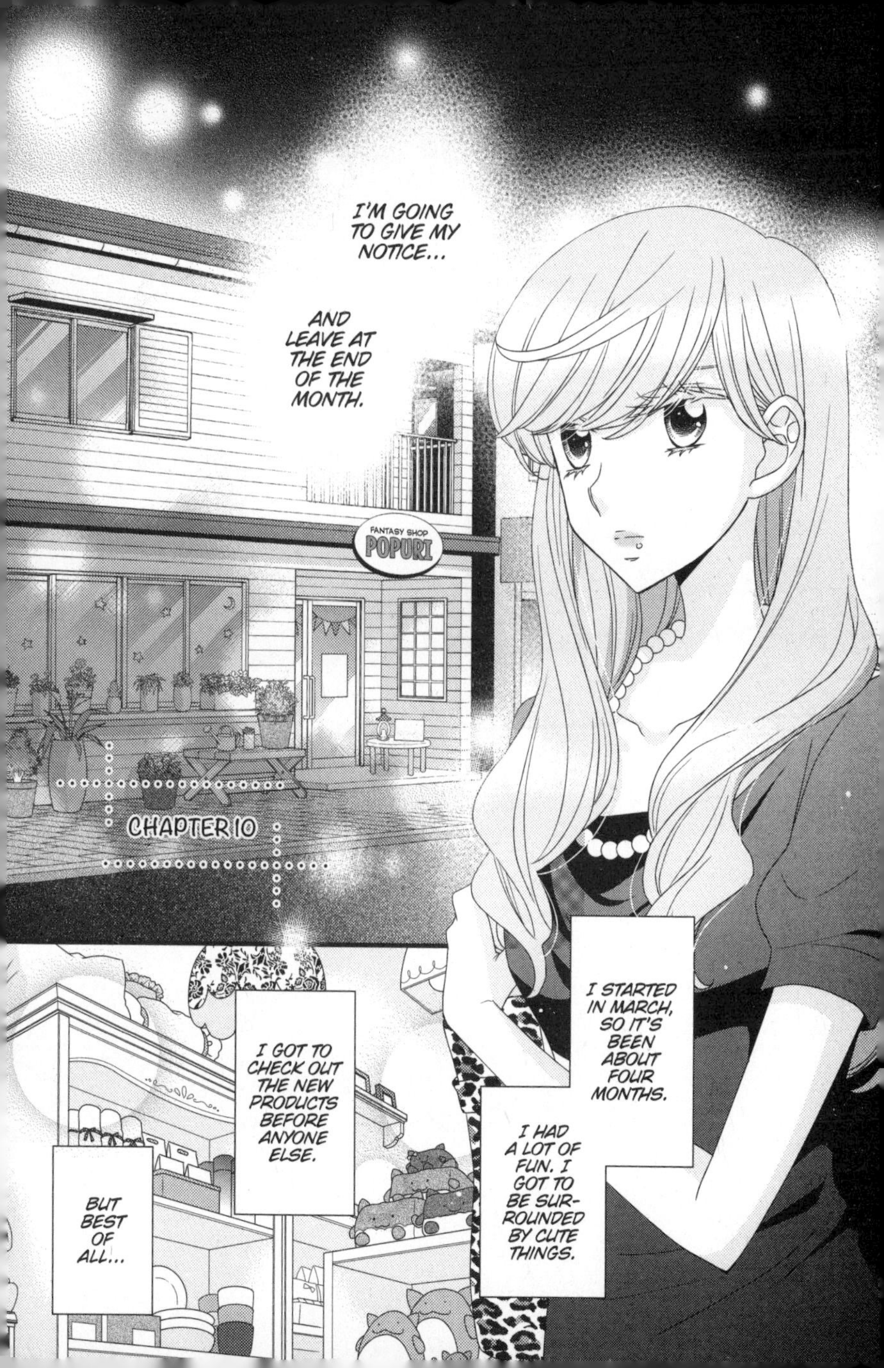
I'M GOING TO GIVE MY NOTICE...
AND LEAVE AT THE END OF THE MONTH.
FANTASY SHOP POPURI
CHAPTER 10
I STARTED IN MARCH, SO IT'S BEEN ABOUT FOUR MONTHS.
I HAD A LOT OF FUN. I GOT TO BE SUR-ROUNDED BY CUTE THINGS.
I GOT TO CHECK OUT THE NEW PRODUCTS BEFORE ANYONE ELSE.
BUT BEST OF ALL...

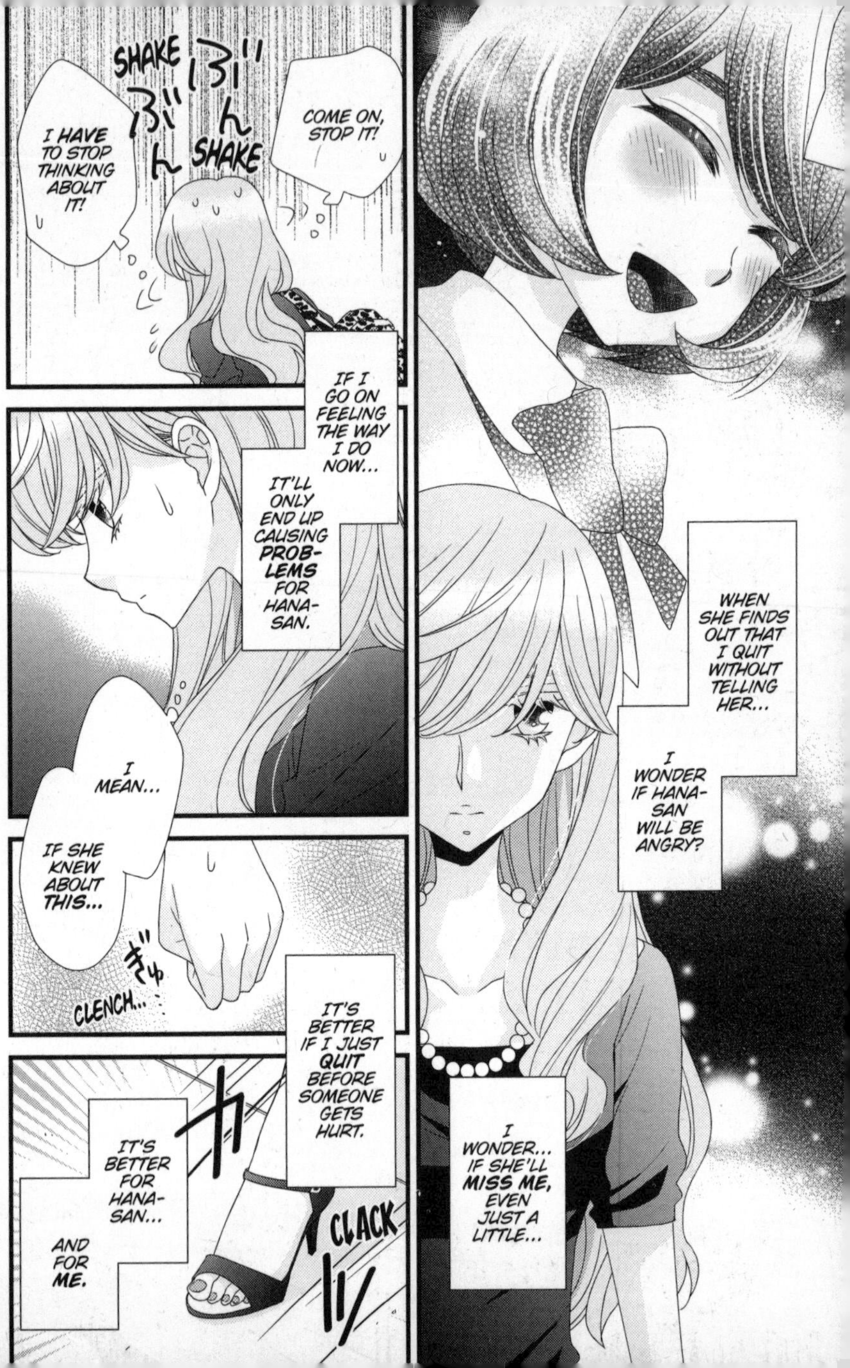
WHEN SHE FINDS OUT THAT I QUIT WITHOUT TELLING HER...
I WONDER IF HANA-SAN WILL BE ANGRY?
I WONDER... IF SHE'LL MISS ME, EVEN JUST A LITTLE...
ぶん ぶん
SHAKE SHAKE
COME ON, STOP IT!
I HAVE TO STOP THINKING ABOUT IT!
IF I GO ON FEELING THE WAY I DO NOW...
IT'LL ONLY END UP CAUSING PROBLEMS FOR HANA-SAN.
I MEAN...
IF SHE KNEW ABOUT THIS...
ぎゅ
CLENCH...
IT'S BETTER IF I JUST QUIT BEFORE SOMEONE GETS HURT.
IT'S BETTER FOR HANA-SAN...
AND FOR ME.
CLACK

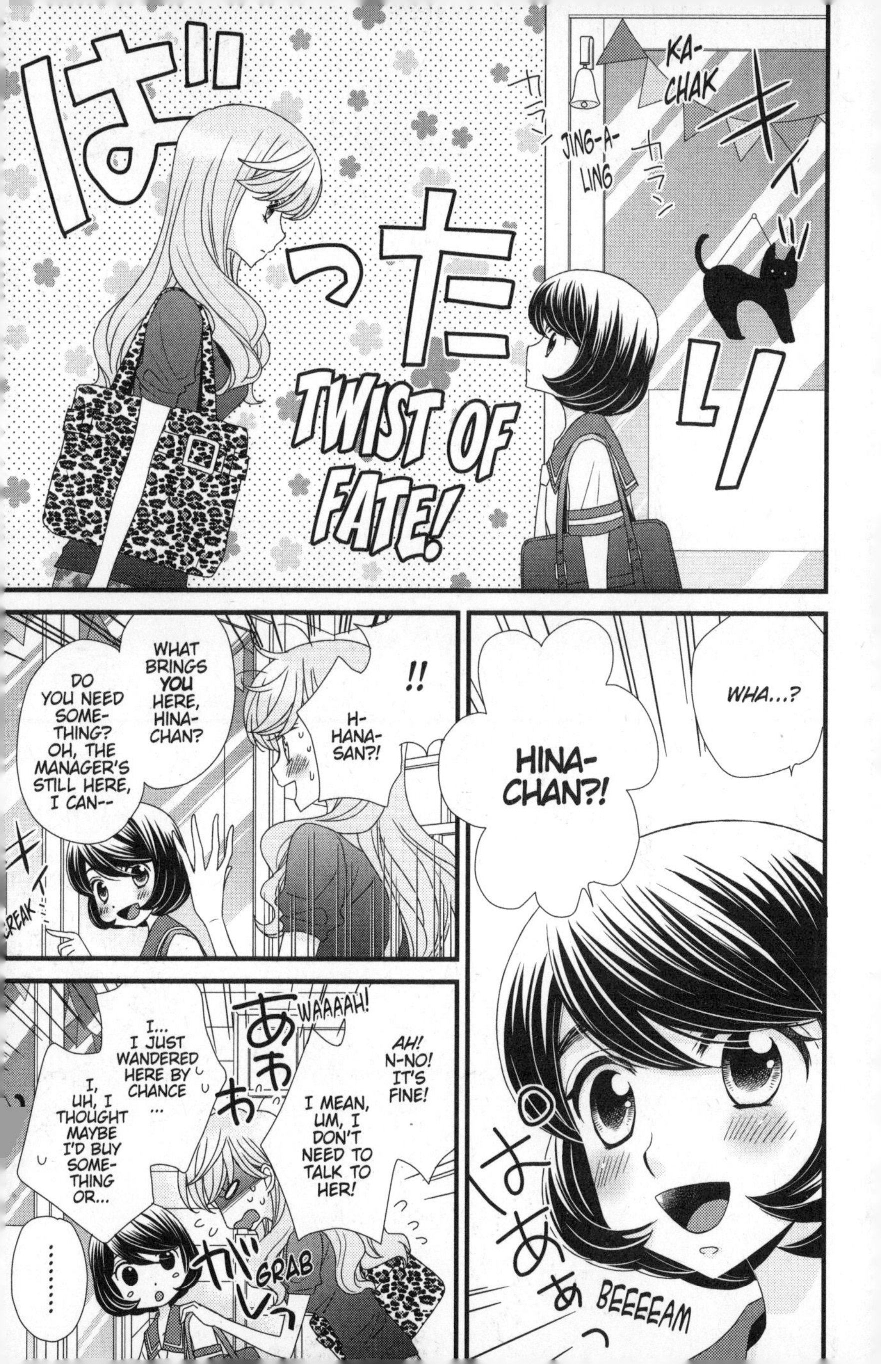
KA-CHAK
キイ
JING-A-LING
カラン
ばったり
TWIST OF FATE!
WHA...?
HINA-CHAN?!
はぁぁ
BEEEEAM
!!
H-HANA-SAN?!
WHAT BRINGS YOU HERE, HINA-CHAN?
DO YOU NEED SOMETHING? OH, THE MANAGER'S STILL HERE, I CAN--
CREAK
AH! N-NO! IT'S FINE!
I MEAN, UM, I DON'T NEED TO TALK TO HER!
WAAAAH!
I... I JUST WANDERED HERE BY CHANCE...
I, UH, I THOUGHT MAYBE I'D BUY SOMETHING OR...
GRAB
....

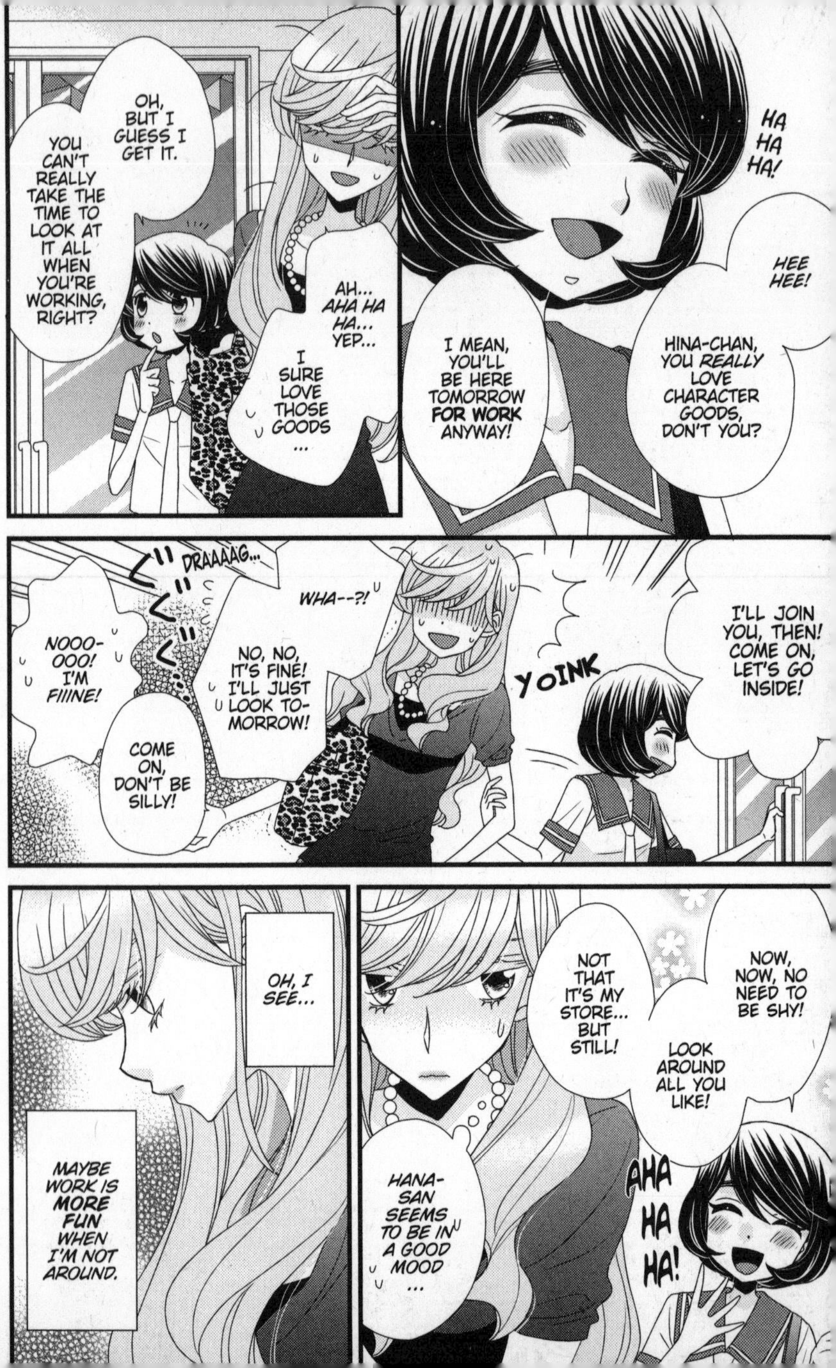
HA HA HA!
HEE HEE!
HINA-CHAN, YOU REALLY LOVE CHARACTER GOODS, DON'T YOU?
I MEAN, YOU'LL BE HERE TOMORROW FOR WORK ANYWAY!
OH, BUT I GUESS I GET IT.
YOU CAN'T REALLY TAKE THE TIME TO LOOK AT IT ALL WHEN YOU'RE WORKING, RIGHT?
AH... AHA HA HA... YEP...
I SURE LOVE THOSE GOODS ...
I'LL JOIN YOU, THEN! COME ON, LET'S GO INSIDE!
YOINK
WHA--?!
NO, NO, IT'S FINE! I'LL JUST LOOK TO-MORROW!
DRAAAAG...
NOOO-OOO! I'M FIIINE!
COME ON, DON'T BE SILLY!
NOW, NOW, NO NEED TO BE SHY!
LOOK AROUND ALL YOU LIKE!
NOT THAT IT'S MY STORE... BUT STILL!
AHA HA HA!
HANA-SAN SEEMS TO BE IN A GOOD MOOD ...
OH, I SEE...
MAYBE WORK IS MORE FUN WHEN I'M NOT AROUND.

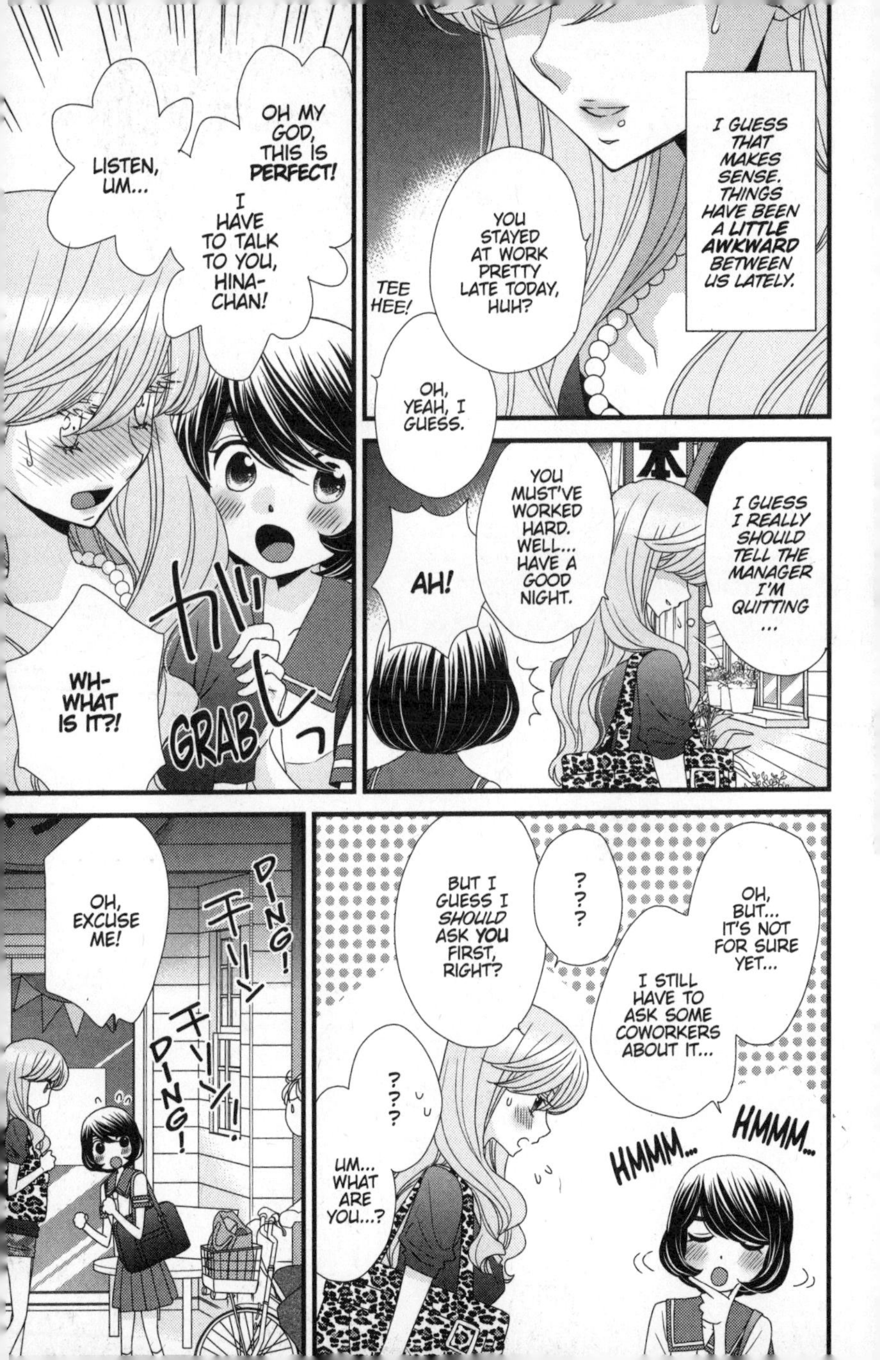
I GUESS THAT MAKES SENSE. THINGS HAVE BEEN A LITTLE AWKWARD BETWEEN US LATELY.
YOU STAYED AT WORK PRETTY LATE TODAY, HUH?
TEE HEE!
OH, YEAH, I GUESS.
I GUESS I REALLY SHOULD TELL THE MANAGER I'M QUITTING...
YOU MUST'VE WORKED HARD. WELL... HAVE A GOOD NIGHT.
AH!
OH MY GOD, THIS IS PERFECT!
I HAVE TO TALK TO YOU, HINA-CHAN!
LISTEN, UM...
GRAB
WH-WHAT IS IT?!
OH, BUT... IT'S NOT FOR SURE YET...
I STILL HAVE TO ASK SOME COWORKERS ABOUT IT...
???
BUT I GUESS I SHOULD ASK YOU FIRST, RIGHT?
HMMM...
HMMM...
???
UM... WHAT ARE YOU...?
OH, EXCUSE ME!
DING!
DING!

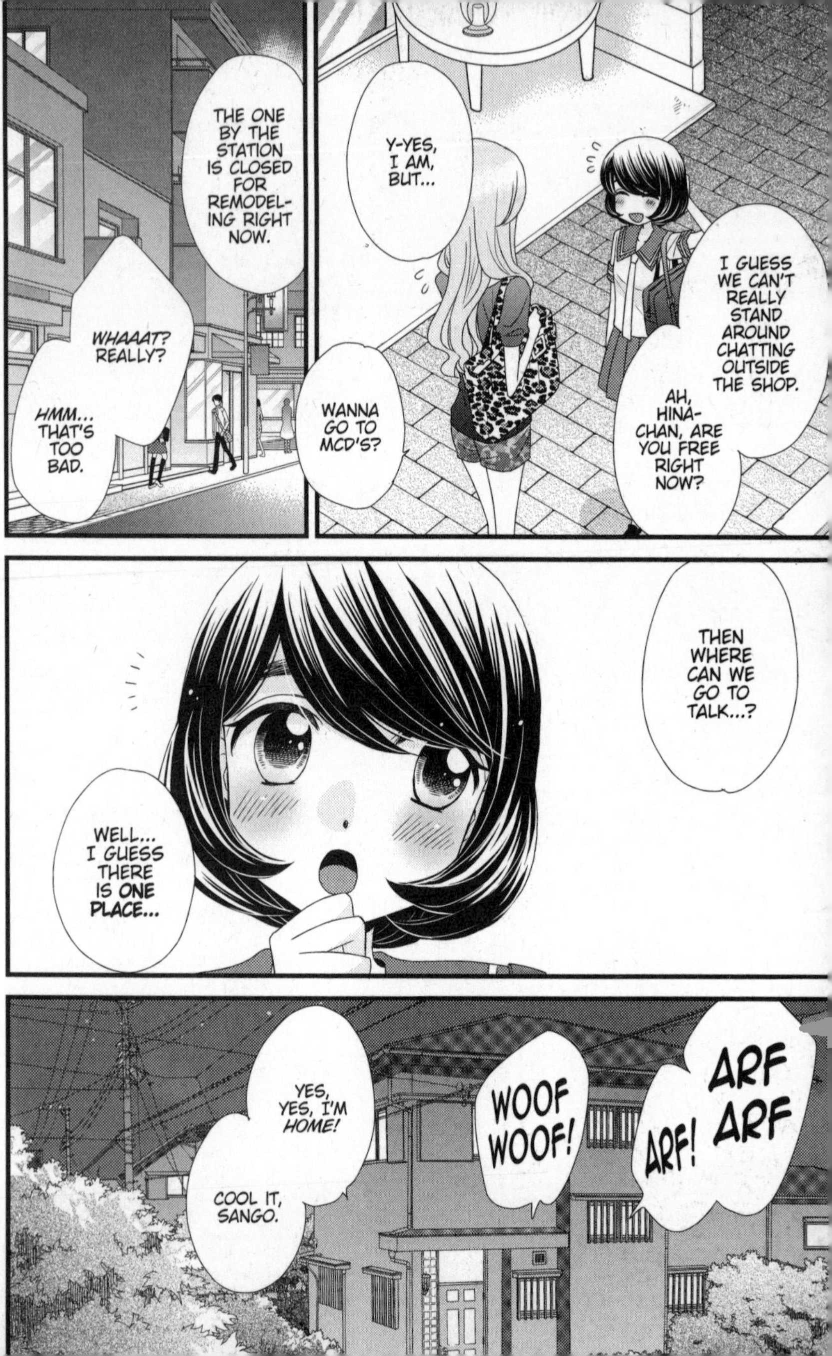
I GUESS WE CAN'T REALLY STAND AROUND CHATTING OUTSIDE THE SHOP.
AH, HINA-CHAN, ARE YOU FREE RIGHT NOW?
Y-YES, I AM, BUT...
WANNA GO TO MCD'S?
THE ONE BY THE STATION IS CLOSED FOR REMODELING RIGHT NOW.
WHAAAT? REALLY?
HMM... THAT'S TOO BAD.
THEN WHERE CAN WE GO TO TALK...?
WELL... I GUESS THERE IS **ONE PLACE**...
ARF ARF
ARF!
WOOF WOOF!
YES, YES, I'M *HOME!*
COOL IT, SANGO.

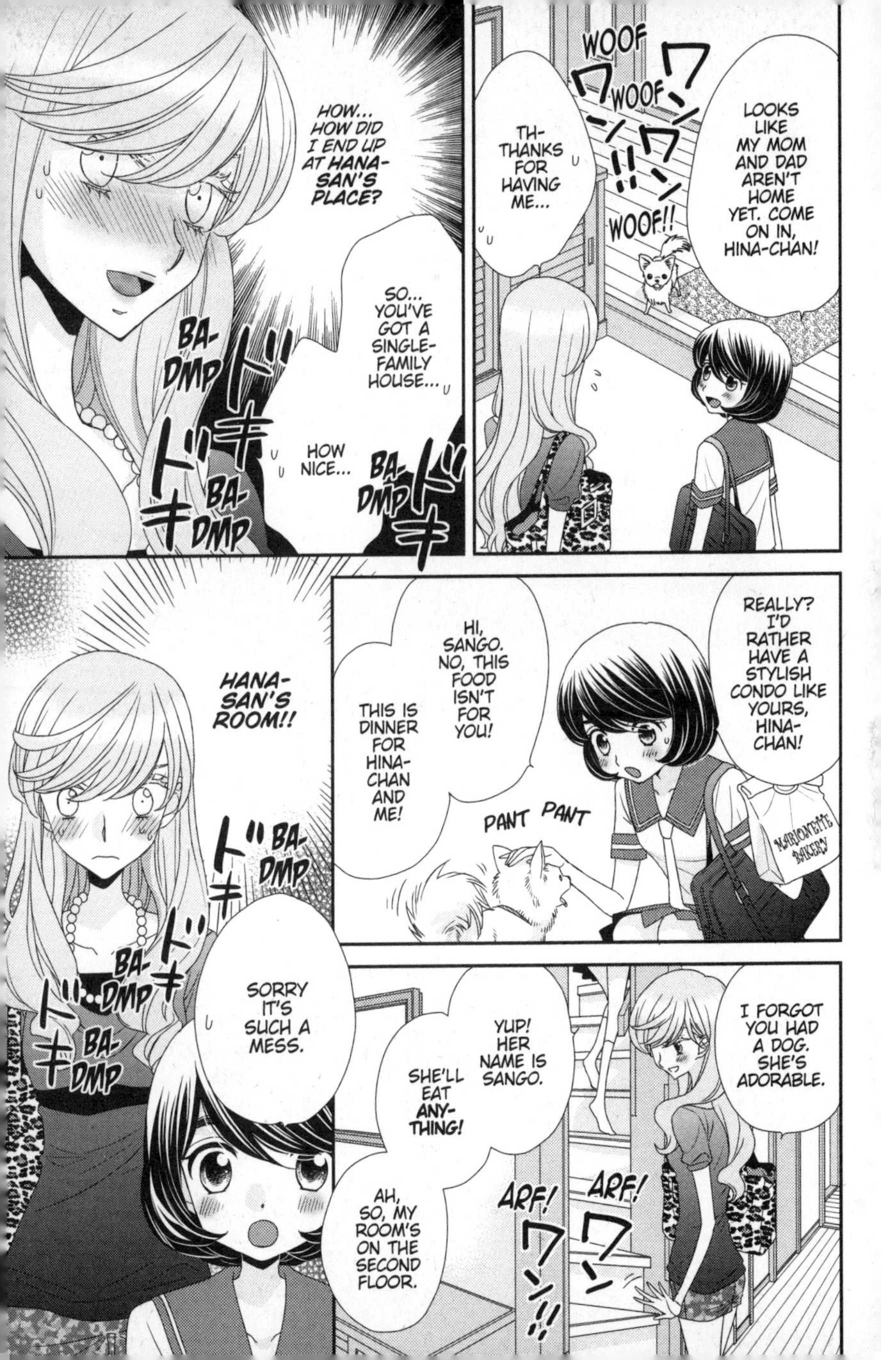
WOOF
WOOF
WOOF!!
LOOKS LIKE MY MOM AND DAD AREN'T HOME YET. COME ON IN, HINA-CHAN!
TH-THANKS FOR HAVING ME...
HOW... HOW DID I END UP AT HANA-SAN'S PLACE?
SO... YOU'VE GOT A SINGLE-FAMILY HOUSE...
HOW NICE...
BA-DMP
BA-DMP
BA-DMP
REALLY? I'D RATHER HAVE A STYLISH CONDO LIKE YOURS, HINA-CHAN!
HI, SANGO. NO, THIS FOOD ISN'T FOR YOU!
THIS IS DINNER FOR HINA-CHAN AND ME!
PANT PANT
MARIONETTE BAKERY
I FORGOT YOU HAD A DOG. SHE'S ADORABLE.
ARF!
ARF!
YUP! HER NAME IS SANGO.
SHE'LL EAT ANYTHING!
AH, SO, MY ROOM'S ON THE SECOND FLOOR.
SORRY IT'S SUCH A MESS.
HANA-SAN'S ROOM!!
BA-DMP
BA-DMP
BA-DMP

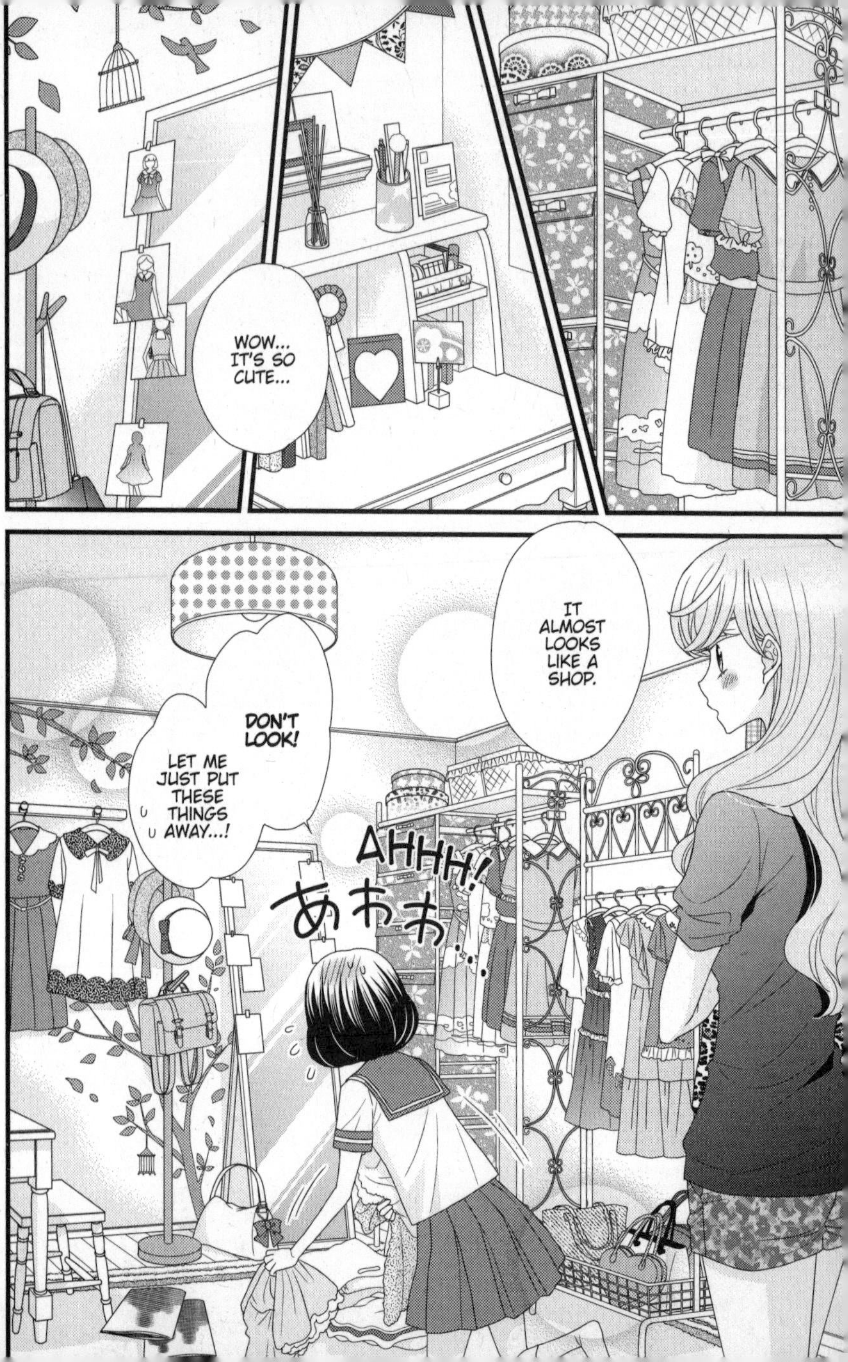
WOW... IT'S SO CUTE...
IT ALMOST LOOKS LIKE A SHOP.
AHHH!
あわわ
DON'T LOOK!
LET ME JUST PUT THESE THINGS AWAY...!

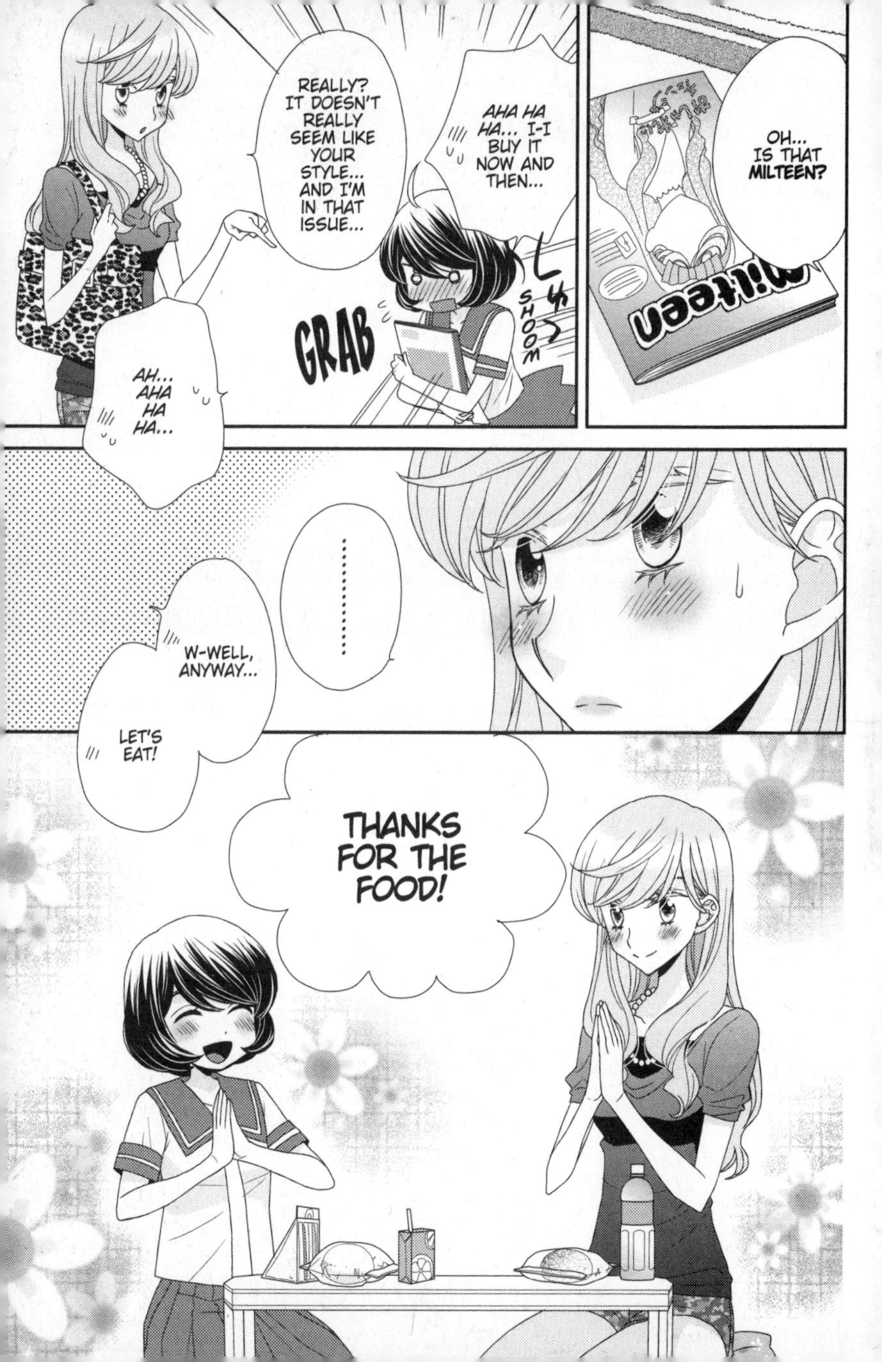
OH... IS THAT MILTEEN?
Milteen
AHA HA HA... I-I BUY IT NOW AND THEN...
REALLY? IT DOESN'T REALLY SEEM LIKE YOUR STYLE... AND I'M IN THAT ISSUE...
SHOOM
GRAB
AH... AHA HA HA...
......
W-WELL, ANYWAY...
LET'S EAT!
THANKS FOR THE FOOD!

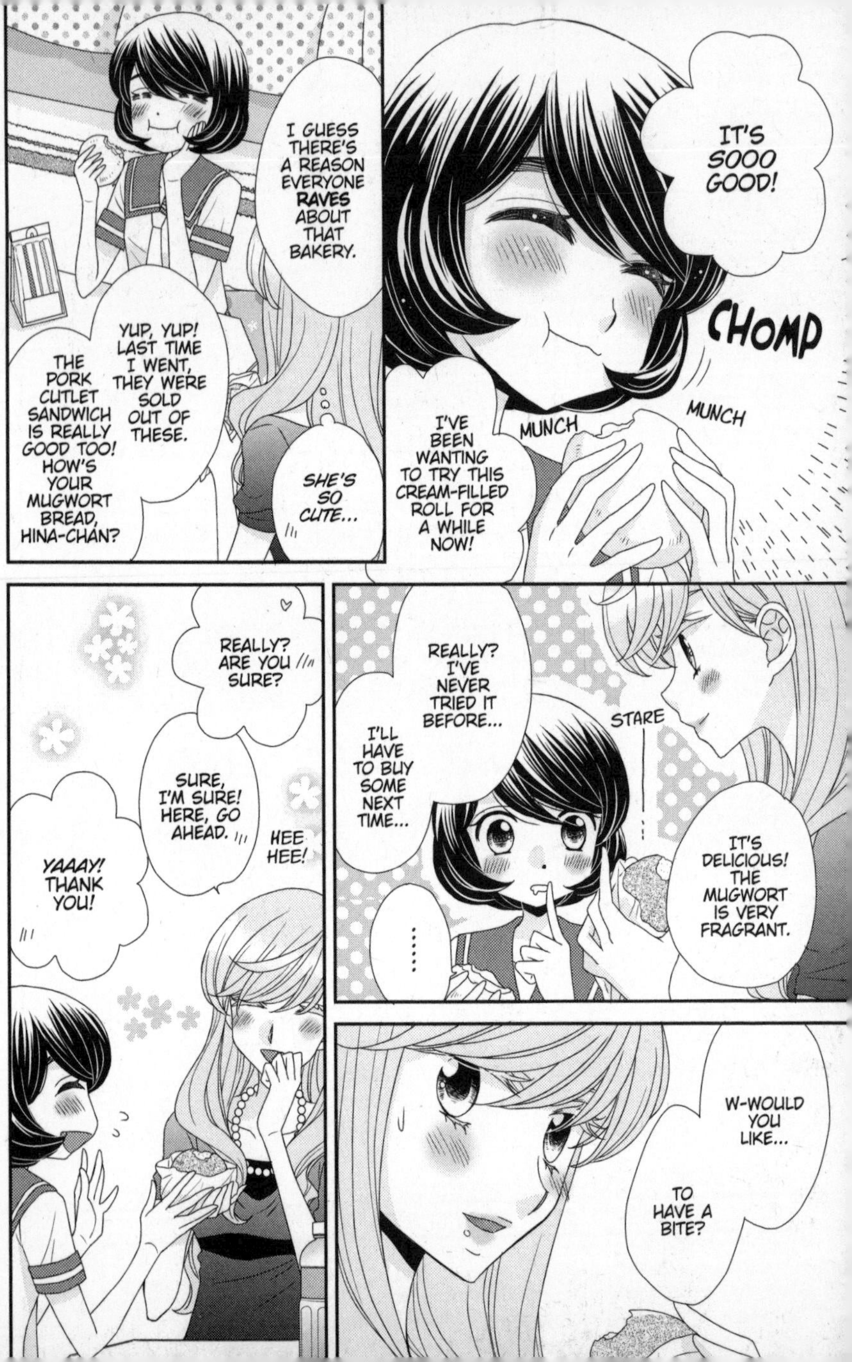
IT'S SOOO GOOD!
CHOMP
MUNCH
MUNCH
I'VE BEEN WANTING TO TRY THIS CREAM-FILLED ROLL FOR A WHILE NOW!
I GUESS THERE'S A REASON EVERYONE RAVES ABOUT THAT BAKERY.
SHE'S SO CUTE...
YUP, YUP! LAST TIME I WENT, THEY WERE SOLD OUT OF THESE.
THE PORK CUTLET SANDWICH IS REALLY GOOD TOO! HOW'S YOUR MUGWORT BREAD, HINA-CHAN?
IT'S DELICIOUS! THE MUGWORT IS VERY FRAGRANT.
STARE
REALLY? I'VE NEVER TRIED IT BEFORE...
I'LL HAVE TO BUY SOME NEXT TIME...
......
W-WOULD YOU LIKE...
TO HAVE A BITE?
REALLY? ARE YOU SURE?
SURE, I'M SURE! HERE, GO AHEAD.
HEE HEE!
YAAAY! THANK YOU!

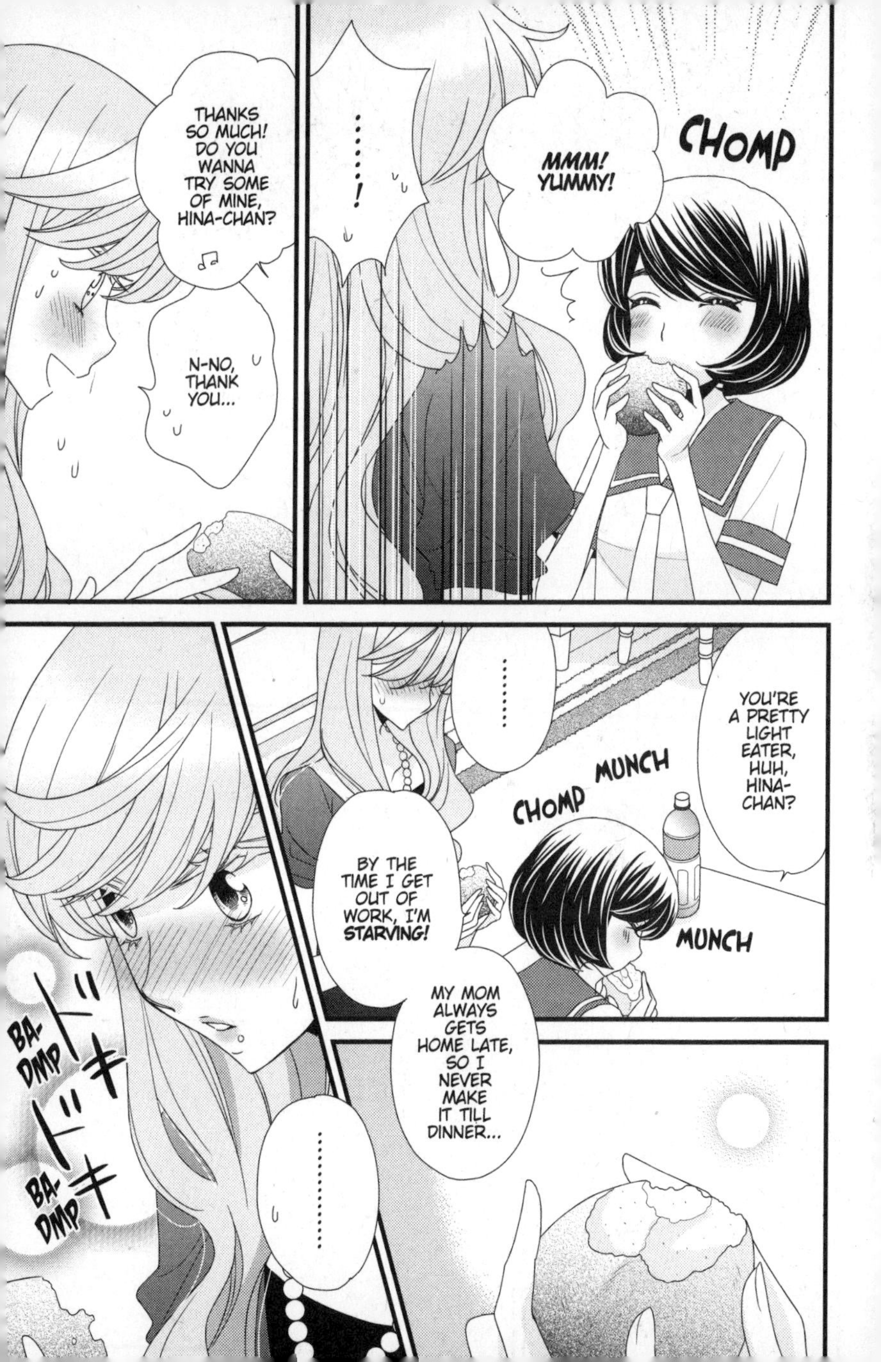
CHOMP
MMM! YUMMY!
......!
THANKS SO MUCH! DO YOU WANNA TRY SOME OF MINE, HINA-CHAN?
N-NO, THANK YOU...
YOU'RE A PRETTY LIGHT EATER, HUH, HINA-CHAN?
......
CHOMP MUNCH
MUNCH
BY THE TIME I GET OUT OF WORK, I'M STARVING!
MY MOM ALWAYS GETS HOME LATE, SO I NEVER MAKE IT TILL DINNER...
......
BA-DMP
BA-DMP

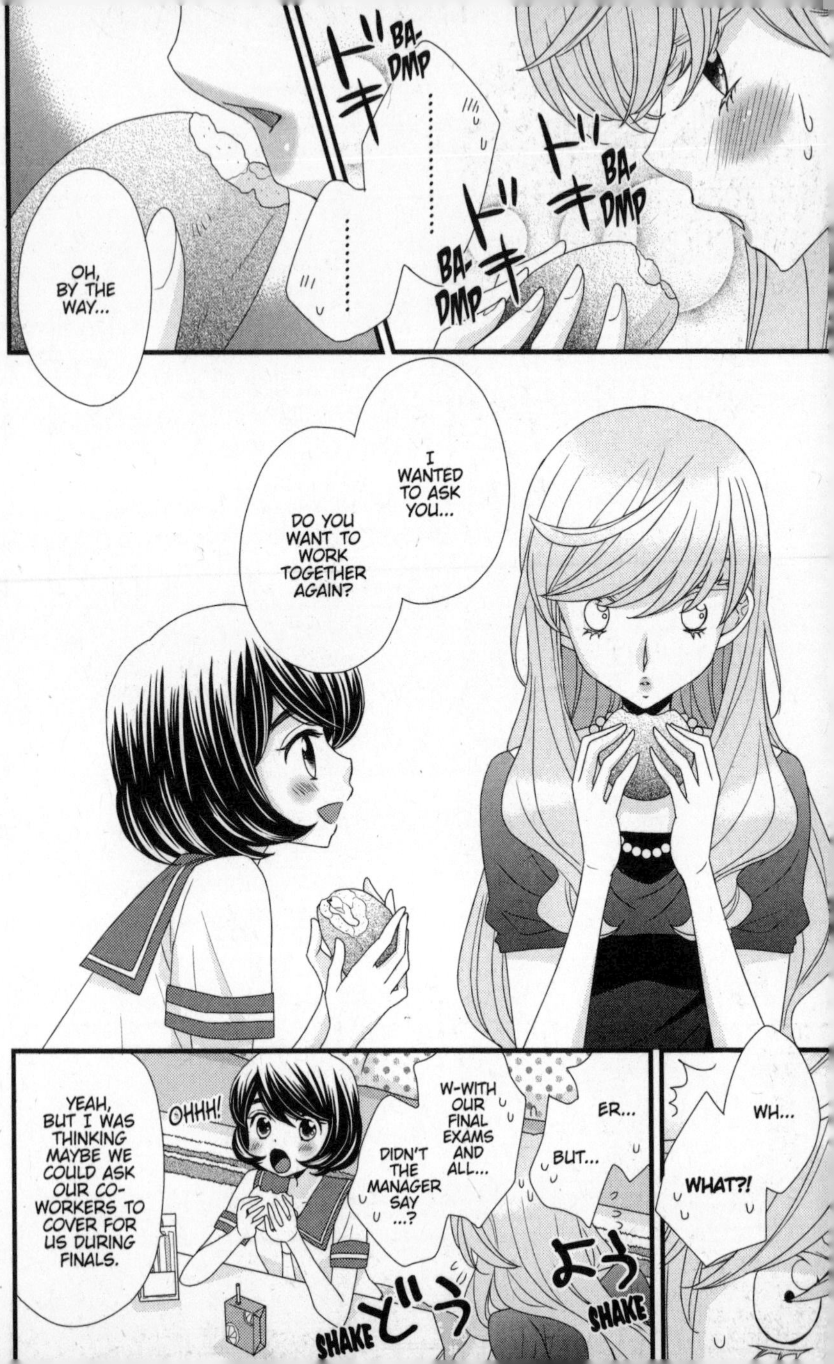
ドキ
BA-DMP
ドキ
BA-DMP
ドキ
BA-DMP
......
......
OH, BY THE WAY...
I WANTED TO ASK YOU...
DO YOU WANT TO WORK TOGETHER AGAIN?
WH...
WHAT?!
ER...
BUT...
W-WITH OUR FINAL EXAMS AND ALL...
DIDN'T THE MANAGER SAY ...?
SHAKE
SHAKE
OHHH!
YEAH, BUT I WAS THINKING MAYBE WE COULD ASK OUR CO-WORKERS TO COVER FOR US DURING FINALS.

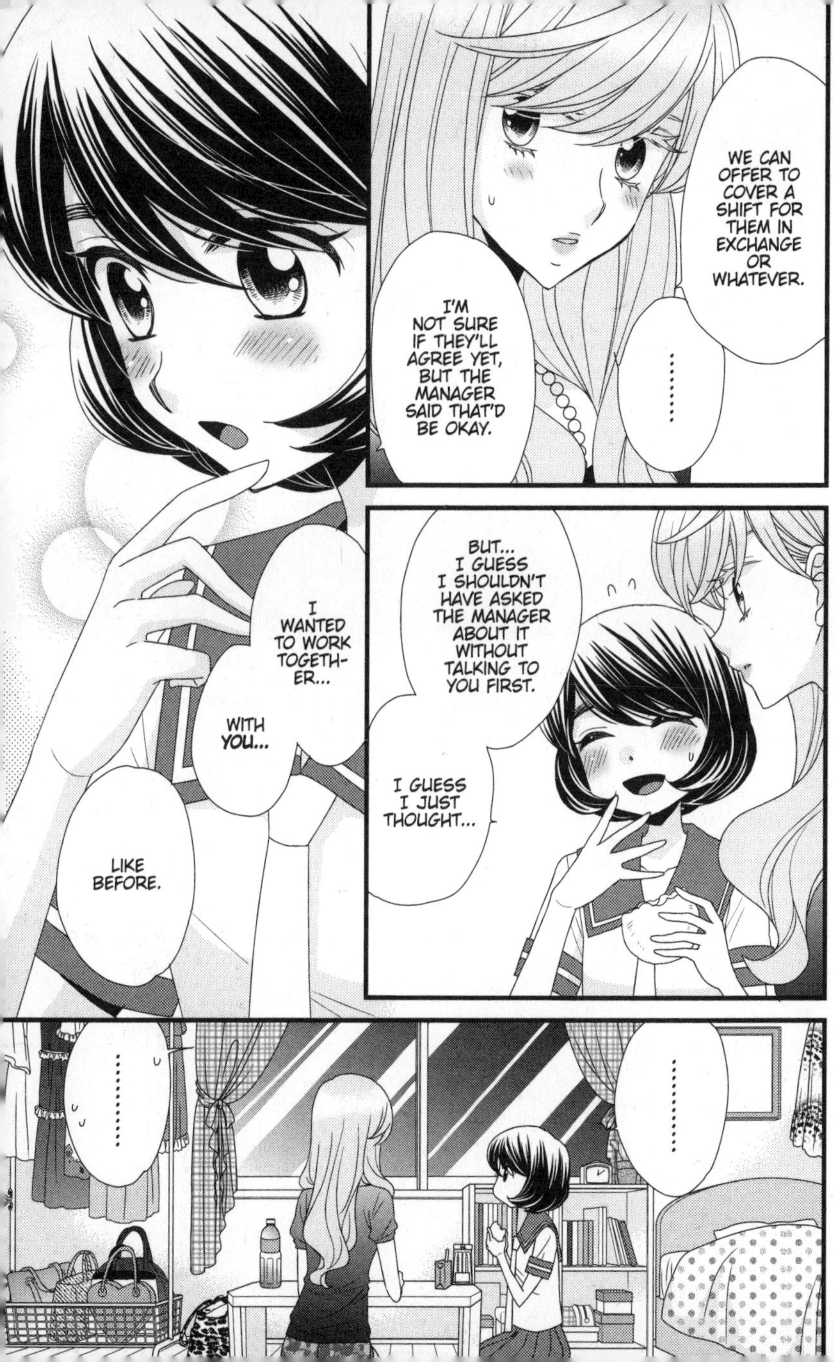
WE CAN OFFER TO COVER A SHIFT FOR THEM IN EXCHANGE OR WHATEVER.
......
I'M NOT SURE IF THEY'LL AGREE YET, BUT THE MANAGER SAID THAT'D BE OKAY.
BUT... I GUESS I SHOULDN'T HAVE ASKED THE MANAGER ABOUT IT WITHOUT TALKING TO YOU FIRST.
I GUESS I JUST THOUGHT...
I WANTED TO WORK TOGETH-ER...
WITH **YOU**...
LIKE BEFORE.
......
......

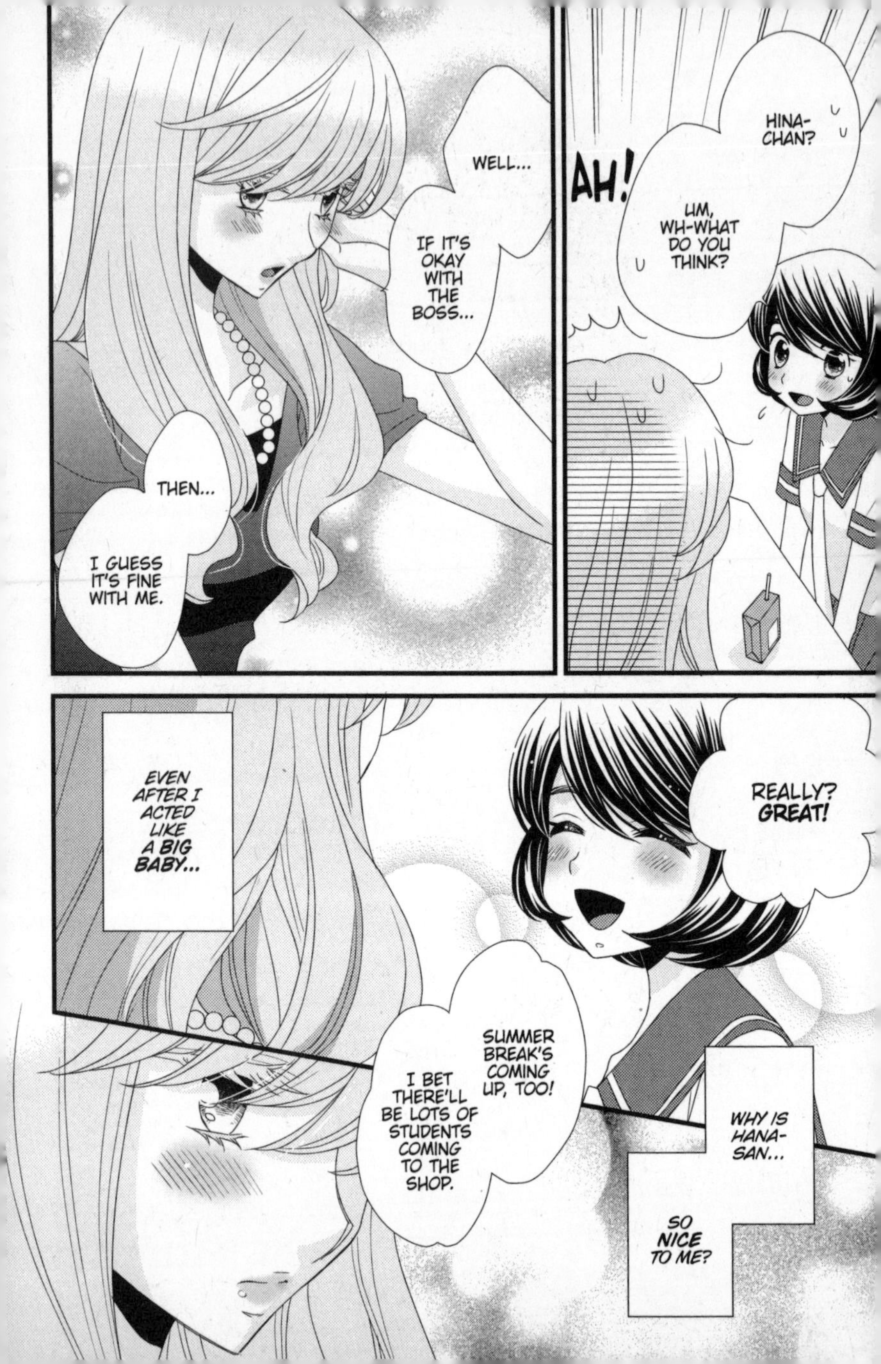
AH!
HINA-CHAN?
UM, WH-WHAT DO YOU THINK?
WELL...
IF IT'S OKAY WITH THE BOSS...
THEN...
I GUESS IT'S FINE WITH ME.
REALLY? GREAT!
SUMMER BREAK'S COMING UP, TOO!
I BET THERE'LL BE LOTS OF STUDENTS COMING TO THE SHOP.
EVEN AFTER I ACTED LIKE A BIG BABY...
WHY IS HANA-SAN...
SO NICE TO ME?

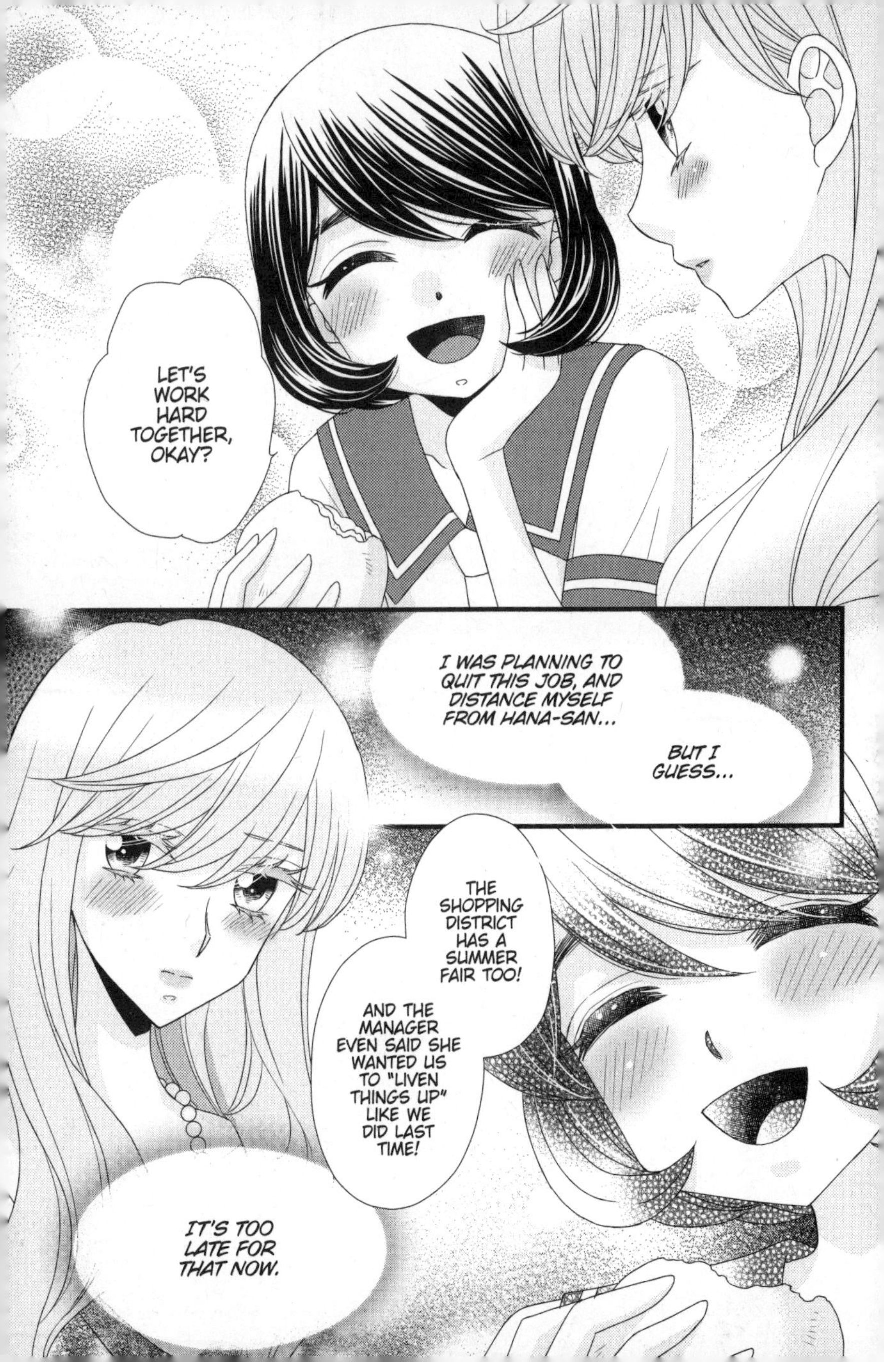
LET'S WORK HARD TOGETHER, OKAY?
I WAS PLANNING TO QUIT THIS JOB, AND DISTANCE MYSELF FROM HANA-SAN...
BUT I GUESS...
THE SHOPPING DISTRICT HAS A SUMMER FAIR TOO!
AND THE MANAGER EVEN SAID SHE WANTED US TO "LIVEN THINGS UP" LIKE WE DID LAST TIME!
IT'S TOO LATE FOR THAT NOW.

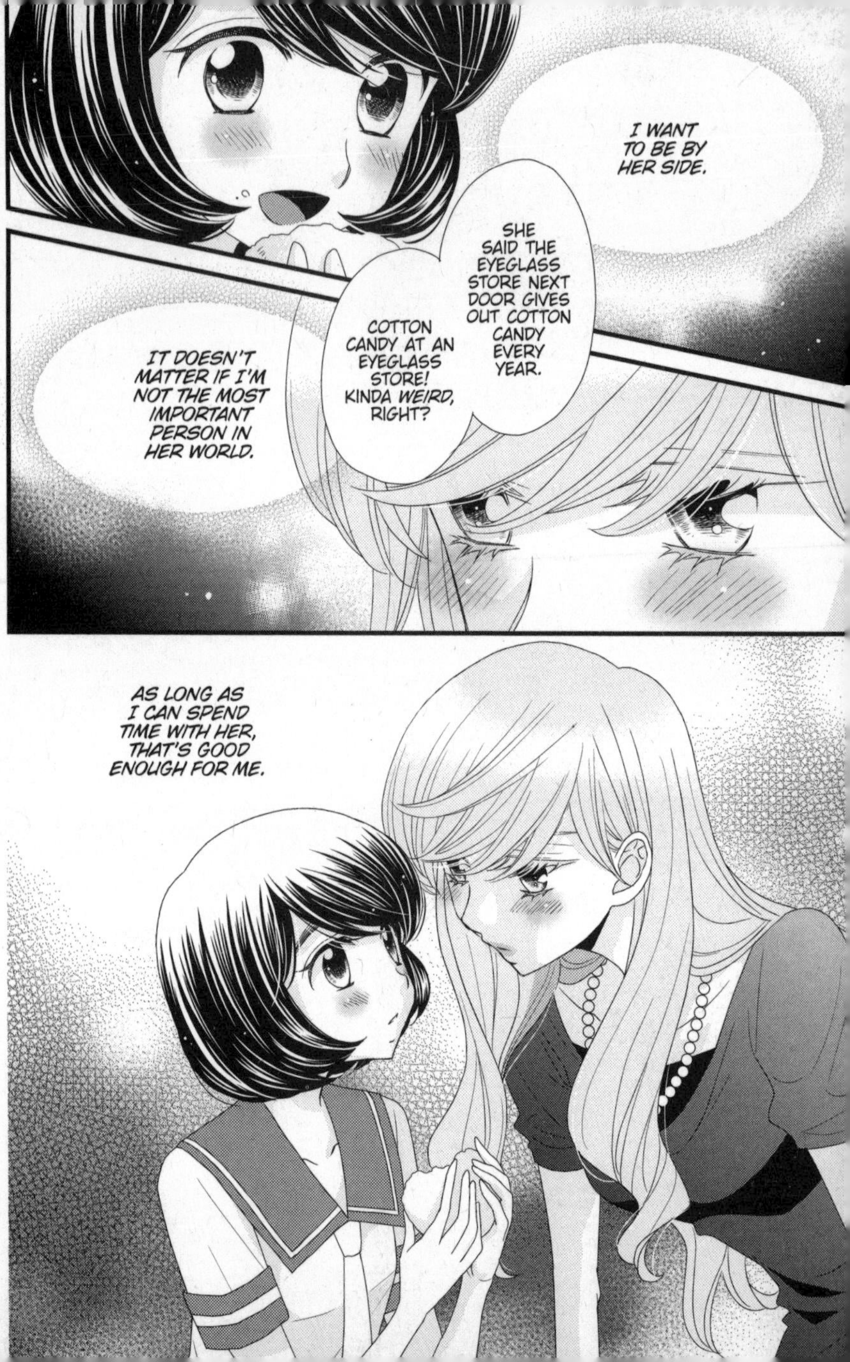
I WANT TO BE BY HER SIDE.
SHE SAID THE EYEGLASS STORE NEXT DOOR GIVES OUT COTTON CANDY EVERY YEAR.
COTTON CANDY AT AN EYEGLASS STORE! KINDA WEIRD, RIGHT?
IT DOESN'T MATTER IF I'M NOT THE MOST IMPORTANT PERSON IN HER WORLD.
AS LONG AS I CAN SPEND TIME WITH HER, THAT'S GOOD ENOUGH FOR ME.

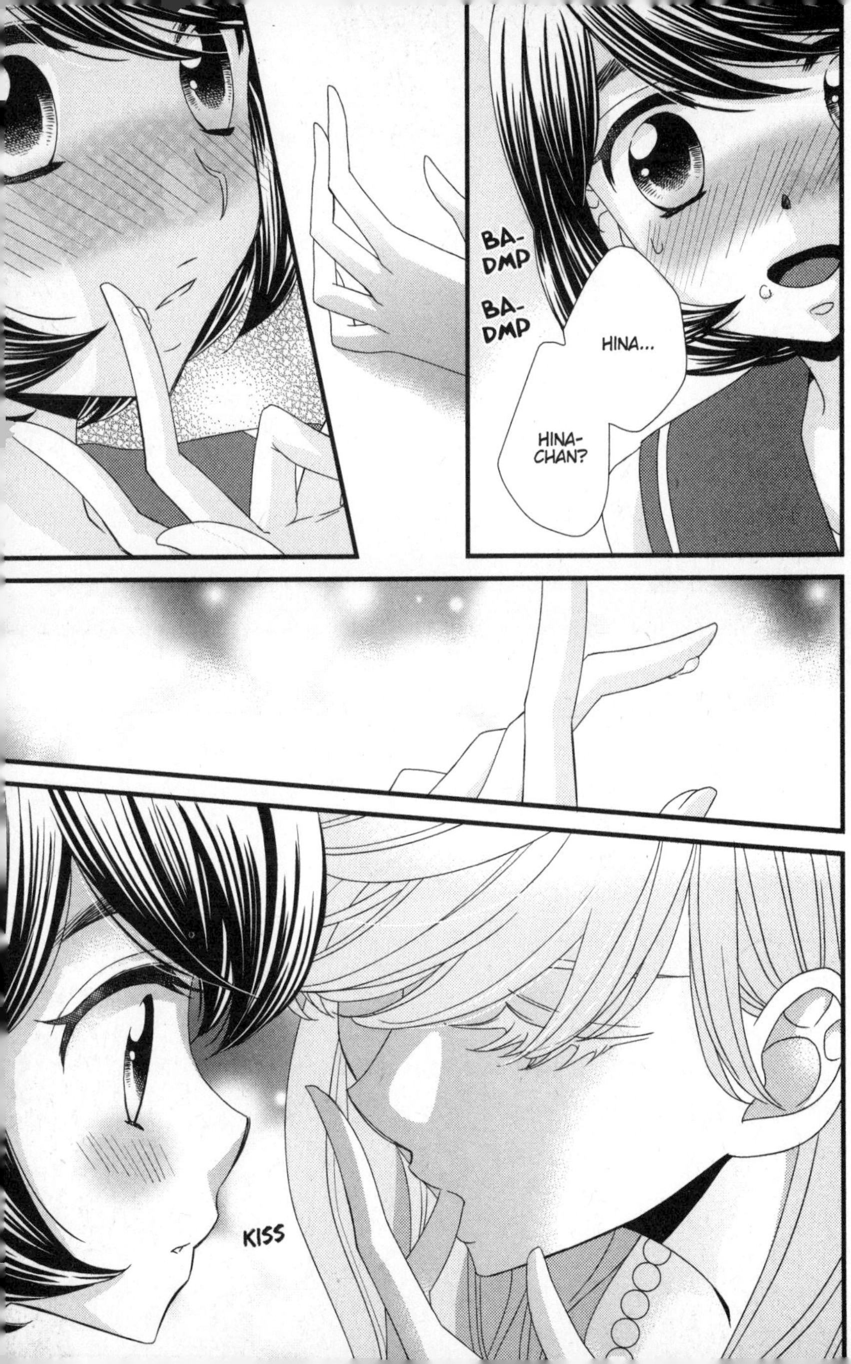
HINA...
HINA-CHAN?
BA-DMP
BA-DMP
KISS

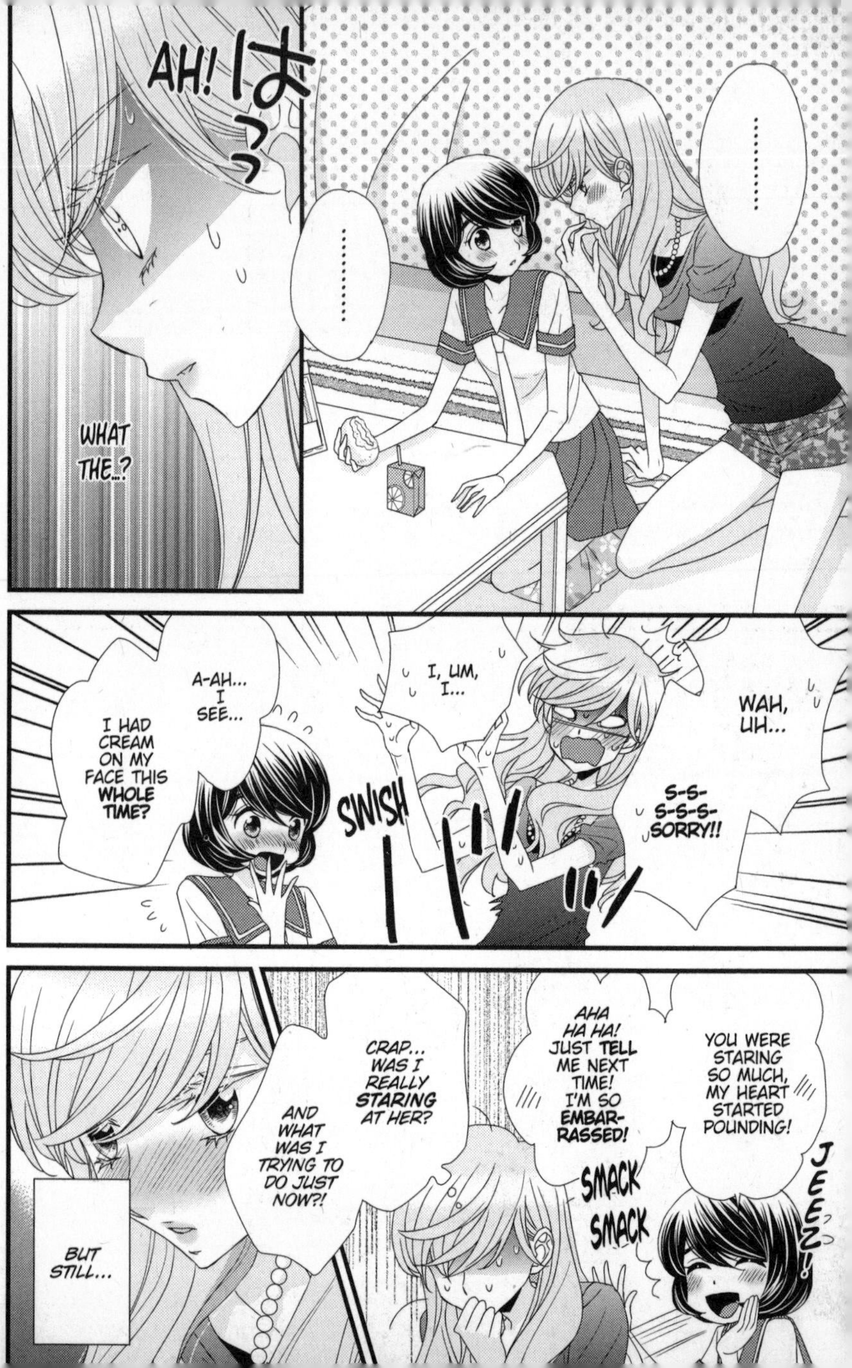
......
......
AH! はっ
WHAT THE..?
WAH, UH...
S-S-S-S-SORRY!!
I, UM, I...
SWISH
A-AH... I SEE...
I HAD CREAM ON MY FACE THIS WHOLE TIME?
JEEZ!
YOU WERE STARING SO MUCH, MY HEART STARTED POUNDING!
AHA HA HA! JUST TELL ME NEXT TIME! I'M SO EMBARRASSED!
SMACK SMACK
CRAP... WAS I REALLY STARING AT HER?
AND WHAT WAS I TRYING TO DO JUST NOW?!
BUT STILL...

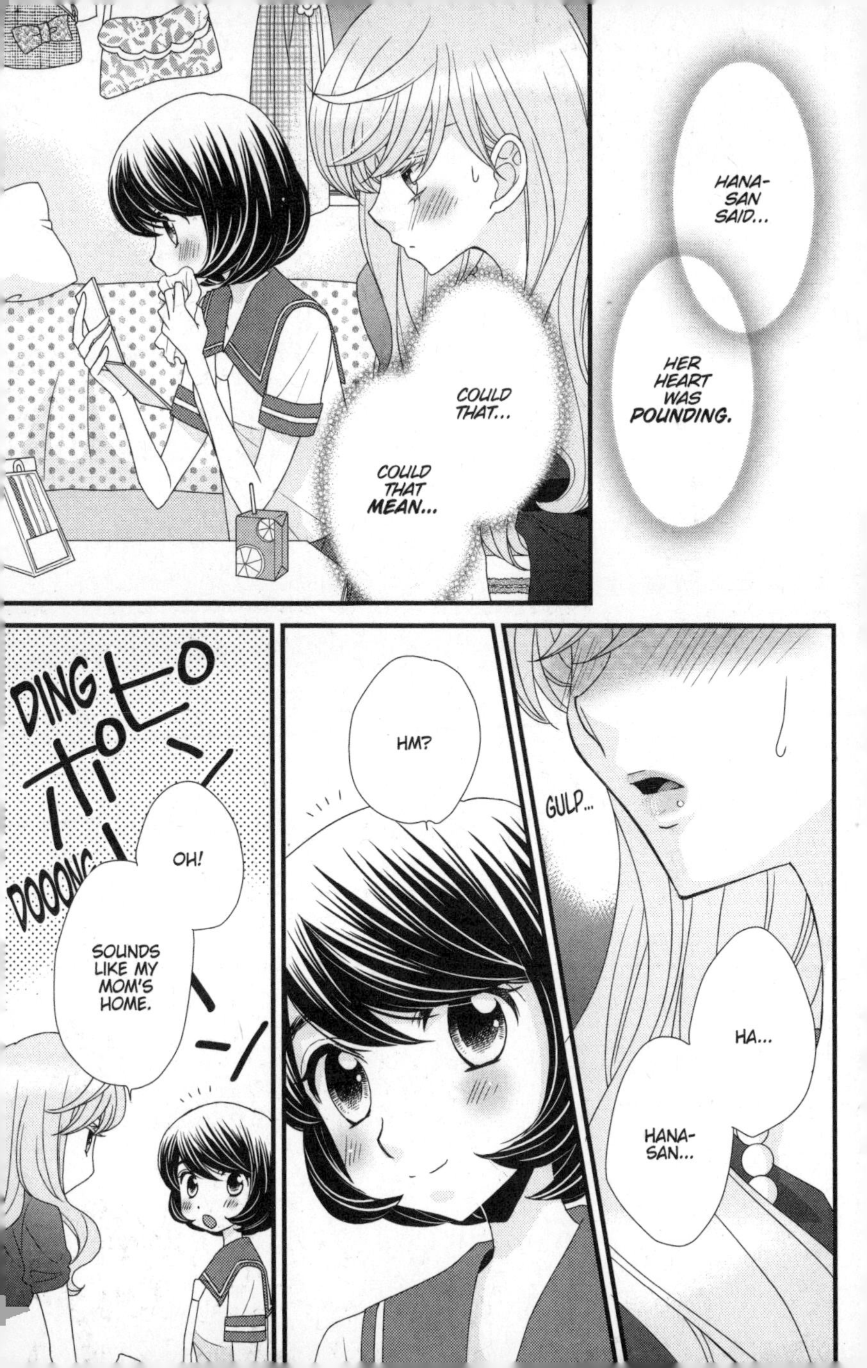
HANA-SAN SAID...
HER HEART WAS POUNDING.
COULD THAT...
COULD THAT MEAN...
GULP...
HA...
HANA-SAN...
HM?
DING DOOONG
OH!
SOUNDS LIKE MY MOM'S HOME.

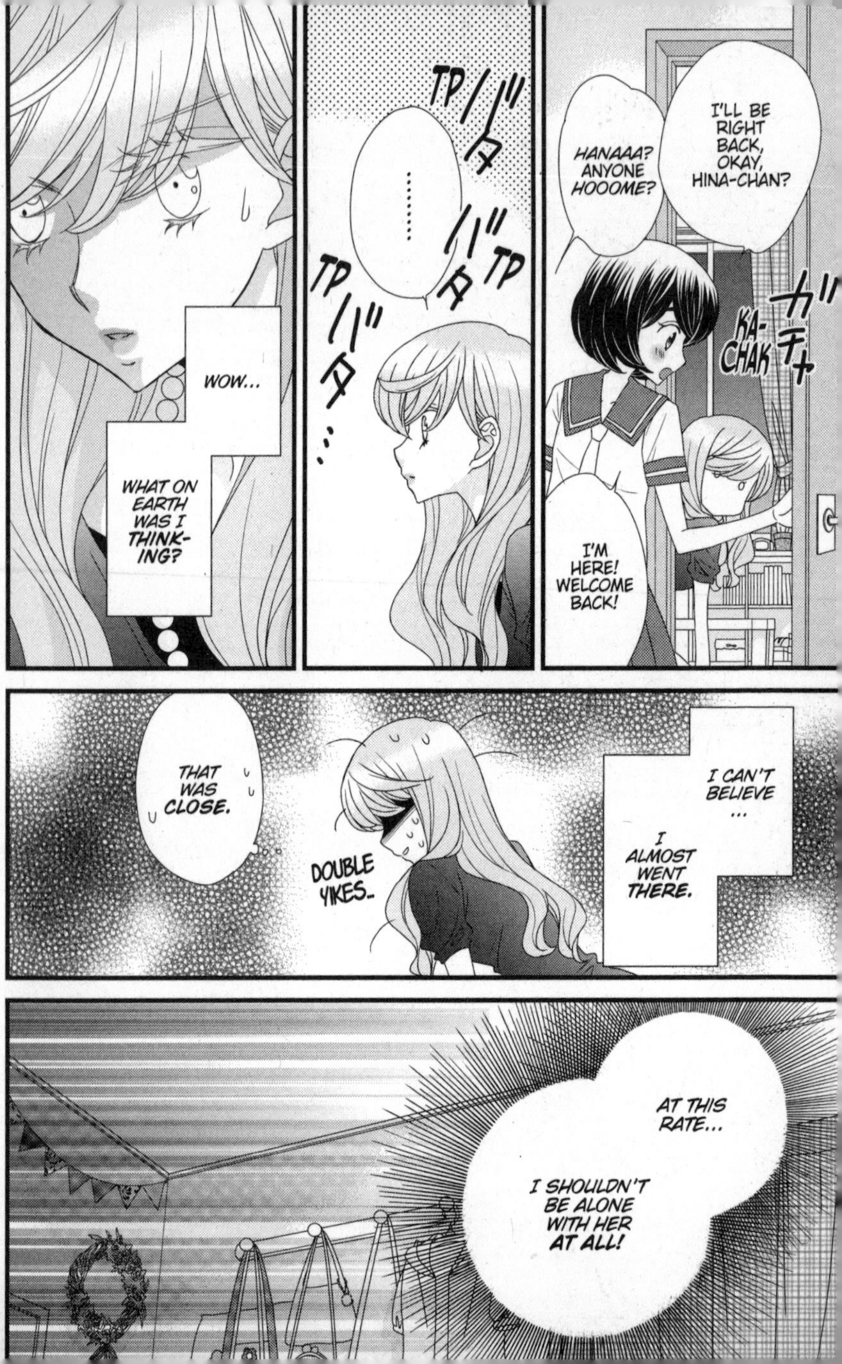
I'LL BE RIGHT BACK, OKAY, HINA-CHAN?
HANAAA? ANYONE HOOOME?
ガチャ
KA-CHAK
I'M HERE! WELCOME BACK!
TP バタ
TP
TP バタ
TP バタ...
......
WOW...
WHAT ON EARTH WAS I THINKING?
I CAN'T BELIEVE...
I ALMOST WENT THERE.
DOUBLE YIKES..
THAT WAS CLOSE.
AT THIS RATE...
I SHOULDN'T BE ALONE WITH HER AT ALL!

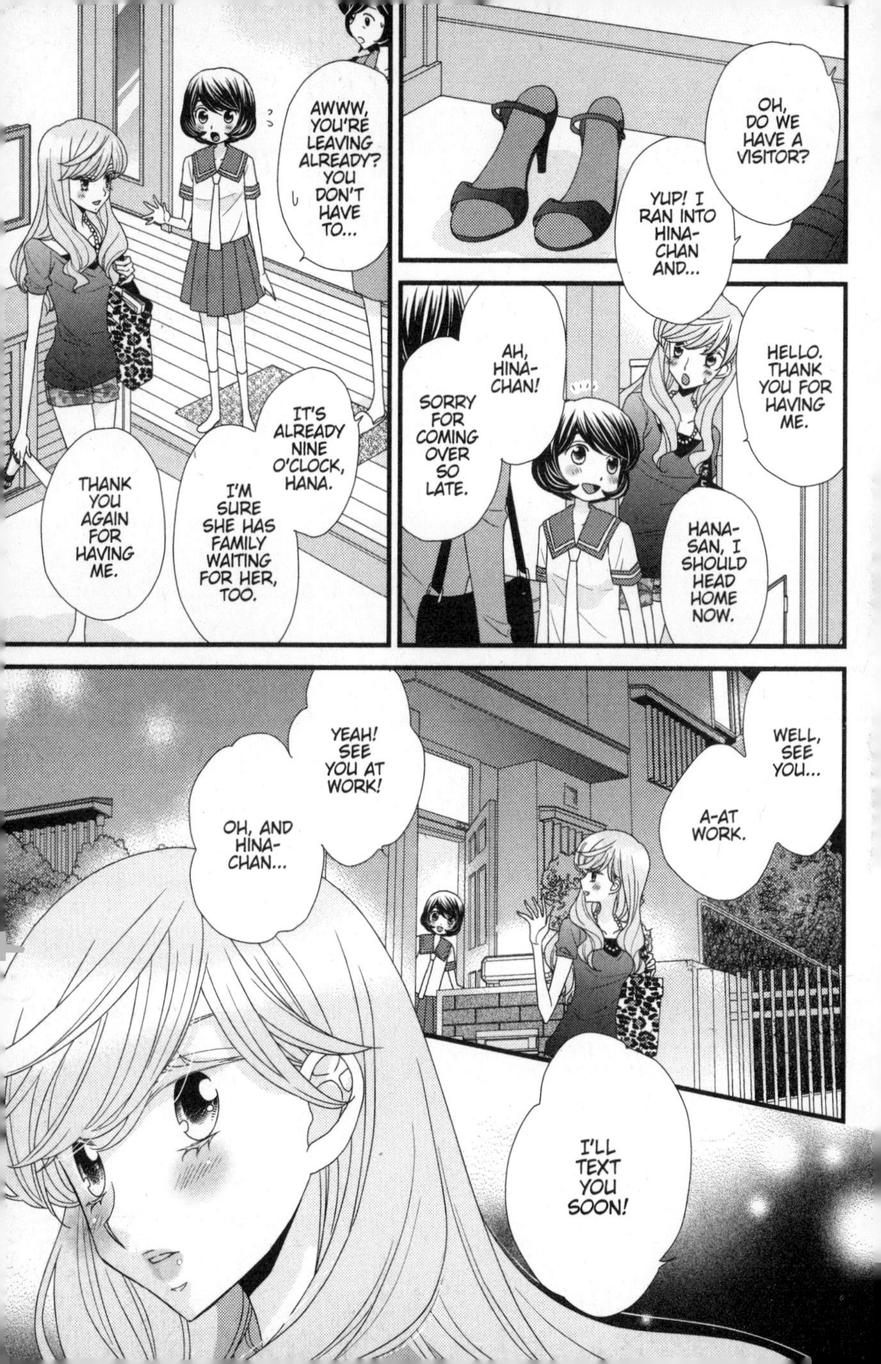
OH, DO WE HAVE A VISITOR?
YUP! I RAN INTO HINA-CHAN AND...
HELLO. THANK YOU FOR HAVING ME.
AH, HINA-CHAN!
SORRY FOR COMING OVER SO LATE.
HANA-SAN, I SHOULD HEAD HOME NOW.
AWWW, YOU'RE LEAVING ALREADY? YOU DON'T HAVE TO...
IT'S ALREADY NINE O'CLOCK, HANA.
I'M SURE SHE HAS FAMILY WAITING FOR HER, TOO.
THANK YOU AGAIN FOR HAVING ME.
WELL, SEE YOU...
A-AT WORK.
YEAH! SEE YOU AT WORK!
OH, AND HINA-CHAN...
I'LL TEXT YOU SOON!

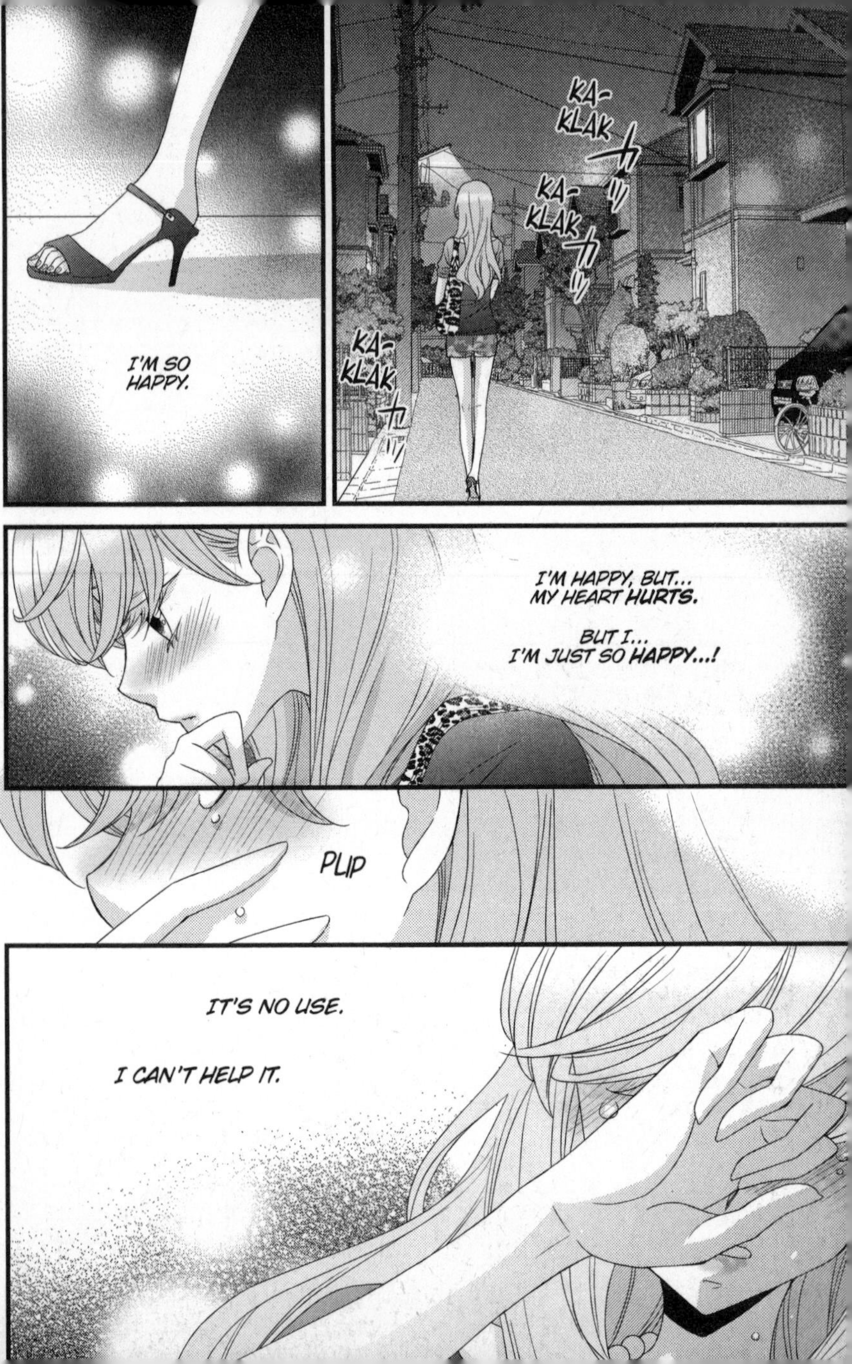
KA-KLAK
KA-KLAK
KA-KLAK
I'M SO HAPPY.
I'M HAPPY, BUT... MY HEART HURTS.
BUT I... I'M JUST SO HAPPY...!
PLIP
IT'S NO USE.
I CAN'T HELP IT.

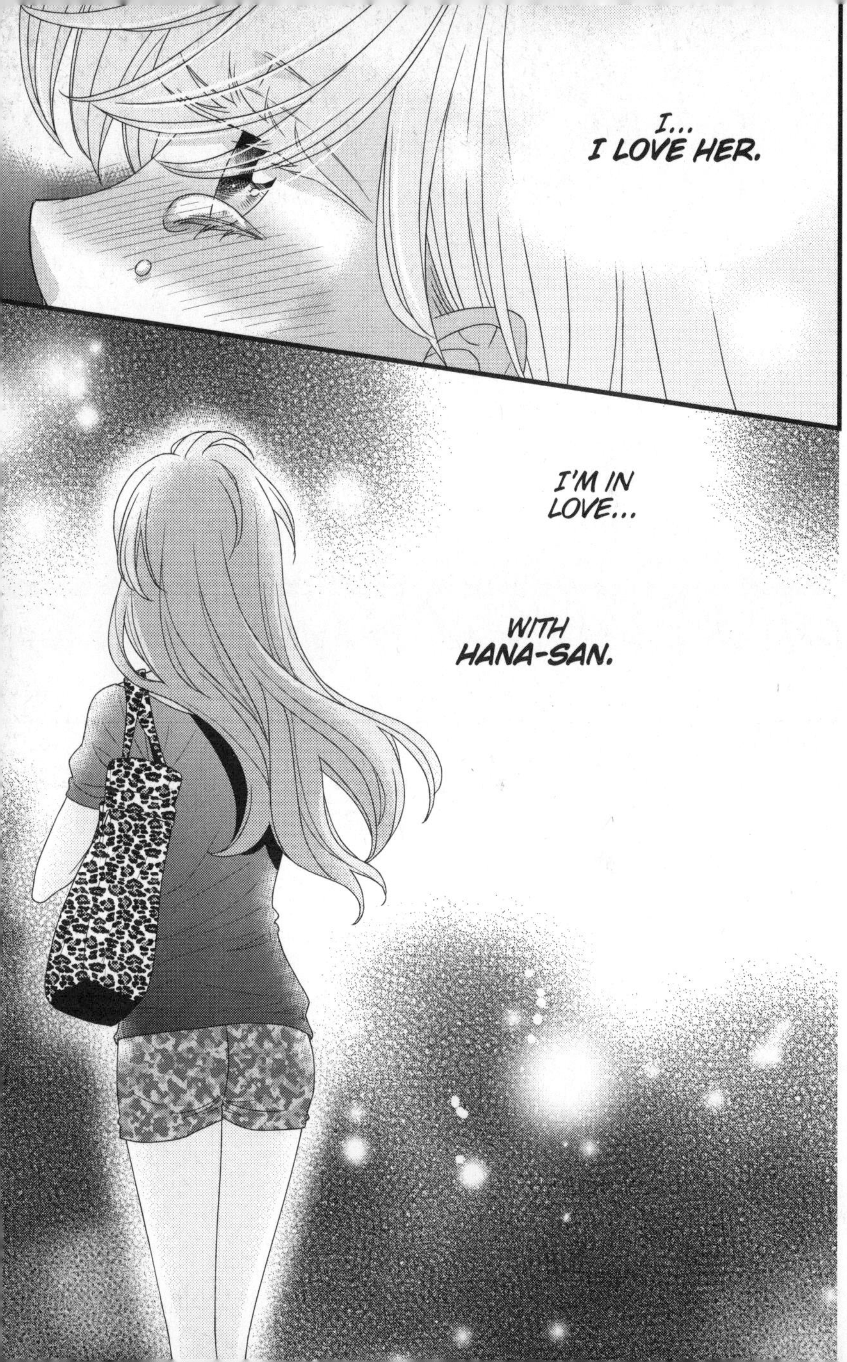
I...
I LOVE HER.
I'M IN LOVE...
WITH HANA-SAN.

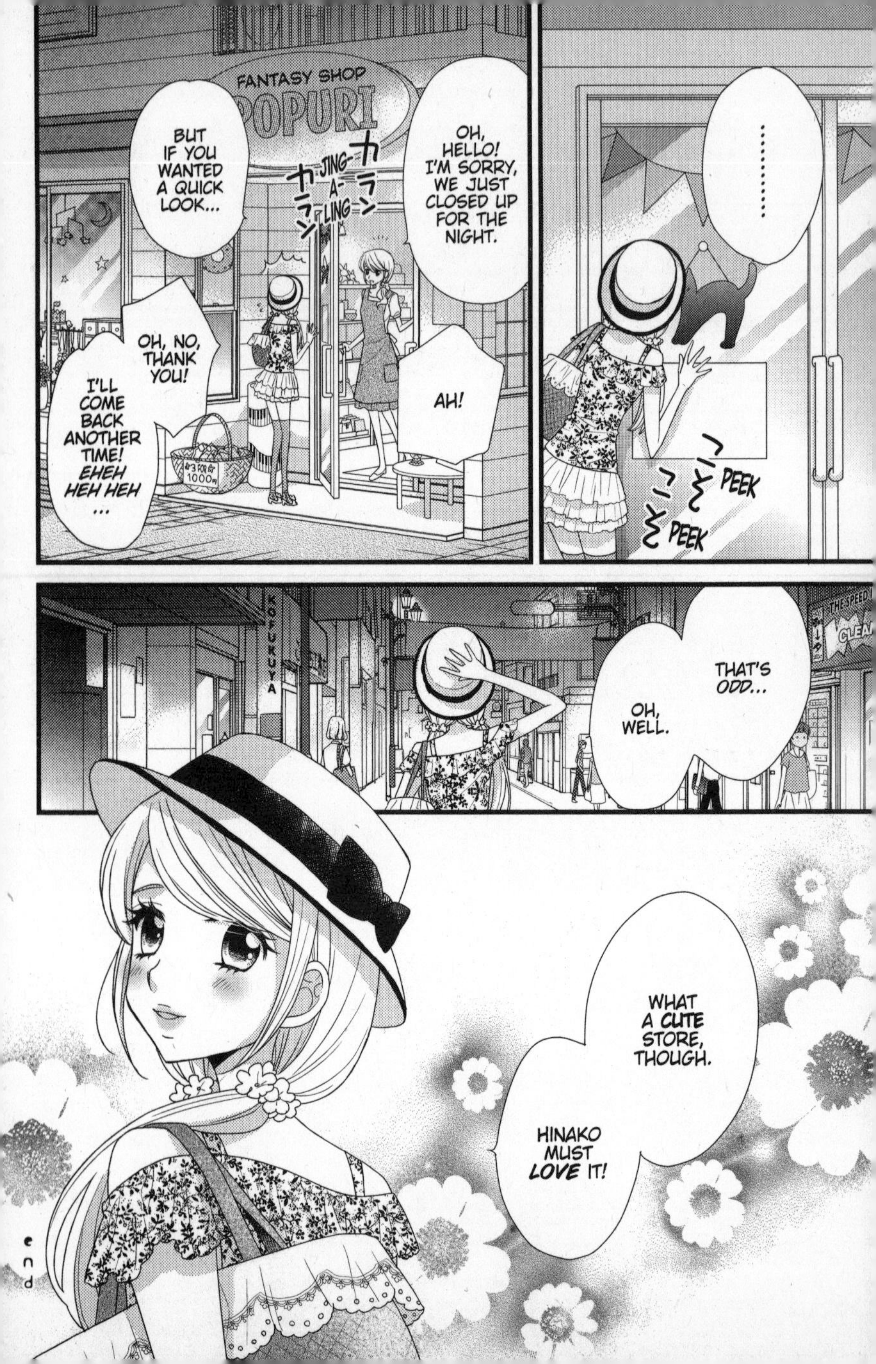
……
こそ PEEK
こそ PEEK
FANTASY SHOP POPURI
カラン カラン JING-A-LING
OH, HELLO! I'M SORRY, WE JUST CLOSED UP FOR THE NIGHT.
BUT IF YOU WANTED A QUICK LOOK...
AH!
OH, NO, THANK YOU!
I'LL COME BACK ANOTHER TIME! *EHEH HEH HEH* ...
KOFUKUYA
THAT'S *ODD*...
OH, WELL.
WHAT A **CUTE** STORE, THOUGH.
HINAKO MUST ***LOVE*** IT!
end

Hana & Hina
AFTER ♡ SCHOOL

Hana & Hina

AFTER ♥ SCHOOL

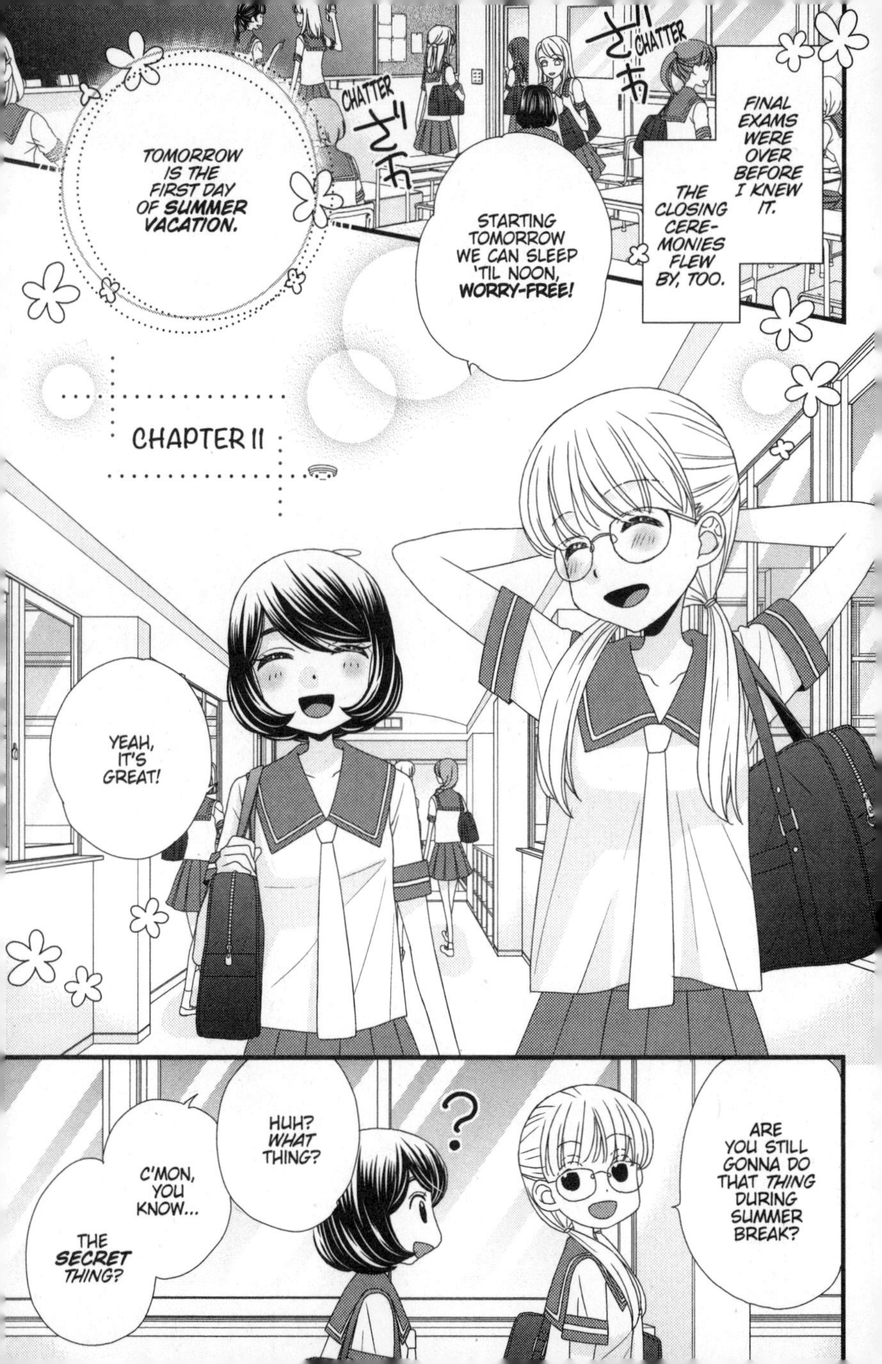
FINAL EXAMS WERE OVER BEFORE I KNEW IT.
THE CLOSING CERE-MONIES FLEW BY, TOO.
CHATTER
CHATTER
TOMORROW IS THE FIRST DAY OF SUMMER VACATION.
STARTING TOMORROW WE CAN SLEEP 'TIL NOON, WORRY-FREE!
CHAPTER 11
YEAH, IT'S GREAT!
ARE YOU STILL GONNA DO THAT THING DURING SUMMER BREAK?
?
HUH? WHAT THING?
C'MON, YOU KNOW...
THE SECRET THING?

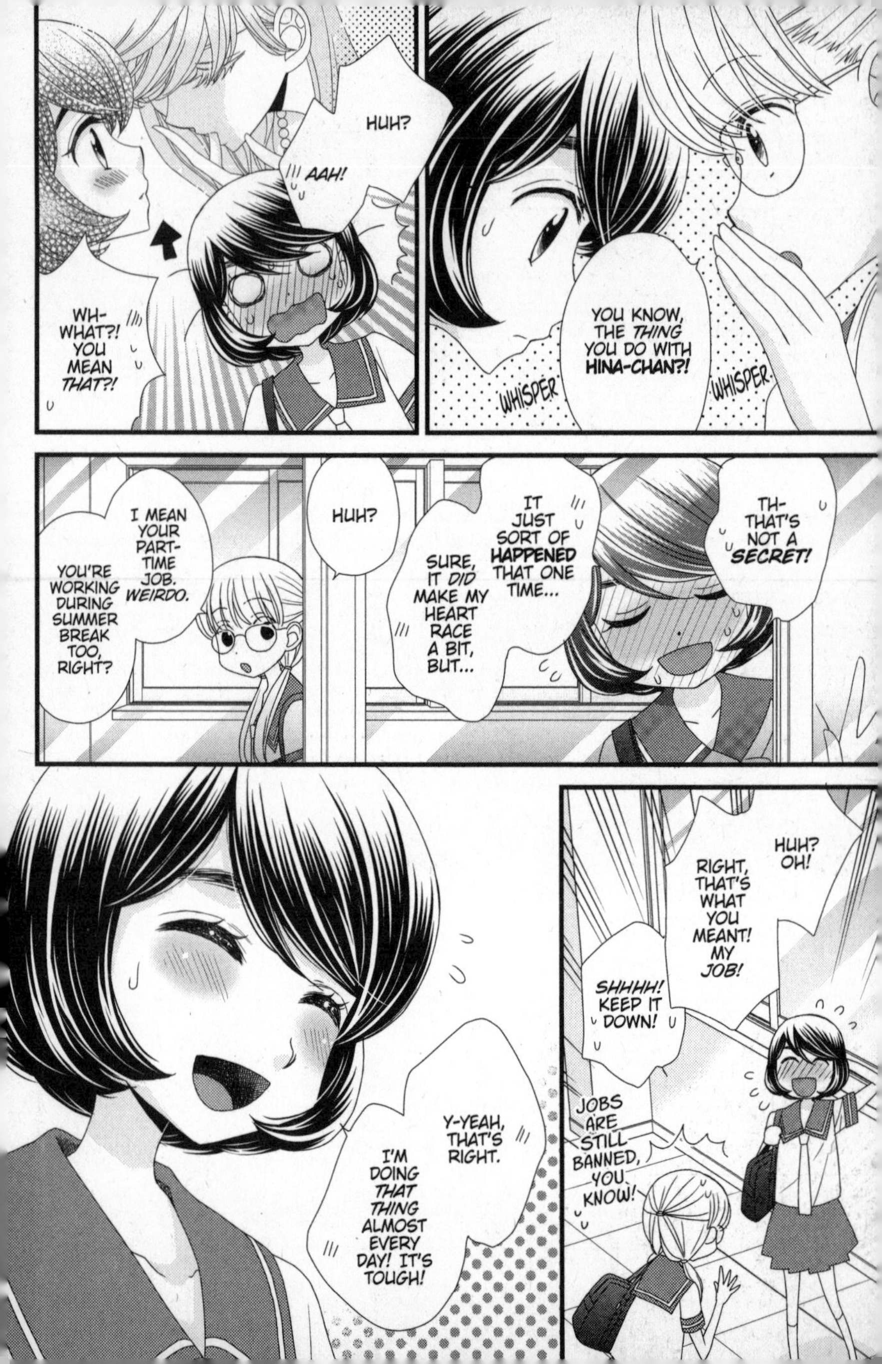

YOU KNOW, THE THING YOU DO WITH HINA-CHAN?!
WHISPER
WHISPER
HUH?
AAH!
WH-WHAT?! YOU MEAN THAT?!
TH-THAT'S NOT A SECRET!
IT JUST SORT OF HAPPENED THAT ONE TIME...
SURE, IT DID MAKE MY HEART RACE A BIT, BUT...
HUH?
I MEAN YOUR PART-TIME JOB. WEIRDO.
YOU'RE WORKING DURING SUMMER BREAK TOO, RIGHT?
HUH? OH!
RIGHT, THAT'S WHAT YOU MEANT! MY JOB!
SHHHH! KEEP IT DOWN!
JOBS ARE STILL BANNED, YOU KNOW!
Y-YEAH, THAT'S RIGHT.
I'M DOING THAT THING ALMOST EVERY DAY! IT'S TOUGH!

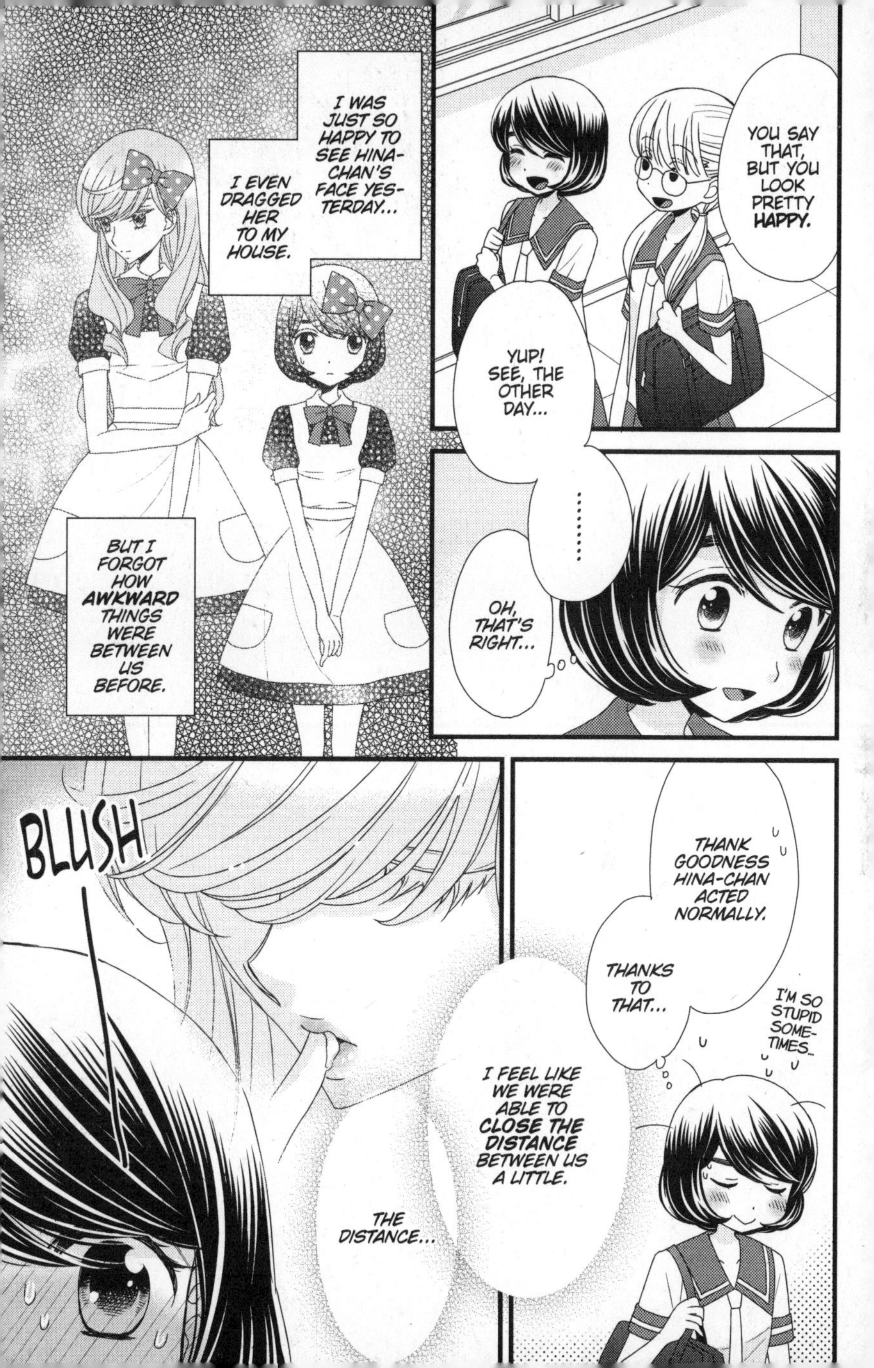
YOU SAY THAT, BUT YOU LOOK PRETTY HAPPY.
YUP! SEE, THE OTHER DAY...
......
OH, THAT'S RIGHT...
I WAS JUST SO HAPPY TO SEE HINA-CHAN'S FACE YESTERDAY...
I EVEN DRAGGED HER TO MY HOUSE.
BUT I FORGOT HOW AWKWARD THINGS WERE BETWEEN US BEFORE.
THANK GOODNESS HINA-CHAN ACTED NORMALLY.
THANKS TO THAT...
I'M SO STUPID SOMETIMES...
I FEEL LIKE WE WERE ABLE TO CLOSE THE DISTANCE BETWEEN US A LITTLE.
THE DISTANCE...
BLUSH

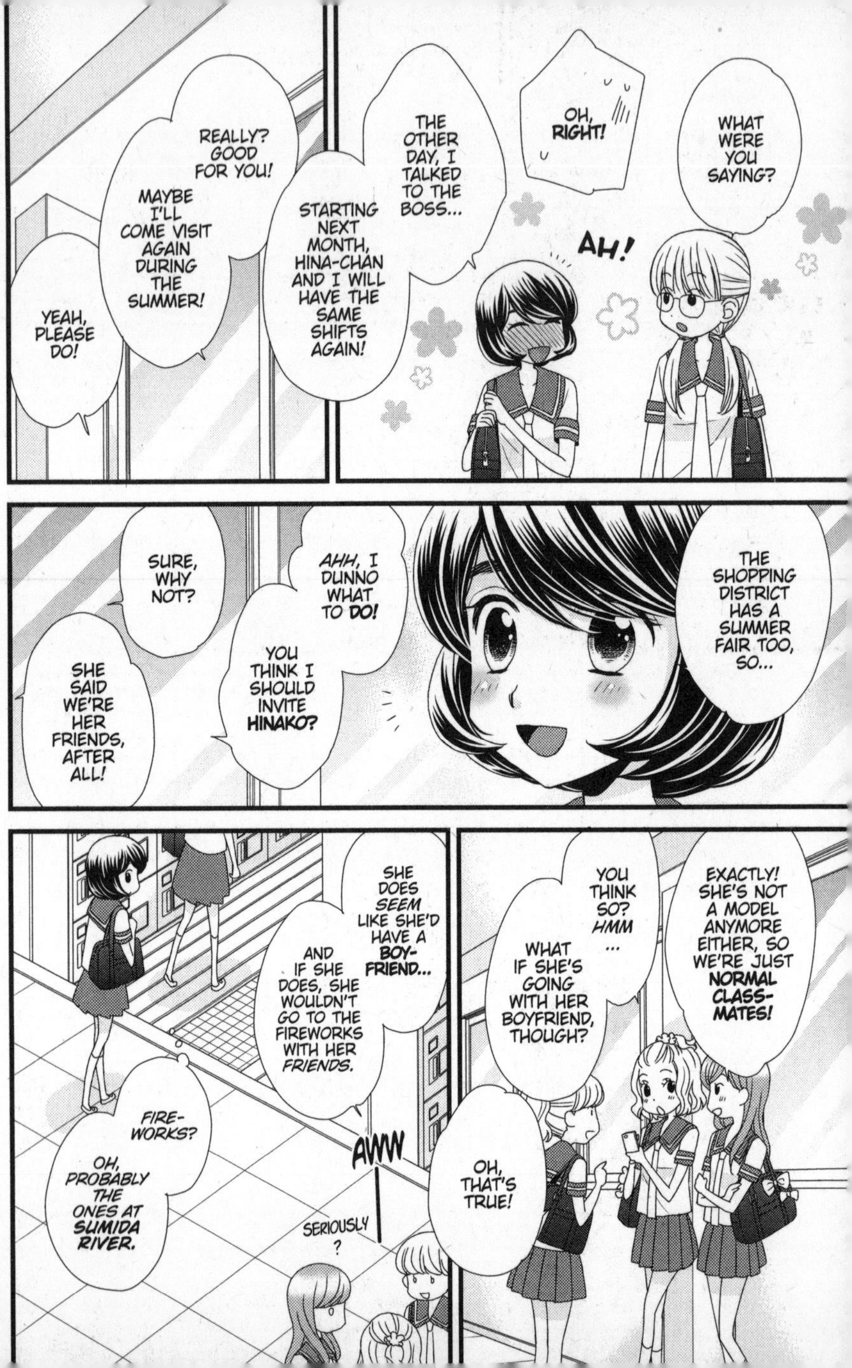
WHAT WERE YOU SAYING?
OH, RIGHT!
AH!
THE OTHER DAY, I TALKED TO THE BOSS...
STARTING NEXT MONTH, HINA-CHAN AND I WILL HAVE THE SAME SHIFTS AGAIN!
REALLY? GOOD FOR YOU!
MAYBE I'LL COME VISIT AGAIN DURING THE SUMMER!
YEAH, PLEASE DO!
THE SHOPPING DISTRICT HAS A SUMMER FAIR TOO, SO...
AHH, I DUNNO WHAT TO DO!
YOU THINK I SHOULD INVITE HINAKO?
SURE, WHY NOT?
SHE SAID WE'RE HER FRIENDS, AFTER ALL!
EXACTLY! SHE'S NOT A MODEL ANYMORE EITHER, SO WE'RE JUST NORMAL CLASSMATES!
YOU THINK SO? HMM...
WHAT IF SHE'S GOING WITH HER BOYFRIEND, THOUGH?
OH, THAT'S TRUE!
SHE DOES SEEM LIKE SHE'D HAVE A BOYFRIEND...
AND IF SHE DOES, SHE WOULDN'T GO TO THE FIREWORKS WITH HER FRIENDS.
AWW
SERIOUSLY?
FIRE-WORKS?
OH, PROBABLY THE ONES AT SUMIDA RIVER.

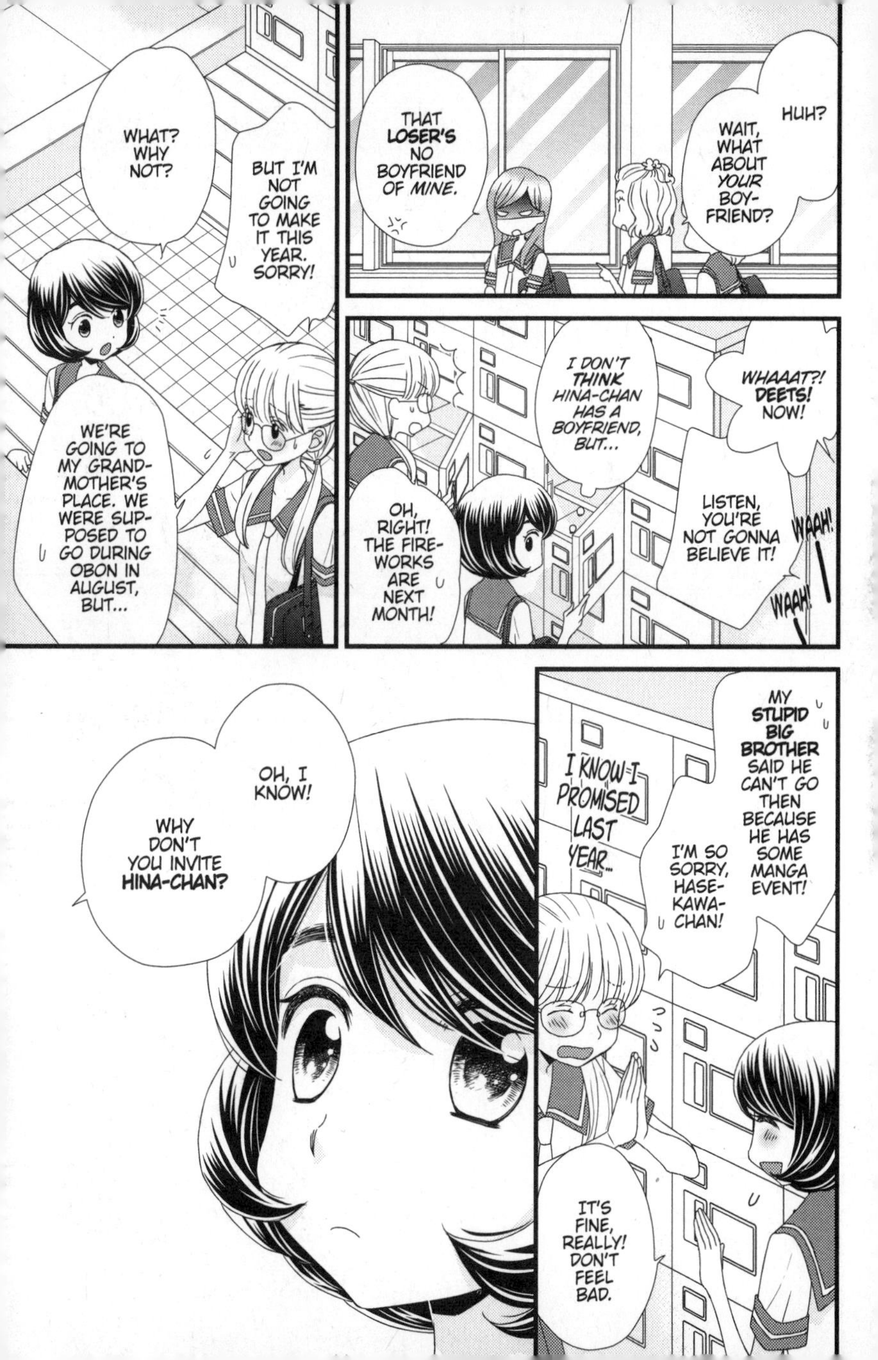
HUH?
WAIT, WHAT ABOUT YOUR BOY-FRIEND?
THAT LOSER'S NO BOYFRIEND OF MINE.
WHAAAT?! DEETS! NOW!
I DON'T THINK HINA-CHAN HAS A BOYFRIEND, BUT...
LISTEN, YOU'RE NOT GONNA BELIEVE IT!
WAAH!
WAAH!
OH, RIGHT! THE FIRE-WORKS ARE NEXT MONTH!
BUT I'M NOT GOING TO MAKE IT THIS YEAR. SORRY!
WHAT? WHY NOT?
WE'RE GOING TO MY GRAND-MOTHER'S PLACE. WE WERE SUP-POSED TO GO DURING OBON IN AUGUST, BUT...
MY STUPID BIG BROTHER SAID HE CAN'T GO THEN BECAUSE HE HAS SOME MANGA EVENT!
I KNOW I PROMISED LAST YEAR...
I'M SO SORRY, HASE-KAWA-CHAN!
IT'S FINE, REALLY! DON'T FEEL BAD.
OH, I KNOW!
WHY DON'T YOU INVITE HINA-CHAN?

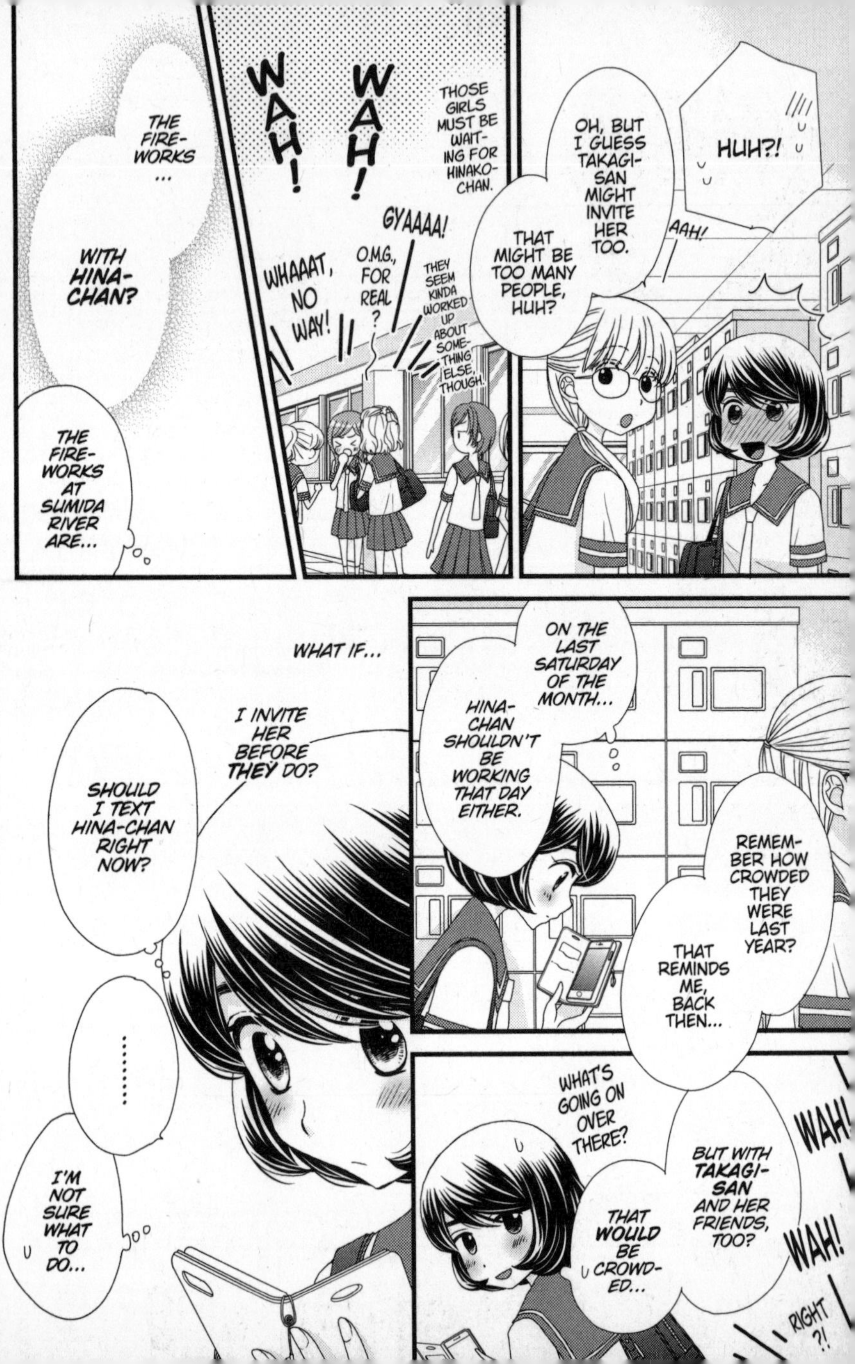
OH, BUT I GUESS TAKAGI-SAN MIGHT INVITE HER TOO.
THAT MIGHT BE TOO MANY PEOPLE, HUH?
AAH!
HUH?!
WAH! WAH!
THOSE GIRLS MUST BE WAITING FOR HINAKO-CHAN.
GYAAAA!
O.M.G., FOR REAL?
WHAAAT, NO WAY!
THEY SEEM KINDA WORKED UP ABOUT SOMETHING ELSE, THOUGH.
THE FIREWORKS...
WITH HINA-CHAN?
THE FIREWORKS AT SUMIDA RIVER ARE...
ON THE LAST SATURDAY OF THE MONTH...
HINA-CHAN SHOULDN'T BE WORKING THAT DAY EITHER.
REMEMBER HOW CROWDED THEY WERE LAST YEAR?
THAT REMINDS ME, BACK THEN...
BUT WITH TAKAGI-SAN AND HER FRIENDS, TOO?
WAH! WAH!
RIGHT?!
WHAT'S GOING ON OVER THERE?
THAT WOULD BE CROWDED...
WHAT IF...
I INVITE HER BEFORE THEY DO?
SHOULD I TEXT HINA-CHAN RIGHT NOW?
......
I'M NOT SURE WHAT TO DO...

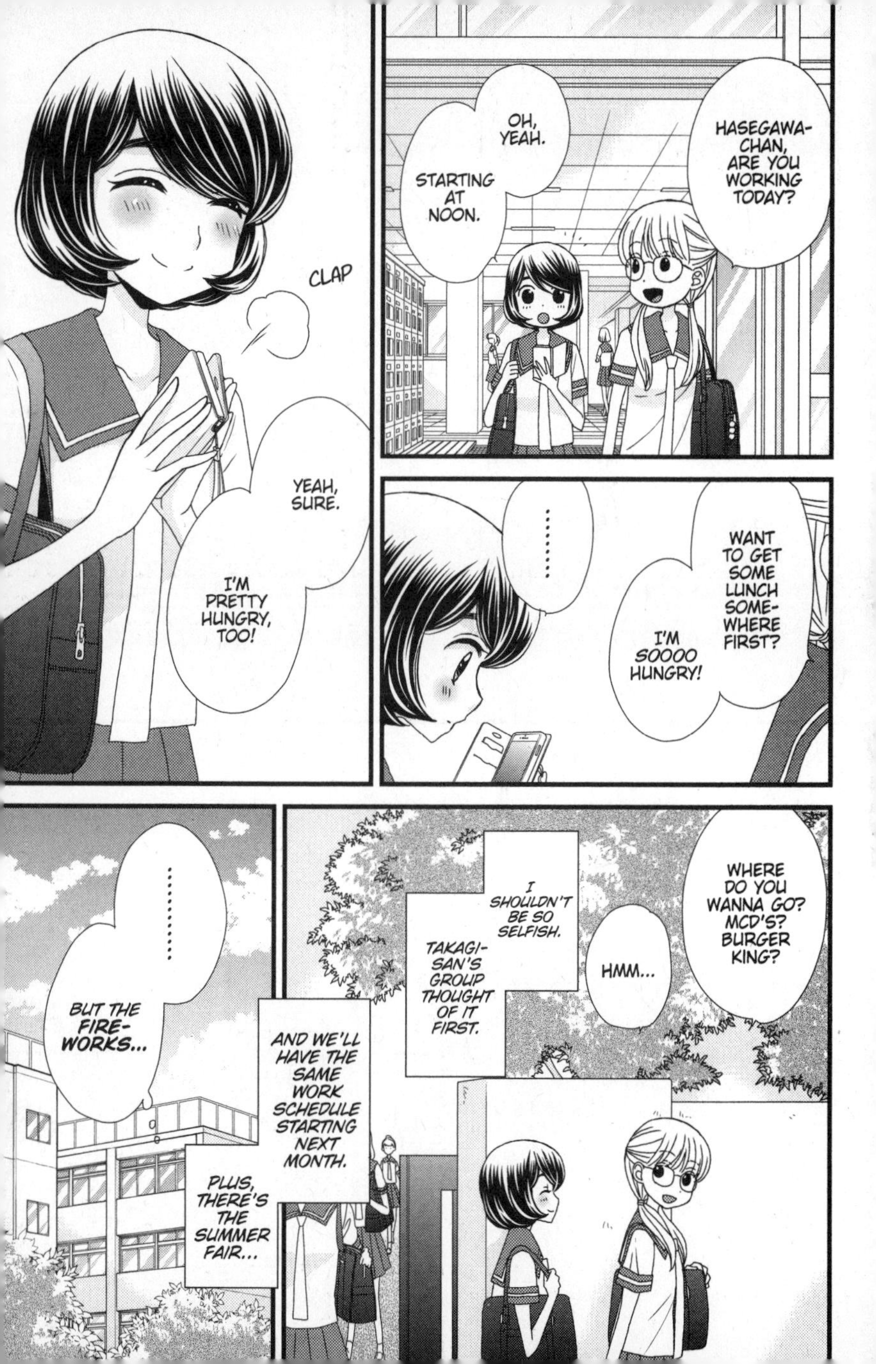
HASEGAWA-CHAN, ARE YOU WORKING TODAY?
OH, YEAH.
STARTING AT NOON.
WANT TO GET SOME LUNCH SOMEWHERE FIRST?
I'M SOOOO HUNGRY!
......
CLAP
YEAH, SURE.
I'M PRETTY HUNGRY, TOO!
WHERE DO YOU WANNA GO? MCD'S? BURGER KING?
HMM...
I SHOULDN'T BE SO SELFISH.
TAKAGI-SAN'S GROUP THOUGHT OF IT FIRST.
AND WE'LL HAVE THE SAME WORK SCHEDULE STARTING NEXT MONTH.
PLUS, THERE'S THE SUMMER FAIR...
....
BUT THE FIREWORKS...

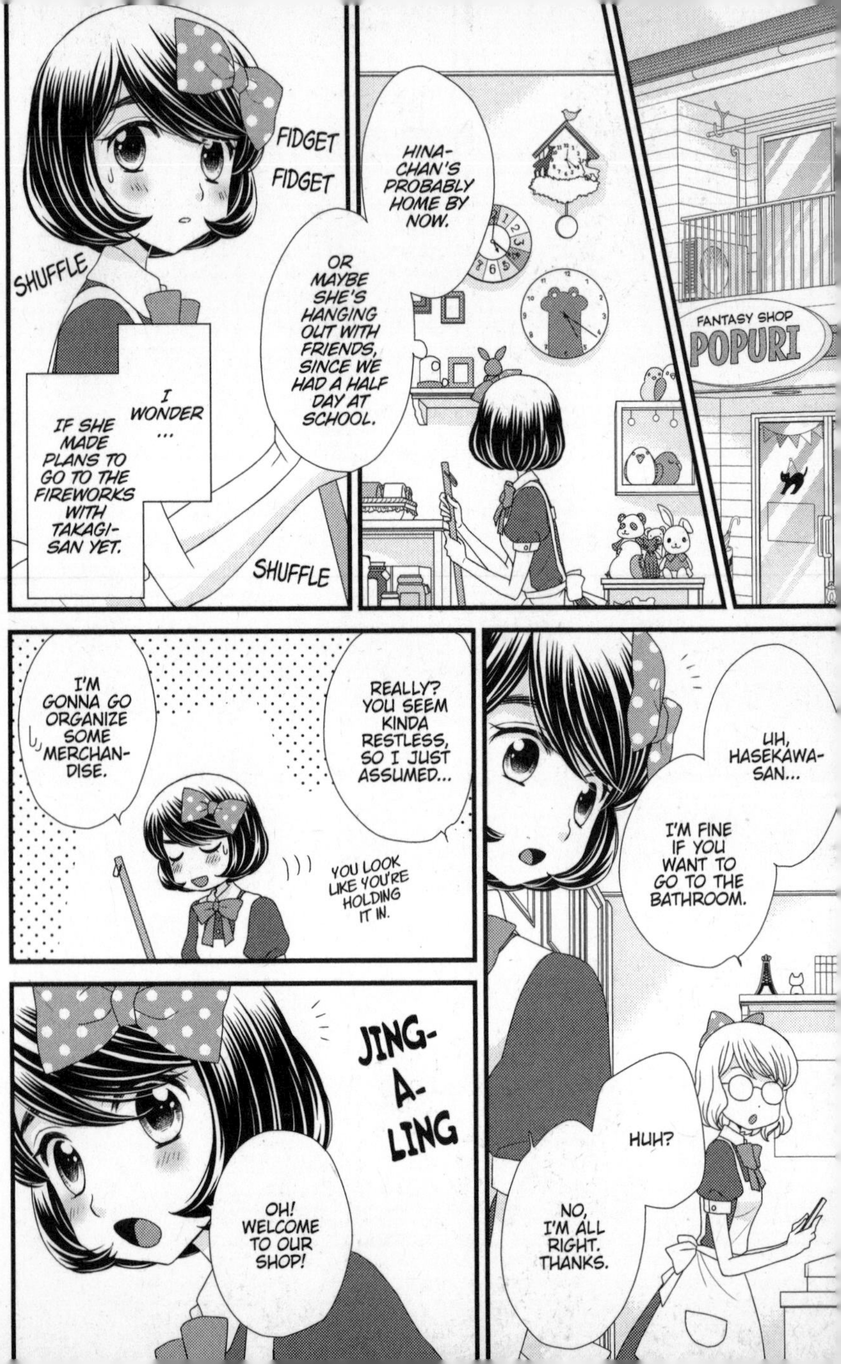
FANTASY SHOP
POPURI
HINA-CHAN'S PROBABLY HOME BY NOW.
OR MAYBE SHE'S HANGING OUT WITH FRIENDS, SINCE WE HAD A HALF DAY AT SCHOOL.
SHUFFLE
FIDGET
FIDGET
SHUFFLE
I WONDER ...
IF SHE MADE PLANS TO GO TO THE FIREWORKS WITH TAKAGI-SAN YET.
UH, HASEKAWA-SAN...
I'M FINE IF YOU WANT TO GO TO THE BATHROOM.
HUH?
NO, I'M ALL RIGHT. THANKS.
REALLY? YOU SEEM KINDA RESTLESS, SO I JUST ASSUMED...
YOU LOOK LIKE YOU'RE HOLDING IT IN.
I'M GONNA GO ORGANIZE SOME MERCHANDISE.
JING-A-LING
OH! WELCOME TO OUR SHOP!

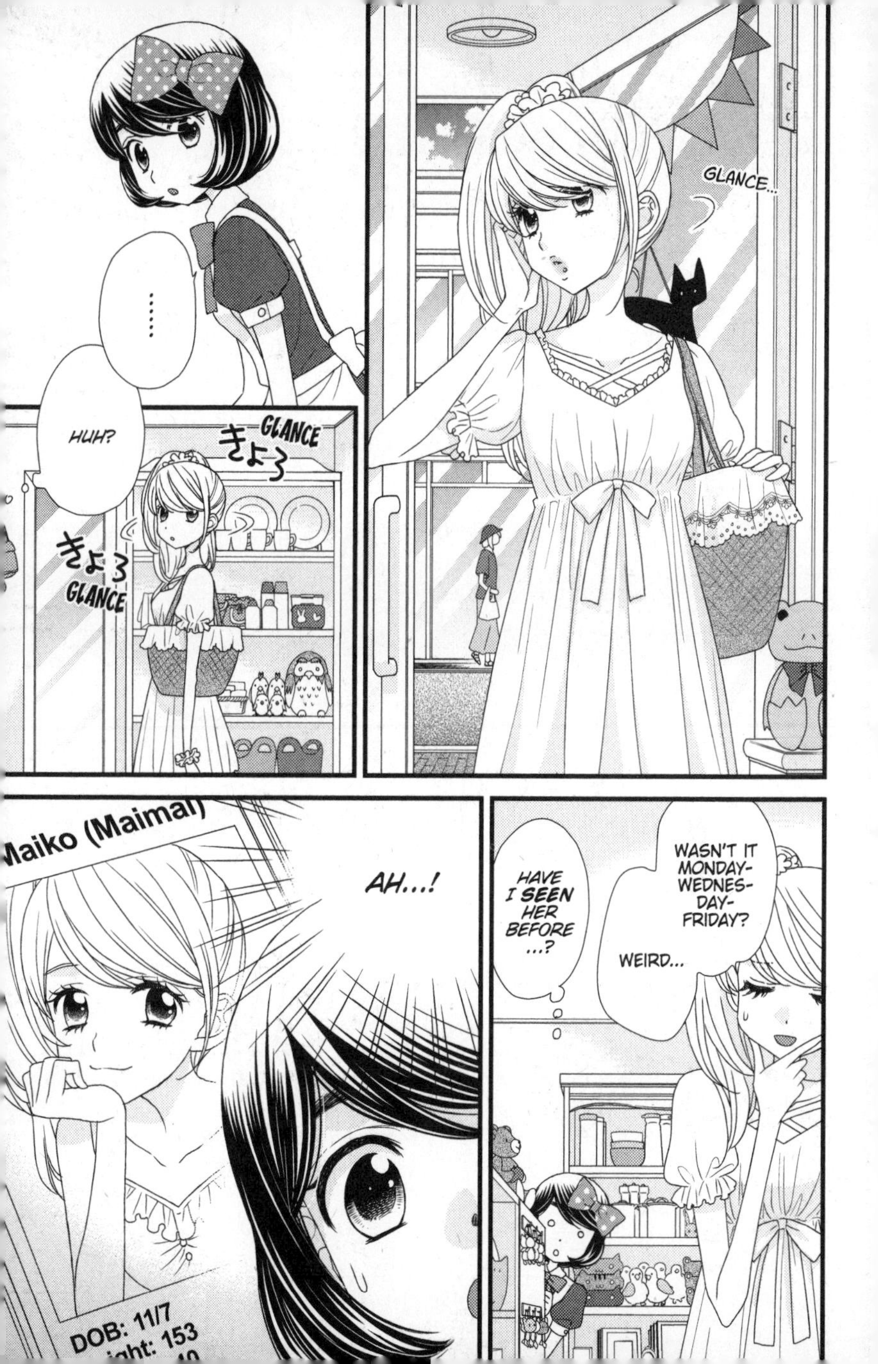
GLANCE...
......
HUH?
きょろ GLANCE
きょろ GLANCE
WASN'T IT MONDAY-WEDNES-DAY-FRIDAY?
WEIRD...
HAVE I SEEN HER BEFORE ...?
AH...!
Maiko (Maimai)
DOB: 11/7

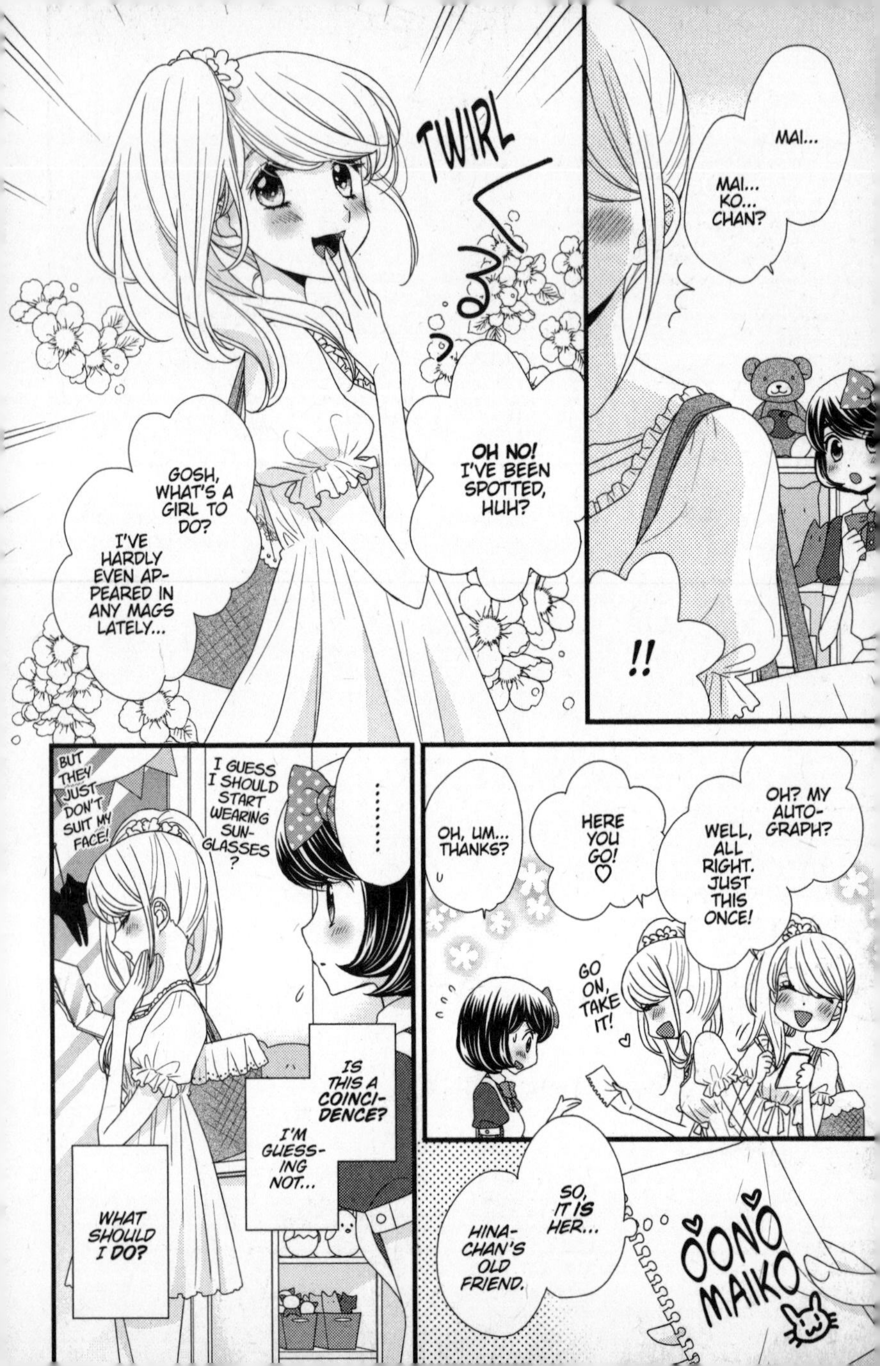

MAI...
MAI... KO... CHAN?
!!
TWIRL
OH NO! I'VE BEEN SPOTTED, HUH?
GOSH, WHAT'S A GIRL TO DO?
I'VE HARDLY EVEN AP-PEARED IN ANY MAGS LATELY...
OH? MY AUTO-GRAPH?
WELL, ALL RIGHT. JUST THIS ONCE!
HERE YOU GO! ♡
GO ON, TAKE IT!
OH, UM... THANKS?
OONO MAIKO
SO, IT IS HER...
HINA-CHAN'S OLD FRIEND.
......
I GUESS I SHOULD START WEARING SUN-GLASSES?
BUT THEY JUST DON'T SUIT MY FACE!
IS THIS A COINCI-DENCE?
I'M GUESS-ING NOT...
WHAT SHOULD I DO?

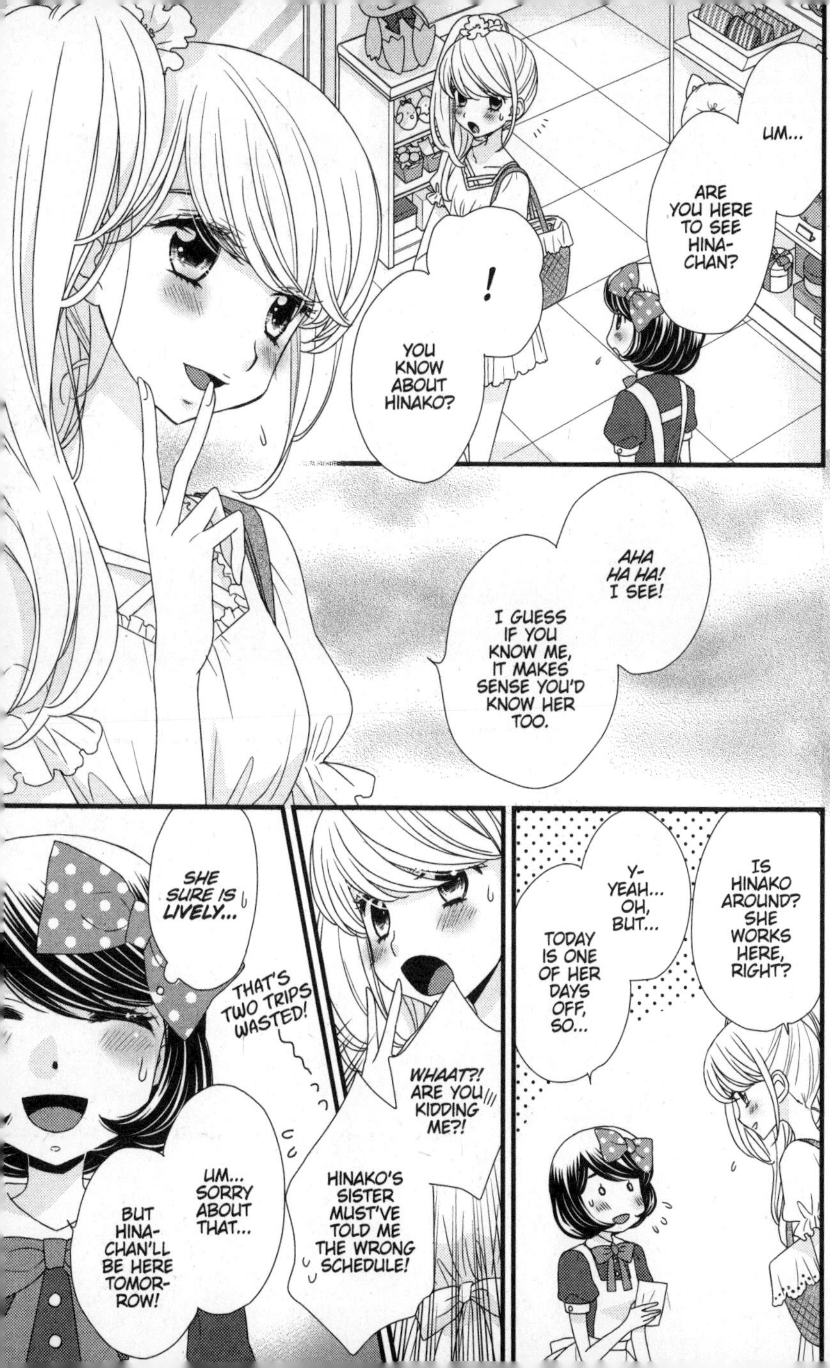
UM...
ARE YOU HERE TO SEE HINA-CHAN?
!
YOU KNOW ABOUT HINAKO?
AHA HA HA! I SEE!
I GUESS IF YOU KNOW ME, IT MAKES SENSE YOU'D KNOW HER TOO.
IS HINAKO AROUND? SHE WORKS HERE, RIGHT?
Y-YEAH... OH, BUT...
TODAY IS ONE OF HER DAYS OFF, SO...
WHAAT?! ARE YOU KIDDING ME?!
HINAKO'S SISTER MUST'VE TOLD ME THE WRONG SCHEDULE!
THAT'S TWO TRIPS WASTED!
SHE SURE IS LIVELY...
UM... SORRY ABOUT THAT...
BUT HINA-CHAN'LL BE HERE TOMOR-ROW!

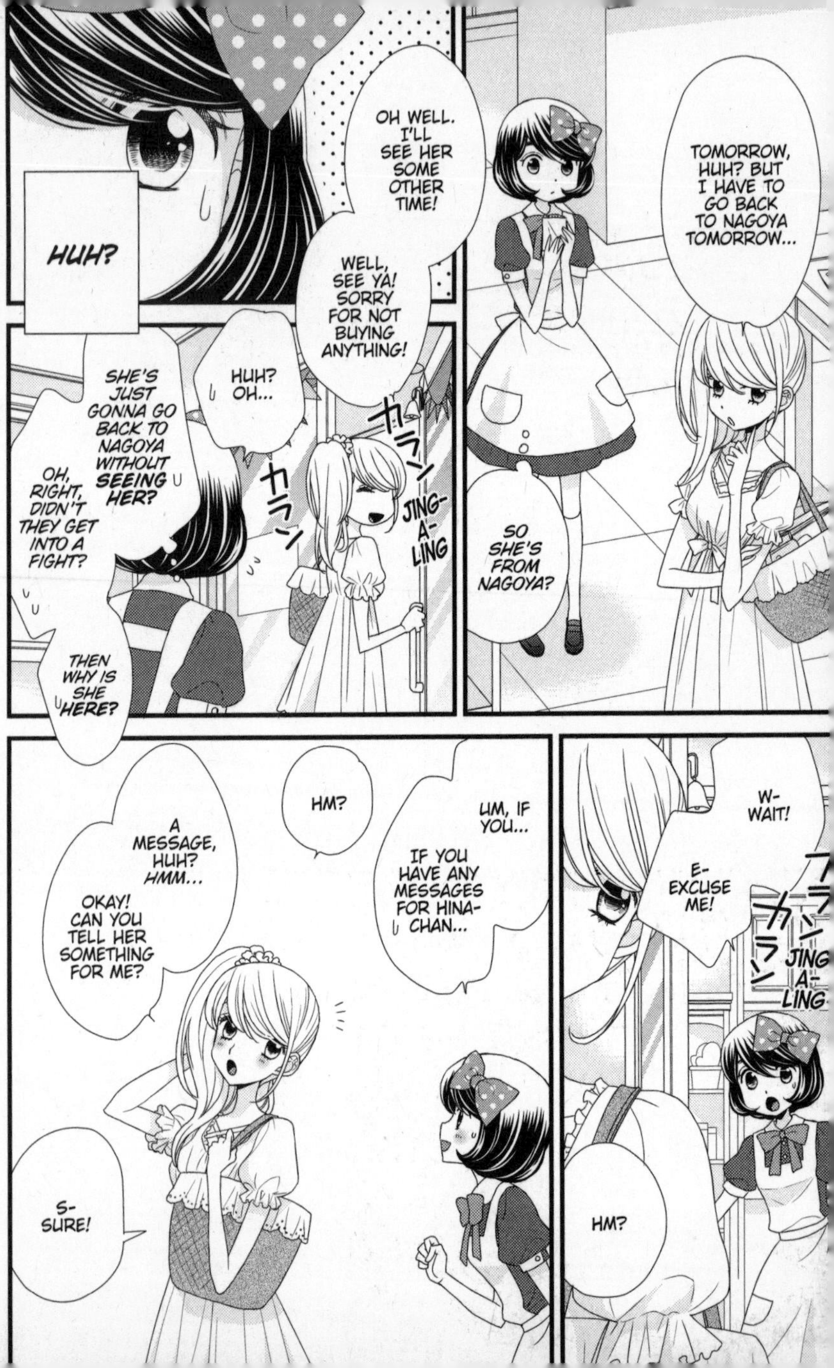
TOMORROW, HUH? BUT I HAVE TO GO BACK TO NAGOYA TOMORROW...
SO SHE'S FROM NAGOYA?
OH WELL. I'LL SEE HER SOME OTHER TIME!
HUH?
WELL, SEE YA! SORRY FOR NOT BUYING ANYTHING!
カランカラン
JING-A-LING
HUH? OH...
SHE'S JUST GONNA GO BACK TO NAGOYA WITHOUT SEEING HER?
OH, RIGHT, DIDN'T THEY GET INTO A FIGHT?
THEN WHY IS SHE HERE?
W-WAIT!
E-EXCUSE ME!
カランカラン
JING-A-LING
HM?
UM, IF YOU...
IF YOU HAVE ANY MESSAGES FOR HINA-CHAN...
HM?
A MESSAGE, HUH? HMM...
OKAY! CAN YOU TELL HER SOMETHING FOR ME?
S-SURE!

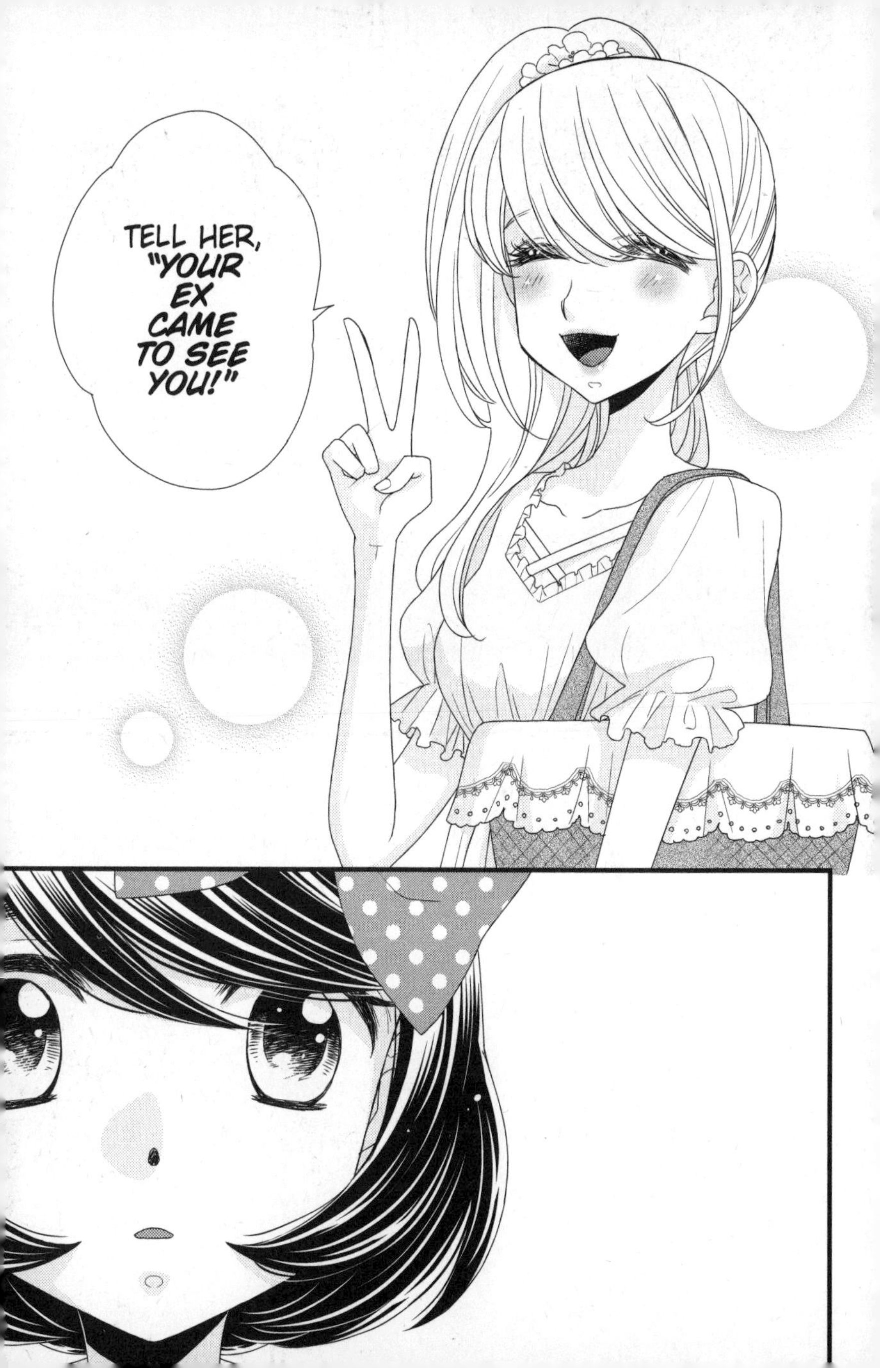
TELL HER, "YOUR EX CAME TO SEE YOU!"

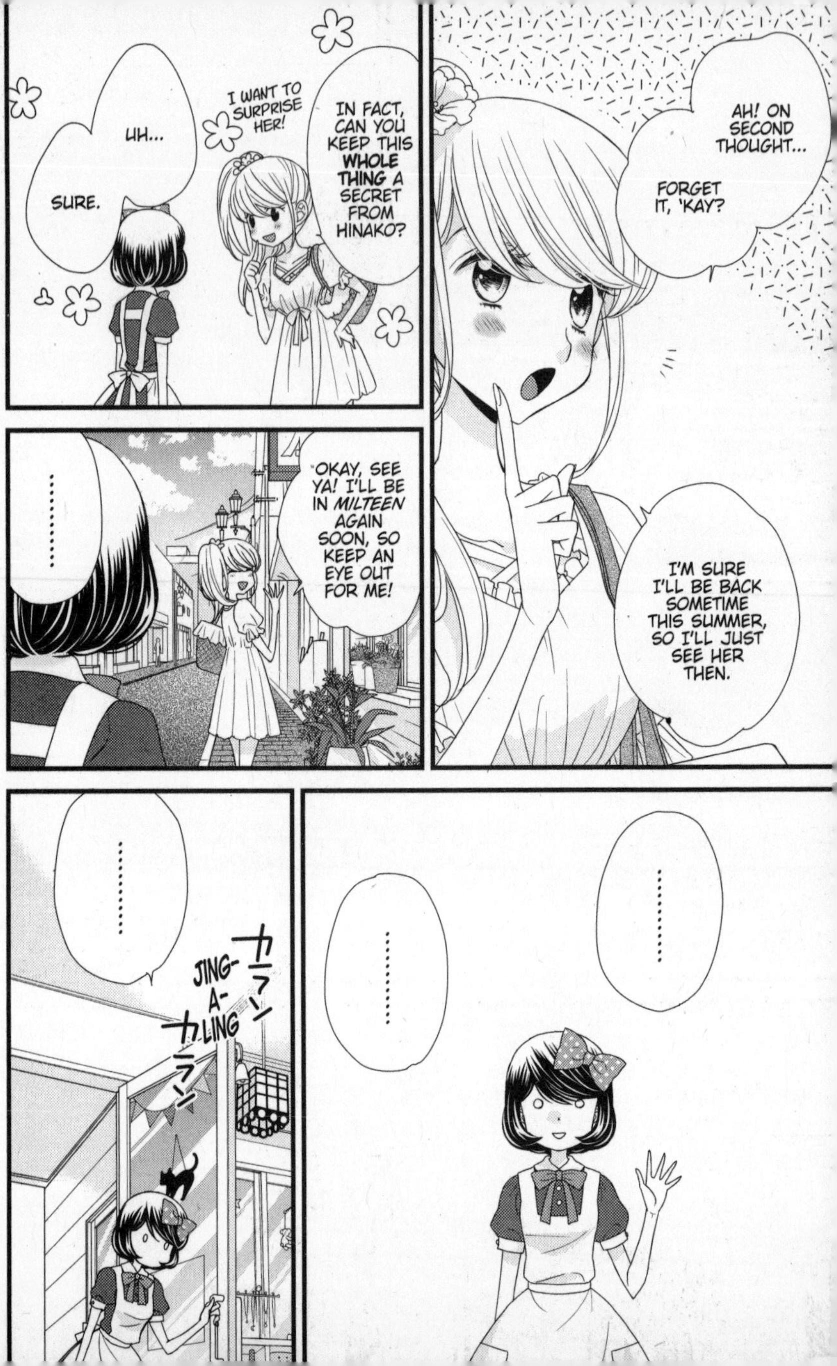
AH! ON SECOND THOUGHT...
FORGET IT, 'KAY?
I'M SURE I'LL BE BACK SOMETIME THIS SUMMER, SO I'LL JUST SEE HER THEN.
IN FACT, CAN YOU KEEP THIS **WHOLE THING** A SECRET FROM HINAKO?
I WANT TO SURPRISE HER!
UH...
SURE.
OKAY, SEE YA! I'LL BE IN *MILTEEN* AGAIN SOON, SO KEEP AN EYE OUT FOR ME!
......
......
......
......
JING-A-LING
カラン
カラン

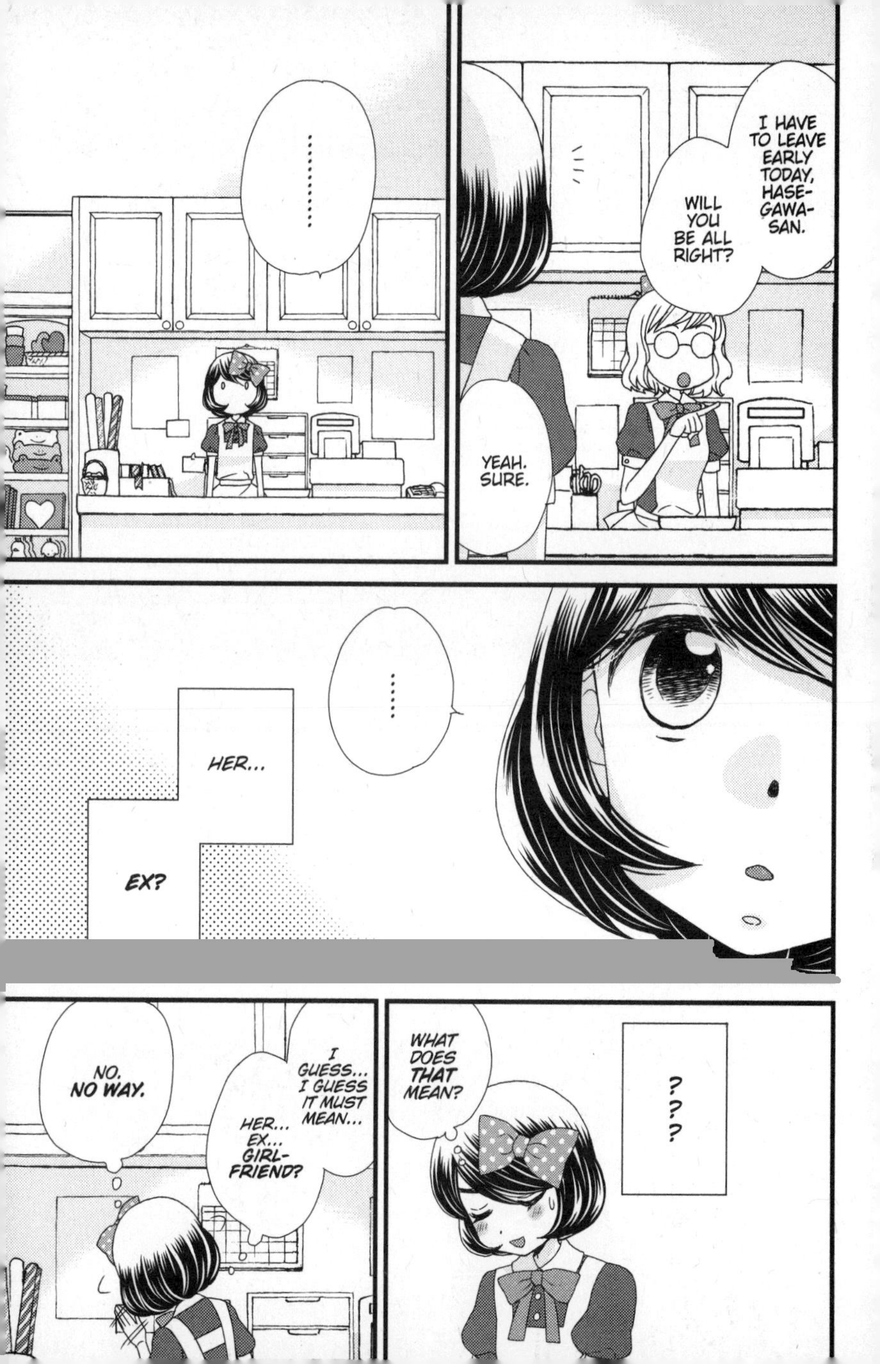
I HAVE TO LEAVE EARLY TODAY, HASE-GAWA-SAN.
WILL YOU BE ALL RIGHT?
YEAH. SURE.
....
......
HER...
EX?
???
WHAT DOES THAT MEAN?
I GUESS... I GUESS IT MUST MEAN...
HER... EX... GIRL-FRIEND?
NO. NO WAY.

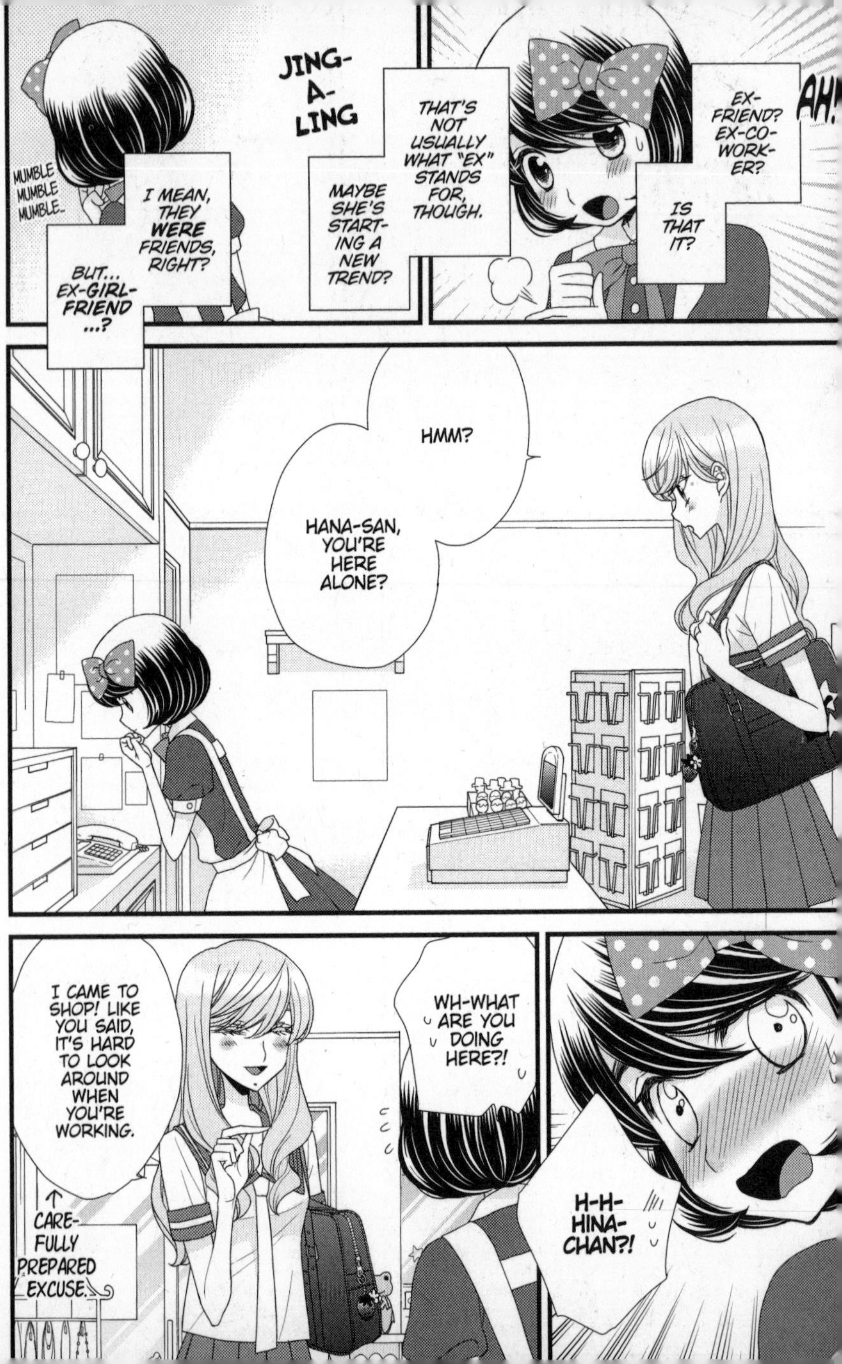
AH!
EX-FRIEND? EX-CO-WORKER?
IS THAT IT?
THAT'S NOT USUALLY WHAT "EX" STANDS FOR, THOUGH.
MAYBE SHE'S STARTING A NEW TREND?
JING-A-LING
I MEAN, THEY WERE FRIENDS, RIGHT?
BUT... EX-GIRLFRIEND ...?
MUMBLE MUMBLE MUMBLE...
HMM?
HANA-SAN, YOU'RE HERE ALONE?
H-H-HINA-CHAN?!
WH-WHAT ARE YOU DOING HERE?!
I CAME TO SHOP! LIKE YOU SAID, IT'S HARD TO LOOK AROUND WHEN YOU'RE WORKING.
CAREFULLY PREPARED EXCUSE.

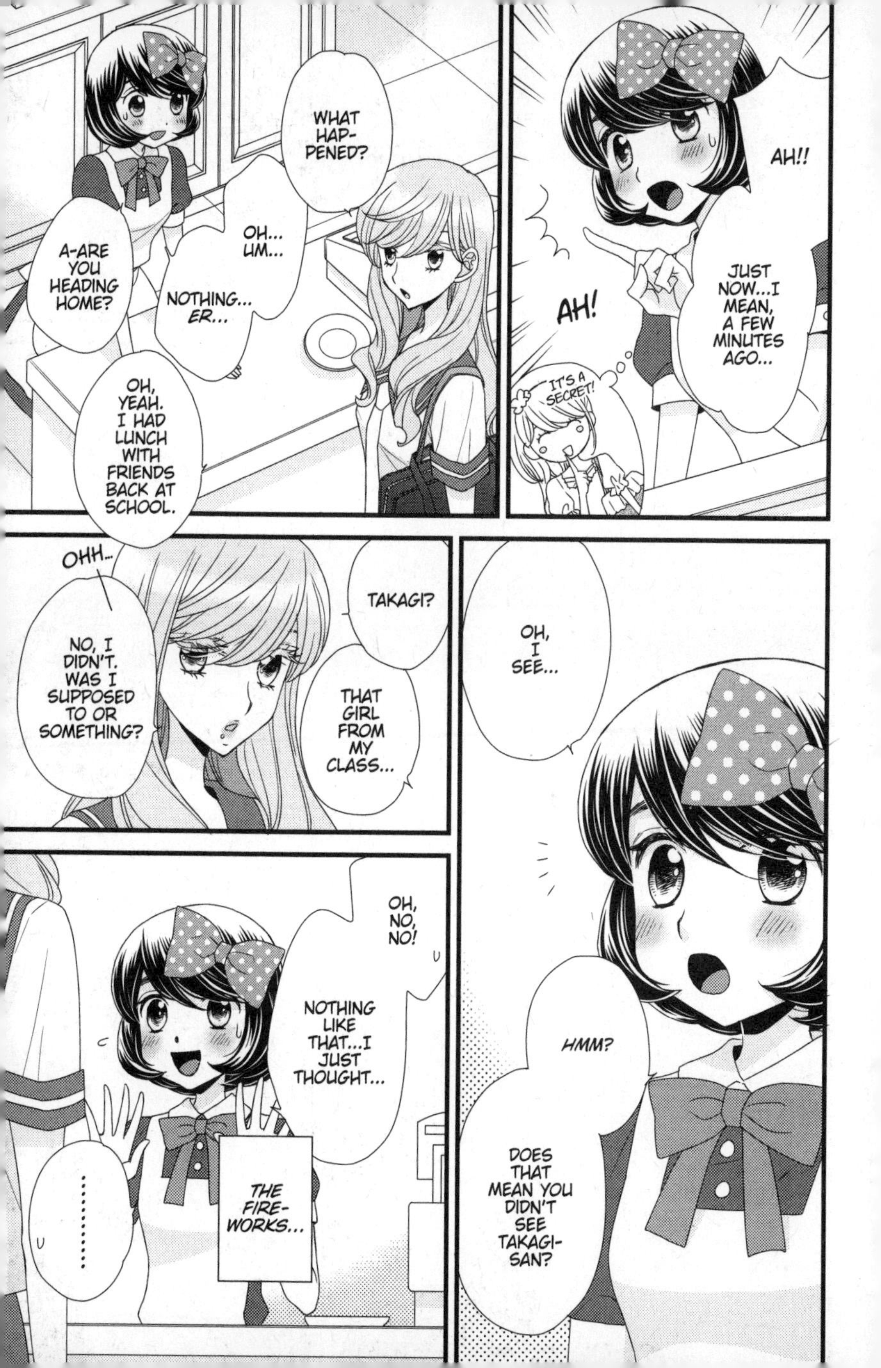
AH!!
JUST NOW...I MEAN, A FEW MINUTES AGO...
AH!
IT'S A SECRET!
WHAT HAP-PENED?
OH... UM...
NOTHING... ER...
A-ARE YOU HEADING HOME?
OH, YEAH. I HAD LUNCH WITH FRIENDS BACK AT SCHOOL.
OH, I SEE...
HMM?
DOES THAT MEAN YOU DIDN'T SEE TAKAGI-SAN?
TAKAGI?
THAT GIRL FROM MY CLASS...
OHH...
NO, I DIDN'T. WAS I SUPPOSED TO OR SOMETHING?
OH, NO, NO!
NOTHING LIKE THAT...I JUST THOUGHT...
THE FIRE-WORKS...
....

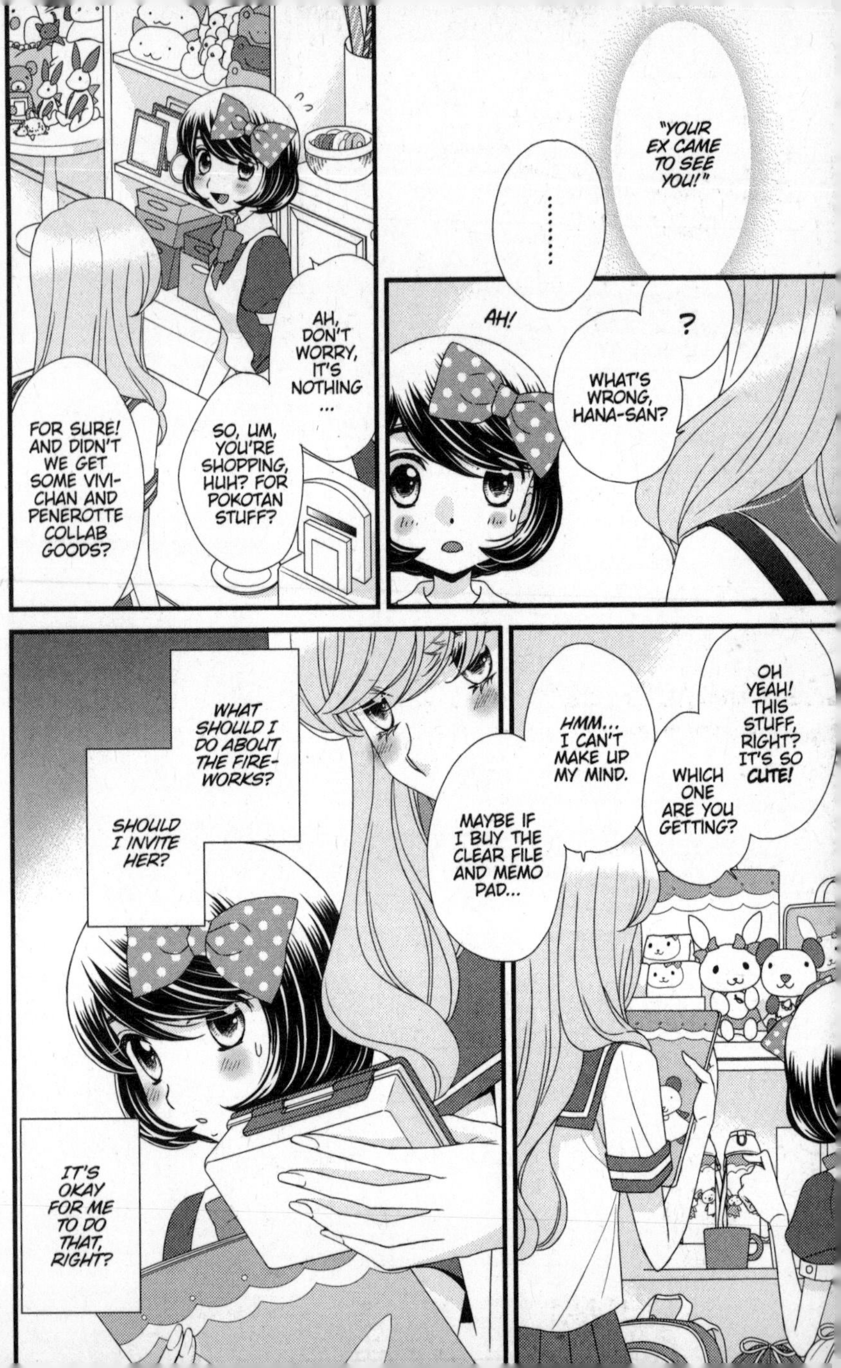
"YOUR EX CAME TO SEE YOU!"
......
?
WHAT'S WRONG, HANA-SAN?
AH!
AH, DON'T WORRY, IT'S NOTHING ...
SO, UM, YOU'RE SHOPPING, HUH? FOR POKOTAN STUFF?
FOR SURE! AND DIDN'T WE GET SOME VIVI-CHAN AND PENEROTTE COLLAB GOODS?
OH YEAH! THIS STUFF, RIGHT? IT'S SO **CUTE!**
WHICH ONE ARE YOU GETTING?
HMM... I CAN'T MAKE UP MY MIND.
MAYBE IF I BUY THE CLEAR FILE AND MEMO PAD...
WHAT SHOULD I DO ABOUT THE FIRE-WORKS?
SHOULD I INVITE HER?
IT'S OKAY FOR ME TO DO THAT, RIGHT?

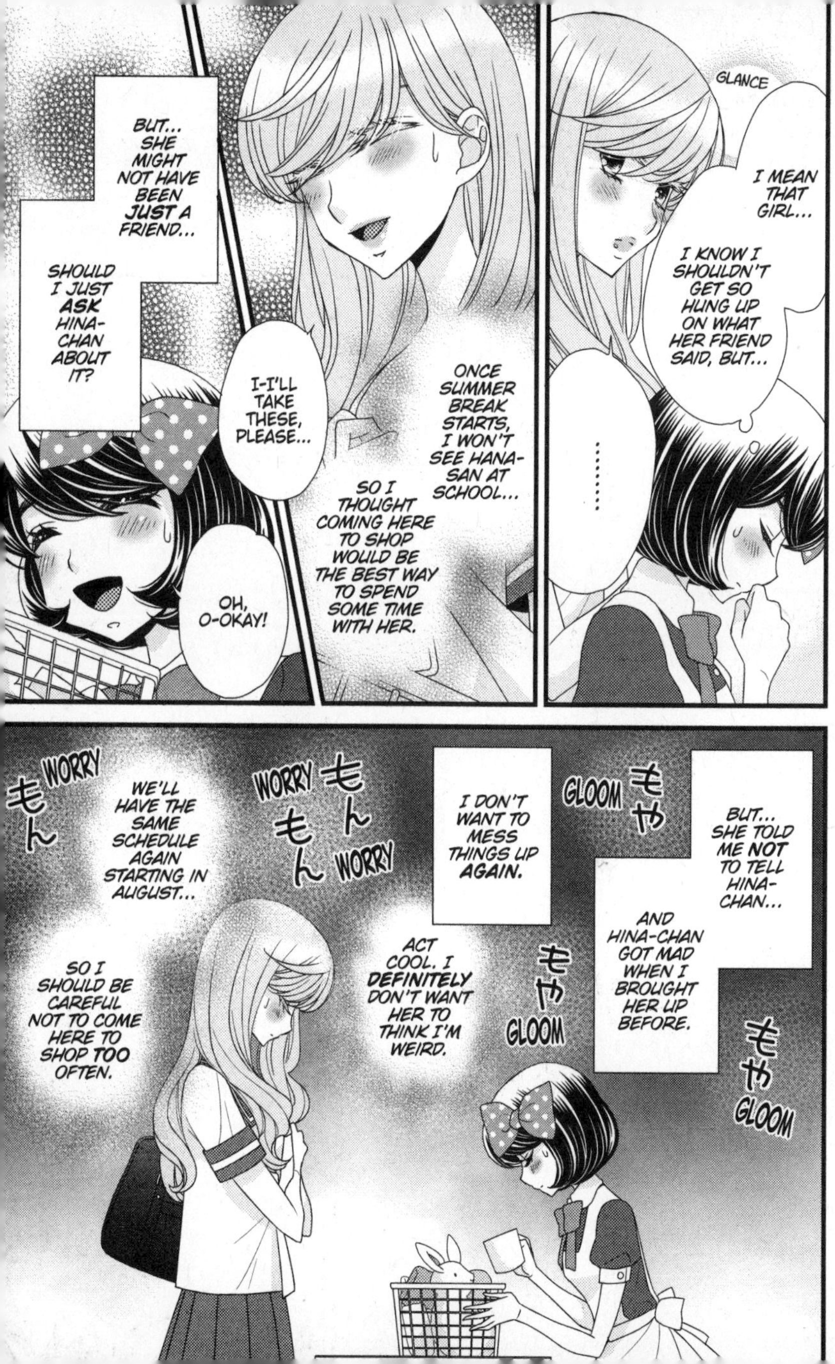
GLANCE
I MEAN THAT GIRL...
I KNOW I SHOULDN'T GET SO HUNG UP ON WHAT HER FRIEND SAID, BUT...
......
ONCE SUMMER BREAK STARTS, I WON'T SEE HANA-SAN AT SCHOOL...
SO I THOUGHT COMING HERE TO SHOP WOULD BE THE BEST WAY TO SPEND SOME TIME WITH HER.
I-I'LL TAKE THESE, PLEASE...
BUT... SHE MIGHT NOT HAVE BEEN JUST A FRIEND...
SHOULD I JUST ASK HINA-CHAN ABOUT IT?
OH, O-OKAY!
BUT... SHE TOLD ME NOT TO TELL HINA-CHAN...
AND HINA-CHAN GOT MAD WHEN I BROUGHT HER UP BEFORE.
もや GLOOM
もや GLOOM
I DON'T WANT TO MESS THINGS UP AGAIN.
もや GLOOM
ACT COOL. I DEFINITELY DON'T WANT HER TO THINK I'M WEIRD.
WORRY もん
もん WORRY
WE'LL HAVE THE SAME SCHEDULE AGAIN STARTING IN AUGUST...
SO I SHOULD BE CAREFUL NOT TO COME HERE TO SHOP TOO OFTEN.
WORRY もん

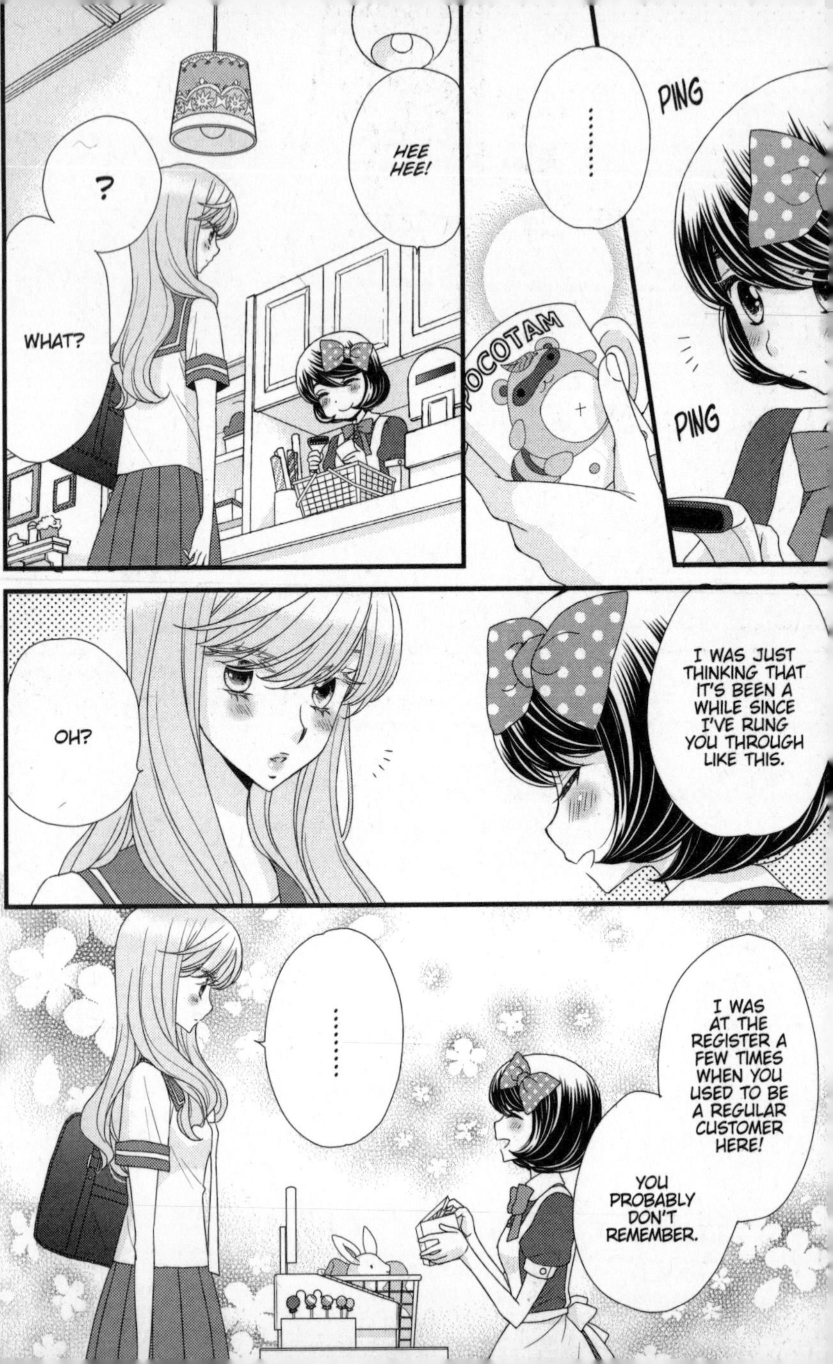
PING
PING
......
POCOTAM
HEE HEE!
?
WHAT?
I WAS JUST THINKING THAT IT'S BEEN A WHILE SINCE I'VE RUNG YOU THROUGH LIKE THIS.
OH?
I WAS AT THE REGISTER A FEW TIMES WHEN YOU USED TO BE A REGULAR CUSTOMER HERE!
YOU PROBABLY DON'T REMEMBER.
......

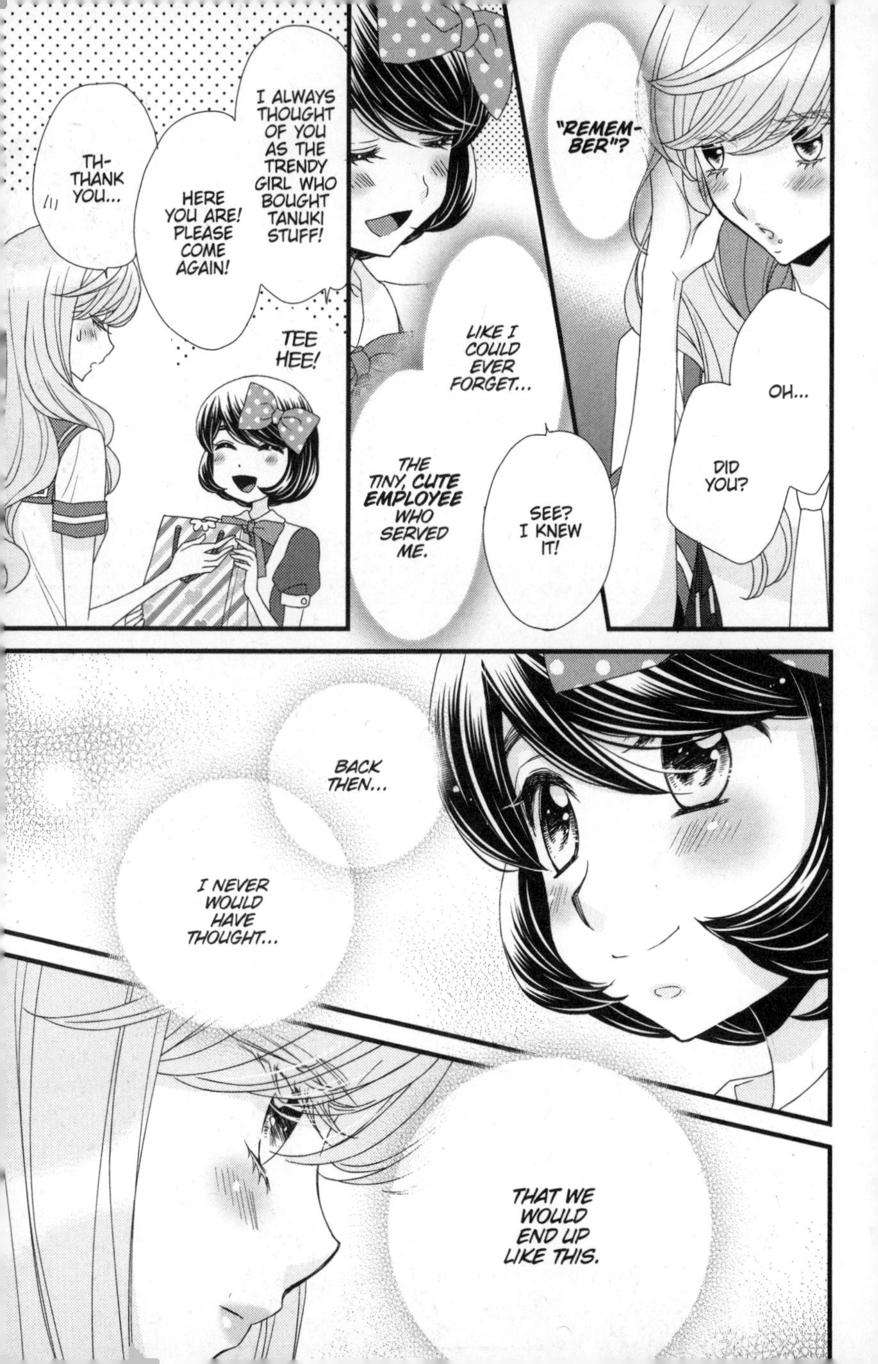
"REMEMBER"?
OH... DID YOU?
SEE? I KNEW IT!
LIKE I COULD EVER FORGET...
THE TINY, **CUTE EMPLOYEE** WHO SERVED ME.
I ALWAYS THOUGHT OF YOU AS THE TRENDY GIRL WHO BOUGHT TANUKI STUFF!
HERE YOU ARE! PLEASE COME AGAIN!
TEE HEE!
TH-THANK YOU...
BACK THEN...
I NEVER WOULD HAVE THOUGHT...
THAT WE WOULD END UP LIKE THIS.

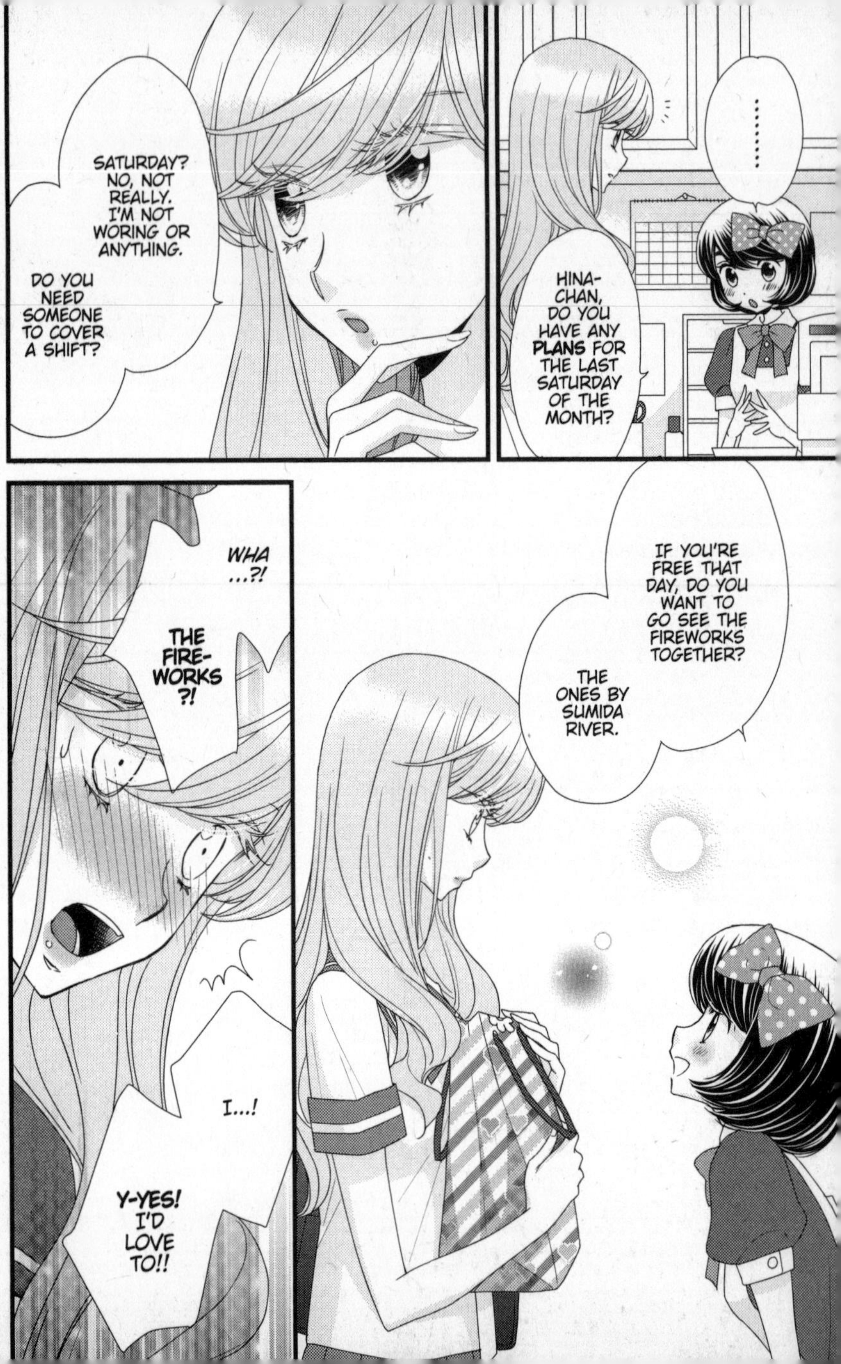
......
HINA-CHAN, DO YOU HAVE ANY PLANS FOR THE LAST SATURDAY OF THE MONTH?
SATURDAY? NO, NOT REALLY. I'M NOT WORING OR ANYTHING.
DO YOU NEED SOMEONE TO COVER A SHIFT?
IF YOU'RE FREE THAT DAY, DO YOU WANT TO GO SEE THE FIREWORKS TOGETHER?
THE ONES BY SUMIDA RIVER.
WHA ...?!
THE FIRE-WORKS ?!
I...!
Y-YES! I'D LOVE TO!!

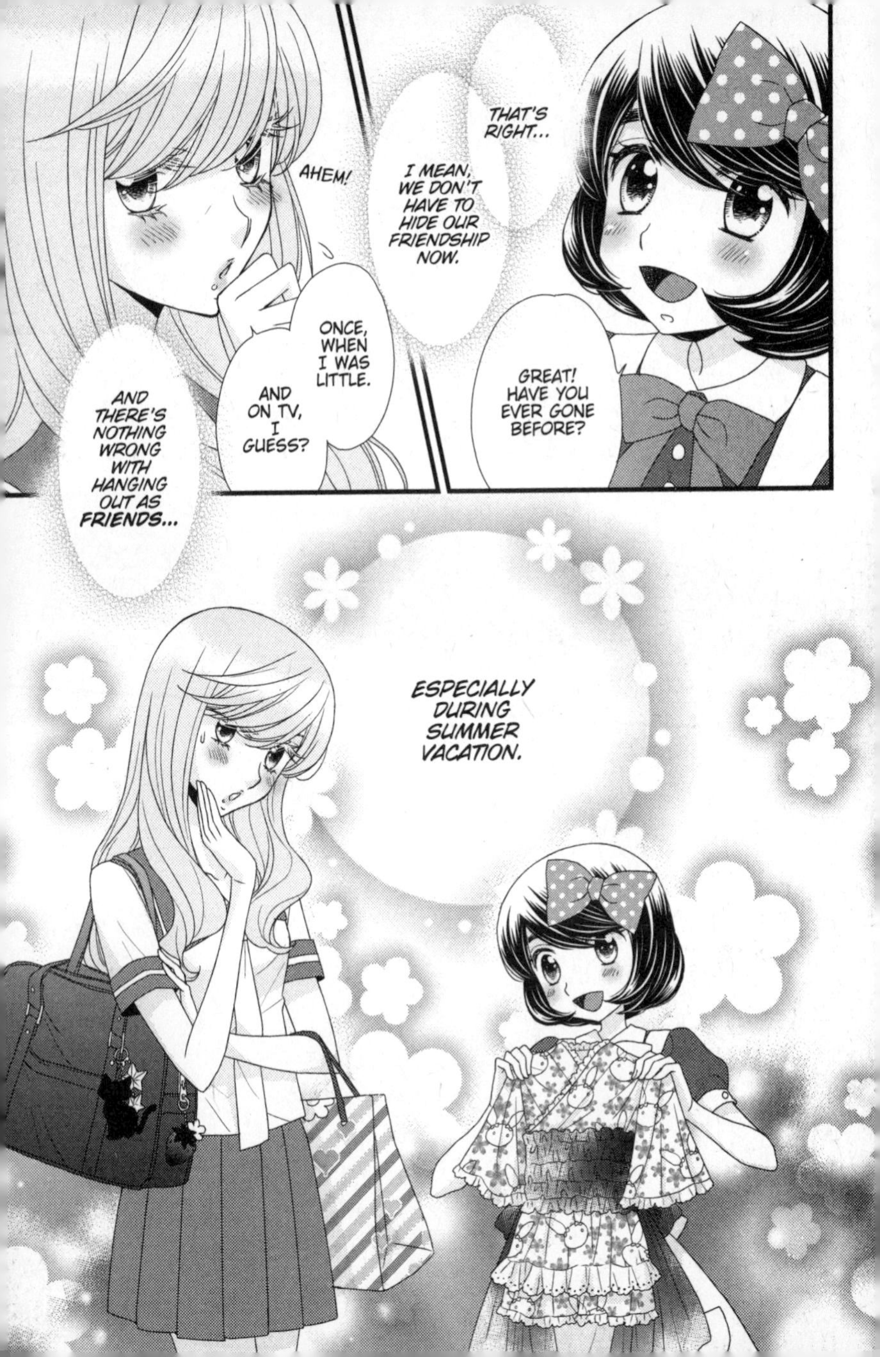
GREAT! HAVE YOU EVER GONE BEFORE?
ONCE, WHEN I WAS LITTLE.
AND ON TV, I GUESS?
AHEM!
THAT'S RIGHT...
I MEAN, WE DON'T HAVE TO HIDE OUR FRIENDSHIP NOW.
AND THERE'S NOTHING WRONG WITH HANGING OUT AS FRIENDS...
ESPECIALLY DURING SUMMER VACATION.

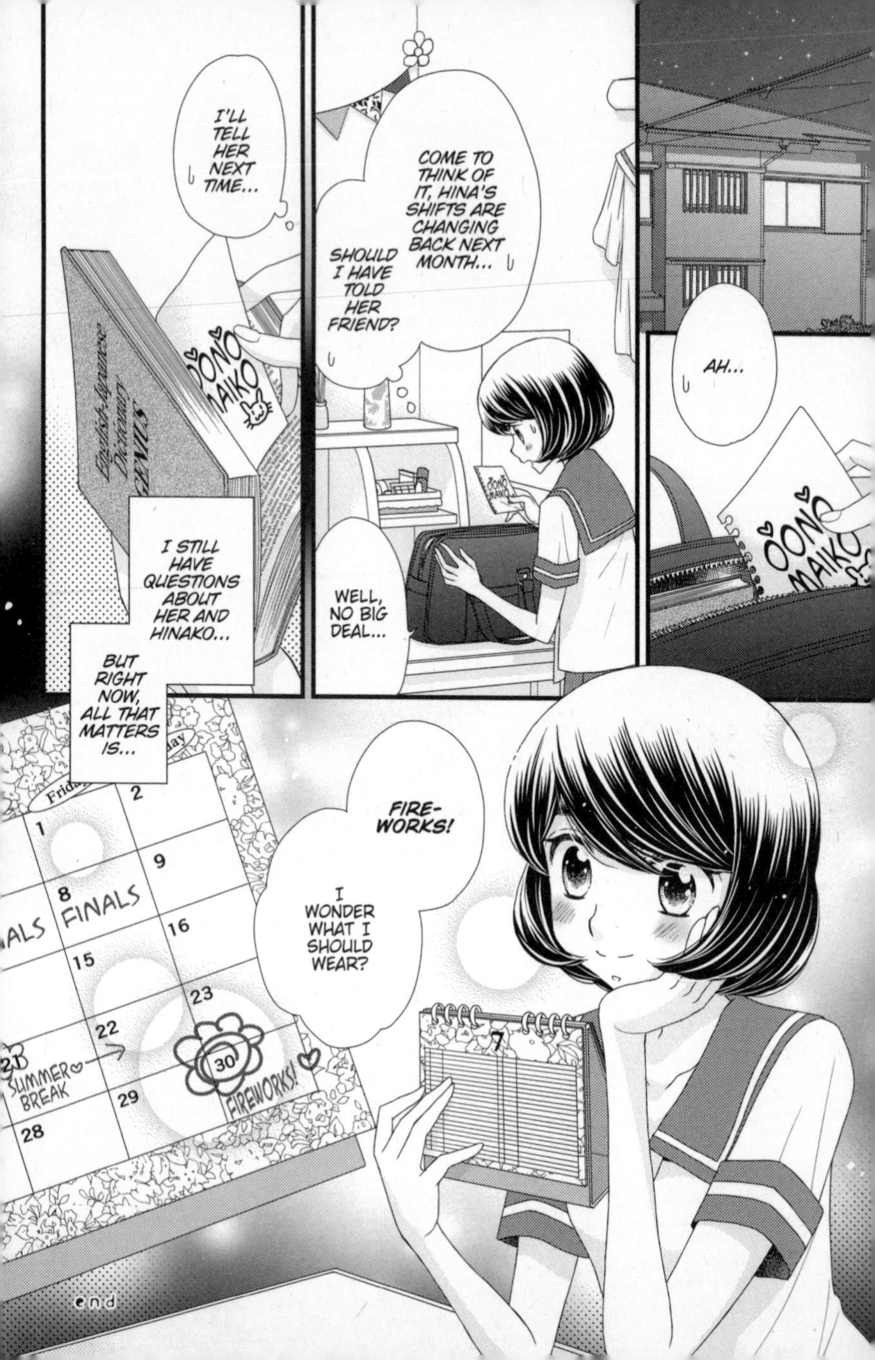
AH...
OONO MAIKO
COME TO THINK OF IT, HINA'S SHIFTS ARE CHANGING BACK NEXT MONTH...
SHOULD I HAVE TOLD HER FRIEND?
WELL, NO BIG DEAL...
I'LL TELL HER NEXT TIME...
OONO MAIKO
English-Japanese Dictionary GENIUS
I STILL HAVE QUESTIONS ABOUT HER AND HINAKO...
BUT RIGHT NOW, ALL THAT MATTERS IS...
FIRE-WORKS!
I WONDER WHAT I SHOULD WEAR?
FINALS
SUMMER BREAK
FIREWORKS!
end

Hana & Hina
AFTER ♥ SCHOOL

Hana & Hina
AFTER ♥ SCHOOL

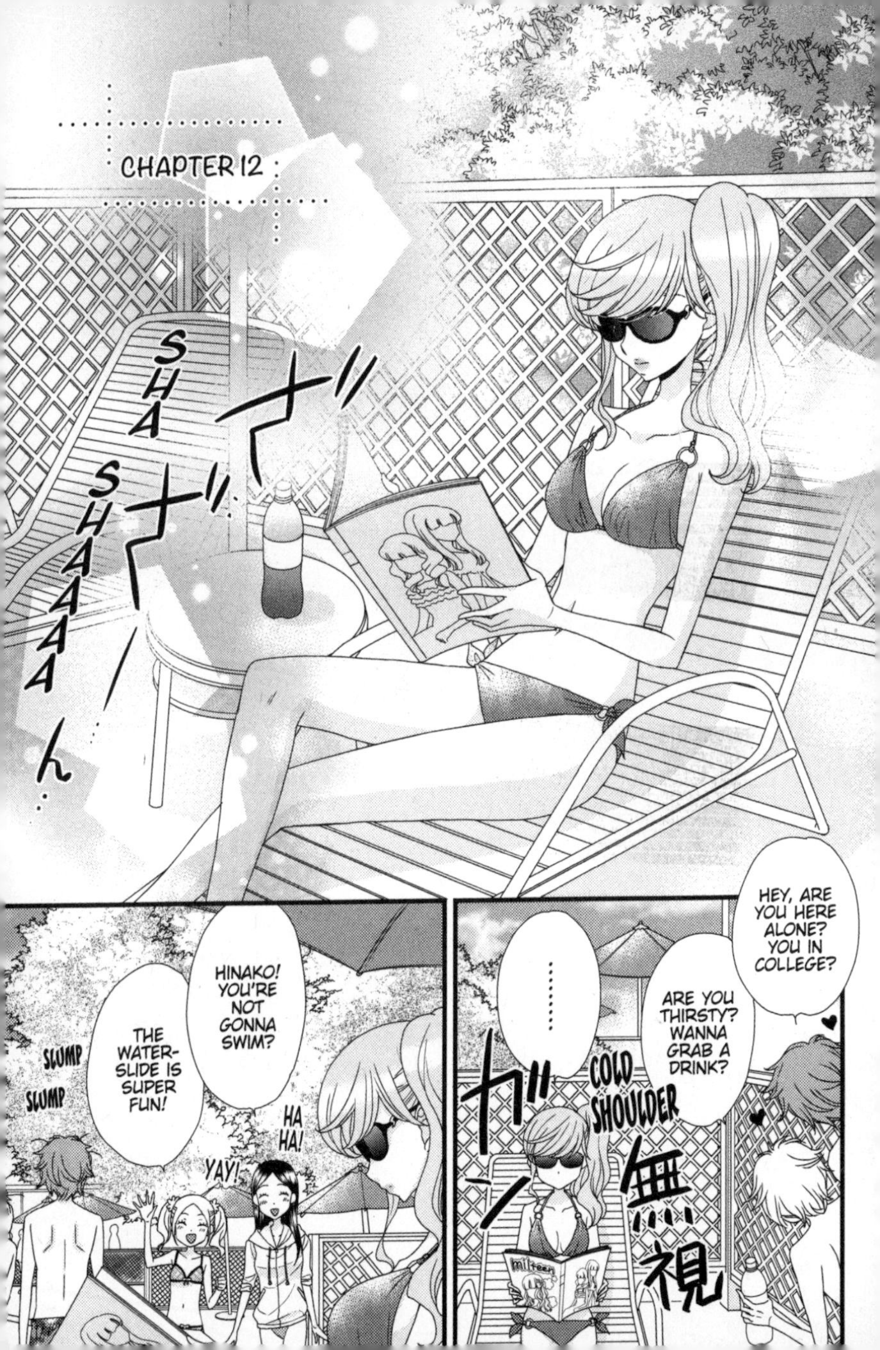
CHAPTER 12
SHA SHAAAAAAん...
HEY, ARE YOU HERE ALONE? YOU IN COLLEGE?
ARE YOU THIRSTY? WANNA GRAB A DRINK?
......
COLD SHOULDER
無視
HINAKO! YOU'RE NOT GONNA SWIM?
THE WATER-SLIDE IS SUPER FUN!
HA HA!
YAY!
SLUMP
SLUMP

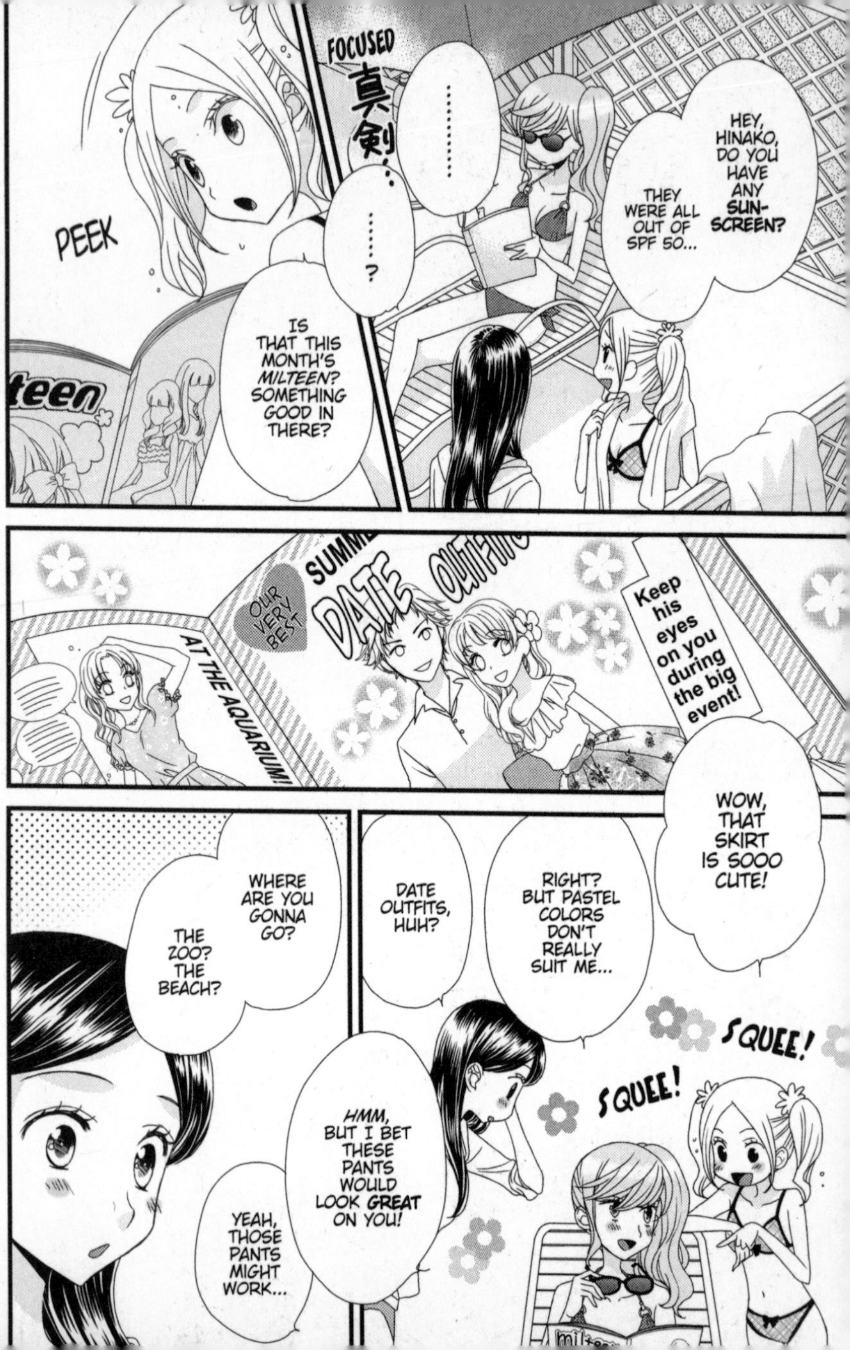

HEY, HINAKO, DO YOU HAVE ANY SUN-SCREEN?
THEY WERE ALL OUT OF SPF 50...
FOCUSED 真剣
......
......?
IS THAT THIS MONTH'S MILTEEN? SOMETHING GOOD IN THERE?
PEEK
teen
SUMM
DATE OUTFITS
OUR VERY BEST
Keep his eyes on you during the big event!
AT THE AQUARIUM!
WOW, THAT SKIRT IS SOOO CUTE!
RIGHT? BUT PASTEL COLORS DON'T REALLY SUIT ME...
DATE OUTFITS, HUH?
SQUEE!
SQUEE!
HMM, BUT I BET THESE PANTS WOULD LOOK GREAT ON YOU!
milteen
WHERE ARE YOU GONNA GO?
THE ZOO? THE BEACH?
YEAH, THOSE PANTS MIGHT WORK...

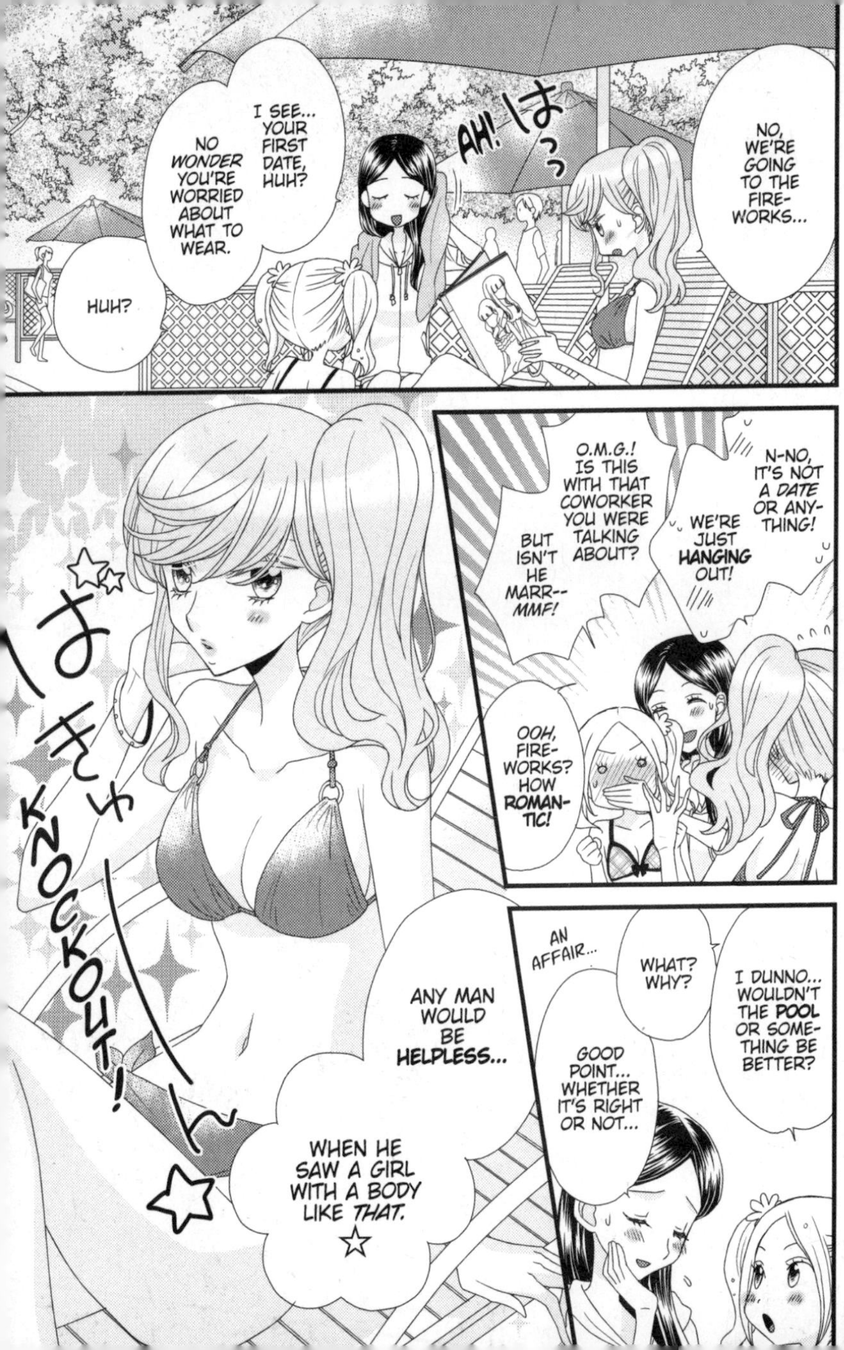
NO, WE'RE GOING TO THE FIRE-WORKS...
AH! はっ
I SEE... YOUR FIRST DATE, HUH?
NO *WONDER* YOU'RE WORRIED ABOUT WHAT TO WEAR.
HUH?
N-NO, IT'S NOT A *DATE* OR ANY-THING!
WE'RE JUST **HANGING** OUT!
O.M.G.! IS THIS WITH THAT COWORKER YOU WERE TALKING ABOUT?
BUT ISN'T HE MARR-- *MMF!*
OOH, FIRE-WORKS? HOW **ROMAN-TIC!**
I DUNNO... WOULDN'T THE **POOL** OR SOME-THING BE BETTER?
WHAT? WHY?
AN AFFAIR...
GOOD POINT... WHETHER IT'S RIGHT OR NOT...
ばきゅーん
KNOCKOUT!
ANY MAN WOULD BE **HELPLESS...**
WHEN HE SAW A GIRL WITH A BODY LIKE *THAT.* ☆

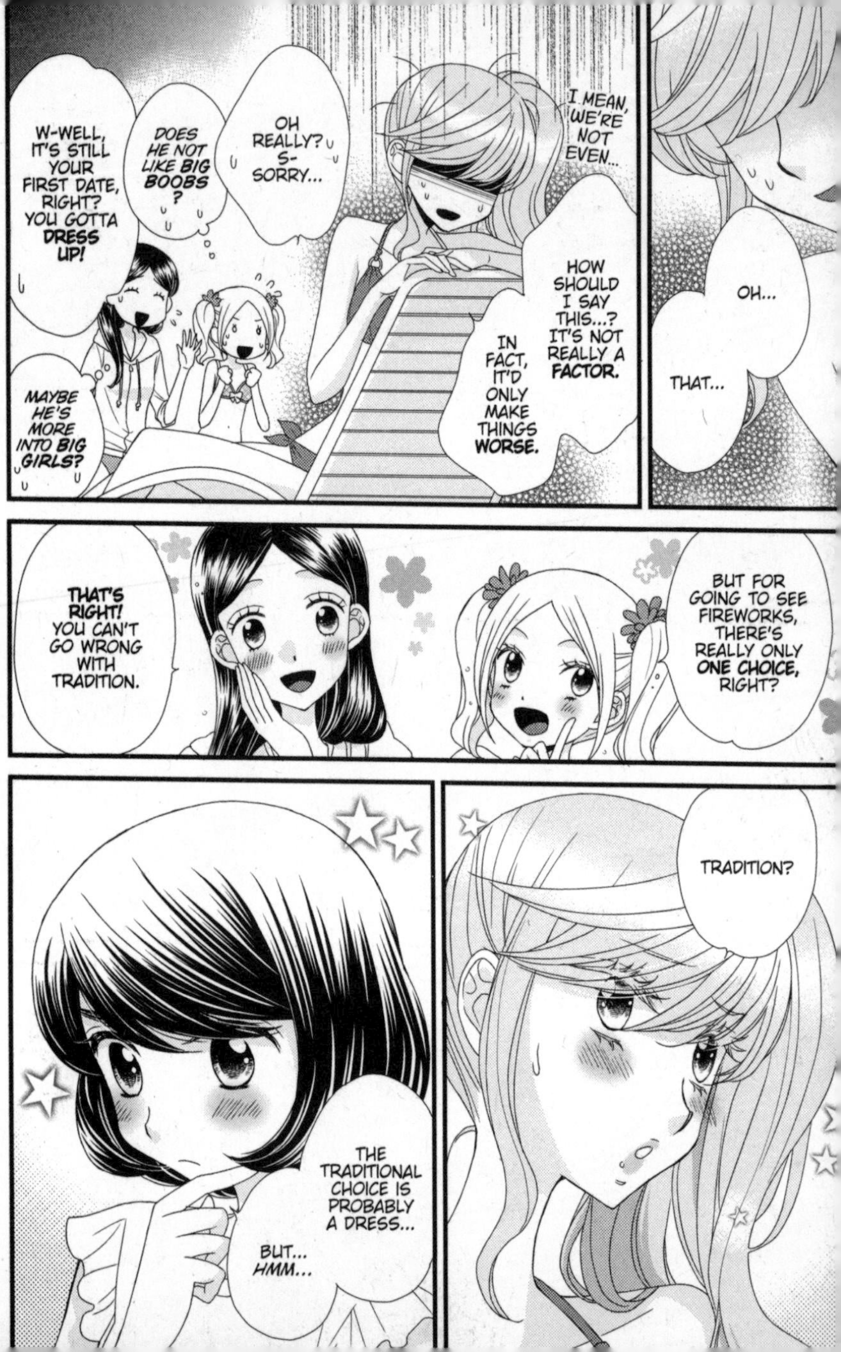
OH...
THAT...
I MEAN, WE'RE NOT EVEN...
HOW SHOULD I SAY THIS...? IT'S NOT REALLY A FACTOR.
IN FACT, IT'D ONLY MAKE THINGS WORSE.
OH REALLY? S-SORRY...
DOES HE NOT LIKE BIG BOOBS?
W-WELL, IT'S STILL YOUR FIRST DATE, RIGHT? YOU GOTTA DRESS UP!
MAYBE HE'S MORE INTO BIG GIRLS?
BUT FOR GOING TO SEE FIREWORKS, THERE'S REALLY ONLY ONE CHOICE, RIGHT?
THAT'S RIGHT! YOU CAN'T GO WRONG WITH TRADITION.
TRADITION?
THE TRADITIONAL CHOICE IS PROBABLY A DRESS...
BUT... HMM...

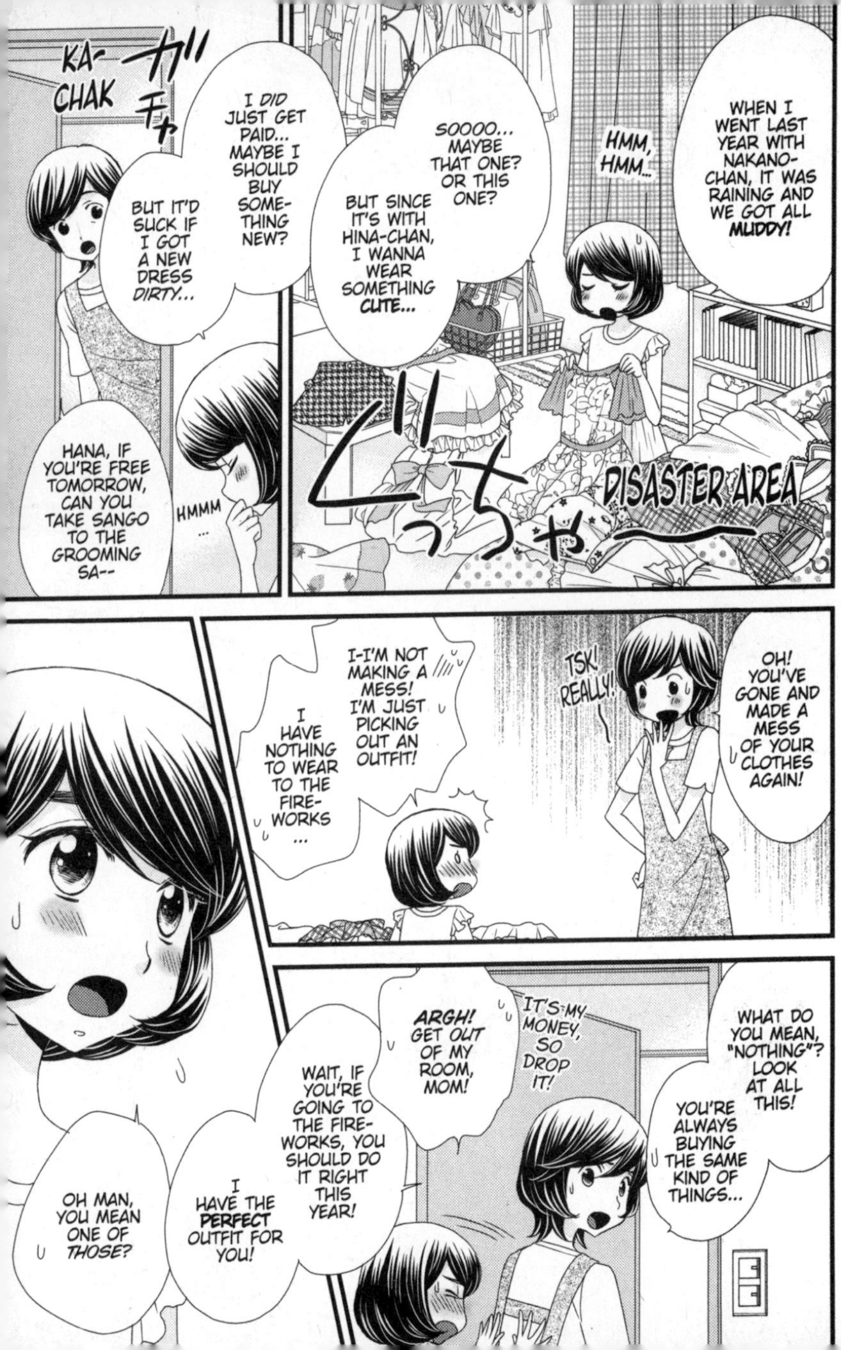
WHEN I WENT LAST YEAR WITH NAKANO-CHAN, IT WAS RAINING AND WE GOT ALL **MUDDY!**
HMM, HMM...
SOOOO... MAYBE THAT ONE? OR THIS ONE?
BUT SINCE IT'S WITH HINA-CHAN, I WANNA WEAR SOMETHING **CUTE...**
DISASTER AREA
ぐっちゃーー
I *DID* JUST GET PAID... MAYBE I SHOULD BUY SOME-THING NEW?
BUT IT'D SUCK IF I GOT A NEW DRESS *DIRTY...*
KA-CHAK
ガチャ
HMMM...
HANA, IF YOU'RE FREE TOMORROW, CAN YOU TAKE SANGO TO THE GROOMING SA--
OH! YOU'VE GONE AND MADE A MESS OF YOUR CLOTHES AGAIN!
TSK! REALLY!
I-I'M NOT MAKING A MESS! I'M JUST PICKING OUT AN OUTFIT!
I HAVE NOTHING TO WEAR TO THE FIRE-WORKS...
WHAT DO YOU MEAN, "NOTHING"? LOOK AT ALL THIS!
YOU'RE ALWAYS BUYING THE SAME KIND OF THINGS...
IT'S MY MONEY, SO DROP IT!
ARGH! GET OUT OF MY ROOM, MOM!
WAIT, IF YOU'RE GOING TO THE FIRE-WORKS, YOU SHOULD DO IT RIGHT THIS YEAR!
I HAVE THE **PERFECT** OUTFIT FOR YOU!
OH MAN, YOU MEAN ONE OF *THOSE?*

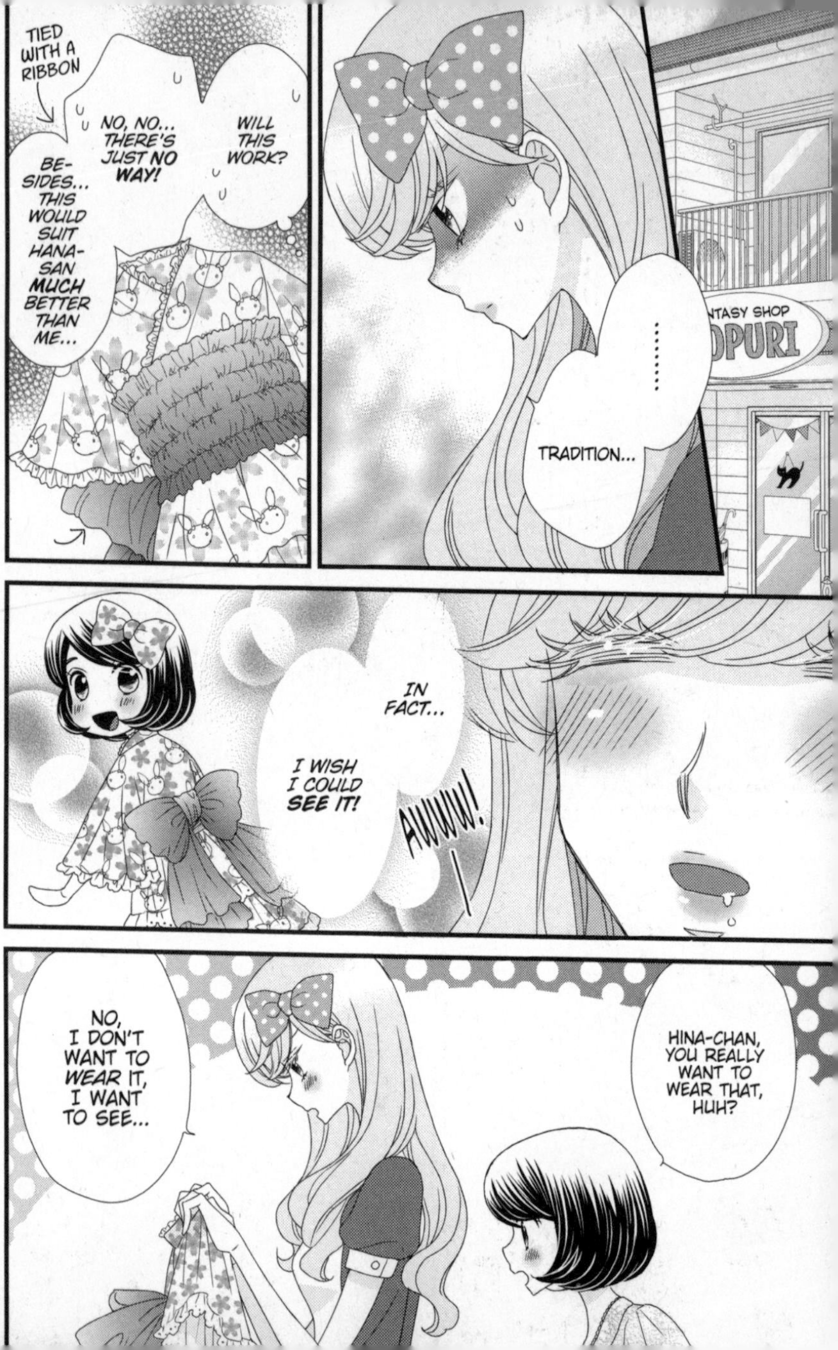
......
TRADITION...
NTASY SHOP
OPURI
WILL THIS WORK?
NO, NO... THERE'S JUST NO WAY!
BE-SIDES... THIS WOULD SUIT HANA-SAN MUCH BETTER THAN ME...
TIED WITH A RIBBON
IN FACT...
I WISH I COULD SEE IT!
AWWW!
HINA-CHAN, YOU REALLY WANT TO WEAR THAT, HUH?
NO, I DON'T WANT TO WEAR IT, I WANT TO SEE...

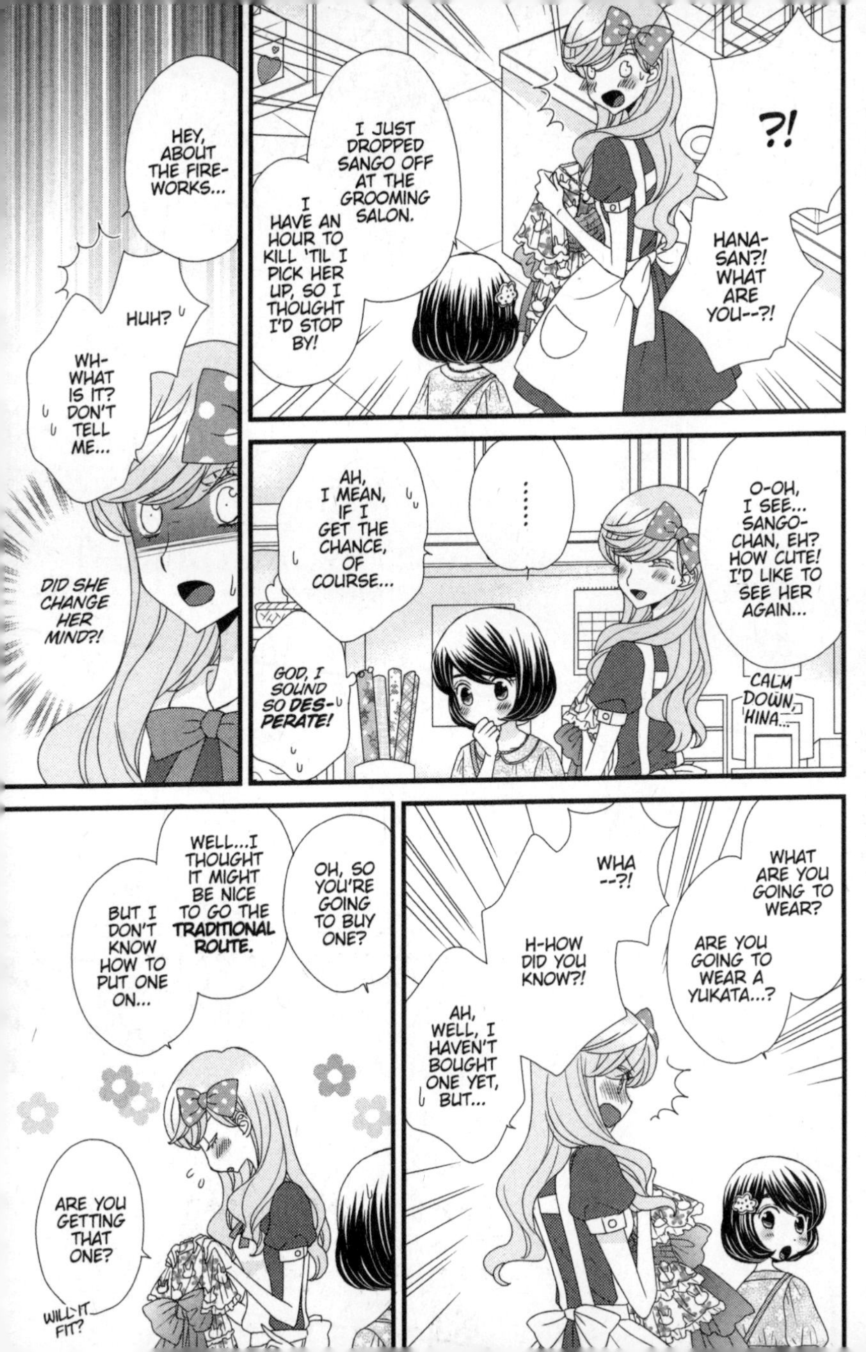
?!
HANA-SAN?! WHAT ARE YOU--?!
I JUST DROPPED SANGO OFF AT THE GROOMING SALON.
I HAVE AN HOUR TO KILL 'TIL I PICK HER UP, SO I THOUGHT I'D STOP BY!
O-OH, I SEE... SANGO-CHAN, EH? HOW CUTE! I'D LIKE TO SEE HER AGAIN...
CALM DOWN, HINA...
......
AH, I MEAN, IF I GET THE CHANCE, OF COURSE...
GOD, I SOUND SO DESPERATE!
HEY, ABOUT THE FIRE-WORKS...
HUH?
WH-WHAT IS IT? DON'T TELL ME...
DID SHE CHANGE HER MIND?!
WHAT ARE YOU GOING TO WEAR?
ARE YOU GOING TO WEAR A YUKATA...?
WHA--?!
H-HOW DID YOU KNOW?!
AH, WELL, I HAVEN'T BOUGHT ONE YET, BUT...
OH, SO YOU'RE GOING TO BUY ONE?
WELL...I THOUGHT IT MIGHT BE NICE TO GO THE TRADITIONAL ROUTE.
BUT I DON'T KNOW HOW TO PUT ONE ON...
ARE YOU GETTING THAT ONE?
WILL IT FIT?

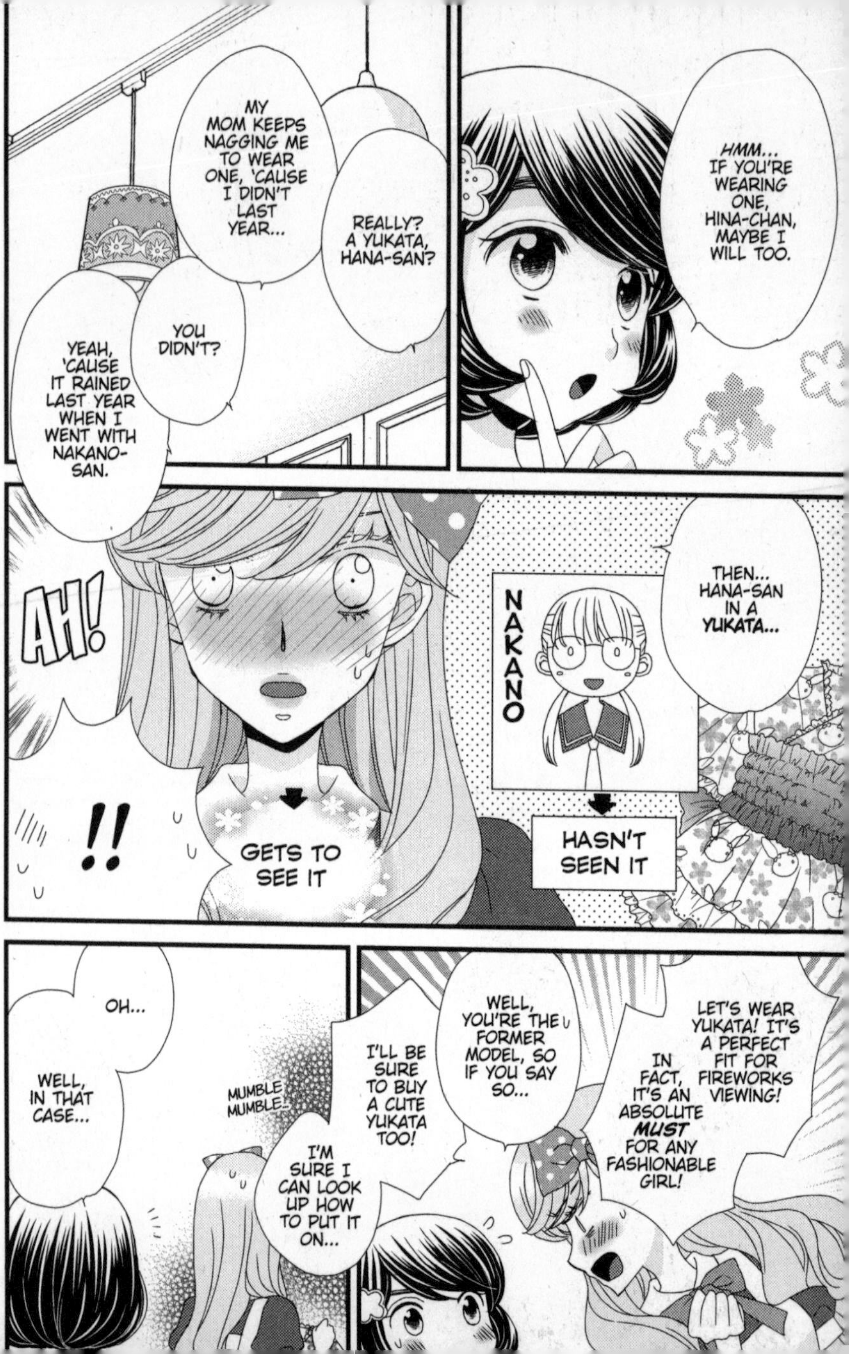
HMM... IF YOU'RE WEARING ONE, HINA-CHAN, MAYBE I WILL TOO.
REALLY? A YUKATA, HANA-SAN?
MY MOM KEEPS NAGGING ME TO WEAR ONE, 'CAUSE I DIDN'T LAST YEAR...
YOU DIDN'T?
YEAH, 'CAUSE IT RAINED LAST YEAR WHEN I WENT WITH NAKANO-SAN.
THEN... HANA-SAN IN A YUKATA...
NAKANO
HASN'T SEEN IT
GETS TO SEE IT
AH!
!!
LET'S WEAR YUKATA! IT'S A PERFECT FIT FOR FIREWORKS VIEWING!
IN FACT, IT'S AN ABSOLUTE MUST FOR ANY FASHIONABLE GIRL!
WELL, YOU'RE THE FORMER MODEL, SO IF YOU SAY SO...
I'LL BE SURE TO BUY A CUTE YUKATA TOO!
I'M SURE I CAN LOOK UP HOW TO PUT IT ON...
MUMBLE MUMBLE
OH...
WELL, IN THAT CASE...

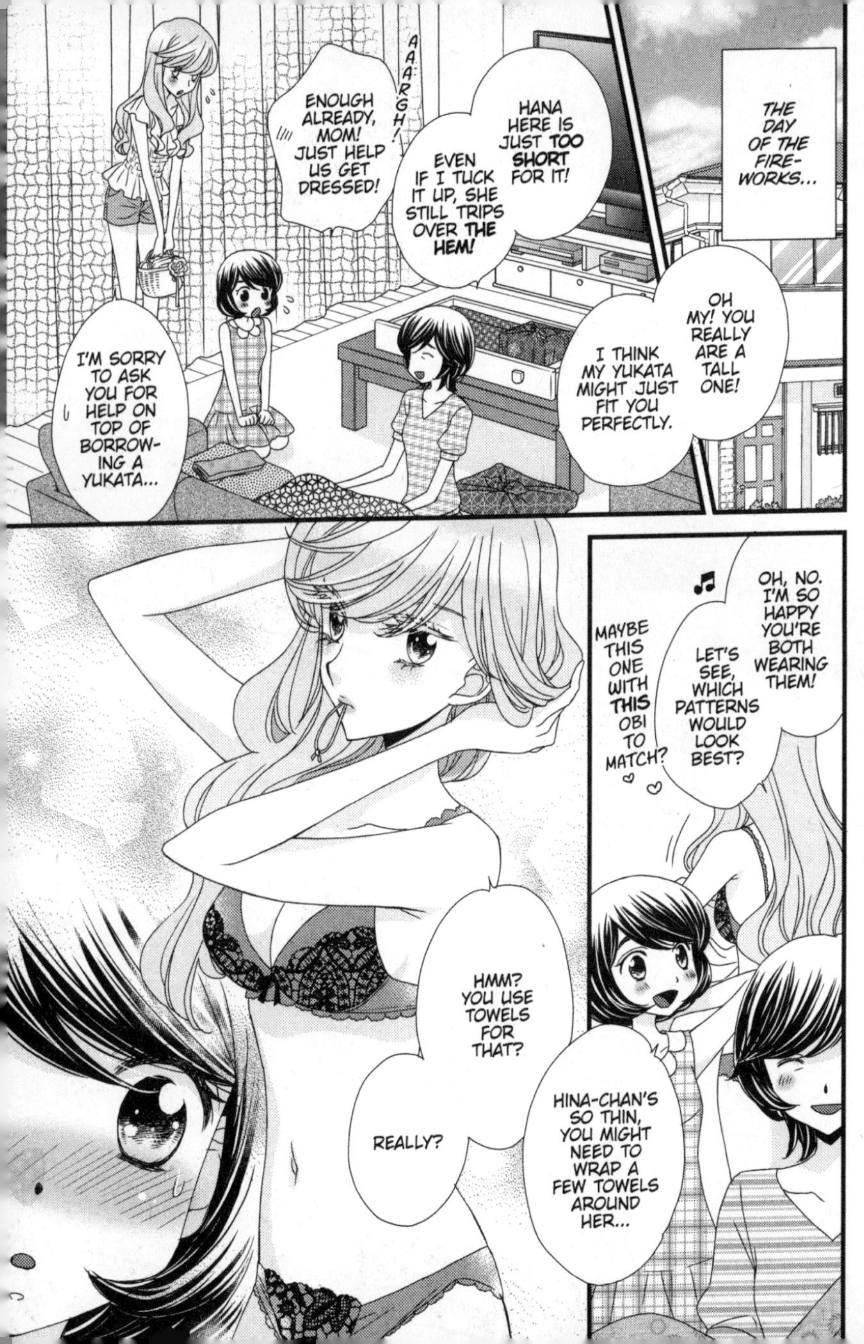
THE DAY OF THE FIRE-WORKS...
OH MY! YOU REALLY ARE A TALL ONE!
I THINK MY YUKATA MIGHT JUST FIT YOU PERFECTLY.
HANA HERE IS JUST TOO SHORT FOR IT!
EVEN IF I TUCK IT UP, SHE STILL TRIPS OVER THE HEM!
AAAARGH!
ENOUGH ALREADY, MOM! JUST HELP US GET DRESSED!
I'M SORRY TO ASK YOU FOR HELP ON TOP OF BORROWING A YUKATA...
OH, NO. I'M SO HAPPY YOU'RE BOTH WEARING THEM!
LET'S SEE, WHICH PATTERNS WOULD LOOK BEST?
MAYBE THIS ONE WITH THIS OBI TO MATCH?
HINA-CHAN'S SO THIN, YOU MIGHT NEED TO WRAP A FEW TOWELS AROUND HER...
HMM? YOU USE TOWELS FOR THAT?
REALLY?

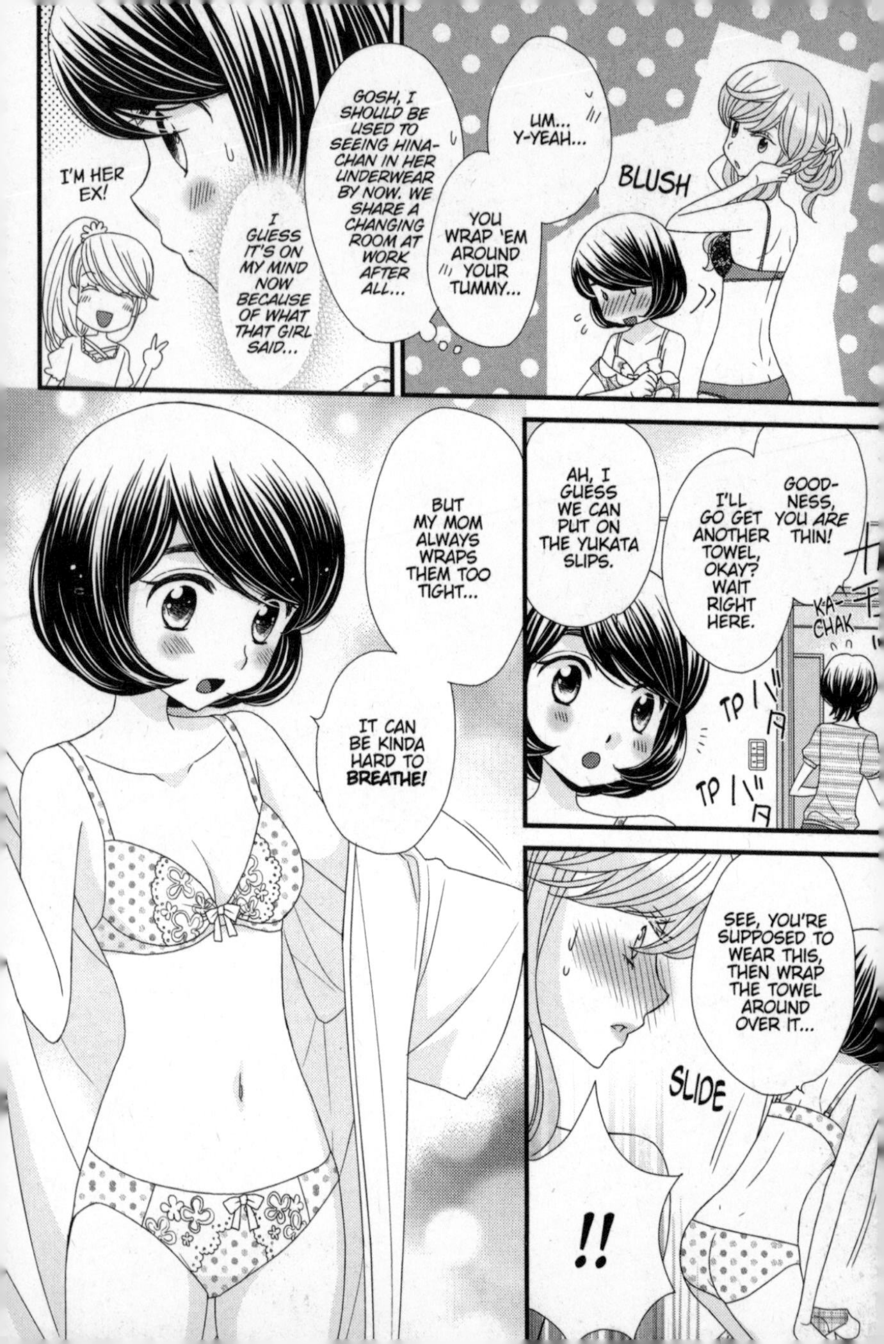
UM... Y-YEAH...
BLUSH
YOU WRAP 'EM AROUND YOUR TUMMY...
GOSH, I SHOULD BE USED TO SEEING HINA-CHAN IN HER UNDERWEAR BY NOW. WE SHARE A CHANGING ROOM AT WORK AFTER ALL...
I GUESS IT'S ON MY MIND NOW BECAUSE OF WHAT THAT GIRL SAID...
I'M HER EX!
GOODNESS, YOU ARE THIN!
I'LL GO GET ANOTHER TOWEL, OKAY? WAIT RIGHT HERE.
KA-CHAK
AH, I GUESS WE CAN PUT ON THE YUKATA SLIPS.
TP
TP
SEE, YOU'RE SUPPOSED TO WEAR THIS, THEN WRAP THE TOWEL AROUND OVER IT...
SLIDE
!!
BUT MY MOM ALWAYS WRAPS THEM TOO TIGHT...
IT CAN BE KINDA HARD TO BREATHE!

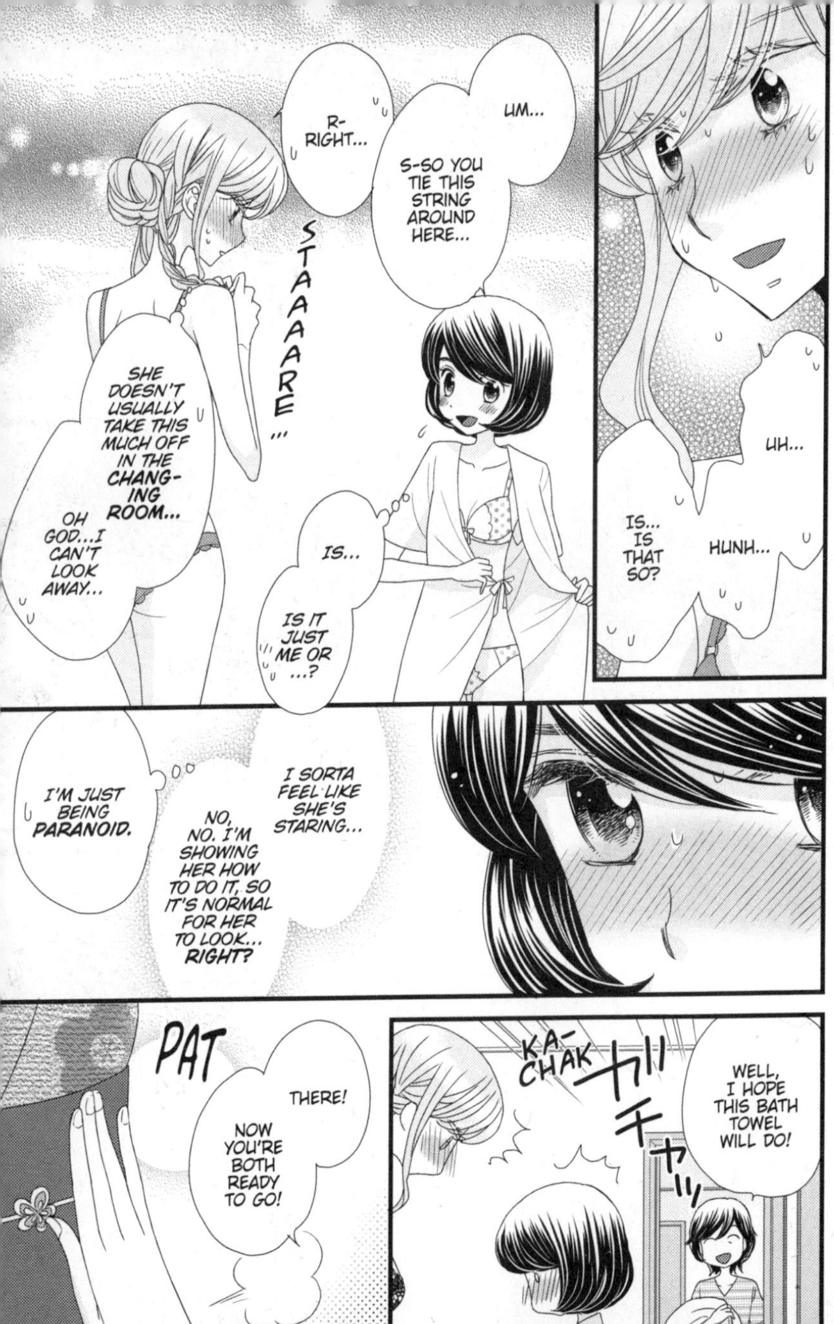
UH...
HUNH...
IS... IS THAT SO?
UM...
S-SO YOU TIE THIS STRING AROUND HERE...
R-RIGHT...
STAAAAARE...
SHE DOESN'T USUALLY TAKE THIS MUCH OFF IN THE CHANGING ROOM...
IS...
IS IT JUST ME OR ...?
OH GOD...I CAN'T LOOK AWAY...
I SORTA FEEL LIKE SHE'S STARING...
NO, NO. I'M SHOWING HER HOW TO DO IT, SO IT'S NORMAL FOR HER TO LOOK... RIGHT?
I'M JUST BEING PARANOID.
WELL, I HOPE THIS BATH TOWEL WILL DO!
KA-CHAK
カチャッ
PAT
THERE!
NOW YOU'RE BOTH READY TO GO!

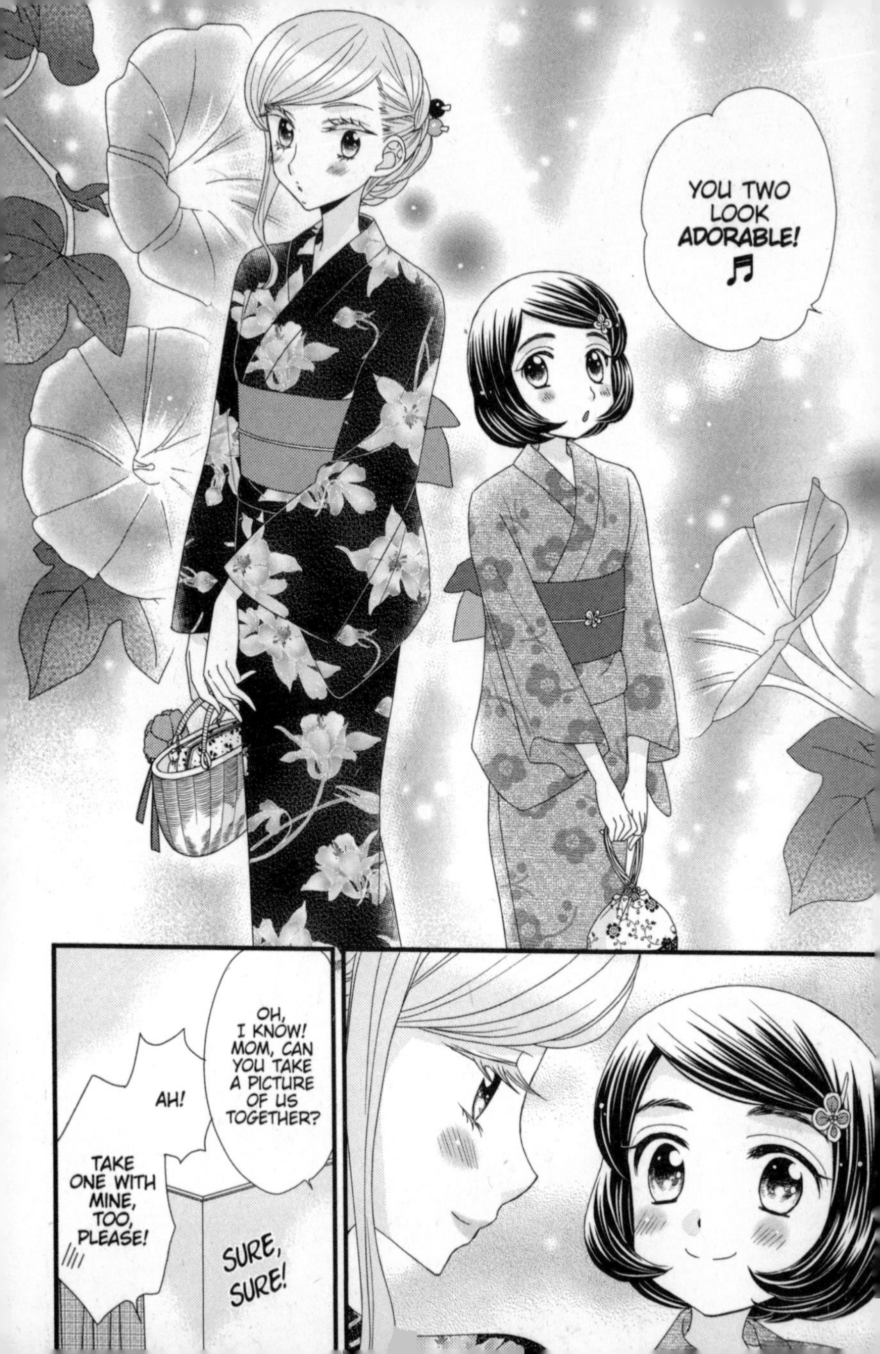
YOU TWO LOOK ADORABLE! ♬
OH, I KNOW! MOM, CAN YOU TAKE A PICTURE OF US TOGETHER?
AH!
TAKE ONE WITH MINE, TOO, PLEASE!
SURE, SURE!

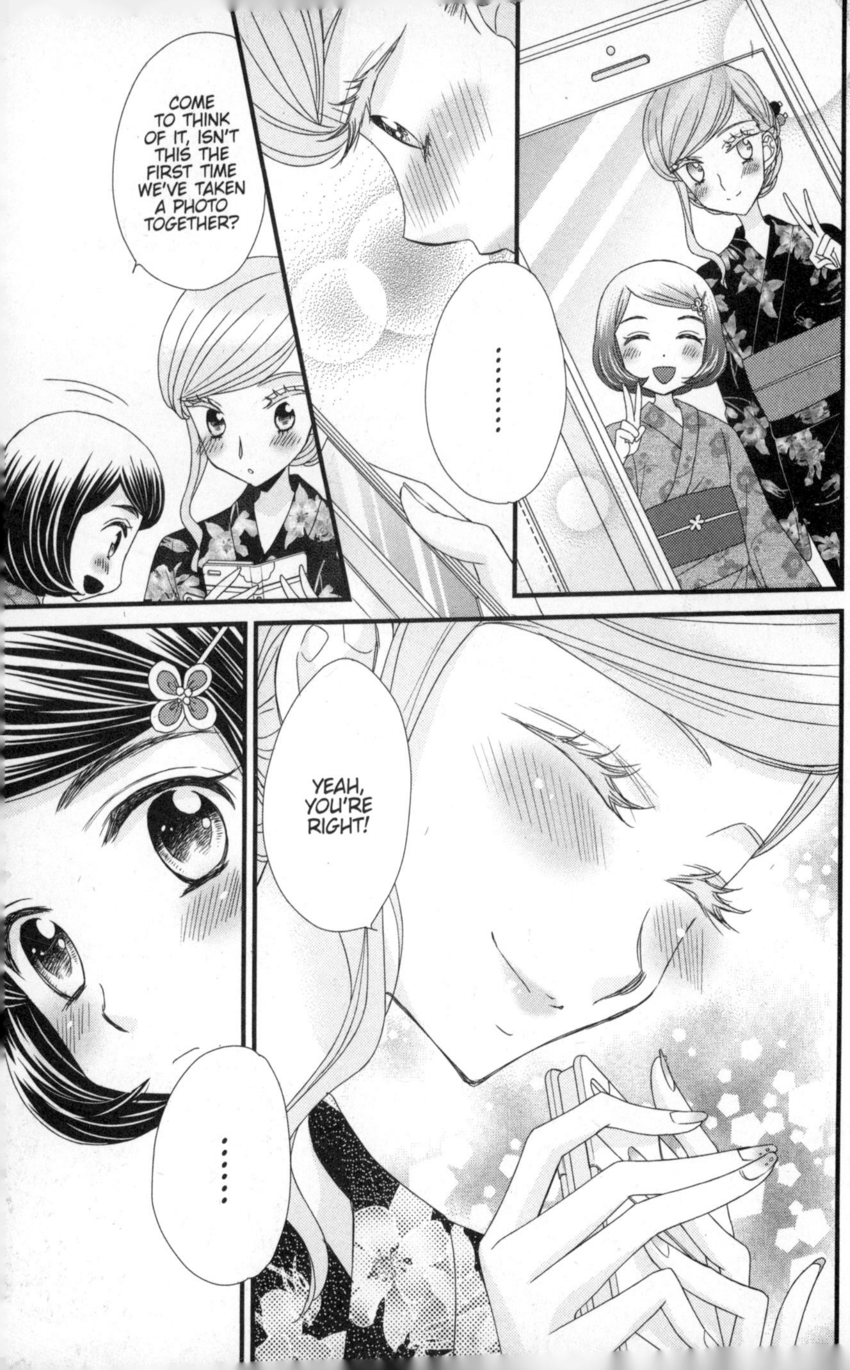
......
COME TO THINK OF IT, ISN'T THIS THE FIRST TIME WE'VE TAKEN A PHOTO TOGETHER?
YEAH, YOU'RE RIGHT!
......

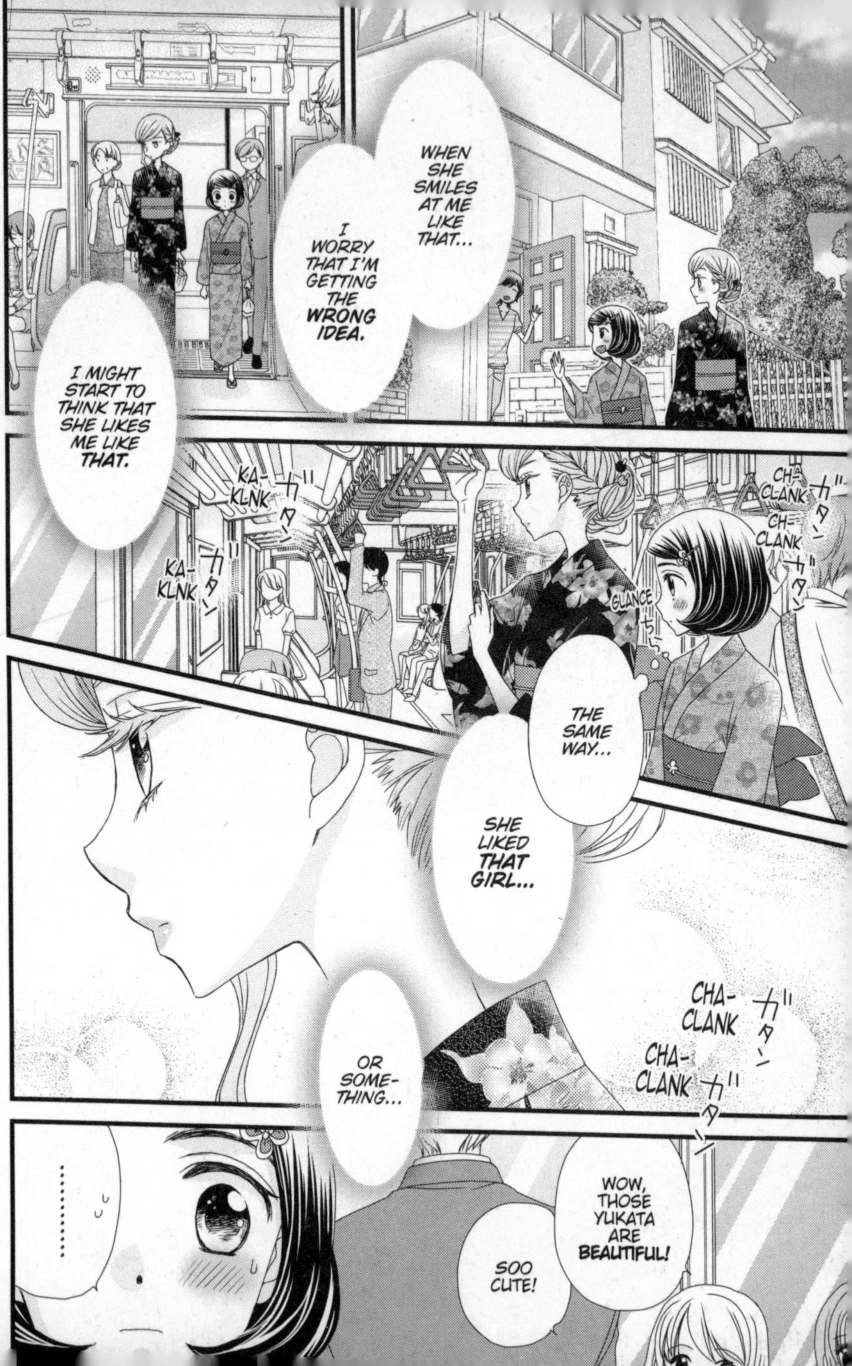
WHEN SHE SMILES AT ME LIKE THAT...
I WORRY THAT I'M GETTING THE WRONG IDEA.
I MIGHT START TO THINK THAT SHE LIKES ME LIKE THAT.
CH-CLANK ガタン
CH-CLANK ガタン
KA-KLNK ガタン
KA-KLNK ガタン
GLANCE ちら
THE SAME WAY...
SHE LIKED THAT GIRL...
OR SOME-THING...
CHA-CLANK ガタン
CHA-CLANK ガタン
WOW, THOSE YUKATA ARE BEAUTIFUL!
SOO CUTE!
......

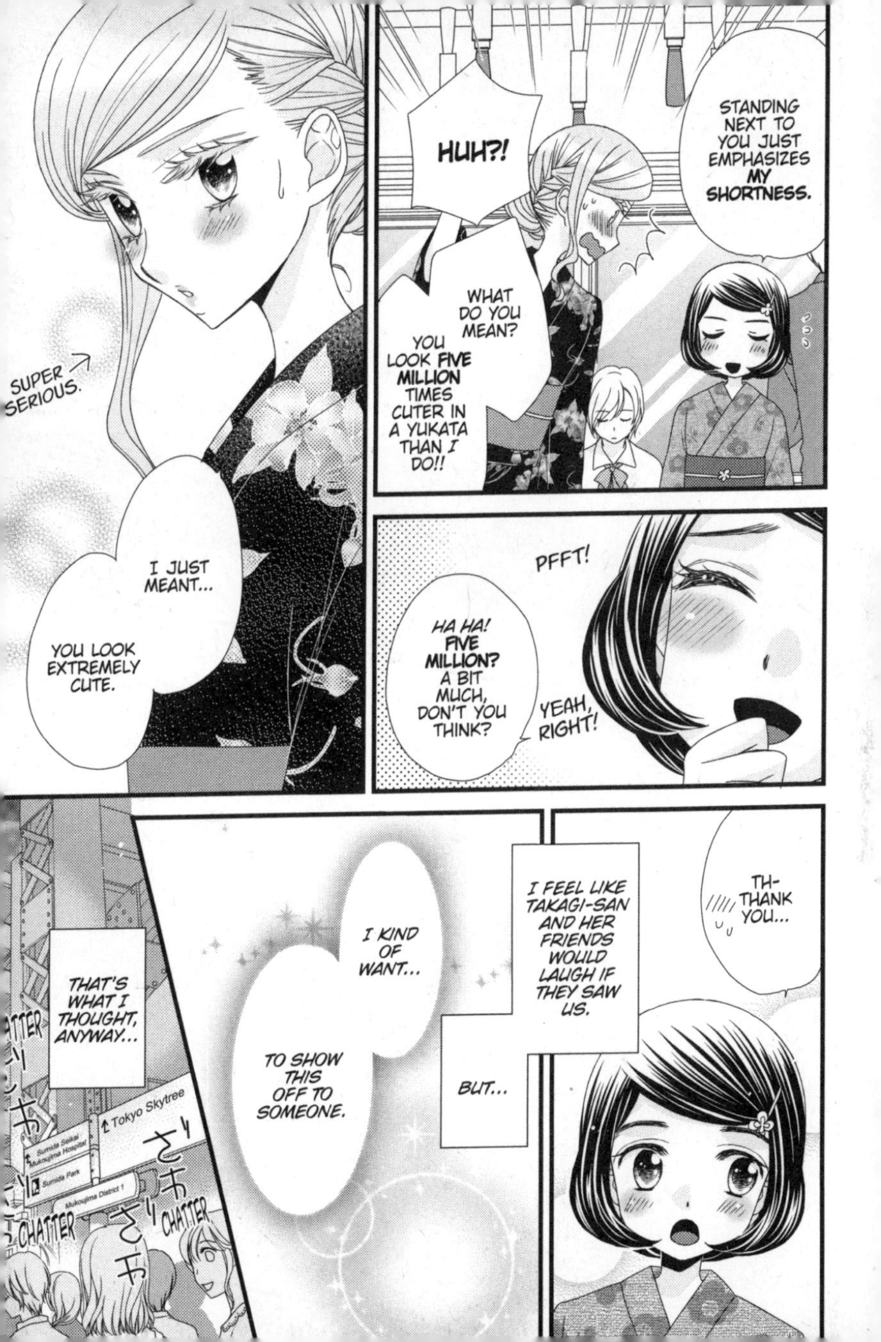
STANDING NEXT TO YOU JUST EMPHASIZES MY SHORTNESS.
HUH?!
WHAT DO YOU MEAN?
YOU LOOK FIVE MILLION TIMES CUTER IN A YUKATA THAN I DO!!
PFFT!
YEAH, RIGHT!
HA HA! FIVE MILLION? A BIT MUCH, DON'T YOU THINK?
SUPER SERIOUS.
I JUST MEANT...
YOU LOOK EXTREMELY CUTE.
TH-THANK YOU...
I FEEL LIKE TAKAGI-SAN AND HER FRIENDS WOULD LAUGH IF THEY SAW US.
BUT...
I KIND OF WANT...
TO SHOW THIS OFF TO SOMEONE.
THAT'S WHAT I THOUGHT, ANYWAY...
Tokyo Skytree
Sumida Seikei Mukoujima Hospital
Sumida Park
Mukoujima District 1
CHATTER
CHATTER
CHATTER

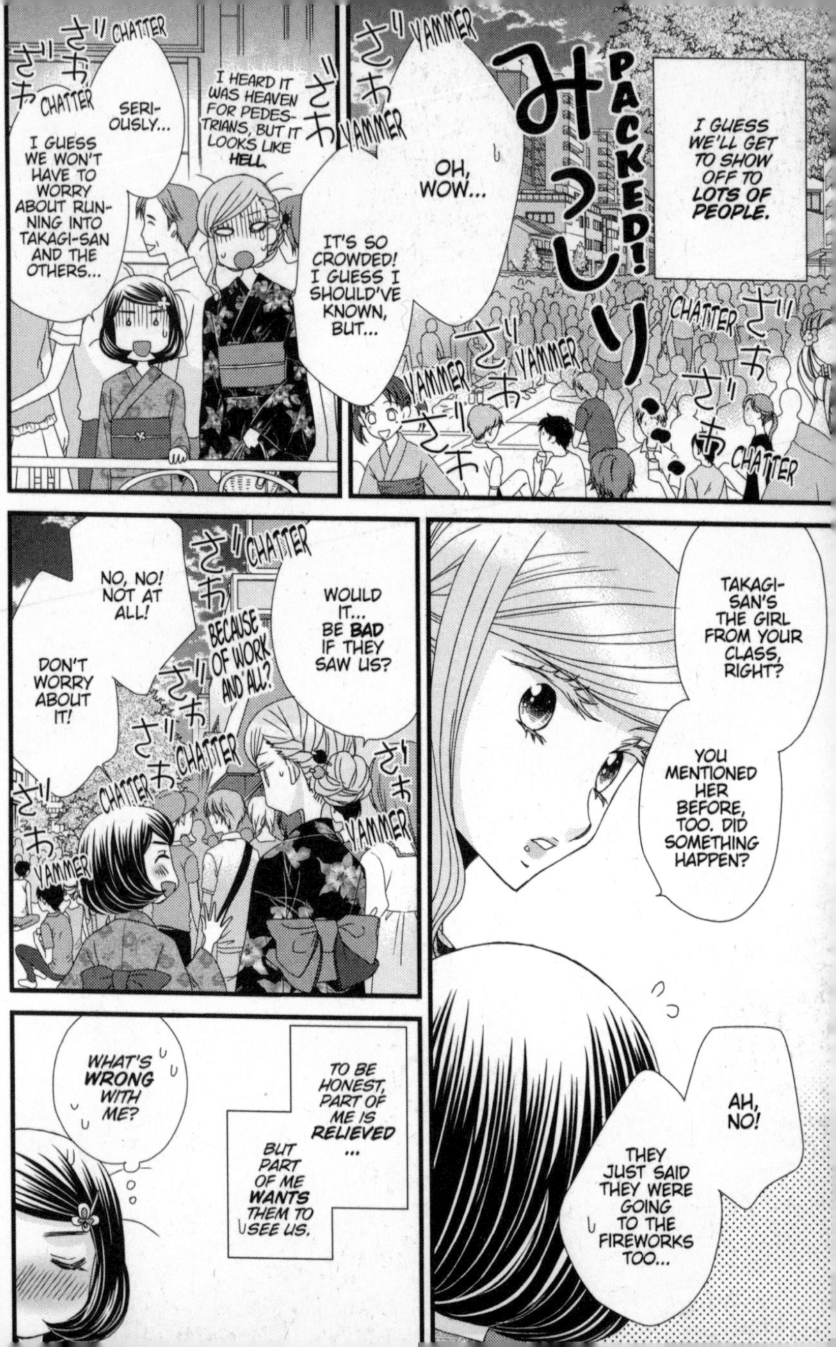
I GUESS WE'LL GET TO SHOW OFF TO **LOTS OF PEOPLE.**
みっしり
PACKED!
ざわ CHATTER
ざわ CHATTER
ざわ YAMMER
ざわ YAMMER
ざわ YAMMER
OH, WOW...
IT'S SO CROWDED! I GUESS I SHOULD'VE KNOWN, BUT...
ざわ CHATTER
ざわ CHATTER
I HEARD IT WAS HEAVEN FOR PEDESTRIANS, BUT IT LOOKS LIKE **HELL.**
SERIOUSLY...
I GUESS WE WON'T HAVE TO WORRY ABOUT RUNNING INTO TAKAGI-SAN AND THE OTHERS...
TAKAGI-SAN'S THE GIRL FROM YOUR CLASS, RIGHT?
YOU MENTIONED HER BEFORE, TOO. DID SOMETHING HAPPEN?
AH, NO!
THEY JUST SAID THEY WERE GOING TO THE FIREWORKS TOO...
ざわ YAMMER
WOULD IT... BE **BAD** IF THEY SAW US?
BECAUSE OF WORK AND ALL?
ざわ CHATTER
ざわ CHATTER
ざわ CHATTER
ざわ YAMMER
NO, NO! NOT AT ALL!
DON'T WORRY ABOUT IT!
TO BE HONEST, PART OF ME IS **RELIEVED**...
BUT PART OF ME **WANTS** THEM TO SEE US.
WHAT'S **WRONG** *WITH ME?*

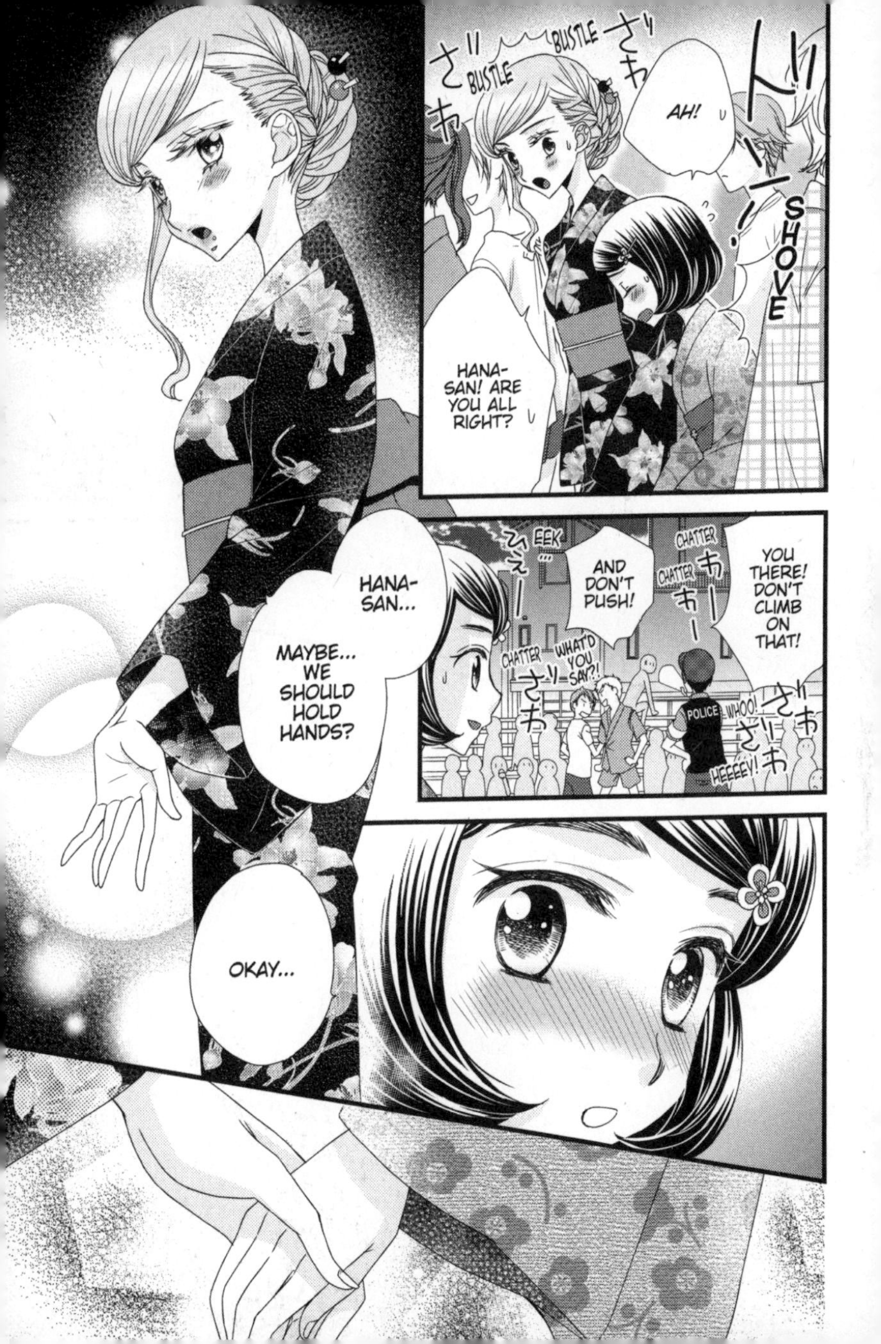
SHOVE
AH!
BUSTLE
BUSTLE
HANA-SAN! ARE YOU ALL RIGHT?
YOU THERE! DON'T CLIMB ON THAT!
CHATTER
CHATTER
AND DON'T PUSH!
EEK...
WHAT'D YOU SAY?!
CHATTER
POLICE
WHOO!
HEEEEY!
HANA-SAN...
MAYBE... WE SHOULD HOLD HANDS?
OKAY...

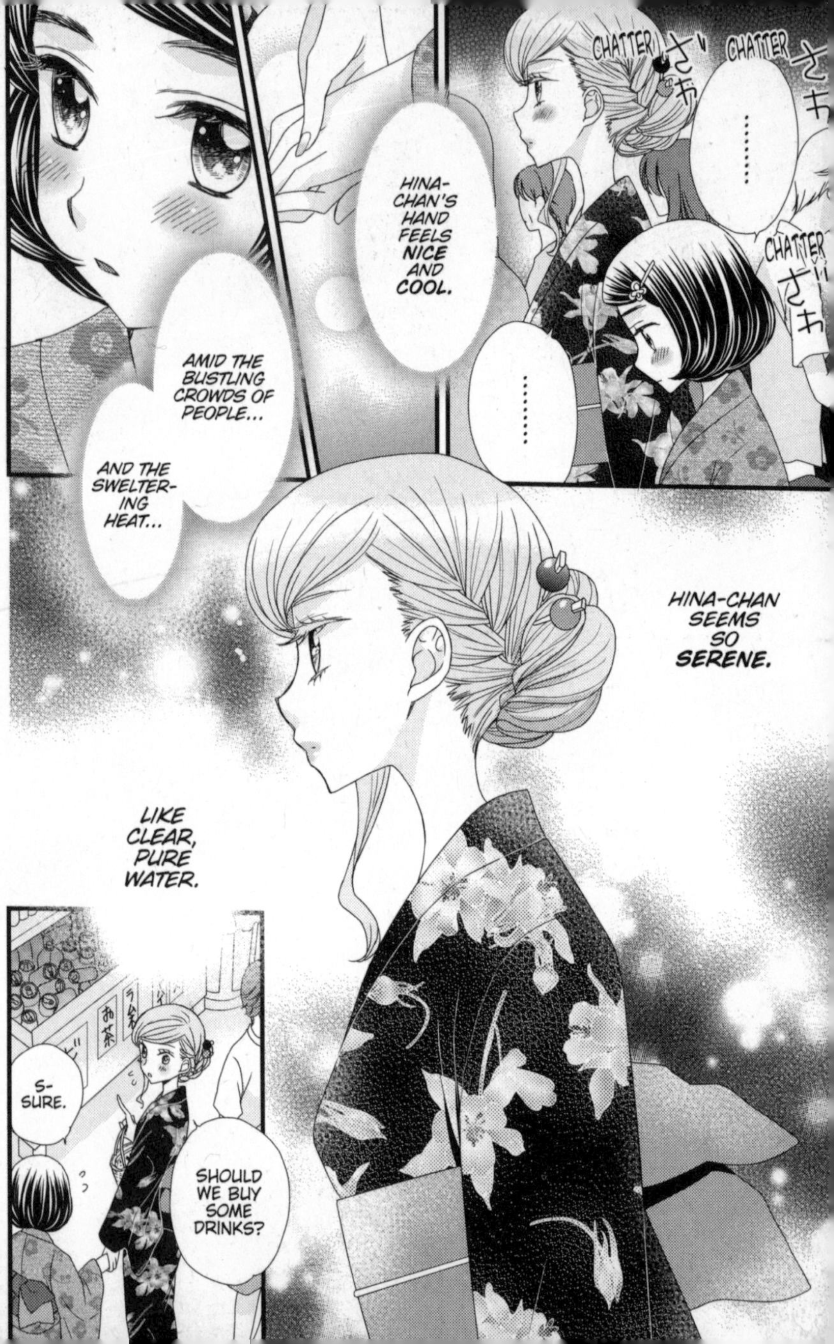

CHATTER
CHATTER
......
CHATTER
......
HINA-CHAN'S HAND FEELS NICE AND COOL.
AMID THE BUSTLING CROWDS OF PEOPLE...
AND THE SWELTERING HEAT...
HINA-CHAN SEEMS SO SERENE.
LIKE CLEAR, PURE WATER.
お茶
SHOULD WE BUY SOME DRINKS?
S-SURE.

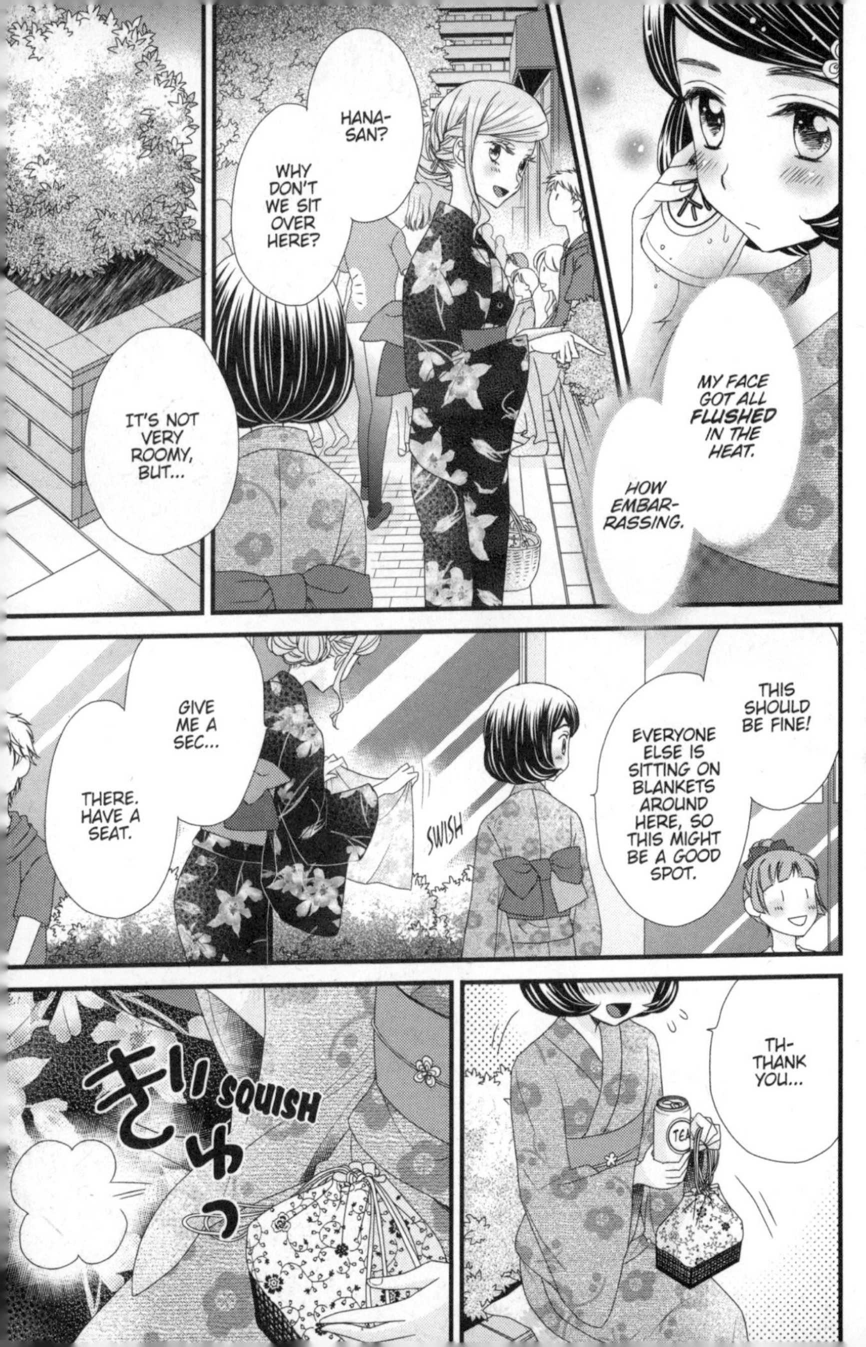
MY FACE GOT ALL **FLUSHED** IN THE HEAT.
HOW EMBAR-RASSING.
HANA-SAN?
WHY DON'T WE SIT OVER HERE?
IT'S NOT VERY ROOMY, BUT...
THIS SHOULD BE FINE!
EVERYONE ELSE IS SITTING ON BLANKETS AROUND HERE, SO THIS MIGHT BE A GOOD SPOT.
SWISH
GIVE ME A SEC...
THERE. HAVE A SEAT.
TH-THANK YOU...
きゅっ
SQUISH

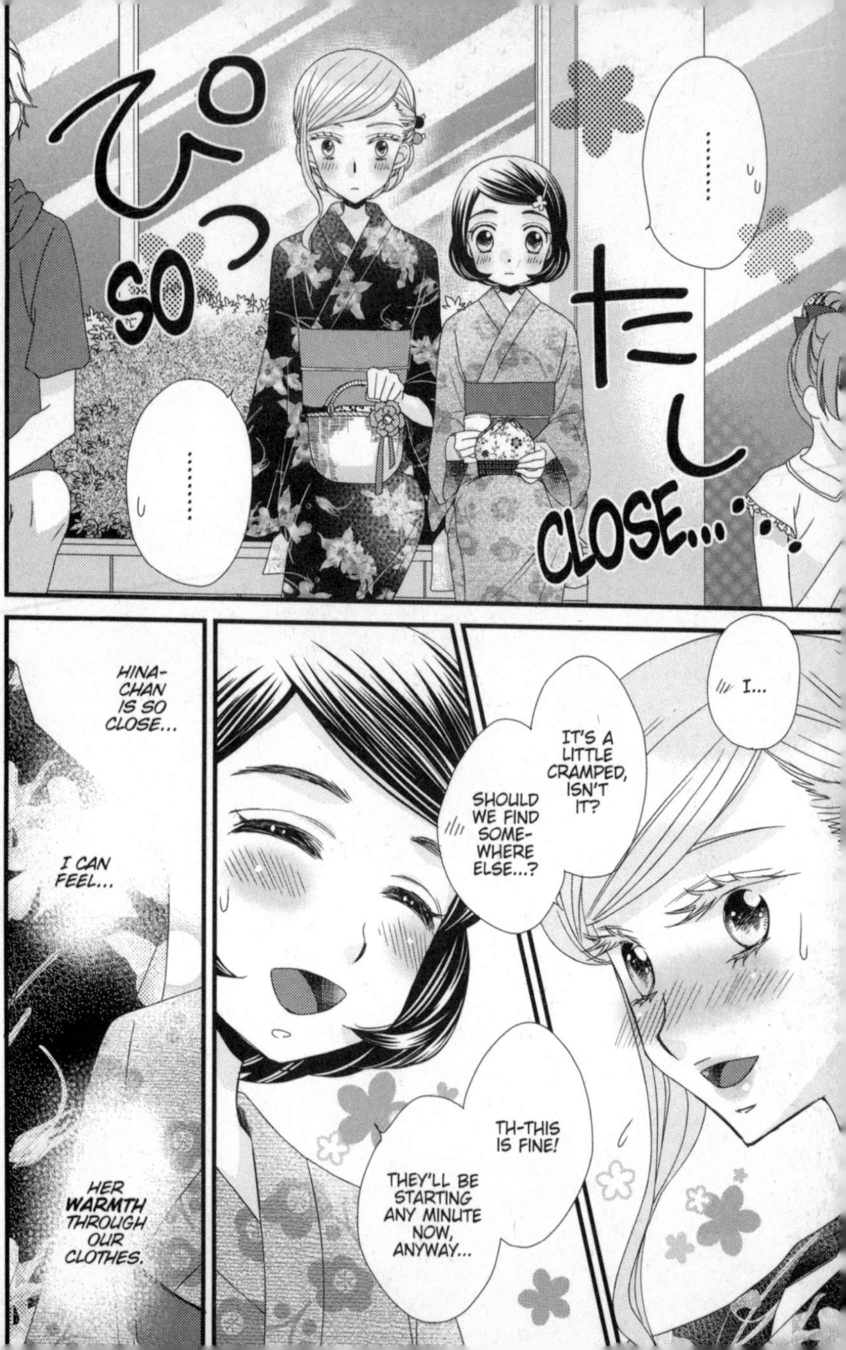
......
たし
CLOSE...
ぴっ
SO
......
I...
IT'S A LITTLE CRAMPED, ISN'T IT?
SHOULD WE FIND SOMEWHERE ELSE...?
TH-THIS IS FINE!
THEY'LL BE STARTING ANY MINUTE NOW, ANYWAY...
HINA-CHAN IS SO CLOSE...
I CAN FEEL...
HER WARMTH THROUGH OUR CLOTHES.

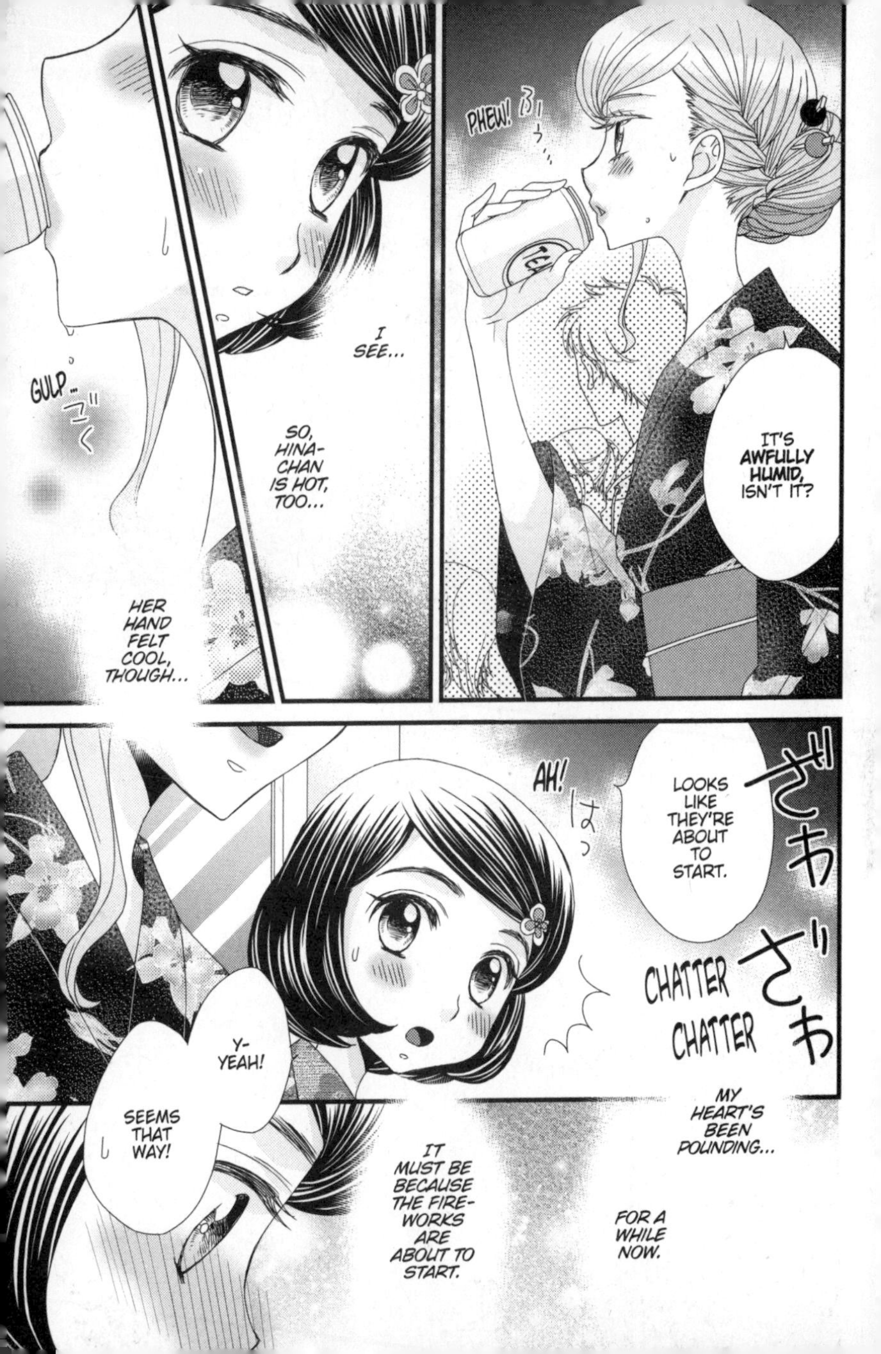
PHEW! ふぅ…
IT'S AWFULLY HUMID, ISN'T IT?
I SEE...
SO, HINA-CHAN IS HOT, TOO...
HER HAND FELT COOL, THOUGH...
GULP... ごく
CHATTER CHATTER
LOOKS LIKE THEY'RE ABOUT TO START.
AH! はっ
Y-YEAH!
SEEMS THAT WAY!
MY HEART'S BEEN POUNDING...
FOR A WHILE NOW.
IT MUST BE BECAUSE THE FIRE-WORKS ARE ABOUT TO START.

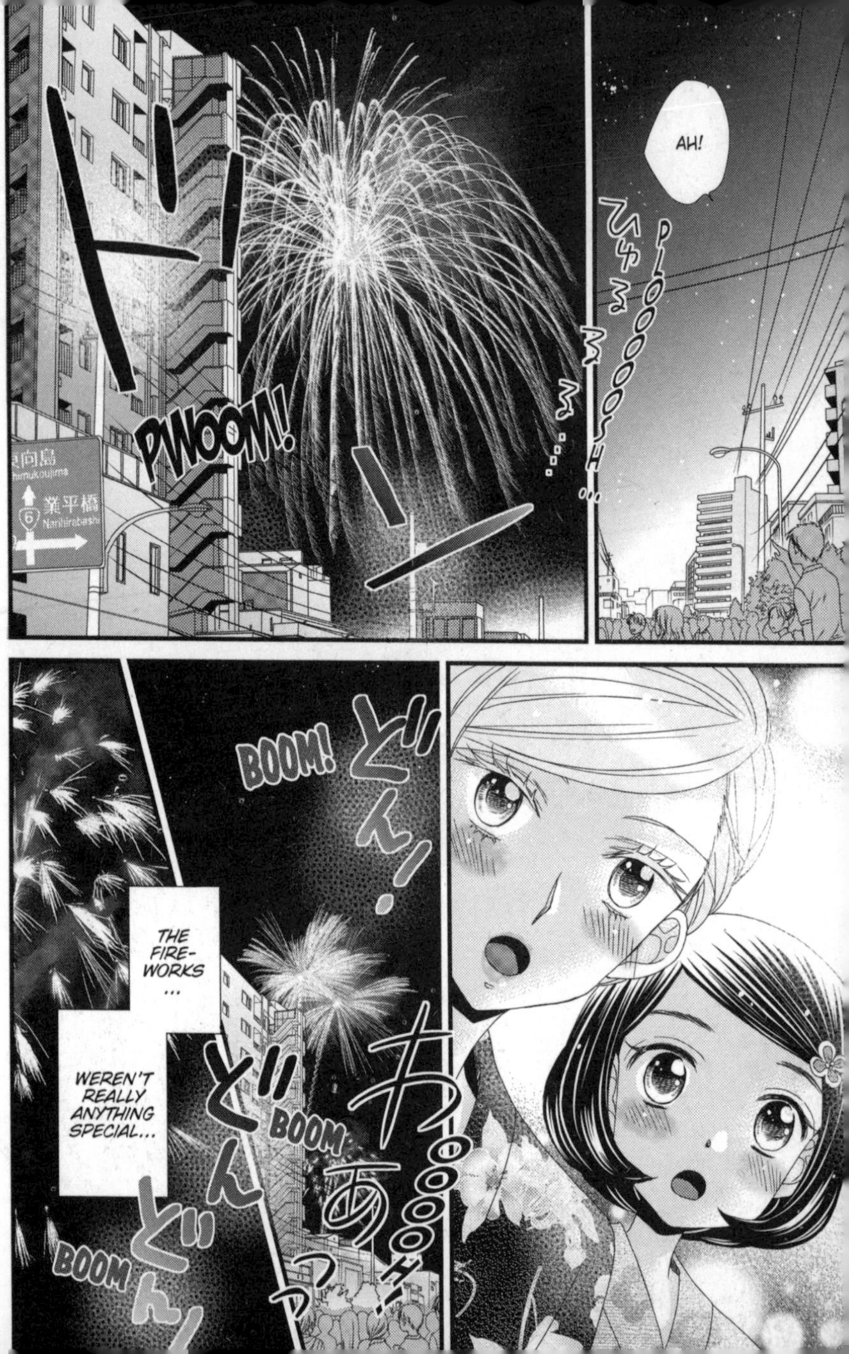
AH!
PLOOOOOOSH...
PWOOM!
BOOM!
THE FIRE-WORKS...
WEREN'T REALLY ANYTHING SPECIAL...
BOOM
BOOM

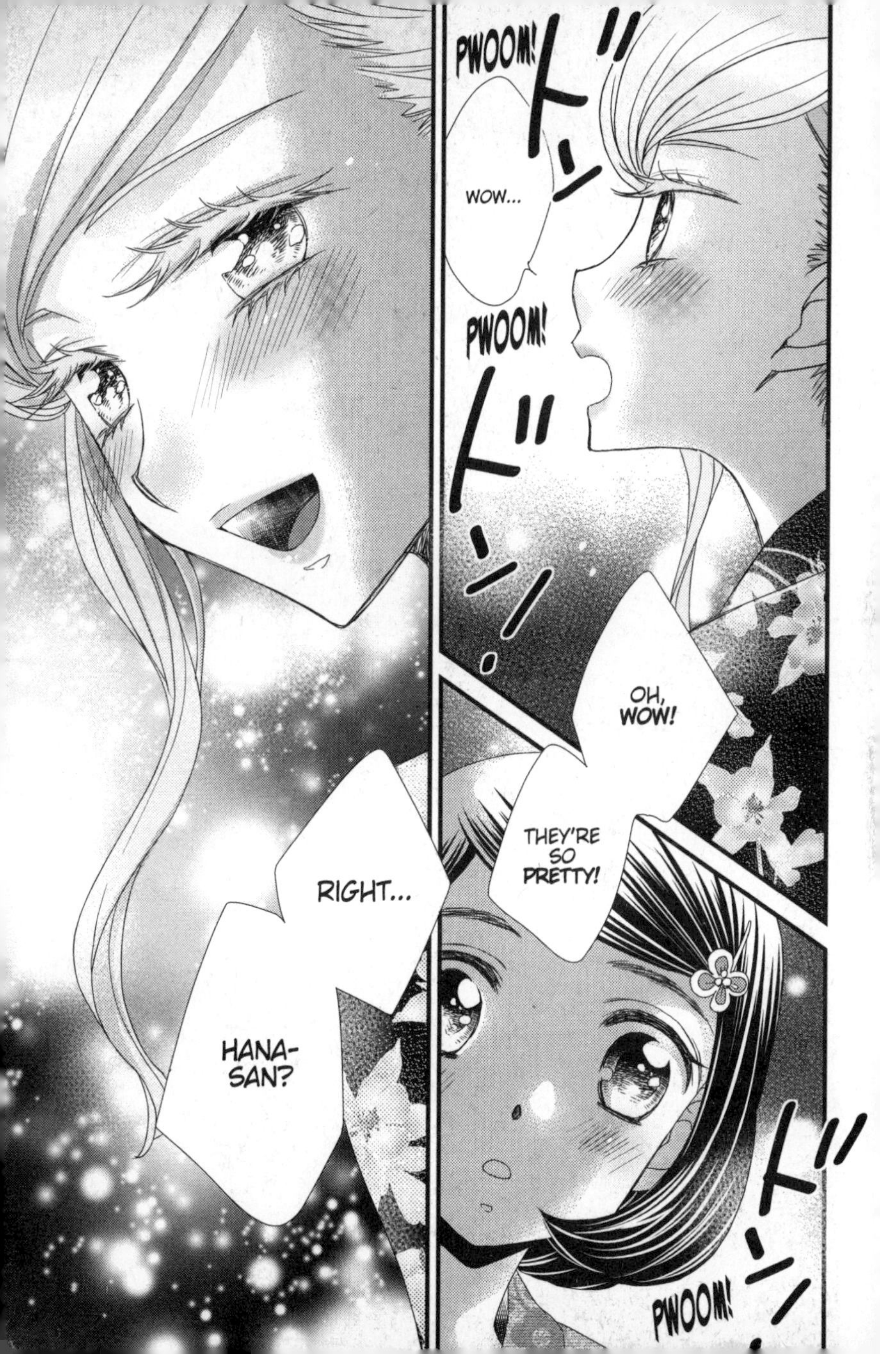
PWOOM!
ドン
WOW...
PWOOM!
ドン!!
OH, WOW!
THEY'RE SO PRETTY!
ドン
PWOOM!
RIGHT...
HANA-SAN?

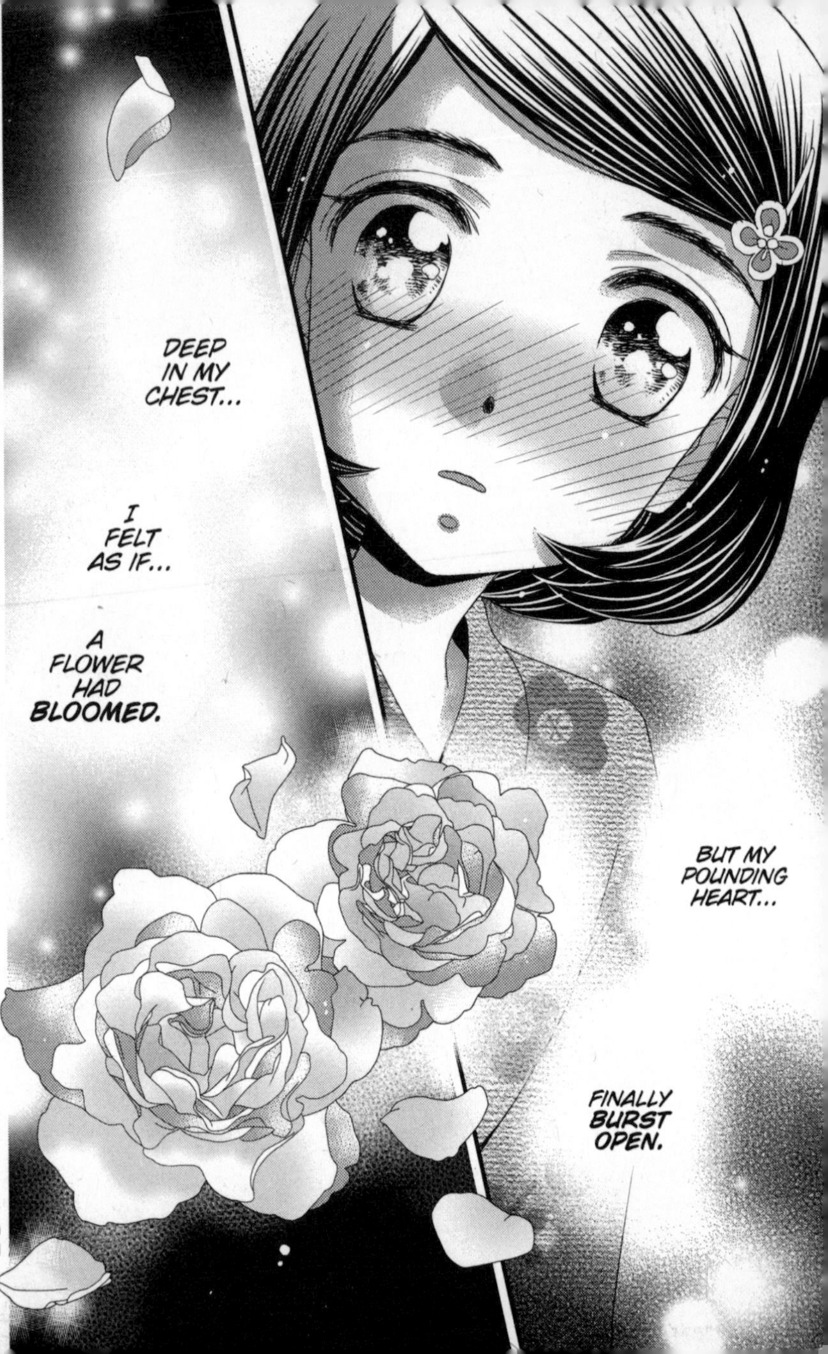
BUT MY POUNDING HEART...
FINALLY BURST OPEN.
DEEP IN MY CHEST...
I FELT AS IF...
A FLOWER HAD BLOOMED.
end

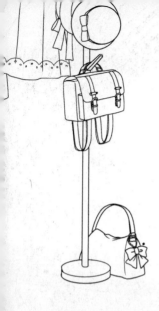

Hana & Hina AFTER ♡ SCHOOL

TO BE CONTINUED...

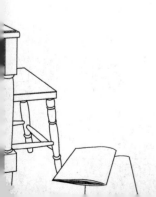

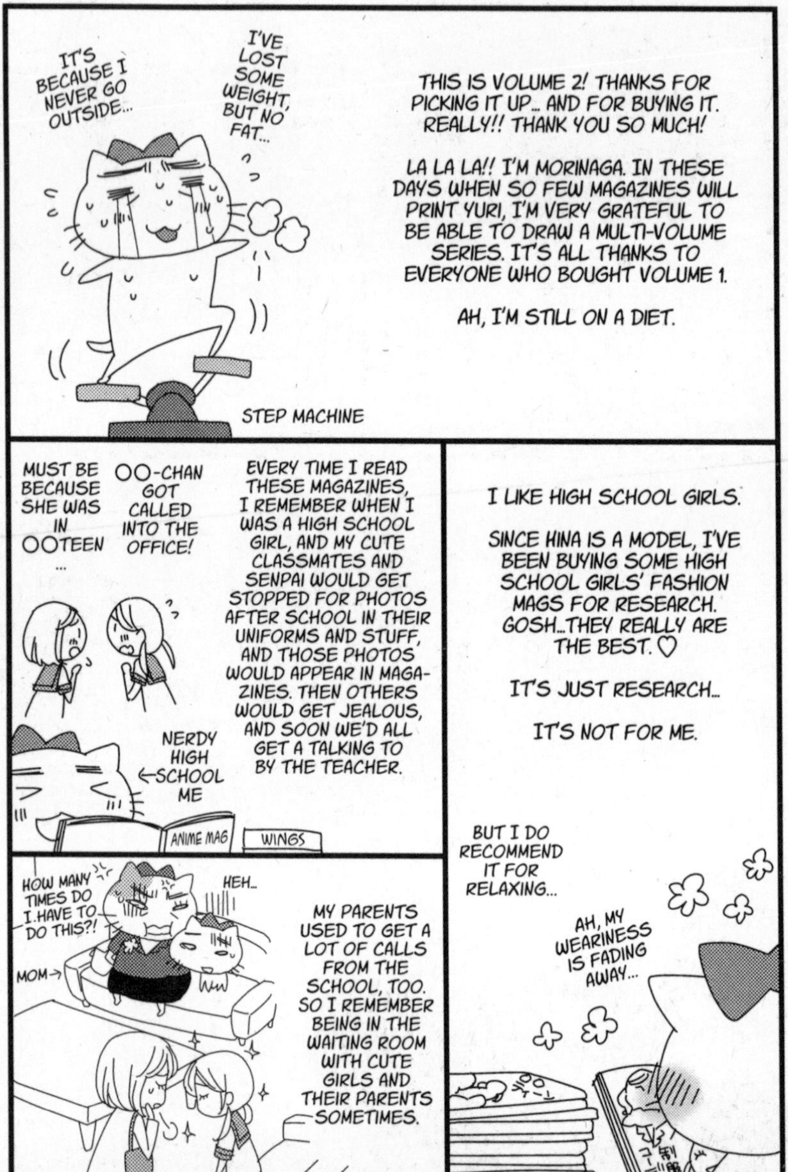
THIS IS VOLUME 2! THANKS FOR PICKING IT UP... AND FOR BUYING IT. REALLY!! THANK YOU SO MUCH!
LA LA LA!! I'M MORINAGA. IN THESE DAYS WHEN SO FEW MAGAZINES WILL PRINT YURI, I'M VERY GRATEFUL TO BE ABLE TO DRAW A MULTI-VOLUME SERIES. IT'S ALL THANKS TO EVERYONE WHO BOUGHT VOLUME 1.
AH, I'M STILL ON A DIET.
I'VE LOST SOME WEIGHT, BUT NO FAT...
IT'S BECAUSE I NEVER GO OUTSIDE...
STEP MACHINE
I LIKE HIGH SCHOOL GIRLS.
SINCE HINA IS A MODEL, I'VE BEEN BUYING SOME HIGH SCHOOL GIRLS' FASHION MAGS FOR RESEARCH. GOSH...THEY REALLY ARE THE BEST. ♡
IT'S JUST RESEARCH...
IT'S NOT FOR ME.
BUT I DO RECOMMEND IT FOR RELAXING...
AH, MY WEARINESS IS FADING AWAY...
EVERY TIME I READ THESE MAGAZINES, I REMEMBER WHEN I WAS A HIGH SCHOOL GIRL, AND MY CUTE CLASSMATES AND SENPAI WOULD GET STOPPED FOR PHOTOS AFTER SCHOOL IN THEIR UNIFORMS AND STUFF, AND THOSE PHOTOS WOULD APPEAR IN MAGAZINES. THEN OTHERS WOULD GET JEALOUS, AND SOON WE'D ALL GET A TALKING TO BY THE TEACHER.
○○-CHAN GOT CALLED INTO THE OFFICE!
MUST BE BECAUSE SHE WAS IN ○○TEEN...
NERDY HIGH SCHOOL ←ME
ANIME MAG
WINGS
MY PARENTS USED TO GET A LOT OF CALLS FROM THE SCHOOL, TOO. SO I REMEMBER BEING IN THE WAITING ROOM WITH CUTE GIRLS AND THEIR PARENTS SOMETIMES.
HEH...
HOW MANY TIMES DO I HAVE TO DO THIS?!
MOM→

YOURS TOO, HUH? ISN'T IT AWFUL?
MY DAUGHTER DOESN'T STUDY AT ALL, SO I KEEP GETTING CALLS TELLING ME THAT SHE'S FAILING! I MIGHT SEND HER TO CRAM SCHOOL.
HEAVYSET, SO SHE SWEATS A LOT.
MOM
AH, MINE HAD HER PHOTO APPEAR IN A MAGAZINE...
OH, BUT WE WANT HER TO GET INTO A GOOD COLLEGE, SO SHE DOES GO TO PREP SCHOOL.
AHH...
YOU HAVE TO, BE MORE CAREFUL...
SMART AND CUTE
GOT CALLED BECAUSE MY GRADES WERE SO BAD.
ANIME NERD
THIS IS THE WORST SCORE I'VE EVER SEEN...
I'LL SEND HER TO CRAM SCHOOL.
TEACHER
SO...I GOT SENT TO CRAM SCHOOL, BUT I JUST SECRETLY READ MANGA THE WHOLE TIME, SO MY GRADES NEVER IMPROVED.
LOOKING BACK, I FEEL BAD FOR MY MOM...

THE NEXT VOLUME WILL SHOW THE REST OF THE FIREWORKS DATE. PLEASE CONTINUE TO FOLLOW ALONG WITH THESE TWO AS THEIR STORY UNFOLDS. I'LL KEEP WORKING HARD, SO I HOPE TO SEE YOU NEXT VOLUME!!

MILK MORINAGA

SPECIAL THANKS

FURI-CHAN • ZOE-SAN
SUGIURA-SAN • KOJIMA-SAN

EDITOR IIDA-SAN
DESIGNER KUSUME-SAMA

EVERYONE AT THE BOOKSTORES
AND EVERYONE WHO READ THIS BOOK

THANK YOU VERY MUCH!

SEVEN SEAS ENTERTAINMENT PRESENTS

Hana & Hina AFTER SCHOOL

story and art by **MILK MORINAGA** **VOLUME 2**

TRANSLATION
Jennifer McKeon

ADAPTATION
Shannon Fay

LETTERING AND RETOUCH
Rina Mapa

LOGO DESIGN
KC Fabellon

COVER DESIGN
Nicky Lim

PROOFREADER
Shanti Whitesides

ASSISTANT EDITOR
Jenn Grunigen

PRODUCTION ASSISTANT
CK Russell

PRODUCTION MANAGER
Lissa Pattillo

EDITOR-IN-CHIEF
Adam Arnold

PUBLISHER
Jason DeAngelis

Seven Seas books may be purchased in bulk for promotional, educational, or business use. Please contact your local bookseller or the Macmillan Corporate and Premium Sales Department at 1-800-221-7945, extension 5442, or by e-mail at MacmillanSpecialMarkets@macmillan.com.

ISBN: 978-1-626925-24-3

Printed in Canada

First Printing: July 2017

10 9 8 7 6 5 4 3 2 1

FOLLOW US ONLINE: ***www.gomanga.com***

READING DIRECTIONS

This book reads from ***right to left***, Japanese style. If this is your first time reading manga, you start reading from the top right panel on each page and take it from there. If you get lost, just follow the numbered diagram here. It may seem backwards at first, but you'll get the hang of it! Have fun!!

1
2
3
4
5
6
7
8
9

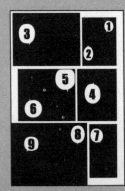